D1238588

R 2 3 2015

Marvin Miller

BASEBALL REVOLUTIONARY

SPORT AND SOCIETY

Series Editors
Randy Roberts
Aram Goudsouzian

Founding Editors
Benjamin G. Rader
Randy Roberts

A list of books in the series appears
at the end of this book.

Marvin Miller

BASEBALL REVOLUTIONARY

Robert F. Burk

UNIVERSITY OF ILLINOIS PRESS

Urbana, Chicago, and Springfield

© 2015 by the Board of Trustees
of the University of Illinois
All rights reserved
Manufactured in the United States of America
C 5 4 3 2 1
∞ This book is printed on acid-free paper.

Library of Congress Cataloging-in-Publication Data
Burk, Robert Fredrick, 1955–
Marvin Miller, baseball revolutionary / Robert F. Burk.
      pages cm
Includes bibliographical references and index.
ISBN 978-0-252-03875-4 (hardcover : alk. paper) —
ISBN 978-0-252-09670-9 (e-book)
1. Miller, Marvin, 1917–2012. 2. Labor unions—Officials and
employees—Biography. 3. Major League Baseball Players
Association—History. 4. Baseball players—Labor unions—
United States—History—20th century. I. Title.
          GV865.M5149B87   2015
      796.357092—dc23   2014021593
                    [B]

Contents

PART III: DEFENDER OF THE FAITH
(1986–2012)

Preface

The subject arose during a telephone interview—one of many sessions we had dubbed "Tuesdays with Marvin" because of the weekday they regularly occurred. When I asked Marvin Miller what element most explained his life's success, to my surprise he stressed the role of luck above all else. Up to a point his claim was valid. Without the happenstance of a double date arranged by a friend, he would have never met the person who would become his life partner of seven decades. Without the good fortune of a job opening up with a different federal agency nonetheless located in the same building where he had been toiling unhappily, he might never have had the opportunity to master the labor-arbitration laws and processes that would pay off so handsomely for him (and his ball-playing membership) three decades hence. Without the luck of not being uncovered as a 1948 supporter of Henry Wallace before CIO and Steelworkers titan Phillip Murray, he might never have been able to relaunch his career in organized labor, much less rise to the rank of chief economist and assistant to the USWA president. And if the inside candidate for the newly created position of executive director of the Major League Baseball Players Association had not thrown away his advantage by persisting in unreasonable demands, Miller might never have gotten the chance to guide an initially rag-tag group of professional athletes during a remarkable era of revolutionary gains.

But if luck had been one necessary ingredient, it was far from the whole story—and even then its role was more accurately that of preparation meeting opportunity. For whether he realized it at the time or not, Marvin Miller had spent a half-century grooming himself for the chance to make his marks upon the union movement and the world of professional sports. The handicap of a right arm crippled from birth had fueled a fiery drive and a stubborn pride that carried him through early discouragements. His family's history of struggle and striving had offered both challenge and inspiration. His Jewish heritage—though his own intellectual evolution took him in a secular direction—still provided powerful examples of collective struggle and solidarity. The Great Depression had been the context for his ideological evolution, as well as providing unforgettable lessons from the school of hard knocks. In college he had witnessed the cruelties of racial and religious prejudice, only to be countered by the basic decency of the impoverished welfare clients he had subsequently met in New York. During the Second World War, first in Washington, D.C., and then in Philadelphia, he had observed the roles of partisan national politics and the law in creating a structure in which the postwar give-and-take of labor-management relations would function. With anguish he had also seen how a cold war climate of fear and persecution could trample individuals' rights while testing one's own integrity. At the Steelworkers union he then had managed to blend ideological conviction with pragmatism to become a cutting-edge labor officer, capable not just of researching policy issues, educating workers, and formulating bargaining positions but also negotiating for his fellow members and defending his union before the public.

After this half-century of personal and professional preparation, it would take Miller less than two more decades—aided, to be sure, by the confusion of his adversaries—to usher in a fundamental transformation of American baseball's labor economics. At the time of his arrival in 1966, Organized Baseball remained marked by an archaic owner paternalism toward its on-field performers, occasionally punctuated by old-fashioned union busting. By the time Miller had stepped down from formal leadership of the big-league ballplayers, he had revolutionized not merely the "national pastime" but also the broader universe of professional sports. Through his hardnosed, shrewd leadership and the solidarity of his membership, his union would successfully dismantle the system of involuntary player servitude known as the "reserve clause," win comprehensive basic workplace rights and outside adjudication of player grievances and salary disputes, and witness a startling rise in prosperity for his constituents. Although the players' surging salaries and benefits dwarfed the earlier gains he had helped secure for the Steelworkers, his fundamental objective in both cases had been the same—to peacefully compel employers to accept a modern system of profit sharing with their workers. And despite the unceasing laments of club owners who had been forced to accommodate themselves to a new industry balance of power, in hindsight they might well have conceded that baseball's modern-day transformation had been achieved with less real disruption than might have been expected given the magnitude of the changes. Instead of decline, the "Miller era," while it had introduced more confrontation, had also ironically driven management innovation and revenue growth through geographic and franchise expansion, internationalization, the diversification of industry revenue, and broader—albeit still oligarchic—on-field competition.

Miller's achievements, to be sure, had not been without their flaws. He had proven unable to extend his union's umbrella either to other employees of the baseball industry or to the professional athletes of other sports. As a consequence the MLBPA would remain the effective equivalent of a small AFL-style craft union, even as it established itself as America's flagship sports-labor organization. Although performers in rival sports leagues copied in bits and pieces the MLBPA's agenda and improved their livelihoods as a result, they remained comparatively weak. And even the success of the MLBPA eventually generated its own dilemmas. Miller would prove unable to harmonize fully the goals of creating a truly democratic, bottom-up union while maintaining both its adversarial identity and its ideological solidarity. Over time—mercifully mostly after he had left his union's daily leadership—the ballplayer membership would become more complacent and less unified, just as the owners finally acquired greater competence and unity and began to chip away at Miller's edifice. And the corrosive effects of player greed and personal recklessness, enabled by Miller's very success in "creating Republicans" out of previously underpaid performers, led directly to the damaging temptations of recreational drugs and to the reckless pursuit of still-higher performance and pay through the resort to performance-enhancing drugs. Both in turn added to the players union's unpopularity in the court of public opinion, alienating fans whose own incomes had stagnated since the 1980s and who increasingly found it difficult to relate to—much less sympathize with—the lives of modern diamond stars. They continued to come to the ballpark or tuned in on television, but could fans ever again see professional athletes as the underdogs they perceived themselves to be?

Despite these storm clouds, however, Miller had continued in retirement to be proud of what he had wrought—as well as the ethical but tough way in which he had achieved it. Those who he had led, who had fought him across the table, or who had covered him in the media all had to acknowledge, albeit sometimes grudgingly, both his impact and his basic integrity. Under him, his union had earned a reputation for cleanliness and toughness in an era in which perceptions of the broader labor movement had eroded badly in both respects. From the liberal 1960s well into the age of Reagan, Miller's MLBPA had stood in marked counterpoint to the accelerating national pattern of union defeats and contract givebacks. Because he had been such a successful catalyst of fundamental changes to the professional baseball industry, the denial of a commensurate place of recognition in Cooperstown grew ever more inexplicable with each passing year and fresh snub. If Albert Spalding had been the architect of baseball's first durable cartel, Babe Ruth had converted the game into a marquee attraction to the masses, Branch Rickey had both pioneered the farm system of talent accumulation and spearheaded management acceptance of racial integration, and Jackie Robinson had changed the literal face of the game, Marvin Miller had been the man who, more than any other individual, had wrenched the national pastime—for better and worse—into a modern industry with modern labor-management relations. On any Mount Rushmore of the sport, unquestionably, he belonged.

And it had been much more than a simple matter of luck.

Acknowledgments

In the preparation of this volume I have accumulated many debts I can never fully repay but wish to acknowledge here. My gratitude to the staffs of the various repositories whose materials contributed significantly to this work is profound, most notably the University Archives of Miami University of Ohio, Catholic University of America Library, the Manuscripts Division of the Library of Congress, Pennsylvania State University Libraries, the National Baseball Library in Cooperstown, and the Robert F. Wagner Labor Archives of NYU's Tamiment Library. To Muskingum University, I am grateful for the support of my colleagues and for the research funding provided through my appointment as Cole Distinguished Professor of American History. To friends who have endured serving as readers of the manuscript at various stages, in particular Ginny Zellers and Connie and Andre Reynolds, I appreciate your keen eyes and your unflagging encouragement. To all who gave of their time to share their thoughts of Marvin Miller, whether in telephone interviews or through correspondence, I am forever grateful to you for helping making this book far better. To Peter Miller in particular, I can never repay you enough for your support, your gentle corrections, your sound advice, and, most of all, your insights into a remarkable man and a remarkable household. To Margaret and to our "children" Zelda, Callie, and Lucy, my devotion only grows for your keeping this retiree as grounded as possible.

Most of all, of course, I wish to express my deep gratitude to the late Marvin and Terry Miller. This is not necessarily the book that they would have written.

It is a biography, and is neither an authorized nor a ghost-written memoir. Any and all errors of fact or interpretation accordingly are mine. But I will forever cherish them for being willing to open up their lives to a total stranger, usually from a distance of hundreds of miles, two to three hours at a time every other week for the better part of a year. They did so without ever ducking a direct question or pulling a verbal punch. I consider it one of the great privileges of my life to have gotten to know them at least somewhat through the research and writing of this work.

Last but not least, this work is dedicated to a person not nearly as famous as Marvin Miller but equally missed by its author and by the others blessed to know her. Few outside Cooperstown will have heard of Rose Edwards, but those who met her during research stays at the National Baseball Library will almost certainly echo the following sentiments. Over the years and spanning the production of three baseball history books, Rose was my host in her hometown. For more than ten seasons I knew her as the matriarch of a tightly-run bed-and-breakfast who saw to her guests' needs while she provided around-the-clock care for an invalid husband. She unfailingly met every challenge life threw at her, whether unruly visitors or the breast cancer that ultimately claimed her life, with a joyful spirit and an unmatchable work ethic. She also freely shared with her ever-growing "family" of regular lodgers her fundamental creed of fairness and equal opportunity for all. She would no doubt have welcomed the election, and then reelection, of the nation's first African American president. Rose never had the chance to meet Marvin Miller, although she certainly heard a great deal about him from me. But I am certain that they would have taken to each other instantly.

Part One

The Making of a
Professional Unionist
(1917–1966)

"It does not take nine months, it takes
fifty years to make a man,
fifty years of sacrifice, of will, of . . .
of so many things."
—Andre Malraux, *Man's Fate*

One

A Brooklyn Boyhood

Marvin Miller—the man working-class chronicler Studs Terkel would later label "the most effective union organizer since John L. Lewis"—entered the world through a small apartment on Beck Street in the Bronx on April 14, 1917. For the newborn's parents, thirty-four-year-old Alexander ("Alex") Miller and twenty-seven-year-old Gertrude Wald Miller, the arrival of their first child marked a new beginning after a series of wrenching trials. Although many of the details evaporated with the passage of time, family descendants would later recall suggestions that the couple had encountered difficulties in conceiving, and possibly a miscarriage as well. Additionally, illness had led to Gertrude's losing both her parents early in her own marriage, at first draining her energies in time-consuming, yet ultimately futile, caregiving and then sinking her in grief that had further postponed childbearing.[1]

Determined to honor her deceased father, Morris, while also giving her first-born a less Old World–sounding name, Gertrude chose to call her new son Marvin. The middle name she and Alex picked—Julian—represented a tribute to Gertrude's deceased mother, Julia. The couple's apartment was situated in an apartment house nestled within a Middle Bronx district populated mainly by Jewish manual laborers and modest entrepreneurs. The neighborhood's residents also reflected a pattern common at the time in New York of young new-lyweds escaping the congestion of lower Manhattan. The location also placed Gertrude closer to her most recent elementary school posting in Harlem. Now with the onset of spring and with the pain of the Millers' past tribulations easing, the pall that had loomed over them seemed finally to be lifting with the start of a new cycle of familial regeneration.[2]

Looking back at prior generations, neither the Millers nor the Walds were strangers to hardship. Alex's father, a tailor by trade, had endured first his wife's death and then a vicious surge of anti-Semitic persecution in Russia more than three decades earlier. The loss of his spouse had left him the sole support of five children—three girls and two boys—none of whom had yet reached their tenth birthday. Alex, the youngest offspring, was less than a year old at the time of his mother's passing. While still dealing with this personal crisis, Alex's father, like other Russian Jews, had been confronted with the choice of either enduring or fleeing a fresh wave of czarist repression triggered by the assassination of Alexander II. The ruler's murder had led to the imposition of the infamous May Laws, triggering a new round of pogroms and state-aggravated famines. From the start of this new round of troubles in 1881 through the next three decades and more, two-and-a-half million Jews would eventually abandon their traditional homelands for America. The widower Miller and his young children emigrated at an early stage of this exodus, embarking on their leap of faith in 1883. Even with the impetus of the events in Russia, the Millers' decision to leave for the New World still demanded considerable courage, for unlike many other immigrants, Alex's father knew no one in the United States, spoke no English, and possessed no prior knowledge of his new home—the Lower East Side of Manhattan.[3]

Although technically an immigrant rather than an American-born citizen, son Alex had been so young at his arrival that he would retain no memory of Russia and would grow up speaking unaccented English. His three older sisters assumed the responsibility for the family's maternal duties, while their father eked out a modest living as a tailor. Years later, Marvin would marvel at his grandfather—by then more than nine decades old—dressed entirely in black and topped by a hat or yarmulke, sporting a long white beard and threading his needle without ever having to look at it despite carrying on an animated Yiddish conversation. While having rapidly adopted his new country's language, Alex had followed his father's example in other ways, likewise embracing the garment trade—albeit as a salesman—and adopting the rituals and responsibilities of Orthodox Judaism. His form of reconciling the Old and New Worlds mirrored that of millions of other southern and eastern European offspring sharing the same environment in turn-of-the-century New York. Not just Russians but also Italians, Romanians, Hungarians, Slovaks, Greeks, Poles, and Turks swelled the Lower East Side to forge the single largest Jewish urban community in the world. Out of choice or necessity, like Alex most of them gradually incorporated not just the language but also the alien work rhythms of their new homeland as necessary concessions for material success and social acceptance.[4]

Alex Miller was inescapably molded by his new environment—the two square miles of the Lower East Side bounded by Division and Houston streets, the Bowery, and the East River. It was a neighborhood during his boyhood in which few organized play areas for children existed, where youths formed gangs and roamed the streets in search of amusement, mischief, or money, and where a few even ended up gangsters. Spurred by the calls for reform from Jacob Riis and likeminded voices, settlement houses had sprouted for the nurture and uplift of the poor, including the renowned Henry Street settlement of Lillian Wald (no relation to Gertrude's family). Various unions, including the United Hebrew Trades, had sunk roots as well, and in such fertile soil, working-class struggle and striving played out and a plethora of class-conscious ideologies dueled. While Tammany Hall's principles-free pragmatism ruled electoral politics, lunch hour at a Russian garment factory might find workers discussing Tolstoy or Kropotkin. Future politicians, professionals, writers, artists, musicians, entertainers—and also labor leaders—found their particular muses in the streets and meeting halls.[5]

In contrast to his father, who remained a humble tailor, the young Alex had quickly advanced within the retail trade to the level of a Division Street women's coat salesman, one who as early as his upper teens had brought home $150 to $200 per week. But rather than embrace the Lower East Side's intellectual ferment, he had continued to follow the traditional patterns of family obligation, limited formal education, and Orthodox religion. Having dropped out of school at an early age for the world of work, he never returned to the classroom, even for vocational training. All his working life his daily setting remained that of the row of competing two-story women's coat shops, huddled between streets featuring larger shoe and clothing establishments, a world where young hustlers stood ready to drag customers into their stores and bearded elders similarly coaxed passers-by into a *minyan.* Dutiful toward the rituals of his faith, Alex donned the prayer shawl each morning, laid *tefillen,* performed *davening,* and delivered his devotions in the language of his ancestors. Although the demands of his sales job would permit no allowance for the Sabbath, and Gertrude stubbornly held to her rival convictions as a nonobservant wife, the adult Alex still always honored the High Holidays—although he was forced to attend *shul* less frequently than in his youth.[6]

Despite his religious devotion, however, to those who knew him, Alex Miller was no pious recluse. His sisters adored him as their fun-loving, albeit protective, sibling. In a slight departure from tradition, as Alex had grown into adult-hood, he had assumed the role of paternal guardian, both to his sisters and to his older, but frail, brother George. His outgoing persona—as much a part of him as his traditional value system—and the reliability that had been ingrained in him from youth had facilitated his rise in the retail trade. The mature Alex would in turn enjoy a special standing with his siblings' children as the favorite uncle. He was uncommonly generous both to them and to hard-up strangers, often to the point of appearing a spendthrift. As a successful purveyor of fine women's coats in Lower Manhattan's cutthroat retail environment, he also insisted upon maintaining a snappy image. Each day of the week he would don a different suit to work. Many years later, Marvin Miller's sister Thelma would recall their fa-ther as a true-life Beau Brummell when it came to his personal appearance. On his infrequent days off from his job, Alex proved himself an avid consumer of Gotham's popular diversions as well, whether Madison Square Garden or Coney Island prizefights, Broadway or vaudeville shows, or afternoon baseball games.[7]

Gertrude Wald Miller, in contrast with her hard-working, fun-loving, yet traditional husband, was seven years younger and displayed a more modern and secular mindset. Like the Millers, the Walds could point to a proud heritage of family daring and sacrifice. They had been but one small part of an even longer-term nineteenth-century migration, that of Hungarians and other central Europeans, spurred on by the failed national revolutions of 1848 and that had swelled after 1870 as the dissatisfied had fled the Hapsburg's reactionary Dual Monarchy. The earliest of them, some of peasant stock but also including a wider swath of social classes and professions, had initially settled in the Lower East Side, just as the later Russian immigrants would do. But over time, those central European migrants with sufficient means—which included Gertrude's parents—had relocated north to the Upper East Side's Yorkville section. There they had settled in windowless, narrow, yet deep multiroom apartments, dubbed "railroad flats," within crowded three- to five-story buildings.[8]

Although Yorkville had previously been settled by Germans and Austrians, by the time Gertrude had been born there in 1890 as the youngest of six daughters (among ten children in total), the neighborhood had already been peacefully conquered by Czechs, Slovaks, and Hungarians. Little Bohemia, encompassing the lower Seventies blocks of the east-west streets, housed many of the Czechs and Slovaks, with each group maintaining its own *sokols* for cultural education. The Hungarians in turn established themselves farther north, on the upper Seventies streets. Farther north still, surrounding and above East 86th Street, resided the resettled descendants of the earlier Teutonic populace. Whether representing "old" or "new" arrivals, however, in all the various enclaves a cauldron of expatriate pride bubbled with fresh vigor.[9]

Like her husband, Gertrude Miller had been raised by parents who had braved America without an awaiting safety net of relatives. Compared with the Millers, however, the Walds had claimed a more venturesome, entrepreneurial spirit. Gertrude's father had not only started a bar in his new neighborhood but even found the time to sell real estate on the side out of his personal roll-top desk. As a household numbering twelve in all, the Wald family was noteworthy for its size even by turn-of-the-century standards—a fact possibly suggesting a persistence of traditional Old World family values and sexual role definitions. But such was not the case. As adults, four of the six Wald sisters would assume the dual responsibilities of housewives and breadwinners. Two ran their own shops. Despite lingering popular resistance to female participation in sports, the adolescent Gertrude roller-skated, rode her own bicycle, played tennis in Central Park, and even took part in organized team basketball. Acknowledged by all in her family as their most intellectually gifted member, she was also the child actively pushed toward postsecondary education. After having attending two years of normal (teachers') school, she began what would eventually stretch into nearly a half-century's career as an elementary-school teacher in the New York City public school system.[10]

Gertrude Wald Miller's modern sensibility similarly extended to matters of religion. Although she had inherited the traditional knowledge of certain ethnic recipes and homeopathic cures from her parents, many of her elders' Orthodox religious customs—including the sexual segregation of women within the synagogue—visibly irritated her. By the time she reached adulthood she had ceased attending religious services save for the High Holidays, and even in that case did so with diminishing frequency. Still more defiant for the spouse of an Orthodox husband, upon her marriage to Alex she refused to keep a kosher home for their children. Because of Gertrude's open nonobservance, Alex's father retaliated by refusing to set foot in his son's abode, even to see his grandchildren. Miller descendants could not recall even one family gathering in which Gertrude and her father-in-law had harmoniously coexisted, even momentarily, in the same room.[11]

Given the stark differences between the Miller and Wald clans, it remained a family mystery how the young adults Alex and Gertrude had ever met, much less fallen in love. But somehow Alex had become acquainted with Tillie, one of Gertrude's older sisters. Had they met by chance at a concert or the theater, or during separate strolls in Central Park? Had they encountered each other on the El, which by that time traversed Manhattan's length along its north-south streets? Had they perhaps become acquainted at Alex's shop when Tillie had been shopping for a new coat? Whatever the particulars, what everyone did know was that upon meeting Gertrude, Alex had quickly shifted his attentions from Tillie to her vivacious little sister. Following a presumably awkward transition, Miller then had ardently pursued his future wife, with their courtship culminating in marriage in 1912.[12]

Given the personal trials Alex and Gertrude had subsequently shared, they had earned the right to have the birth of their first child unfold as an occasion of unqualified joy. Unfortunately, it was not to be the case. The couple had opted to have the delivery occur in their home rather than in a hospital, apparently sharing an all-too-common superstition that persons who checked into hospitals frequently failed to leave them. But the doctor summoned to the Millers' apartment for the in-home birth was overmatched and underprepared. The difficult delivery required the use of instruments, owing to Gertrude's narrow pelvis, and the physician's mishandling of forceps in the extraction managed to wrench the newborn's right shoulder and cause initially imperceptible but severe damage. As the parents discovered only when the infant started to attempt to crawl, only to be unable to employ his right arm for support, one or more primary nerves in Marvin Miller's shoulder region had been irreparably harmed. The malady, today known in medical parlance as "Erb's palsy" or "brachial plexus paralysis," meant that the newborn's right arm lacked the essential nerve stimulation to develop full motor control and would remain in an atrophied state with the limb positioned at an awkward angle for the rest of his life.[13]

Over the next seven years, Alex and Gertrude Miller tried virtually everything to gain their son's complete use of his arm. Marvin's mother used up two years' worth of maternity leave to be with him, and for five more she regularly took her boy to a specialist in upper Manhattan for manipulation sessions. At that same physician's advice, the Millers even bought a mechanical rubbing machine for Marvin's home use. The electrical contraption required the patient—either solo or with the help of another person—to hold the unwieldy contraption against his damaged upper arm while the device vibrated upon the skin. While in operation the machine's motor gave off a sickening smell of burning lubricant and rubber. Not only would the device prove useless, but for the rest of Marvin Miller's life the mere memory of the acrid burnt-oil odor would trigger acute sensations of nausea.[14]

Even before Marvin had reached his first birthday, his parents had decided to relocate to roomier accommodations in the Flatbush section of Brooklyn. Besides the obvious need for more space to accommodate a growing family, Gertrude's postpregnancy return to teaching—this time at a Coney Island elementary school—dictated a closer location to work. Fortuitously, the city's recent expansion of the subway system now provided Brooklyn–Manhattan transit connections that linked both boroughs from end to end, and thus offered both parents practical work transportation in opposite directions. Facilitating the Millers' move was also the presence in Brooklyn of Gertrude's brother Rudy, who had purchased a house on East 19th Street. With Rudy acting as a scout, Alex, Gertrude, and Marvin soon joined him in Flatbush. The Millers bought a semidetached house (one sharing a wall with another home in a fashion similar to a modern duplex) at 1939 East 19th—one in a string of eight such structures on the same side of a still-developing residential block. For Gertrude the location's proximity to the subway put her but four southbound stops from her new school, while Alex would have nearly as quick a commute across the East River to his Division Street workplace.[15]

The Millers' new home borough had maintained a proud history of independence from New York City, despite its many linkages to it. Long known as the "city of churches," Brooklyn carried forward a strong civic commitment to education and to the care of the less privileged. Among the borough's civic attractions was Prospect Park, featuring numerous picnic areas, tennis courts, ball fields, ponds, a municipal zoo, parade grounds, and a bandstand. The Brooklyn Ice Palace afforded an indoor skating rink with house organist and offered such enticing refreshments as hot dogs and hot chocolate. At Brooklyn's south end, Coney Island and Brighton Beach enticed patrons with varied diversions that included bathing pavilions, handball courts, beaches, boardwalks, amusement rides, food stands, and contestant booths. At its core, however, modern Brooklyn had evolved into a residential bedroom community for the swelling numbers of commuters to Manhattan.[16]

With the borough's native industry largely restricted to an area a few blocks from the waterfront and its retail business district contained in the downtown area, most of Brooklyn consisted of an expanding collection of suburban-style neighborhoods whose pace of growth was dictated by the extent of the subway network and the accompanying tempo of new construction. When Marvin and his parents arrived in their new neighborhood, the unpaved street in front of their house and the still-vacant lots farther down the other side of the block spoke to the area's transitional status. Horse-drawn wagons still delivered blocks of ice and milk bottles. Nearby community fields suited equally well for ball playing or for planting corn and tomatoes. At the end of the Millers' side of the block, an old three-story, wooden structure remained that had once housed Sheepshead Bay jockeys. Close by was a large barn with horses where in the hayloft an adventurous lad could thumb through stacks of old newspapers and magazines. Times, however, were changing. Within the year Gertrude would be startled by the unfamiliar sound of neighbors celebrating the Armistice not with traditional church bells but with a cacophony of car horns. Vehicle traffic proliferated once street paving arrived. The old barn was eventually converted into a rental garage. For neighborhood boys, the resurfaced streets offered smoother surfaces for pickup games, but also more cars to dodge. Responding to the challenge, the youngsters defended their turf by threatening to push away "foreign" vehicles.[17]

As more newcomers arrived and more new homes sprung up, the block's character evolved in other ways, too. For generations the prominence of well-to-do Protestant families had been a hallmark of the area. Though such a presence did not completely disappear, now Jews and Catholics constituted a growing majority. As a visitor strolled down the Millers' side of the street from one end of the block to the other, the other families sheltered within its eight residences included the Howells (a Protestant household); Marvin's Uncle Rudy and his family (who shared a wall with the Howells); the Walters and Cohens (two more Jewish households); the Millers' immediate Protestant neighbors the Swensons; and finally a pair of Catholic families. As the other side of the street also filled in, it came to include a plurality of Jewish residents, as well as two sets of Italian Catholic neighbors. The construction of a Catholic church and rectory on the corner during Marvin's childhood accelerated further the influx of Irish and Italian co-religionists.[18]

To the children of the neighborhood, though, adult distinctions of class, ethnicity, or religion counted for little. One of the two lawyers on the block, Mr. Walter, was a partner in a prominent Manhattan firm that at one time retained the young Franklin Roosevelt. The youngest Walter child, Jimmy, not only was about Marvin's own age, but he shared the reality of a physical handicap. In Jimmy's case, polio had rendered him severely hunchbacked. Given his own frustrations, the young Miller could well appreciate his friend's determination to earn acceptance from his playmates. The two boys bonded, and together they eagerly plunged into East 19th Street's raucous sports competitions. At any given time, fifty or more children of varying ages could be found roller-skating or playing spontaneous stickball, stoopball, punch ball, and touch football games. Teenagers migrated to the closest sandlots and schoolyards for more structured contests of baseball or tackle football. In all these battles, a hard-earned meri-

Marvin Miller age three, with parents Alexander and Gertrude (Peter Miller)

tocracy tended to prevail, with a youngster succeeding or falling based upon his combination of seniority, physical maturation, and skill. Typically a boy rose from a pee-wee to novice status, then to the respect of a veteran. Once a child reached his teens, further recognition came within reach as role model or coach to others below.

Fueling a Brooklyn lad's dreams of athletic glory, of course, was the presence of the borough's own major-league baseball team . . . if you defined the term loosely. The Dodgers, nicknamed after Brooklyn's trolley-dodging denizens, seemed destined—with rare exceptions—to service as sacrificial lambs to the National League's stronger aggregations. But despite of—or sometimes because of—the squad's often-comical deficiencies, its fans, especially the young ones, loved their "Bums" and proudly ignored the ridicule that rained down from high and mighty Yankee and "Jints" (Giants) backers. With Ebbets Field just a five-cent subway ride away, and with Saturday afternoon double-header bleacher seats going for a mere fifty-five cents, what local boy could resist—particularly once the borough's schools had let out for the summer?[19]

Not surprisingly, Marvin Miller grew up both an avid ballplayer and a devoted Dodger fan. Although the awkward angle of his right arm prevented him from reaching out to snag balls with his glove one-handed, he could field routine grounders with both hands, and he honed his skill as a left-handed pitcher in part to minimize his need for the defensive prowess required of the other position players. He discovered to his delight both that his damaged shoulder did not hamper him that much at bat, and his foot speed and quick reaction made him an excellent base runner. His love of the Dodgers led him to eagerly collect and trade baseball cards, using his allowance money as his means of purchase, and he zealously memorized the Brooklyn roster, batting order, and player statistics each season. Ranking highest on his personal list of heroes stood hurler Dazzy Vance, the team's aging but still hard-throwing star.[20]

Given his father's work schedule and his mother's strictures against skipping school, most of Marvin's visits to Ebbets Field awaited the summertime. When circumstances permitted, however, Alex—a Giants fan since childhood—accompanied his son, usually opting for the cheaper bleacher seats. In contrast, Marvin's indulgent Uncle Sid, a real-estate contractor from the Jersey outlands, treated his nephew to Dodger box seats and even took him to Yankee Stadium to watch the incomparable Babe Ruth. Besides its value in securing baseball cards and game tickets, the boy's allowance money helped finance other kinds of diversions. Some of it ended up as youthful wagers with friends, including costly bets on another of his idols, boxer Jack Dempsey. For the young Miller, the financial stakes only deepened the gloom at the Manassa Mauler's loss to challenger Gene Tunney in 1926, which Marvin listened to on the radio. A year later the scenario was repeated when Dempsey's chance to win the rematch was thwarted by a referee's infamous "long count." Motion pictures offered still another focus of the boy's youthful adulation, and thus a new name joined Vance and Dempsey in his pantheon of heroes—Tarzan the Ape Man.[21]

Attendance at other, "mature" forms of entertainment, however, required Marvin's strenuous lobbying of his parents. One of the family's more colorful older relatives on Gertrude's side was Uncle Jack, whose past included running away from home at the age of sixteen to become a burlesque actor, followed by the marriage and then divorce of a Protestant minister's daughter and a second set of nuptials with a chorus girl young Marvin came to know as Aunt Mildred. When Jack would loudly arrive in town, he would arrange to leave special passes that enabled the underage boy to gain admittance into Minsky's or the old Gaiety with Mildred as his adult escort. By the time Marvin reached ten years of age, his persistent campaigning had not only worn down his father's objections to his attending the burlesque but also to nighttime New York Rangers hockey games. But while Alex reluctantly let Marvin travel solo to the Garden, he insisted for safety reasons that his son not tarry afterward—not even for an ice cream—but return home immediately via the earliest well-populated train.[22]

Despite the youthful Miller's vicarious love of professional sports and more raucous entertainments, they were no substitute for direct participation. Ignoring his handicap, he plunged fully into the rough-and-tumble of the neighborhood competitions. The reactions from his parents to his complete lack of restraint could hardly have contrasted more sharply. Alex maintained a stern disapproval of his son's indifference to his own safety, and he tried in vain to steer him toward lower-impact or noncontact activities. Marvin, however, saw a harsher meaning in his father's approbations, still insisting decades later that Alex "always had low expectations for me." But when his father would raise his voice to oppose his son's stubborn participation in rough play or even to Marvin's being assigned hard household chores, Gertrude emphatically would counter with the discussion-ending statement, "Yes, he can!" Not only did she accept her son's competitive need to take part in rough sports, she even enlisted him to help her relearn how to roller-skate.[23]

Even without the ongoing friction between father and son over "dangerous" sports, the relationship between Alex and Marvin was likely destined to be more distant. The larger-than-normal age gap between the two, combined with Alex's work regimen (which kept him away from home from midmorning to late night save for a single weekday, Friday evening, and Sunday each week) inhibited a greater forging of father-son intimacy through shared experiences. And whether owing to his own guilt over Marvin's crippled arm or an obsessive need to protect his son as his way of measuring up to his own father's sacrifices, Alex's open disquiet before Marvin's peers caused his son unbearable embarrassment. "Be careful!" his father would shout to him in the middle of a ball game, or "Watch out for the cars on the street!" demanding that he slow up for his own safety. Alex would even take Marvin's playmates publicly to task for any infractions of what Alex deemed excessively rough play toward his child.[24]

Given Alex's lengthy absences from home, his exaggerated overprotection of Marvin when he was present often resembled the behavior of a fussy grandparent more than that of a father. But his excessive protectiveness almost certainly reflected nothing worse than a misguided excess of devotion. It did not come from any personal physical timidity or moral disapproval of sports. As a young man—probably at the urging of his fellow salesmen—Alex had not only taken up bowling but had become so good at it to win local amateur tournaments. The father's victories even resulted in spoils for the family, including a Lionel train, a set of luggage, and fireworks. Family members would long remember fondly how, on each subsequent Fourth of July, Alex conducted impressive fireworks shows despite city regulations. Given bowling's one-armed and noncontact nature, not surprisingly Alex had tried to instill in Marvin a similar passion for the sport as an alternative to his son's more aggressive pursuits. But the boy's superior agility and his determination to prove his toughness and fit in as one of the neighborhood gang led to his clear preference for baseball (in all of its various street and sandlot forms), handball, roller and speed skating, and even tackle football and hockey.[25]

If Alex's attitude toward Marvin's need for validation only raised the intensity of their verbal skirmishes, Gertrude for her part displayed a defter touch. She demanded that, in light of his father's long work hours, Marvin should help out with the more masculine household chores. Without making any reference to her son's handicap, she assigned him a range of tasks that required him to both confront and adapt to his condition, not just such "one-handed" duties as painting the front stoop or the kitchen stools. Each spring Marvin was called upon to put up, and each fall remove, the Miller house's cumbersome, hooked exterior windows screens. Until the family ultimately replaced the home's coal-burning furnace with an oil burner, Marvin also drew the task of collecting the ashes twice weekly in wintertime. The chore required him to shovel the residue into tall metal cans, hoist them up the basement steps to street level, roll them curbside, and after each pickup collect the empties and return them to the house by himself. Gertrude also assigned him the strenuous task of breaking up the ice from the front steps and walkway and shoveling it away.[26]

Although daily life in the Millers' neighborhood did not exhibit racial diversity, the mix of ethnicities and religions did promote a reflexive tolerance. Typical of Gotham's Gilded Age immigrant influx, Alex and Gertrude were reliably Democratic in their voting habits and supported New York's symbol of immigrant ascendancy, Al Smith. Mr. Keeley, the contractor who had built the nearby Catholic facilities, also doubled as the local Democratic precinct captain. But politics in the Miller household, unlike that of Marvin's own family later, was never a subject for deep discussion or strong debate. Public issues rarely surfaced as dinner-table conversation save immediately before an election, and often not then. But regardless of his own essentially apolitical nature, no one could doubt Alex Miller's social conscience or compassion for the needy regardless of background. As one example, the neighborhood sanitation teams regularly consisted of a white driver with two African American laborers, the latter outside handling the cans. On winter days when the crews would come to empty residents' containers and return them curbside, without fail Alex would invite the soot- and snow-covered workmen inside to break the chill. Ushering them into the living room, he would offer them a seat on the family sofa while he fetched them hot coffee laced with Four Roses or Canadian Club, Prohibition notwithstanding. When Gertrude would return home from school in the afternoon she would find Alex gone but ashes and puddles of dirty water left on the furniture and the floor. When he returned she would berate him for the mess and expense of his hospitality, but he never stopped.[27]

A personal window for the young Marvin Miller into his father's world were the Saturday and summertime midday transit rides he took from age eight to visit Alex at work. At first—but with declining frequency as her son grew older—Gertrude accompanied him and dropped him off at the Division Street address when she had shopping to do. Once Alex's lunch break arrived, father and son would spend the hour strolling down adjacent streets in a kind of walking tutorial. Then as now New Yorkers enjoyed a deserved reputation as schmoozers, and Alex personally ranked among the best. Walking northward from the coat store, the duo would take in the sights of the Bowery, with its rough assortment of pawnshops, flophouses, missions, and makeshift "barber schools," where unemployed "students" cut hair for fifteen cents a head. More exotic and captivating to the young Marvin were the sights and smells of nearby Chinatown, with its bustling import houses, groceries, restaurants, and apartments.[28]

The most important regular destination of these walks, however, was the neighborhood in which Alex had grown up and where he now brought Marvin to pay homage to his grandfather. As they headed toward their destination, the boy observed how his father delighted in exercising his generosity. Alex kept a ready supply of coins for plucking out of his pocket, and would push them into the palms of those down on their luck. He would engage acquaintances in casual banter, switching effortlessly from English to Yiddish to even rudimentary Chinese. Out of a desire not to offend his father by visibly violating the Sabbath, Alex never took Marvin to see the family patriarch on a workday Saturday. On the occasions they did visit, Marvin's inability to speak Yiddish precluded conversation with his grandfather, but he observed as the old tailor chatted with Alex in the tiny one-and-a-half-room apartment. During these stops Alex also sometimes gave money to his father without Gertrude's knowledge. The weekday visits to Grandfather Miller lasted until Marvin was ten years old, only to end tragically when the ninety-three-year-old patriarch died of injuries when hit by a truck while walking to shul.[29]

When the young Miller's noon visits to his father were paired with a practical need, such as clothes shopping, Alex the genial companion abruptly transformed into Alex the seasoned *hondler*. Both Miller parents prized quality and value over mere cheapness even in times when finances proved tight. During these shopping forays, Marvin was forced to endure humiliations not unlike those when his father attended his ball playing. On one occasion the boy suffered through modeling nineteen different coats while Alex administered the third degree to a clerk over the respective fabric and cut. Such haggling invariably spilled out into the street, including a feigned rejection by Alex, before the two sides would reach their pact. For those lucky enough to have witnessed in the flesh Marvin Miller's father as a negotiator, the son's later success at the bargaining table would have seemed unsurprising, but instead testament to a family legacy.[30]

While Alex alternated between long hours of work and holding court on Division Street, after her own workday Gertrude Miller ran an organized—and decidedly non-Orthodox—home. Although Alex insisted upon keeping up his own religious obligations, and the Miller home's front and back doors bore mezuzahs, as a unit the family did not celebrate Chanukah or the seder. Though delegation of some household chores to Marvin eased Gertrude's burden modestly, occasionally she still required outside assistance. Both in Marvin's first few years and again after the birth of his younger sister Thelma, a sequence of six-day-a-week domestic workers aided with the household duties. The timing of Thelma's birth just a few months after five-year-old Marvin had started school helped Gertrude balance the additional demands from a second child—as did the rush of curious visiting relatives. Even without the presence of Grandfather Miller, the house was often abuzz with the sounds of kin from all across the city and the surrounding outlands who had dropped by on their way to Coney Island and Brighton Beach.[31]

Within the Millers' modest but comfortable home, Gertrude was the leader in providing the children an intellectually rich environment. Books filled the house, in keeping both with the mother's own curiosity and out of a determination to stimulate her son's mind. Different rooms were renovated at various times, and as a result the accumulation of household amenities came to include both a ping-pong table and a baby grand piano—which Marvin equally mastered. In the case of the former he discovered that he could hold a ping-pong ball in his right hand and, employing a short underhand motion, propel the sphere for serving. As for the musical instrument, playing it did not require him to lift his arm above waist level, and thus it became a staple of his life going forward. As an adult, Miller would regularly regale family members and guests alike with impromptu medleys of popular standards and classical works.[32]

Being a professional teacher, Gertrude also took the natural lead in preparing Marvin for his formal schooling. At her prodding he had already learned to read by age three. A year later he was writing his name and doing arithmetic. In 1922, at just five years and five months of age, he started elementary school. Despite beginning early he earned a follow-up promotion to second grade after but one semester. Two more such advances occurred in elementary school. He eventually attended three different primary-school institutions—the first an old, wooden, four-grade schoolhouse on Ocean Avenue with outhouses for restrooms. After it was torn down between his fourth and fifth-grade years, it was replaced by a new P.S. 96 on Neck Road and then followed by P.S. 153, on Homecrest Avenue and Avenue T, for the seventh and eighth grades. Months before the arrival of his twelfth birthday he was already a high schooler. Gertrude's identification of Marvin as her most intellectually gifted child was in sharp contrast to her perception of daughter Thelma, who accordingly did not receive similar academic attention from her mother. Owing to this apparent greater intellectual identification of Gertrude with her son, outside family relatives perceived Marvin to be her favorite, while Thelma was Alex's pet.[33]

Even if the young Marvin possessed obvious intelligence, however, he was not particularly diligent about developing it. It irritated him that school's demands afforded him less time for sports and other diversions. But even less tolerable to him than the demands of public education, however, was an additional obligation forced upon him—one that represented an uneasy bargain his parents had struck concerning Marvin's religious instruction. With Gertrude's insistence that the boy's home upbringing be primarily secular, Alex Miller had demanded in return that once Marvin reached age ten he would attend after-school Hebrew training to prepare for his bar mitzvah. Four afternoons a week he would thus be drilled in the language, traditions, and ceremonies of Orthodox Judaism. For Alex this was not a matter for renegotiation. Nonetheless his son rebelled. But Alex, convinced of the inescapability of his son's physical limitation, saw the imposition of the educational "double shift"—whether or not it compromised Marvin's afternoon freedom—as reasonable and necessary. The tragedy of his own father's abrupt death likely only reinforced Alex's imperative that the Orthodox way should not die with his own son. But to Marvin, it made no sense to sacrifice a normal adolescence for the sake of boring hours of Hebrew tutorials.[34]

Barely four months into his hated after-school regimen, Marvin abruptly bowed up and refused to attend any more sessions. More angry confrontations with Alex in turn led to extended bitterness between the pair, marked by telling silences. With Marvin having triggered the showdown anew, and with his father's absences from home depriving him of the leverage to enforce his edict, it now fell upon Gertrude to forge a pragmatic compromise. Perhaps predictably, she did so in a form closer to Marvin's position. The son would no longer have to attend the Hebrew school. But starting six months before he reached age thirteen and the date of his bar mitzvah, Marvin would have to submit to home tutoring from a private teacher to prepare him for the occasion. An unhappy Alex complained that the plan would not sufficiently instill the necessary mastery, and he lamented to his son, "You're not even going to be able to say *Kaddish!*" Gertrude, however, had effectively decided the matter for good.[35]

Despite—or perhaps partly because of—Marvin's short-term victory, the emotional tug of war between father and son would continue for years. Thanks to the intercession of Uncle Sid, Marvin soon prevailed once more, this time in a parent/child dispute over whether he would be allowed a shiny blue bicycle to ride on the neighborhood's busy streets. The boy quickly employed his new acquisition delivering the *Brooklyn Daily Eagle* on an afternoons-and-Sundays paper route. With the money he earned from the delivery job, he then bought a new ball glove and even—once more over Alex's misgivings—a pair of ice skates. Ironically, Marvin's subsequent success in weekly speed-skating races at the Brooklyn Ice Palace rink earned him treasured praise from his father. And now possessing his own source, albeit modest, of independent spending money, Marvin was also freer to attend Ebbets Field, Madison Square Garden, and his other escapes from home.[36]

Beyond the self-acquired possessions and the greater feeling of independence the paper route gave the young Miller, however, the paperboy job also enabled him to begin forging a more mature relationship with both parents. In an adult fashion, he could now afford to buy his parents and sister birthday and holiday gifts. He took on more of the family babysitting duties overseeing Thelma, which in turn afforded Alex and Gertrude greater opportunity to go out together. The expansion of Marvin's adolescent responsibilities and success with the physical demands of the paper route also helped instill self-pride. At the same time, though, his seemingly unquenchable drive to challenge any affront to his capabilities as a young man led him to bristle still at anyone who posed even innocent questions regarding his arm or—worse yet—expressed sympathy. He did find relief in these awkward situations now taking place less frequently than in his younger years.[37]

In 1929—fully two years ahead of schedule—twelve-year-old Marvin Miller entered James Madison High School. Despite the institution's prestige, for Marvin the start of his secondary education would bring fresh challenges to his hard-won independence. A surge in New York's student population in the 1920s and the continuing outmigration to the city suburbs had forced schools such as

Madison to operate with two separate shifts. The first group of students—the juniors and seniors—attended from 8 A.M. to 1 P.M., while the second wave of first-year and sophomore classes commenced at 1 P.M. and ran until 6 o'clock. Besides allowing the school to maximize its now-inadequate space, the two-shift policy saved the district money by enabling closing of the lunch room, on the rationale that first-shift students could wait and have lunch at home and afternoon attendees could eat before leaving for class. But for Marvin, the second-shift school schedule meant the loss of his *Eagle* delivery job since the paper was an afternoon daily. Fortunately, he then managed to secure a morning paper route delivering the *New York Times*.[38]

Although the adolescent Miller was not yet fully aware of it, he was about to enter a much more challenging phase of his life. From birth, even before he had been conscious of the reality of it, he had been rendered damaged goods. But his disability, however emotionally traumatic, had not proven to be the determining factor shaping his life. There had been the contrasting environments of Brooklyn and Lower Manhattan, the religious and secular influences of his parents, and the family's ongoing tensions between tradition and modernity. Taken as a whole, they had molded a slight yet determined youngster eager to assert his independence beyond his protective cocoon on East 19th Street. But he was also in many respects still a boy, with all of the preoccupations and pressures typical of someone his age. Before his first year of high school had even concluded, however, an economic cataclysm would begin to shake his world—one that would shatter much of his remaining innocence and sow in him a lifelong antipathy toward the harboring of illusions. Ironically, though, instead of the Great Depression shattering the young Marvin Miller's future prospects for good, the emerging crisis would ultimately help him to define his personal identity and point him on his adult path.

Two

Hard Times

The Great Depression fundamentally altered the lives of millions, not just in New York but throughout the nation and the world. For Marvin Miller it was the formative period of his life. It offered up brutal testimonials to the ties that bound people together, and how swiftly those ties could fray under stress. It tested the solidarity of working people while underscoring the importance of that same principle to their well-being. It helped lead the young Miller toward a decision to pursue a degree in economics. It began his personal history in the union movement and introduced him to its struggles for economic justice. It facilitated the rise of international fascism and forced him to face his own clash of principles between the imperative of confronting brutal dictators and the equally powerful view that war did little but enrich profiteers. Above all else, it was in Depression-era New York that he met the love of his life—a woman who would prove a soul mate of the mind as well as the heart.

For the Miller family and other New Yorkers, the Depression's full impact would not be felt until several years after the initial 1929 Wall Street crash. For the young Marvin, the immediate pressures that preoccupied him were those of an underage and awkward high-schooler. James Madison was larger by far than any school he had ever attended before, and most classmates were older and physically more mature than him. Although cousin Malvin (Uncle Rudy's youngest son) was younger still, the latter had succeeded in joining a self-identified circle of "nerds" that included future ecologist Barry Commoner. (As an adult, Malvin would make his own mark as well in Hollywood as a script-

Miller at age thirteen (Peter Miller)

writer of the Academy Award–nominated film *The Naked City*.) In contrast to Malvin, however, Marvin anxiously sought the regular crowd's acceptance. But his slight build and bum arm prevented him from garnering the status that accompanied success on any of the school's athletic teams. Even without his physical handicap Marvin's making a varsity squad would have been improbable, given that Madison ranked among the top city sports powerhouses. Its gridiron team alone was talented enough to best rival Erasmus in spite of the presence of the great Sid Luckman on the latter squad. Madison's own great star, Marty Glickman—one year ahead of Marvin and a multisport hero in track, basketball, and football—would make the 1936 U.S. Olympic track team as a sprinter and enjoy still greater renown later as a professional broadcaster.[1]

Although frustrated at his athletic shortcomings, Marvin initially earned good grades. But his social and sexual awkwardness around the older boys made for an increasingly difficult time. Adding to his adolescent stresses, his deferred obligation to study for and then complete his bar mitzvah was coming due. For the six months leading up to the April 1930 ceremony, he unhappily subjected himself to thrice-weekly Hebrew tutorials over and above his high-school classes and his paper route. On the appointed day, at the Midwood temple at Avenue P and 17th he managed to stumble his way through the traditional Jewish ritual of manhood. Father Alex's open dismay at each verbal miscue only added to the torture. But if the father was underwhelmed at the performance, at least Marvin had the satisfaction of having met his duty. And, besides the relief at surviving the ordeal, young Miller found that completion brought him tangible rewards, in the form of fountain pens and books from proud relatives.

Soon enough, however, the Millers and their neighbors and extended family would all find themselves confronted by concerns far more dire. By the winter of 1931–1932 the economic devastation presaged by the Wall Street collapse had become all too real and had put the lie to earlier conventional wisdom that had stubbornly insisted the downturn had already bottomed out or was soon to do so. By the following spring fully one-quarter of New York City's labor force was jobless, and in one year alone nearly sixteen hundred inhabitants committed suicide. In the garment industry, unemployment characterized fully one-third of the workforce. Makeshift shanties—Gotham's version of Hoovervilles— sprouted like weeds in Central Park and along the Hudson and East rivers. Confusion and political paralysis in Washington, D.C., and the corruption of Tammany Hall's playboy mayor, Jimmy Walker, fed the deepening despair that sparked a growing working-class militancy.[2]

Neighborhoods within the city's boroughs, including Brooklyn, saw anti-eviction groups launch rent strikes, and in turn, the spreading resistance triggered violent retaliation from property owners' armed enforcers. To some of the protesters being beaten, shot, or arrested, this new version of stick-wielding brutality seemed little different from what their ancestors had once fled back in the Old World, and accordingly they dubbed their current assailants "Cossacks." But if the strikers feared and loathed their attackers in equal measure, in truth the latter were as panicked by them as the tangible vanguard of revolution. Years later an adult Marvin Miller would retell a familiar Depression-era anecdote in which a pedestrian accidentally found himself in the midst of a mass protest in front of City Hall. As he became caught up in the melee of police retaliation and a uniformed rider bore down upon him, swinging his club, the trapped bystander desperately pleaded, "I'm an anti-Communist! I'm an anti-Communist!" Undeterred, the advancing officer shouted back, "I don't care what kind of Communist you are!"[3]

As the metropolitan economy sank, it submerged the Miller family's prospects with it. None of Marvin's adult male kin were business owners, and as employees of others, not only were their jobs at the mercy of their bosses but they were in no position to assist a younger relative in securing part-time work after school or summer jobs. Uncle Rudy toiled as a traveling salesman for Interwoven Socks. Uncle Ben, in far-off Kansas, was also a salesman, not an entrepreneur. As for Uncle Jack, his performing gigs in burlesque had dried up and he now sustained himself as a carnival barker at Luna Park. While he still procured Marvin passes to the boardwalk and the Steeple Chase, he had no useful job connections. And if the young Miller postponed entry into the workforce by applying for college, would his parents be able to support him? Were there enough savings to pay for related expenses, even if his grades qualified him for local tuition remission? And if his academic standing slipped and he lost his eligibility for the tuition waiver, where then would he turn?[4]

Marvin did have one ace in the hole. His mother, as an early enrollee in the municipal teachers' union, claimed a seniority-protected teaching job, and her relative economic security helped stabilize the family's otherwise uncertain employment circumstances. But farther on the horizon, if Marvin entertained thoughts of following in his mother's footsteps as a teacher, the growing backlog of qualified but unemployed candidates seemingly doomed his prospects. Given its school system's worsening budget crunch and teacher glut, New York City had already suspended its qualifying examination for new education graduates. As his horizons narrowed, at the worst possible time Marvin's innate restlessness then took on a self-destructive path of indifference toward his studies. His acts of truancy spiked and his grades plunged. For Gertrude in particular, such a turn of events was simply unacceptable given her son's intellectual potential. Indicative of his mental maturity for one of such a tender age, one of the young Miller's twelfth-birthday gifts had been a copy of Erich Maria Remarque's renowned antiwar novel *All Quiet on the Western Front*. But even in easier times, maintaining Marvin's attention to his schoolwork had been a struggle. Though particular subjects such as French, biology, European history, and economics challenged him and drew out his potential, others simply bored him. And continued tensions with his father and the mounting distress of relatives and neighbors accelerated his downward spiral. By his junior year, in the company of similarly aimless pals from the neighborhood, Miller was regularly cutting classes for the escapes of Brooklyn and Manhattan.[5]

By then, Marvin's immediate family had already endured the first of a series of financial hits. As early as 1931, business at Alex's coat shop had slumped, triggering cuts in hours, wages, and commissions. Over the next few years, Alex's work schedule further contracted from fifty weeks (with two weeks' vacation time) to forty, then thirty-six, twenty-four, and eventually fewer than ten. The adult Marvin would later recall unemotionally, "My father got more and more anxious and concerned, and I was old enough to be aware of all that." A single incident drove home Alex's grim new reality to his son. On a particular workday morning, the younger Miller walked into the bathroom only to almost collide with his father—who was intently engaged in applying hair dye to his scalp to appear younger. An embarrassed Alex then confessed that for more than a year his boss had been issuing warnings about the impression his graying locks potentially made upon the store's female customers—and that remediation was required if he wanted to keep his job.[6]

To Alex Miller's credit, however, he had also chosen to respond to his own economic crisis with an act of genuine courage and even defiance. For the first time in his life he had joined a union—that of the Retail, Wholesale, and Department Store Employees. He even took part in an organizing drive that spanned his entire retail block. Alex kept his union membership secret initially from his children, and so it came as a shock when Marvin dropped by unannounced at the shop to find his father walking a picket line. The teenager quickly recognized virtually everyone engaged in the organizational picket as Alex's work friends. Some of them the boy knew to be socialist in their leanings, and a few were communists. What the vast majority had in common, however, was membership in the Workmen's Circle—a mutual aid society established years earlier by immigrant eastern European Jews and that, among its various activities, sponsored a summer camp the young Miller had attended for several years. Alex explained the details of the organizing campaign and then added that the two of them would need to wait twenty minutes more, until the father's replacement showed up, before they could leave on their customary noontime stroll.[7]

As they walked the nearby streets, the pair could not fail to notice how the sights and sounds along their route had drastically changed. In place of the jocular schmoozing of better times, downcast men in long lines shuffled toward soup kitchens. Once limited to the Bowery, but now just as evident on streets that had earlier teemed with pushcart peddlers, desperate beggars now sat pleading for a handout. As for the Bowery itself, the population of those barely subsisting had swollen by several-fold. Middle-aged men, some of them ex-garment salesmen who since their teens had faithfully reported for work, now sold apples or other fruit procured by the crate from dockside wholesalers. Using empty boxes as makeshift stands or stools, they offered samples to passers-by at five to ten cents apiece. Besides their shared destitution, Lower Manhattan's swollen population claimed one other feature in common—its race. For the city had already become sharply segregated, with the African American share of unemployed largely invisible to the rest of Gotham, unless an observer either encountered a multiracial protest or ventured north to Harlem's neighborhoods.[8]

Despite the heroic efforts to defend his livelihood, Alex Miller's circumstances continued to contract. He never fell completely jobless, and the new union contract he and his coworkers won preserved his paid holidays and sick leave. But shrunken work schedules meant longer stretches of involuntary idleness that further exacerbated household pressures. In response Gertrude urged her husband to seize the moment to start his own business, even volunteering her own savings to the cause, and she prodded him to seek entrepreneurial advice from her older sister, who ran a New Jersey dry goods business. A prideful Alex, however, rejected the entreaties, calling his sister-in-law's firm "penny-ante." In all fairness, the risk in his taking such a financial gamble in the midst of the Depression would have been substantial. The fact also remained, though, that Alex was too completely wedded to the only occupation he had ever known to be able to summon a career change. His professional identity was as much of a fixture to him now as his Orthodox faith, and no matter how dire his circumstances became he would not abandon it.[9]

In contrast to her husband, whose mounting anxieties could not be hidden, Gertrude at least projected a greater equanimity toward the economic crisis. On the few occasions she talked openly of the Depression, she did so in the abstract. Despite the family's ever-tightening finances, she continued to demand quality over cheapness in her shopping. Tellingly, she refused to sell off the family piano. But many of the Millers' immediate neighbors, lacking an economic anchor comparable to Gertrude's job, were less fortunate. Men Marvin had never been used to seeing on the block in the morning when he left for school or present when he returned were now visibly languishing. The idled included not just the once-affluent lawyer across the street but even the seemingly unconquerable Uncle Rudy. Extended-family members dropped by more often than ever before, but the motives were not the same as in better times. Now the young Miller saw reddened eyes and heard trembling voices that belonged to his own aunts and uncles. Down the length of the street, the extra money in storage fees that neighbors had once collected from car owners lacking personal garages had dried up as ever more vehicles had been repossessed. On one particularly awkward occasion, Marvin walked to the transit station to catch a ride into the city, only to run into next-door neighbor Mr. Swenson. Wordless, they boarded the train together for Manhattan, but as they rode the older man suddenly began to explain the reason behind his commute, only to break down sobbing. He had just recently been laid off from the only work he had ever known, and being newly unemployed and in his fifties, he now faced the daunting prospect of never finding gainful work again.[10]

It was into such an unforgiving world that Marvin Miller came from James Madison High in the spring of 1933. Over his last two years of secondary school he had been lucky that his mounting absences had not prevented his graduation. But plummeting grades had still disqualified him from a scholarship or even free tuition at an area college. For the sixteen-year-old, the humbling immediate reality was that he would have to continue living under his parents' roof. He proceeded to scrounge up temporary work as a delivery boy, then a chain-store soda jerk, and finally a short-order cook. He later characterized the series of dead-end positions as "one stupid job after another which didn't mean anything." At his mother's pestering, over the next year and a half he also took two night classes each term at Brooklyn College. To boost his marginal prospects, he bought an instructional manual and taught himself to type. Seeking a more mature appearance, only in part out of employment reasons, he also began to sport a thin mustache—a feature that would become a lifelong trademark. Additionally, he took up smoking, at first a pipe and then cigarettes, soon becoming a chain-smoker. (He would maintain his habit for more than five decades, until a heart attack eventually forced him to quit cold turkey.)[11]

Even after his graduation, Marvin insisted upon frequenting the venues he had sought out earlier when cutting classes. He ducked out from menial chores and familial tensions at home to engage in various recreations or to attend sports contests with his friends. Ebbets Field, Brighton Beach, and the Ice Palace continued to be frequent hangouts. At Brighton Beach pavilion he newly took up a racketless sport dubbed "hand tennis," which was played on abbreviated indoor courts. This variation on handball allowed the wiry, 5'8" lad to exploit his superior hand-eye coordination, reflexes, and agility while minimizing the limitations of his weak right shoulder. Rapidly mastering the sport, he twice reached a tournament's singles final. At the Ice Palace, where as a boy he had raced in weekly in-season speed-skating contests and had won age-group medals, he continued to triumph. But as for a more adult engagement in the "real world," the young Miller remained aimless and adrift.[12]

By summer's end in 1934, however, Marvin's fortunes began to turn. Having accumulated enough in savings to enroll full-time at an area college and eager to finally escape his mother's badgering, he signed up for an undergraduate pre-law program at St. John's University. In truth, he had no interest in becoming a lawyer despite the examples of several attorneys on his block. Instead, repeating what was a familiar tendency to tag along after others, he followed behind a neighborhood friend, Seymour Simon, who had always carried the expectation of following in his father's footsteps in the legal profession. Miller lasted at St. John's for only one year before withdrawing. Only belatedly he grasped what he should have realized before even enrolling—that the school's law curriculum would require more than four years to complete. In any event, the only profession in which he had ever shown a slight spark of interest had been teaching, owing to his mother's example. Even then, it had been the relative security of a unionized teaching job and not a genuine calling that had prompted his modest curiosity.[13]

Now that he was leaving St. John's, where would he go next? While looking into both local and out-of-state colleges, Marvin heard about Miami University of Ohio, thanks to a second cousin from Yonkers who had visited the Oxford campus and had decided to enroll there. The impulsive Miller abruptly sent off for his own catalogue. Miami was a land-grant school situated in the southwestern part of the Buckeye state. At a modest $80 yearly tuition to Ohio residents and only $25 more for outsiders, it was relatively cheap. Dormitory rent was similarly reasonable, and a three-times-a-day meal plan cost a mere $5 extra per week. Miami possessed a strong teaching program, with its original founder having authored the *McGuffey Reader*. Gertrude helpfully arranged an interview for her son with members of the city board of education, who confirmed Miami's solid reputation. The school's distance from home would provide Marvin an additional bonus by enabling him to escape his parents' intrusive oversight. By the time he finished his studies, likely in just three years, his chances to land a teaching job, whether in New York or elsewhere, might well have improved. So once again, Miller followed upon the heels of another and enrolled in the fall of 1935 at Miami with sophomore standing.[14]

As the son of two unionized breadwinners and already acutely aware of the realities of economic hardship in New York, Miller already possessed a greater awareness of matters of economic and social injustice than most eighteen-year-olds. His home city had been battling the economic crisis for fully half a decade, and the New Deal programs of state favorite-son Franklin Roosevelt had belatedly begun to funnel hundreds of millions of dollars in supplemental relief spending and in subsidized, large-scale public works projects. But Marvin's new environment of Oxford, Ohio, would soon seem a world away. At Miami he found a college and a host community that appeared to have intentionally cut themselves off from awareness of the suffering and tumult that lay beyond. The school's administration was traditional to the point of hidebound. Fraternities were populated by the legacy offspring of well-connected alums who, like their fathers had done, dominated student affairs and zealously guarded their status from any "outsider" incursions. As for adjacent Oxford, it rested comfortably within the political orbit of Robert A. Taft and embraced a blend of complacent domestic conservatism mixed with foreign-policy isolationism.[15]

Miller's stay at Miami, though it would end in his departure after but two years, did serve to revive his intellectual ambition and, ironically, sharpen his social convictions. But if his time at the school was not a complete waste, it was nonetheless frustrating. On the positive side of the ledger, his grades bounced back, and his interest in economics blossomed. He also qualified for the college's education honorary. As for nonacademic growth, Miami's policy of accepting female students, albeit in segregated dorms, and the presence of a women's school a short walk from his dorm facilitated his sexual emergence. As he had demonstrated for years in response to a restless need to prove his manhood, once more he plunged into all manner of sports and paid no heed to his physical shortcomings. He unsuccessfully tried out for the varsity baseball team as a left-handed pitcher, then after the rejection became a hurler for his dorm team. Ignoring his crippled arm, he volunteered as a workout partner for the welterweights on the school boxing team. Active in intramural sports, Miller excelled at table tennis, even reaching the college's singles championship.[16]

Where his grit and his reflexes combined for greatest effect, however, was in handball. In both years at Miami he shared the school doubles title. In his junior season, despite never having played the local version of four-wall singles before arriving at the college, he won the championship after coming back from two points down in the last game of a best-of-three match with his opponent serving for the title. Even in that moment of triumph, however, campus caste distinctions nearly denied him his tangible embodiment of victory—a silver cup inscribed with the names of past years' winners. So accustomed were the fraternities at having one of their own claim the prize that when Miller—a mere dorm resident and a Jew besides—showed up to take it from the previous champion's house, he was refused entry for "lack of identification." The furious victor walked back to his residence hall and explained the situation to his dorm mother, an imposing figure who proceeded to march back to the frat house herself and secure the cup for a full year's display on the Ogden Hall mantelpiece.[17]

As the handball confrontation reflected, anti-Semitism of a casually cruel nature thrived at Miami. On campus Miller found that some of his classmates would become visibly ill at ease in his presence and would reflexively display prejudice directed at him. When they asked for his hometown, for example, his reply of New York typically occasioned the follow-up, "Are you Jewish?" If the conversation lurched into the subject of personal possessions, such as clothes, then a student might blurt out the stereotypical comment, "You get everything wholesale, right?" But if Miller found insulting such unthinking prejudice toward those of his background, the indignities he suffered were nothing compared to what the handful of African Americans on campus experienced. Out of a student body of three thousand, fewer than ten Negroes attended the school. A majority of them were athletes. Although Miami had admitted its first African Americans as far back as 1903, in 1936 they were still officially excluded from campus housing. Black student-athletes managed to circumvent the color ban by sleeping surreptitiously on mattresses in the basement quarters of Swing Hall dormitory's black cook. Other African American attendees, however, were pushed off campus and into Oxford's scarce supply of minority public accommodations. Sporadic racial harassment in town would continue until after the Second World War, when the college at the same time finally lifted its racial housing ban. (Ironically, in 1964 civil rights workers preparing for Freedom Summer in Mississippi would train in Oxford before their journey south to face intimidation or even death.)[18]

Immediately prior to the start of the 1936 school year, not just at Miami but on other campuses across America, the Berlin Olympics had earned its place in sports history and in the annals of race through the heroics of Jesse Owens. Far less publicized than Owens winning four gold medals, however, had been the collusion by American officials and their Nazi hosts in denying Marvin Miller's Jewish former high-school classmate Marty Glickman his own chance for Olympic glory. Having trained for the U.S. 400-meter relay team, Glickman had been abruptly dropped from the American quartet the day of the preliminary heats and forced to watch as teammates—including Owens—won the gold in world-record time. At the same time in Oxford, Ohio, the Miami football team was preparing for what would eventually be the school's best football campaign for many years. At the end of the season, the home squad, nicknamed the Redskins (a label that would be shed only decades later), would tie for the Buckeye Conference championship with a 7-1-1 record. The team's impressive results would owe in no small measure to the talents of sophomore halfback Jerry Williams—the team's lone African American starter and one of but two blacks on that year's roster.[19]

On a Saturday afternoon late that season, Miller and several dorm friends attended the Redskins' home contest against archrival Toledo. With Jerry Williams as the game's star, Miami triumphed by a 13–0 score. Along with other students, the Ogden Hall contingent rooted their team to victory and then marched triumphantly from the stadium back to their dorm. During that particular week,

Marvin and his pals had opted not to take the two-meal plan but instead just one meal a day, meaning they would need to go into Oxford for dinner. When they went out again and arrived at the local diner, they encountered a situation that immediately made the young Miller's blood boil. Jerry Williams, who had been the toast of campus and community mere hours before, was being refused service by the proprietor of the establishment. The outraged Miller immediately stormed in and tried without success to persuade the already seated customers to walk out in protest. But no one—not even any of his companions—would join him in the effort, and he strode away in humiliation.[20]

The shocking incident solidified what was already Marvin's tentative decision to return to New York for good at the end of the current academic year. He was homesick, but more importantly he had a second, powerful reason to pursue the remainder of his college education in Gotham. Her first name was Terry. Back in the previous spring after his first year at Miami, he had returned home for summer vacation. A neighborhood friend named Herb Parmet had invited him to tag along on a double date. Herb's companion that evening had been an attractive seventeen-year-old sophomore he had met in a classics course at nearby Brooklyn College. For Miller the occasion would likely have been recorded in the annals of teenage courtship as yet one more blind-date disaster—except he had instantly fallen for Herb's partner.[21]

As soon as the awkward circumstances had permitted, Marvin had obtained Herb's permission to ask out Terry. But for an agonizing stretch she had continued to rebuff him, seeing in his solicitations a snub to the friend who had been Marvin's arranged date that previous occasion. All through that summer, Marvin had continued to press his case, only to be routinely rejected. Because the combatants had both rented lockers at Brighton Beach, run-ins had frequently recurred, but Terry had maintained her vigilance. The cold shoulder lasted even past Miller's return to Miami. Finally, however, just before the end of the fall term and following still more written entreaties from Marvin, Terry had relented to a date upon his return to Brooklyn for the winter holidays. Imbued with a special combination of romantic ardor and ideological zeal—and knowing the similar political leanings of the target of his affections—the enterprising Miller managed to secure two of Manhattan's toughest tickets: seats for the WPA Federal Theater Project production of Sinclair Lewis's *It Can't Happen Here*. In a move meant to boost FDR's electoral prospects, the government agency had staged the controversial antifascist satire not just in New York but also twenty-one other cities. Even though Roosevelt had already won his landslide reelection weeks earlier, the stage production had proven so popular with audiences that its run had been extended into 1937.[22]

At first glance, Miller's choice of entertainment for his first real date with Terry might have seemed questionable. At the least, it was not likely to provide the setting for encouraging passions of a nonpolitical nature. If his ulterior motive in taking her to such an overtly class-conscious political production had been to test their compatibility—not just sexually but also of beliefs—she had her own test ready for him. Once the curtain had been drawn and Miller had escorted his date to her doorstep, his request for a good-night kiss ran smack into a counterdemand from Terry. Before she would agree, she insisted, he must first provide her with "ten good reasons" as to why she should comply. With the evening abruptly at an impasse, Miller rushed home and through the night composed his ten-point thesis assignment, successfully turning in his assignment to Terry the next morning.[23]

It would prove the most important bargaining proposal he ever drafted. Notwithstanding her initial refusal to date him for months and her blunt test of his sincerity, the future Terry Miller later admitted that from her first encounter with Marvin Miller she had found him "very handsome." He, of course, had never tried to hide his attraction to her. But as the deferral of an actual courtship had given them more time to discover traits about each other, they had found that they possessed a strong compatibility not just in attraction but of shared passions and convictions. Both of them were secularized Jews, despite the respective efforts of Miller's Orthodox father and Terry's observant, if more modern, parents. Terry saw in Marvin a young man with intelligence, idealism, and grit. She observed approvingly that he was one who demanded vigorous give-and-take from her, who disdained appeals to superstition or emotion, and who possessed the ability to listen as well as argue. For his part Miller saw in Terry not just the love of his life but a best friend, an ideological soul mate and sounding board, and a fellow lover of both sports and music.[24]

With much more now awaiting Miller in New York, the impatient student returned to Miami of Ohio to finish up that year's academic obligations. Before he could sever his ties to the school for good, however, he needed to line up an alternative in Gotham that would accept his transfer credits and thereby enable him to finish his degree as promptly as possible. After only modest haggling, New York University agreed to admit him for his senior year. With both him and his girlfriend planning to graduate from their respective schools in the spring of 1938, as their relationship continued to progress rapidly, Miller's thoughts increasingly turned to contemplating the contours of a shared life with Terry. The

Depression was stubbornly persisting, and reactionary fascism was aggressively on the march overseas. How would they manage to harmonize their ideological fervor with the practical necessities of earning a living and securing their future together? The road ahead was filled with uncertainties, but more and more it now seemed that they would travel it together.

Three

Avenues of Discovery

By the time Marvin Miller returned to New York to complete his college education, class-conscious activism had become even more visible in his home city. In 1937, local theater audiences still arose to chant "Strike!" at each curtain close of Clifford Odets's agitprop, *Waiting for Lefty*. Garment-union leaders David Dubinsky and Sidney Hillman had formed the American Labor Party as a political vehicle for Gotham's leftist trade unions. Michael Quill, a former Irish revolutionary now head of the Transport Workers Union (TWU), launched a sit-down strike against the Brooklyn-Manhattan Transit Company. On the national scene, with the aid of Dubinsky and Hillman, the United Mine Workers' John L. Lewis had broken decisively with the AFL to form the Committee for Industrial Organization (later the Congress of Industrial Organizations, or CIO). A CIO affiliate called the Steel Workers Organizing Committee (SWOC), headed by Lewis's subordinate Philip Murray, had been assigned the daunting task of conquering that industry. In the aftermath of FDR's 1936 landslide, the United Auto Workers fought for and won union recognition from General Motors, and SWOC soon achieved the same from U.S. Steel. But by the spring of 1937, brutal tactics had temporarily thwarted similar pushes at Ford and at the "Little Steel" firms.[1]

During his two years in Ohio, Miller had been largely isolated from the turmoil in New York. But his return to Gotham and to NYU potentially offered him the prospect of direct engagement with the city's ongoing ideological struggle. Adjacent to the NYU campus's main Washington Square building stood the

Museum of Living Art, which featured the works of such European avant-garde artists Picasso and Mondrian and American painters Marin, Demuth, Sheeler, and Hartley. Around the corner was a row of apartment buildings that turn-of-the-century literary pioneers of realism Theodore Dreiser, Frank Norris, Stephen Crane, and John Dos Passos had once called home. Less than a block farther on, the Triangle Shirtwaist Company Building remained standing as a stark monument to industrial exploitation and workplace tragedy. But the image of social ferment projected by the setting proved deceiving. To his dismay Miller found that despite the Depression's impact in radicalizing thinking on his major subject, the university's economics curriculum still largely ignored contemporary issues and Marxist social critiques. And though his new classmates were less parochial than those he had encountered at Miami, they too rarely focused long on matters outside their grades and social lives.[2]

While Miller hunkered down to the task of completing his bachelor's degree, his fiancée was similarly engrossed in her English major at Brooklyn College. Reflecting the underdog nature of its home borough, Terry's school often exhibited greater ideological passion than that of her boyfriend. Although at least one member of her English departmental faculty used his position to quote from right-wing literature to his students, her own views had migrated steadily leftward even before she had met Marvin. Briefly she had even dated a young man, named Bill Schultz, who had subsequently volunteered in the Spanish republican cause and had died in the brutal civil war. By 1937 few who met Terry could have ever imagined that her family had voted Republican in the 1920s, or that she had once campaigned for Herbert Hoover in a grade-school mock election.[3]

Despite the young couple's deepening leftist convictions, the necessities of coping with everyday matters kept them from immediately plunging headlong into political activity. Although compared to their childhood friends and family they were more ideologically radical, Marvin and Terry were still, as she would later describe herself and her boyfriend, a "committed bourgeois couple." Their favorite diversion was outdoor sports, whether summer or winter. As an adolescent, Marvin had attended summer camps upstate and had enjoyed the company of teenage friends on outings to the Adirondacks and Lake George. Now he and Terry continued the latter as a couple, overcoming the lack of an automobile by borrowing Gertrude's car. Another shared passion was music, both classical and popular. While both admired the orchestral works of Bartok, Stravinsky, Schubert, and Brahms, Marvin particularly delighted in performing medleys of Porter, Gershwin, and Berlin on the piano in the fashion of a Tin Pan Alley entertainer.[4]

Miller (second from top) the college graduate (Peter Miller)

Once the couple had finished their college studies, they shared the daunting challenge of securing gainful employment in the still-stagnant New York job market. Failure meant having to delay marriage and the start of their own family. Miller's fading hopes of an immediate teaching career had fully evaporated with the word that not only was the school system extending its half-decade-long moratorium on teacher-certification exams, local education officials were winnowing down the number of postcertification candidates on grounds of their having unacceptable (as in "foreign") accents. At Gertrude's instigation Marvin conferred once again with city Board of Education members to weigh his prospects. They candidly informed him that in his case his arm injury—despite its seeming irrelevance to his competence—was now an insurmountable barrier to his chances. As one board bluntly defended the policy, "Look, we have become progressively more choosy."[5]

Though Miller had little control over it, the timing of his entry into the job market that spring of 1938 could not have been much worse. A second downturn, dubbed the "Roosevelt recession," had caused unemployment to spike once more. Joblessness nationwide, which had fallen from 25 percent in early 1933 to under 15 percent at the end of 1936, now swelled by two additional million more to more than 19 percent of the labor force. As early as the summer preceding his senior year, Marvin had been denied even the application forms for temporary employment at the various government work agencies. During that experience he had learned the dismaying truth that the employment offices' usual requirement was for the job seeker first to run the gauntlet of a screening interview by a staffer. Only if the questioning revealed a unique talent or specialized work experience would application forms even be disbursed. In effect, first-time job seekers had no chance. As Miller now renewed his forays into the job market after graduation, he learned the hard way when—and when not—to reveal his level of education. As one example, he soon discovered that businesses that advertised clerical positions regularly would reject any college man as "overqualified" even if he claimed such skills as typing aptitude.[6]

Miller was finding out the hard way that his freshly minted bachelor's degree was of little or no immediate worth. Determined to exhaust every employment avenue, he signed up for each available job-placement test. The only apparent "payoff" for his diligence, however, which he later noted sardonically, was that "I found I was very good at taking exams." His parents tried to help him by passing along word-of-mouth information, tipping off their son that a family friend and insurance salesman for Metropolitan Life might be able to scrounge up work for him. But when he went to the firm's Manhattan office, before he had even talked to a representative, Marvin overheard in the waiting area that the company's reputation for anti-Semitism in its hiring practices meant he was wasting his time.[7]

For well over a year Miller's quest for steady work came up empty. In the meantime he toiled at a series of dead-end jobs to make ends meet. The first of these was working for a wholesaler of gift-shop products, including cheap necklaces and cigarette cases. Next was a customs-broker job in Manhattan near the docks with the Majestic Shipping and Forwarding Company—a firm that prepared paperwork for importers and exporters to ensure compliance with U.S. customs law. From there he moved on to a position as a stock runner in the financial district, toting transaction documents between securities buyers and sellers. The pay in all these jobs was low and the hours terrible. Each opportunity placed a premium on his foot speed and physical stamina rather than his brainpower. As an example, in the case of the Majestic job, the goods being shipped out frequently left on vessels with departure times of midnight or even later. Meeting those deadlines required the prompt delivery of the necessary papers by the runner regardless of the time of night. Although Miller received modest meal payments while on shift, the company refused to make good on his transportation costs to and from the dockyards. The firm's manager, a female stand-in for the Majestic's absentee owner, took apparent pride in being a petty tyrant. If Miller or any coworker showed up as little as five minutes late for whatever reason, she imposed fines and docked pay with an unconcealed relish.[8]

Although Miller's post-NYU sequence of temporary jobs failed to provide stability or security, they did offer at least a ground-floor window on American capitalism. Although his job at Majestic did not require him to interact with sailors and dockhands, nevertheless their presence was inescapable. Showing little fear of consequences, longshoremen would bitterly voice their contempt for the procedure known as the "shape-up"—the demeaning process by which several times daily the boss stevedore selected temporary hands from the much larger throng milling about the gates. In turn, Miller's subsequent posting as a Wall Street runner placed him at the heart of finance capitalism's complex banking, credit, and securities markets. Shortly before 9:00 A.M. the financial district's streets would awaken like beehives and the army of swiftly moving clerks, tellers, stenographers, office boys, and runners would pour out of the subways, ferries, and elevated trains of Lower Manhattan. Then the bankers and brokers would arrive, carried by chauffeur-driven automobiles or even airplanes landing on a ramp at the foot of Wall Street. As a human speck in this chaotic multitude, Miller toted securities from opening bell to close and beyond, hustling to and fro between the brokerage houses.[9]

Eager to escape such day-to-day grind whenever possible to spend time with his fiancée, Miller delighted in bringing Terry to favorite spots in the Adirondacks. When time and distance did not permit these escapes, the couple took in musical shows such as *42nd Street* and partook of the diversions of Brighton Beach as their finances allowed. But for them and many other residents of the metropolis, in the spring of 1939 a grander entertainment diversion now presented itself. New York's World's Fair consisted of a sprawling playground of government and corporate exhibits and popular amusements that gave spectacular testimony to the ideal, if not yet the actual reality, of material progress. Erected on Flushing Meadows' marshland, the fair dedicated itself to the premise that science and technology were ushering in a "world of tomorrow" characterized by peace and prosperity and linked by futuristic transportation. Like many fellow attendees, Marvin and Terry were especially awestruck by the GM-sponsored Futurama, in which chair-borne spectators were symbolically transported from "coast to coast" above a model United States of thirty-years hence and from which they peered down upon an orderly, mechanistic utopia of cities with suspended walkways, and tied together by high-speed expressways.[10]

The world of the moment, of course, bore scant resemblance to this technology-driven utopia. Fascism was on the march, threatening to tear apart an increasingly fragile peace. Ironically, just days after the Nazi invasion of Poland on September 1, 1939, and the formal outbreak of European war, Miller received word of a promising job opportunity. His earlier persistence and foresight first in learning how to type and then constantly enlisting for battery after battery of job tests finally had paid off. One of his more recent exams had been a typing test meant to screen candidates for federal civil-service office employment. He had managed an eighty-words-a-minute pace with an acceptable error rate. Miller now received formal notification in the mail that he had been approved for just such an entry-level position in Washington, D.C., at the Treasury Department. The new job would carry with it a $1,440 annual salary before pension deductions, and a twice-monthly take-home figure of $57.90.[11]

Quickly packing their modest belongings, Marvin and Terry immediately moved to Washington and secured a small rental apartment at $50 per month. Once he had settled into the new job, Marvin promptly joined a union for the first time in his life—the AFL-affiliated American Federation of Government Employees. Of greater immediate importance to him than his union membership, however, was that his new job finally enabled the couple to schedule a wedding. Coordinating their nuptials and their honeymoon with the limited Christmas vacation time Miller's position allowed, Marvin and Terry wed on Christmas Eve 1939 in their native Brooklyn. Herb Parmet, the pair's unwitting matchmaker, served as best man. In spite of the patience they had been forced to exhibit, Marvin was still just twenty-two years of age and his bride but twenty. With all of the seemingly interminable waiting, just slightly over three years had passed since their first real date.[12]

Having yearned for the security of a civil-service position or comparable stable job, the Millers' first tour of duty in Washington nonetheless would last but two-thirds of a year. Even so, the time the couple spent in the nation's capital proved an eye-opening experience. Like other informed Jews, Marvin and Terry had followed through the media the ominous ascent to power of Adolf Hitler and the mounting catalog of fascist aggression and repression. They had noted with mounting alarm the Nazi seizures of Austria and the Sudetenland, the virulent anti-Semitism of *Kristallnacht,* and the invasion of Czechoslovakia. The West's shameful passivity toward these outrages, and the U.S. government's indifference to the plight of Jewish refugees aboard the *S.S. St. Louis,* infuriated the couple. The signing of a nonaggression pact by the Soviet Union with Nazi Germany, however, was perhaps the greatest shock to the pro-Soviet Millers, given the two countries' obvious ideological contradictions and their support of opposing sides in the Spanish Civil War.

Barely weeks later, in September 1939, Hitler's troops stormed into Poland and the British and French governments declared war on Germany. Inside the United States, the fact of European war now fueled an increasingly strident debate over whether the nation should pursue isolationist or interventionist paths. Like other young people of the time holding passionate leftist beliefs, the Millers were now convinced that history had reached a fundamental crossroads, but Stalin's appeasement of Hitler posed a painful dilemma for such Popular Front supporters as they. Was the Soviet dictator's action a cold-blooded betrayal deserving condemnation, or a necessary pragmatic avoidance for the time being of a war against fascism that bought time and space for an underprepared Russia? With a revulsion against imperialism and war that had been recently refreshed by reading Dalton Trumbo's *Johnny Got His Gun,* and contradicting his strong hatred of fascism, Miller naively accepted the Soviet government's rationalization of its actions, as did his wife. In doing so they minimized the roles of Stalin's purges and of collectivism-induced famine in contributing to Russia's lack of preparedness. Over the ensuing winter of 1939–1940, the deceptive calm of the "phony war" only muddled the issue of American intervention by offering domestic advocates of pacifism additional hope that the conflict could be contained or halted. In the spring of 1940, such naiveté was cruelly shattered by German conquests of Norway, the Low Countries, and France.[13]

That same spring of 1940, a new job opening drew the Millers back from Washington. In April, Marvin was notified that he had been offered a job as a social investigator in New York City's Welfare Department. Even after he and Terry had first moved to Washington, the low-level nature of his Treasury position and their strong ties to New York had led Marvin to continue signing up for professional examinations for positions there. Among the most recent of these had been a general civil-service exam qualifying the applicant for municipal employment. Eighteen thousand applicants had taken the test, with the city anticipating the hiring of only five hundred. Being selected also required not merely attaining a high score on the written test but possession of either a bachelor's degree or a minimum four years of social welfare work experience, an oral exam, and finally endorsement by a department personnel panel. Miller had placed in the top fifty on the formal test, and in his oral interview, he impressed his inquisitors with both his knowledge and his dedication. When the offer materialized, the couple eagerly packed their bags once again for a welcomed return to New York.[14]

Miller would be employed by the Welfare Department for more than two years, from spring 1940 to the early fall of 1942. It proved to be a life-changing experience. His work in close contact with the city's destitute profoundly shaped his views on the nature of poverty and reinforced a budding awareness of the importance of unions and solidarity to the attainment of political influence and economic and social progress. His new job at first paid only slightly more than his old one, with a starting salary of $1,500 a year and $120 in future annual increases. But the welfare-department position also meant membership in a CIO union for the first time—the State, County, and Municipal Workers of America. Dedicated to his local, Miller quickly won election to the grievance committee and soon was elevated to the rank of its chairman, from which he helped lead a brief sit-down strike. Marvin and Terry also both signed up with the labor left's electoral vehicle in New York, the American Labor Party, and distributed campaign literature door to door during the 1940 fall campaign. True to their commitment, they voted for all of the ALP's endorsed candidates, including President Roosevelt—in so doing ignoring the quixotic pleadings of CIO national leader John L. Lewis in behalf of Republican Wendell Willkie.[15]

Still carrying with him the memory of the dispossessed people of his old neighborhood and those he had seen on his walks with his father in earlier times, Miller found himself working directly with and for similar men on a daily basis. His role was not limited to representing the city in its dealings with poor clients, but included serving as an advocate for the latter. One of New York's more remarkable features during the Depression was its recognition of formal representation of the various segments, whether employed or not, of the city's labor force. In other words, not only was Miller a union member, but so too were those he was retained to help. Men receiving non-workfare forms of general public assistance, for example, belonged to the Workers Alliance. At the same time, the smaller share of the unemployed who had gained temporary public jobs through the Works Progress Administration (WPA) claimed the right to be represented by the Unemployed and Project Workers Union.[16]

When Miller started at the Welfare Department, the American economy was just beginning to experience a positive boost from rising defense spending. However, New York City continued to lag well behind. Compared to other urban economies more tied to vehicle or ship manufacturing, Gotham's greater reliance upon the garment trade and upon financial services meant that the early stages of preparedness had less of an impact upon its employment picture. Combined with national cuts in government relief spending, New York's slow recovery meant that Miller's first month on the job was the one in which the city's public-assistance rolls climbed to their Depression-era high. With his client load swollen, he did not have the luxury of being able to review each new case file before making an initial home visit. Thus without warning, on one of these get-acquainted sessions he discovered that among his clients were several past "employees" of New York's organized-crime syndicate Murder, Incorporated.[17]

Miller's charges were like human pinballs in careening from one type of public assistance to another. Some had joined the WPA workers' organization when they had been hired onto federal projects, only to fall back onto general assistance rosters once their temporary work had concluded. Others were men whose savings had been exhausted but who had still not secured private or public employment of any kind. Still more were seasonal workers, who appeared on welfare rolls between periods of short-term hiring only to come off again as soon as another such job materialized. Whatever the individual circumstances of each, these men of all races and backgrounds had lost any real economic security and been forced to choose between often demeaning and consistently inadequate welfare or back-breaking toil on city public-works projects. Given New York's private-sector occupational profile, many of Miller's clients were former white-collar salesmen who resembled his own father and who either had never been required to perform manual labor of the type required in the WPA or were now too old or infirm to do so. Marvin learned that the unjust yet widespread idea of relief workers as lazy individuals leaning on shovels often stemmed from their utter exhaustion and not laziness. In related fashion, he was amazed at the numbers of those with notations of strenuous-work injuries such as hernias in his case files.[18]

Eye-opening as well, but inspirationally, was the color-blind solidarity frequently exhibited by those struggling alike for economic survival. On one of his earliest client visits, Miller came upon the all-too-familiar Depression scene of a local sheriff's deputy removing furniture from an apartment and piling it on the curbside in response to a repossession order. White neighbors of the evicted African American family first milled about the building feigning indifference, while they cast furtive glances toward the lawman. But as soon as these seemingly innocent loiterers had satisfied themselves that not only all of the unfortunate's furniture had been set outside but the police had also disappeared to carry out their next eviction, the neighbors hurriedly snatched up the items and toted them back inside the building—not for use in their own fleabag apartments, but to return the belongings to their original holder.[19]

Miller's contact with his destitute clients offered a kind of daily practical tutorial in the real world that contrasted with his formal education in economics.

Combined with his innate curiosity and his already strong underdog instincts, it led him increasingly to ponder basic questions about the nature and roots of such glaring need amid plenty. Fortuitously for a young man in search of answers, among the side benefits available to such Welfare Department employees as he who had compiled superior performance records was free tuition for graduate classes at the New School for Social Research. The New School, which had been founded in 1919 by progressive academics James Harvey Robinson and Charles A. Beard, also claimed a lineage with the pioneering scholar of social status, Thorstein Veblen. More immediately relevant to New School attendees of the early 1940s, however, was the presence of a cadre of ten exiled German professors, a "University in Exile," who upon fleeing the Nazis had migrated to New York and who now constituted the institution's core graduate faculty. The expatriates included such luminaries as anthropologist Claude Levi-Strauss, political scientist Hannah Arendt (who would gain fame as the author of "The Origins of Totalitarianism"), and renowned musician and composer Hanns Eisler. It was another one of the refugee professors, however, who made the strongest impression upon Miller. Frieda Wunderlich arguably had been the single greatest female public figure of Weimar Germany. As principal architect of the German government's pioneering social-welfare system, she had held the post of judge of the German Supreme Court for Social Welfare from 1930 until her exodus in 1933. For ten years prior to her escape she had also been editor of a leading German antifascist journal, *Soziale Praxis,* as well as contributing frequent articles on various aspects of employment, labor, and welfare policy.[20]

Prodded by both his clients' everyday experiences and by his New School classes, Miller sought out literature that could illuminate for him the historical and theoretical contexts of, and prescriptions for, the present crisis. Despite the Millers' modest income, which discouraged purchases of expensive first editions, Marvin and Terry both frequented 4th Avenue's secondhand bookstores. For the first time in his life, having not been required to do so for his undergraduate classes at Miami or NYU, he read Marx's *Das Kapital* and Engels's *Origins of the Family, Private Property, and the State.* The Millers also avidly consumed fiction with an historical materialist bent, most notably the works of British novelist and social critic Robert Briffault. In *Europa* and *Europa in Limbo* they eagerly absorbed the two volumes' accounts of pre–World War I Europe's excesses and self-delusion, the Great War's leveling of the old aristocratic order, and Russia's revolutionary convulsions.[21]

For Marvin, however, the book that left a particularly lasting impact was a different Briffault work—a collection of essays entitled *Reasons for Anger.* In the work its author defiantly rejected innate explanations, whether spiritual or biological, for the evolution of human classes, institutions, and culture. Instead, Briffault found their root in man's drive for material self-interest and, through it, social control. Societies at any given moment were a mix of classes and interests holding greater or lesser power. This blend of dominant and subordinate groups also included interests that survived and even thrived by buttressing the dominant classes. In modern times, such mainstays of the status quo could include established political parties, popular religions, and mainstream press organs. For Briffault, then, it was not merely the combination of social injustice and the role played by rulers, but also the responsibility shared by its apologists that gave the contemporary social critic his justifiable "reasons for anger." The pursuit of justice and peace, in turn, required the rigorous and courageous application of cold reason by the individual, as well as his and others' mobilization and collective assertions of power to change such unacceptable objective realities as inequality. Those determined to confront the social ills of their times held in themselves the human potential to do so, but only if they took the initiative directly rather than expecting salvation from others.[22]

As Miller continued to work with his welfare clients and privately wrestled with the weighty questions of his times, by 1941 belated improvement was finally taking hold in New York. And like his fellow citizens, he followed attentively as the tide of news poured in from both Washington and abroad. In March Congress passed the controversial Lend-Lease Act providing U.S. military assistance to Great Britain. Across the nation, labor unrest was again on the rise, as CIO steel, auto, electrical, and farm-implement unions took advantage of the leverage offered by the growing demand for workers to strike against those firms still resisting organization. Actions at Allis-Chalmers and North American Aviation drew sharp rebuke, however, and not just from the usual sources but even pro-mobilization trade unionists such as Sidney Hillman. As spring became summer, however, the most dramatic news development came from the European war. Reported by radio dispatches and then shouted in boldface newspaper headlines, on June 22 Germany shattered the nonaggression pact with Russia and launched a massive invasion of conquest. If there was any silver lining in the news for those such as the Millers, it was that the advocates of American intervention and the champions of isolationism among Popular Front leftists could now once more unite behind the common antifascist cause.[23]

By the fall, American destroyers and German U-boats were exchanging salvoes in the Atlantic and U.S. warships had been authorized to attack Nazi submarines "on sight." On the other side of the world, a continuing Japanese military aggression in the Far East threatened to conquer not only all of China but the resource-rich lands of Southeast Asia as well. It seemed more and more obvious to Americans—including the Millers—that soon the United States would become, voluntarily or not, a direct participant in global war. Nonetheless, it was still a shock when, on the morning of December 7, 1941, a carrier-borne Japanese airstrike hit the U.S. Pacific Fleet at Pearl Harbor. The sneak attack upon the Hawaiian Islands would not only propel a reluctant nation into a war, but it would also succeed in uniting virtually all Americans, regardless of their prewar ideologies and interests, in support of the goal of total victory over the Axis. For many citizens, the dawn of war would mean a personal decision to enlist and to fight on distant shores. For Marvin Miller, who was barred from volunteering for such service by a handicap of birth, the nation's call to arms would instead return him to Washington, D.C., for bureaucratic service in the government that would direct America's "arsenal of democracy."

Four

Working for Victory

Barely one month after Pearl Harbor, president Franklin D. Roosevelt set forth before Congress the immense challenge that now confronted the United States as a nation engaged in a two-front, global war. The production goals he outlined as necessary were daunting, and included 60,000 military aircraft in 1942 and more than double the number the following year; 120,000 tanks; 55,000 antiaircraft guns; and sixteen million deadweight tons of merchant shipping over a comparable two-year span. Because of the military disasters already suffered by the Russians and British, the speed with which the United States could convert its factories into an "arsenal of democracy" would be vital to the attainment of Allied victory over the Axis.[1]

Marvin Miller, like his fellow Americans at home, would be directly engaged in this massive mobilization effort. He and his wife would relocate twice as they shuttled from post to post in the war economy and bureaucracy. With one serving in the federal government and the other alternately in both the public and private sectors, they would make their contribution while adapting to the conflict's impact on their daily lives. As home-front warriors they would be forced to adjust to such shared sacrifices as longer hours, fewer and shorter vacations, controls on wages, shortages of consumer goods, and rationing. On the positive side of the ledger, they would see their financial security get better, and—most significantly—they would welcome a new member into the family.

It was not until November 1942—almost a year after Pearl Harbor—that the Millers returned to Washington to begin jobs in the expanding wartime federal bureaucracy. Not surprisingly Marvin had been rejected for enlistment in the military as a 4-F because of his crippled shoulder. Determined to do his part, he had enrolled in a new round of civil-service and professional examinations in the hopes of landing a federal post. Included among this battery of tests was a junior-level federal exam in economics. After weeks of waiting, he received notification that based upon his prior experience in Washington and his high test score, he had been selected for a job on the research staff of the War Production Board (WPB). Miller quickly accepted, and he and Terry packed again, returning to the city they had left just two years before.[2]

The lingering effects of the Great Depression as late as 1941 ironically had left the American economy with sufficient slack to now make a rapid mobilization possible. Still, this untapped potential would not magically transform itself into reality. The Roosevelt administration's earlier preparedness effort had spawned a host of new agencies geared to accelerating war production, but with mixed results. A fumbling Office of Production Management already had been replaced by the WPB. The Office of Price Administration (OPA) had been given primary responsibility for restraining price inflation and mitigating the adverse impact of consumer-goods shortages. In April 1942 it had issued the famous General Maximum Price Regulation, or "General Max," which had set price caps indefinitely at the previous month's levels. The OPA had followed up its price edict by creating ten separate rationing programs for basic domestic products, including ones for meat, shoes, fats, coffee, tires, and gasoline. Business and labor leaders in turn demonstrated reciprocal patriotism by offering to eschew strikes and lockouts for the war's duration. In the absence of a normal collective-bargaining environment in wartime, the Roosevelt administration back in January 1942 had created yet another new agency as well—the National War Labor Board (WLB)—consisting of four representatives each from government, business, and labor and serving as the temporary adjudicator of labor-management conflicts. On the heels of the OPA's "General Max," the WLB through its "Little Steel" rulings followed suit and set the wartime pattern of linking the size of civilian wage adjustments to the rate of consumer price increases.[3]

Miller joined the WPB in the expectation that his new position would both challenge him and enable him to make a tangible contribution to the war effort. He was soon disappointed on both scores. Already the WPB was being outmaneuvered by the military-procurement departments it had been tasked with overseeing. Reflective of the armed services' scorn toward the WPB were reported comments by army Lt. Gen. Brehon Somervell, who had attacked the bureaucrats' efforts as a scheme by "[Vice President] Henry Wallace and the leftists to take over the country." Public opinion toward the WPB was proving no more favorable. Back in March, the agency had issued a controversial edict designed to conserve scarce wool supplies that banned vests, patch pockets, cuffs, or extra pair of pants from inclusion in men's suit purchases and mandated instead the production of single-breasted, narrow-lapelled, and short-pocketed "victory suits." But the new suits' lower material costs had led in turn to lower retail prices, and the subsequent sales jump that ensued shattered the board's conservation limits. Of broader consequence than this fiasco, however, was the agency's inability to adjudicate effectively competing raw-materials demands from rival service branches and private companies. As a result, aircraft production stalled from insufficient supplies of aluminum and cargo-vessel construction hogged available steel stocks. Military trucks languished for lack of tires and spark plugs, while troops trained with rocks and firecrackers rather than scarce grenades and live ammunition.[4]

In response to the worsening gridlock, over the summer of 1942 WPB staffers had labored to draft a new overall scheme dubbed the Controlled Materials Plan to impose more effective control over materials allocation. Under the agency's proposed guidelines, once the military services had each taken their initial bites out of the apple, second-tier federal departments such as the Maritime Commission, the Lend-Lease Administration, and the Office of Civilian Supply would submit their needs estimates. The WPB would then assign materials shares out of the remaining stockpiles for these agencies to distribute to their respective subcontractors. Even the revised system, however, still failed to give the WPB the authority it needed to rein in the armed forces' gargantuan appetites. It also failed to provide the board with the practical clout to press the services to award more contracts to small businesses or to demand fair hiring of women and minorities by military contractors.

Lacking the necessary statutory authority, the newly hired Marvin Miller and fellow junior staffers found themselves required to project future civilian resource demands and availabilities without having the necessary data to do so. To take but one case, having to do with the allocation of steel supplies, once military production had gotten its share, which civilian claimants should be granted higher priority than others? Should manufacturers of fire trucks, for example, be given a superior place on the pecking order over ambulances? Given the frustrating and even surreal nature of these assignments, Miller soon wanted out of the WPB and Washington. But Terry, for her part, had landed a more congenial post on the editorial staff of the Office of Price Administration's newsletter, the *OPA Calendar*. Having tagged along while Marvin had pursued a succession of jobs after graduation, she was now finally utilizing her English degree drafting advice columns directed at the agency's female workers. The OPA's reach—and that of Terry's publication—extended well beyond Washington to encompass not just seventy-five thousand regular employees but also the three hundred thousand additional volunteers across the country, the majority of them women, who served as merchandise price and quality checkers.[5]

For the unhappy Marvin, however, a seemingly more promising opportunity now popped up outside Washington. Coworkers aware of his discontent had tipped him off about an opening in the Philadelphia regional office of the War Manpower Commission (WMC). After spousal heart-to-heart discussions of the implications of another move for both partners, Miller applied for the job and landed it in June 1943. To their subsequent frustration, however, Marvin's new posting proved even more frustrating than his previous post. Unbeknown to him until after he had already assumed his new job at the WMC, the agency had already garnered a reputation for intense hostility toward unions and toward agency employees with open prolabor opinions. As the civilian-labor market in America had grown tighter in 1942 and 1943, the commission had made it a top priority to fill all businesses' requests for workers as rapidly as possible, even those calls emanating from firms with blatantly antilabor, antifemale, and antiminority hiring practices. And even in comparison to other mobilization offices, almost all of which were unabashedly pro-industry, the WMC demonstrated a special animus toward anything that smacked of union-organizing campaigns among its personnel.[6]

In a more general sense, hostility across the federal bureaucracy toward labor activism had intensified by the spring of 1943. One catalyst for the backlash had been John L. Lewis's leading UMW members out of the soft-coal mines in violation of no-strike pledges and the WLB-imposed "Little Steel" wage ceilings. Congress had retaliated by passing the Smith-Connally War Labor Disputes Act, which had expanded presidential executive power to seize war plants, criminalized the encouragement of strikes at such facilities, ordered thirty-day mandatory cooling-off periods, and outlawed direct union monetary contributions to federal election campaigns. Within this negatively charged atmosphere—nowhere more so than at the War Manpower Commission—Miller's open effort to organize his fellow employees in behalf of the CIO's United Federal Workers drew the wrath of his superiors in the Philadelphia office. Despite receiving exemplary efficiency ratings, after just three months at the agency Miller lost his job in September in a WMC "reduction in force."[7]

With deserved guilt pangs for having been fired from his own posting after having made Terry give up a good job, Miller scrambled to land another federal position. He returned to Washington and interviewed for an economist opening at the U.S. Department of Agriculture. When he returned home, however, Marvin learned with some embarrassment that back in Philadelphia, the Wage Stabilization Division of the War Labor Board's regional office—located in the very same building as his former WMC job—was actively looking for trained researchers. As had been detailed in the original executive order creating the WLB in 1942, then refined in the Smith-Connally bill, if a labor-management dispute threatened war production, the opposing parties were first required to attempt direct resolution of their differences. If that failed, they could in turn solicit the help of the Labor Department's Federal Mediation Service (FMS). But if both these avenues failed, the WLB then assumed the role of a court of last resort. In contrast to the NLRB, the WLB's powers in such instances went well beyond merely overseeing the fairness of the adjudication process to addressing the substantive issues and determining a settlement. It could set wages, hours, and other employment terms and conditions and then enforce the results it had itself dictated. Undergirding the WLB's wartime authority were each side's earlier promises not to unilaterally undermine military production, the deterrent effects of public opinion against any party that defied the WLB, and as a last resort the presidential hammer of possible government seizure and operation of war plants.[8]

The timely opportunity afforded Marvin Miller with the WLB in fall 1943 would make a major contribution to his subsequent career in labor. Years later he acknowledged his debt in observing, "At the National War Labor Board during World War II I received an advanced education in labor-management relations and the resolution of disputes." He added appreciatively, "The War Labor Board was the greatest training ground for labor, management, and arbitrators." Service in the WLB provided Miller an unforgettable lesson in the importance of federal labor law and its impartial and effective implementation in fostering an environment in which worker rights and wages were protected. Early on, even before its landmark Little Steel rulings, the WLB in spring 1942 had adopted policy guidelines intended to preserve unions' prewar membership strength. Cognizant of labor's vulnerability to management counterattack if the unions patriotically foreswore the strike option, the WLB's "maintenance-of-membership" guidelines afforded new hires in plants with existing union contracts but a fifteen-day window to opt out of union membership. Those fresh employees who had not formally withdrawn from the union by the deadline were then obligated to pay dues and uphold all other "good-standing" requirements through the end of the particular labor contract. The policy did not relieve organized labor of its problem with so-called "free riders"—nonunion employees who nonetheless received union-negotiated rights and benefits. But the WLB "maintenance of membership" policy proved a boon to wartime union membership growth since, whether by choice or inertia, most new workers in the organized industries stayed on union rolls. As a consequence, by war's end organized labor's ranks were 50 percent stronger and counted approximately fifteen million men and women.[9]

Despite the WLB's stance, labor-management battles persisted over worker representation rights—including unions' authority to recruit supervisory personnel and those whose job classifications had been redefined "upward" as a result of wartime plant conversions. But by the time Miller joined the WLB Philadelphia office in 1943, an increasing share of disputes now stemmed not from representation issues but instead from basic wage disagreements or grievances and wildcat stoppages triggered by unilateral changes in employee schedules and work rules. This mushrooming caseload of wage and work-rule grievances was what had actually led to the War Labor Board's establishment of twelve decentralized offices—including that of the Third Region, which included not just the City of Brotherly Love but all of Pennsylvania, western New Jersey, and Delaware. Ever since OPA's General Max directive and the WLB's adoption of its Little Steel formula, union workers had been growing restive at what they perceived as rank favoritism toward rival economic interests, in particular big business and agriculture. FDR's "hold the line" wage/price order of April 1943 had sparked even more grumbling. Labor had taken note that although the UMW's earlier, controversial walkout had drawn John L. Lewis the label of the "most hated man in America," the end result of his defiance nonetheless had been impressive wage hikes for his membership. Unsurprisingly a surge in WLB wage cases had followed, generating the need for the talents of Miller and fellow agency staffers in generating the evidentiary material regional-office hearing examiners required.[10]

The WLB's surge in such wage and work-rule cases also provided Miller eventually with his opportunity to move up the ranks. Receiving plaudits from his superiors for his research work, the twenty-six-year-old staffer gained promotion to the post of hearings officer in early 1944. In his new role, he would later admit with gratitude, "the experience I gained . . . dealing with almost every type of disputed issue in a wide variety of industries, could not have been duplicated anywhere or at any other time." Now, rather than preparing background data for others to base rulings upon, Miller himself was either a sole adjudicator on one-man panels or chair—and swing vote—on tripartite boards consisting also of labor and management representatives. It was his responsibility to study the research others provided, listen to the testimony from spokespersons representing the dispute's competing parties, draw conclusions on the merits and determine a preferred remedy, and draft official conclusions and recommendations for final sign-off or reversal by his higher-ups.[11]

Miller's calm and rational demeanor and his materialistic conception of society meshed well with the requirements of a WLB hearings officer. Proceedings mirrored those of courtrooms in using an adversarial process that nonetheless maintained strict decorum and based decisions upon evidence, precedent, and law rather than raw clout. At the same time, the formal recognition of the opposing status of labor and management in the hearing structure underscored the continuing reality of class conflict even in a wartime America that asserted a patriotic unity of purpose. While Miller strongly held as a personal article of faith that in normal times vigorous, direct labor-management combat should be allowed to play out with a minimum of governmental interference, given the war's exigencies he saw WLB's binding resolution as a practical and necessary departure that prevented economic disruption while still protecting workers' rights and well-being.[12]

Although disputes over union-security provisions—including employers' requirement that they honor dues check-offs and closed-shop arrangements (requiring union membership in the hiring and retention of workers) that pre-dated the war—still occasionally reached Miller's panels, the lion's share of the cases he fielded involved disagreements over the size of wartime wage adjustments. These included disputes over the level of base hourly boosts relative to inflation; the appropriate value assigned to shift differentials and night-shift premium pay; questions of overtime, jury duty, and vacation pay; and whether and how much compensation to award for down-time and on-call reimbursements. The industries affected by his rulings ran the gamut, from dairies, power companies, electrical manufacturing plants, locomotive works, and mines to restaurants and consumer retail establishments. A typical outcome in a dispute over what constituted appropriate wage and overtime adjustments was a retroactive increase of 2½ cents in the hourly rate since the expiration of the previous contract, additional premiums of 4 to 6 cents for second- and third-shift workers, and time-and-a-half pay for work in excess of eight hours daily or for work weeks that exceeded five days.[13]

Given his prolabor sympathies, Miller might have been expected to exploit his hearings authority to orchestrate one-sided findings. But as the public representative on his panels, he was officially obligated to harmonize his recommendations with federal wage-and-price statutes, presidential executive orders, and WLB national-office precedents. As a result his personal latitude was limited. He did share the conviction of other activist-minded colleagues that despite the boundaries of WLB flexibility, he should not check his own life experience at the door and only base his decisions upon the varying quality of the presentations from either side. But his integrity and obligation to uphold established national benchmarks occasionally resulted in decisions that upset those on the labor side. In one such case in 1945, he sided with industry in a dispute between the Continental Diamond Fibre Company and a United Mine Workers local. Rejecting the union's demand for a starting hourly wage of sixty-five cents, Miller endorsed a lower immediate figure of 57½ cents, coupled with a 2½-cent annual raise. Overall in his tenure at the WLB, the general pattern of his rulings showed a tendency to pair modest upward adjustments in basic wages with flexibility and generosity in overtime-pay boosts and shift-differential distinctions.[14]

Although they did not appear frequently, disputes involving race and gender occasionally surfaced in Miller's cases. In those instances, too, a pragmatic approach was usually applied. Perhaps his most innovative ruling, once more from 1945, was a Pittsburgh-based case involving the city's Labor Standards Association, the Hotel and Restaurant Employees International Alliance, and the AFL bartenders' local. The controversy focused upon the disparity in rates of overtime pay awarded to restaurant workers and those of other department-store employees. A key underlying issue, however, was the persistent wage inequality between male and female retail workers. Besides the ultimate recommendation of a general base-wage hourly increase of 2½ cents, overtime pay at a 1⅓ rate for those working forty to forty-four hours a week, and time-and-a-half rates for employees with weekly schedules in excess of that, Miller and his panel majority additionally specified that while males' overtime rate should kick in upon eight hours' daily work, that of female employees should start after just seven hours and twenty minutes.[15]

Miller's acknowledgement of the unique challenges women faced in the workplace was informed by his wife's experiences. When he and Terry had first moved to Philadelphia, she had secured a research assistantship in Bendix Aviation's engineering department despite her lack of academic training in that field. (Ironically in view of both Millers' ideological convictions, Bendix was not just a vital manufacturer of aviation instruments for the U.S. military but at the same time the target of an investigation by the Roosevelt administration,

Marvin and Terry Miller (Peter Miller)

accused of prewar international patent-cartel violations of antitrust laws and of attempting a similar illicit relationship with a German company's Spanish subsidiary.) At her facility, Terry worked in a department of twenty engineers and their aides in a separate section of the factory from the line workers. One of her main responsibilities was to test magnetic drag tachometers—instruments used for measuring aircraft engine speed—under conditions of great heat and cold. To re-create the appropriate extremes, she constructed a box with a light bulb inside to generate high temperatures and retrieved dry ice for the opposite test using a small red cart, drawing whistles from male factory hands as she walked by.[16]

Although the United Electrical Workers (UE) represented Bendix's five thousand shop-floor employees, the company's professional staff remained nonunion despite the successes of the CIO's Federation of Architects, Engineers, Chemists, and Technicians in penetrating the firm's rivals. As a consequence Bendix's production-line women workers were better protected against discrimination than was Terry. The representation divide inside the factory between line workers and white-collar employees was replicated by an equally stark partisan split. After the CIO had suffered its 1942 midterm debacle and had been forced to swallow the poison pill of Smith-Connally, the federation in advance of 1944 contests had formed a political action committee to raise campaign funds, prepare and distribute voter guides, and generate a larger working-class turnout. Despite the CIO's disapproval of Roosevelt's dumping of Henry Wallace as running mate in favor of Senator Harry Truman, it nonetheless marshaled its resources behind the FDR fourth-term effort. Inside the Bendix plant, Terry Miller estimated conservatively that forty-nine hundred of Bendix's five thousand shop-floor employees were sporting FDR buttons that Election Day. In sharp contrast, virtually all the engineering department save Terry were lined up solidly behind Thomas Dewey.[17]

November 1944 was a particularly noteworthy month for both Marvin and Terry, and not merely for political reasons. Not only did it bring the reelection of Roosevelt and significant gains for the Democrats in the Congress, it marked the conception of the Millers' first child. Within a few months, the physical demands of the pregnancy and the specter of looming job reductions at Bendix as victory grew closer forced Terry to resign and to seek a less-taxing post with an area employer. Ironically, her search for a desk job then landed her at the nearby Camden district offices of the Federation of Architects, Engineers, Chemists, and Technicians—the same CIO affiliate that had failed to organize Bendix. In her more compatible new environment, she soon ascended to the position of district director.[18]

As the war played out its brutal endgame, the Millers continued parallel countdowns toward victory and the arrival of their firstborn. Via the newspapers and the radio they tracked the Allied drives into Germany from east and west and the American island-hopping march toward Japan. They observed with deep sadness the sudden passing of President Roosevelt that April, cheered Adolf Hitler's suicide in his Berlin bunker later that month, and observed the subsequent celebrations of V-E Day in early May. As summer approached and then advanced, Terry's August delivery date neared and she reluctantly quit her union job to make last-minute preparations for her baby's arrival. Given the life-changing complications that had marked Marvin's entry into the world less than three decades ago, the Millers found themselves holding in their emotions more than usual as the expected day neared. While they waited anxiously, on the morning of August 6, 1945, an American B-29 bomber dropped an atomic bomb on the Japanese city of Hiroshima. Three days later, a second explosion followed over Nagasaki. Keeping their promise made at Yalta the previous February, the Russians now declared formal entry into the Japanese war and advanced into Korea. Within a week of these dramatic developments, at around seven o'clock in the evening on August 14, radio broadcasts interrupted regular programming to announce that Emperor Hirohito had ordered his nation to surrender. Just one hour after hearing the news, Marvin and Terry Miller welcomed their first child, a son they named Peter Daniel, into a world that had minutes before been restored to peace.[19]

But what kind of world would their son now inherit? With the end of the war, the Miller family faced renewed uncertainties about their financial security and their country's direction. Did Marvin's success at the War Labor Board mean that his employment instability was over, or would peace lead to government cutbacks and a return to his economic insecurity? More broadly, would a postwar economy mean a return to mass unemployment and Depression-style hardship, as some officials feared? And at home and overseas, would the Allies' hard-won victory over the Axis improve the prospects for a new era of progressivism at home and cooperation abroad, or would wartime unity disintegrate into cold war confrontation and anti-Communist hysteria? The answers for the Millers personally, and for their countrymen, would not be long in coming.

Five

Issues of Loyalty

In the months following the end of World War II, a return to Depression-era mass unemployment did not materialize. But return to a peacetime economy nonetheless produced short-run dislocations and turmoil. Organized labor, which had exercised restraint for the cause of victory, now expected rewards for its sacrifices. Spurred by long-festering discontent over wage inequities and in anticipation of the end of the no-strike pledge, workplace actions already had begun to surge. By November 1945 a strike wave was sweeping the country. Before it finally started to subside in 1946 it encompassed hundreds of thousands of workers in the automobile, steel, rubber, meatpacking, oil-refining, and electrical-appliances industries.[1]

In response the Truman administration scrambled to retain its wartime regimen of wage and price restraint. At the War Labor Board and at its successor, the Wage Stabilization Board, Marvin Miller and other holdover staffers tried in vain to moderate the inflationary spike. Signaling the disintegration of the government's wartime controls, fact-finding boards in the steel and auto disputes endorsed 20 percent wage boosts, amounting to roughly 18½ cents an hour, which despite their generosity failed to match industry's even heftier price hikes. Businesses justified their moves by citing rising costs from reconversion to civilian production. WLB and WSB regional wage panels—effectively circumscribed by the steel and auto benchmarks—ordered 15- to 20-cent hourly raises. Typical of such findings was Miller's recommendation in an early 1946 dispute between the Campbell's Soup Company of Camden and the local of the Food, Agricultural, Tobacco, and Allied Workers (CIO). Miller and the panel majority called for a 15-cent hourly hike for the five thousand regular employees and a 12½ cent boost for an equal number of temporary "tomato-season" workers. Five cents' worth of each group's increase was made retroactive to late September 1945, with the remainder taking effect at the end of March.[2]

Fanned by antilabor business interests, a reinvigorated GOP eager to exploit the public's ire at labor strife and high prices and its doubts about Harry Truman looked forward to major midterm electoral gains. From her new postpregnancy job as a free-lancer for the Amalgamated Meat Cutters' *Union Reporter,* Marvin's wife Terry warned her readers of the high cost of apathy if they failed to show up at the polls. But the efforts of her and others to rally the working-class Democratic base failed to stem the massive Republican tide. On Election Day of 1946, an estimated ten million blue-collar voters stayed home, and for the first time since the 1920s the GOP reclaimed control of both houses of Congress.[3]

Even before the new 80th Congress claimed its seats, its lame-duck predecessor voted to consign the Wage Stabilization Board to the scrapheap. For Marvin it meant a new round of job interviews and the return, however temporary, of economic insecurity. Fortunately, his wartime government experience combined with the ongoing labor-management strife gave him a leg up in securing a new position in Washington as a "counselor" in the Labor Department's U.S. Conciliation Service (USCS). Ironically, his primary duty consisted of training fresh-faced USCS apprentices in the arbitration and mediation skills and processes that the WLB and WSB had wrested away from the USCS in wartime. From 1942 through 1946, the Conciliation Service had been effectively reduced to the status of messenger boys, fielding and certifying initial adjudication requests from labor or management and forwarding them to the likes of Miller. Now that the shoe was on the other foot, the return to prewar lines of authority created an awkward working environment for Miller as he retrained his charges on how to carry out their prior functions.[4]

When Miller returned to Washington in early 1947 to assume his training duties, it was obvious how much the political ground had shifted since his family's last time in the capital. In just the eighteen months since the Axis surrenders, more than seventy anti-union bills had been introduced in the U.S. House of Representatives, and many of the most-hated provisions were about to become law in the form of the Taft-Hartley Act. This antilabor statute claimed to restore "balance" within the "one-sided" NLRB by putting the worker's right to reject unionization on an equal or greater footing than organized labor's ability to recruit. Taft-Hartley made decertification elections, special referenda to overturn union shops, and employer dissemination of anti-union literature all easier. And by expanding the number of intentionally dilatory ways in which business could trigger NLRB intervention, the bill threatened to strangle the agency in procedural requests and red tape and thereby restore an effective equivalent to the injunction. Seeing the Conciliation Service's very presence inside the Labor Department as evidence of prounion "one-sidedness," Taft-Hartley also called for its separation as an independent Federal Mediation and Conciliation Service (FMCS).[5]

If these changes were not troubling enough for prounion federal bureaucrats like Miller, Taft-Hartley further weakened organized labor by mandating eighty-day "cooling-off" periods during periods of "national emergency" that effectively gutted the strike power; barred secondary union boycotts; exempted supervisory employees from federal labor-law coverage or organizing rights; and allowed individual states to pass "right-to-work" laws that effectively preempted the further spread of unionization beyond its prewar base in the industrial Northeast and Midwest. Also, amid rising national cold war fears of internal subversion fueled not just by Republican accusations but by the Truman administration's own creation of loyalty boards to weed out suspected Communists from the government, Taft-Hartley now required loyalty oaths from union officialdom—but not from business executives—disavowing loyalty to Communism in both affiliation and belief. If a labor leader refused to comply, he forfeited his own and his organization's legal standing in the eyes of the NLRB and with it the government's ability to protect his rank and file from company predations.[6]

Motivated in part by the passage of Taft-Hartley over Truman's veto, Miller left the federal government in the summer of 1947. He insisted that he had not personally been at risk of firing because of the loyalty program, but rather that working in the reshaped policy environment created by Taft-Hartley would only have brought him mounting frustration. Choosing instead to enter the labor struggle directly, he joined the New York City office of the AFL's International Association of Machinists (IAM) as a district organizer. The IAM regional that Miller entered claimed jurisdiction beyond Gotham's metropolitan limits to include upstate New York, all of Connecticut, parts of Massachusetts and of northern New Jersey, and the city of Baltimore. Upon the Millers' return to their native New York, they moved into a modest house in Long Island's Queens Village. Terry continued with her free-lance reporting, contributing commentary and profiles for the *Jewish Daily Outlook* and *Southern Jewish Outlook* on such figures as Menachem Begin and Albert Einstein. As for Marvin, thanks to his

Miller organizing for the Machinists (International Association of
Machinists/Tamiment Library, NYU)

government experience in dealing with the postwar maze of collective-bargaining
issues and grievance processes, his responsibilities soon expanded well beyond
his official title as an organizer. When IAM negotiations with Yale and Towne—
maker of Yale Locks—deadlocked, the union's counsel Jerry Sturm called upon
Miller to join his regional bargaining panel—a request that evolved into a regular
pattern.[7]

While Miller took part in the Machinists' regional battles for union rights,
the labor movement both nationally and in New York approached a political
and ideological crossroad. Since the late 1930s, the AFL and CIO federations had
separately integrated their political operations with the Democratic Party and
had subordinated their own election strategy to the latter's direction. CIO-PAC
had already proven its value in this regard in 1944 and, following the Democrats'
1946 electoral disaster, the AFL launched a similar political action committee,
Labor's League for Political Education (LLPE). But despite such political mobili-

zation by unions, an increasingly vocal minority within the labor movement—particularly inside the CIO—believed that the time was overdue for the birth of a distinct national Labor Party. In New York the American Labor Party had been operating as early as 1936, and four years later a separate ALP ballot line had generated 40 percent of the total vote received by all of the ALP's endorsed candidates—many of them Democrats—in the Empire State.[8]

True believers in a national version of a Labor Party—including Marvin and Terry Miller—insisted that a third-party strategy would free labor from its supplicant position with the Democrats and ultimately force the latter to redefine itself as an uncompromising progressive vehicle or else risk losing not merely individual elections but its major-party standing. Labor Party supporters pointed to local successes not just in New York but also in Wisconsin, Washington, California, and Michigan, and to the rise of a social-democratic labor party in the Canadian province of Ontario. A similar national third political force in America, advocates insisted, would revive the New Deal–Popular Front coalition of the Depression years and advance a broad agenda of domestic progressive causes, including civil rights and national health insurance, as well as a more cooperative postwar relationship with the Soviet Union.[9]

The leadership majority of both the AFL and CIO, nonetheless, opposed this third-party vision on both ideological and practical grounds. It was technically true that labor's own voting-age membership of fifteen million, if combined with family members, small farmers and agricultural laborers, racial minorities, and other low-income Americans, constituted the numerical basis for a national party. But even by the late 1940s union members still represented barely one-third of the national workforce, and the nonunion majority of blue-collar America was not so easily mobilized. Working-class turnout often fell under 50 percent, and crosscutting divides of race, religion, and ethnicity splintered its electoral impact. And among those workers who did vote, the very success of the New Deal in having won the political loyalty of a majority of them for the Democrats now made persuading them to reconsider their partisan identity all the harder. While to leftists within its ranks, labor's commitment to the party of FDR had too often proven a "barren marriage," it was not just a majority of mainstream union leaders but of the rank and file whose political identity had become fused to that of the Democrats.

Inseparable from the growing warfare within the labor movement over third-party politics was the deepening cold war. As most anti-Communist unionists saw it, labor's internal advocates of severing ties with the Democrats for the sake of more radical alternatives were almost always Soviet loyalists or their misguided lackeys. Advocates of a third party that embraced American Communists as part of a broad progressive vanguard countered that the Communist Party had earned a place at the table as a stalwart champion of the union movement and of antifascism, anticolonialism, and racial justice at home and abroad. To the party's defenders, the slogan "Communists are only liberals who mean it" had proven to be more than mere words. Despite such arguments, as but one early sign of the widening split within organized labor over the degree of Communist inclusion and influence, David Dubinsky himself had abandoned the ALP in New York in 1944 to form an anti-Communist rival called the Liberal Party.

Now, as the 1948 election year loomed, the choice for leftist unionists such as the Millers lay between continuing to strategically back the Democrats, while awaiting a larger shift of a progressive nature in the national political winds, and launching an immediate third-party bid to jump-start the desired change. For those, like Marvin and Terry, who were inclined to support the riskier latter course, the logical alternative candidate was former Vice President Henry Wallace. A combination of austere moralist and devout social gospel advocate, Wallace had burnished his progressive credentials since his early days as Roosevelt's secretary of agriculture by positioning himself as a champion of civil rights, full-employment policy, and partnership with the USSR. Having been pushed off the ticket in 1944 at the insistence of the Democrats' urban and southern bosses, Wallace's status as party pariah had been confirmed in late 1946 when President Truman had dumped him from his subsequent cabinet post as commerce secretary for having criticized the administration's "get tough with Russia" policies. In the immediate aftermath of the firing, a Gallup Poll showed that roughly one-quarter of the Democratic Party backed him for the 1948 presidential nomination and fewer than half of registered Democrats favored the incumbent. A little over a year later, in late 1947, the former vice president made his White House bid official in a Chicago radio address.[10]

As Popular-Front leftists of almost a decade, Marvin and Terry Miller enthusiastically embraced the Wallace candidacy. Both had been active ALP supporters since 1940 and shared the challenger's policy stances. Adding fuel to the fires of Marvin's support for Wallace was his visceral contempt for Truman, the former haberdasher turned politician who in age and affinity for snappy attire strikingly resembled Miller's own father. Marvin and Terry also shared a view of Truman as a petty, crude Kansas City machine pol who had failed to measure up to the standards of his office or of his venerated predecessor FDR. As they saw it, the Missourian's entire presidency, from his morally troubling decision to deploy the atomic bomb to his failed stewardship of the FDR domestic agenda, his bellicose hostility toward Russia, his acquiescence in the restoration of Western colonialism, and his hesitancy in endorsing a Jewish state in Palestine (although Truman would eventually do so) provided ample justification for backing the Wallace alternative.[11]

Even with the support of passionate backers such as the Millers, the Wallace campaign lost altitude almost from the start—a result of the candidate's personal idiosyncrasies; the pro-Truman impact on public opinion of international crises; and the withering criticism from the mainstream press, Democratic regulars, and anti-Communists both inside and out of the labor movement. On the heels of the Communist coup in Czechoslovakia and the initiation of the Soviet blockade of West Berlin, Wallace's criticism of the Marshall Plan aid proposal to western Europe seemed particularly tone-deaf. Publication of the Progressive Party candidate's odd private exchanges (dubbed the "guru letters" by vitriolic columnist Westbrook Pegler) with a Russian-born mystic reinforced the emerging caricature of Wallace as "wooly-minded." Pro-Truman unionists such as the UAW's Walter Reuther blasted the challenger as "a lost soul" and, underscoring the candidate's backing from "fellow travelers," added, "Communists perform the most complete valet service in the world. They write your speeches, they do your thinking for you, they provide you with applause, and they inflate your ego." Even New York's militant Mike Quill, well aware of Republican nominee Thomas Dewey's record of hostility to labor, became sufficiently alarmed at the prospect of a leftist third party gift-wrapping a GOP sweep that he broke with the ALP—Wallace's official ballot line in the Empire State—and added his own accusations of Communist manipulation of the Progressive ticket and platform.[12]

Loyally—but foolishly—Wallace refused to disavow those supporters who were Communists, even as he insisted he was not their puppet. But even as the polls registered the plunge in Wallace support, the Millers and fellow diehards remained steadfast in their loyalty to the cause. When the Progressives' nominating convention arrived in Philadelphia in late July, Marvin and Terry attended as ALP delegates. Some three thousand supporters in all rode to the City of Brotherly Love on chartered trains respectively labeled the "Common Man" and "World Peace" specials. By background, ideology, and age, the Millers were stereotypical of Wallace delegates, who as a group averaged thirty years of age and contained a mix of housewives, teachers, students, veterans, union activists, and African Americans. Amid loud chants of "One, two, three, four, we don't want another war," Wallace's thirty-two-thousand-strong army gathered in Shibe Park to hear their leader exhort them to fulfill "the dream of the prophets and the founders of the American system."[13]

Despite the ridicule the Wallace campaign attracted from such newspapers as the Scripps-Howard chain and from major-party surrogates, the Wallace campaign at times demonstrated political courage and principle. One month after the convention, the candidate bravely stumped before desegregated audiences in seven southern states calling for voting-rights legislation. In other policy areas, too, the 1948 Progressive platform when viewed with the benefit of hindsight today seems less radical and more prescient than it did at the time. Crafted by the likes of former "brain-truster" Rexford Tugwell and ex-CIO counsel Lee Pressman (who had been forced out of his federation post over links to Communists and his support of Wallace), party planks included the eighteen-year-old vote, national health insurance, federal aid to education, antilynching and anti–poll tax legislation, a fair-employment bill, desegregation of the armed forces and interstate transportation, the elimination of corporate tax loopholes, public ownership of offshore oil reserves, and full equality for women. More problematic given the similarity to Soviet policy stances were foreign-policy statements calling for an international pact to outlaw atomic weapons; internationalization of the Dardanelles, Suez, and Panama waterways; and Big Four shared control of western Germany's industrial Ruhr.[14]

Wishing to boost Wallace's New York turnout, the state ALP recruited a full slate of candidates for lesser offices, even in impossible-to-win jurisdictions. One such race was in a state assembly district that contained the Millers' Queens neighborhood, and Terry gamely agreed to stand in for the Ninth Assembly seat. Outside New York, however, similar efforts were undermined by successful legal challenges brought by Democratic officials. More than any such major-party electoral maneuvering, however, the Wallace effort fell far short primarily because of its inability to shake its pro-Communist label, combined with the incumbent president's belated but effective embrace of New Deal liberalism. The latter lost Truman the support of southern Dixiecrats, who fled to segregationist Strom Thurmond, but not enough of the party's "yellow-dog" supporters to cost the incumbent victory in most of the region. At the same time, Truman's successful rebranding as defender of the Roosevelt domestic legacy enabled him to recapture disaffected voters in other parts of the nation.[15]

Completing a stunning political comeback, Harry Truman won a hard-fought reelection in November. Making the result all the more discouraging to Wallace backers was that their candidate had garnered an even smaller popular-vote total than the reactionary Thurmond. Nor did Progressive Party congressional candidates prevail, save for Harlem's Vito Marcantonio. Only in New York did Wallace mange a respectable vote total. As for Terry Miller's quixotic campaign for the state legislature, it resulted in a third-place finish in the heavily Republican district. But she and Marvin took pride that with more than nineteen hundred votes, her total had placed her ahead of the Liberal Party candidate.[16]

Years later, democratic socialist and author of *The Other America* Michael Harrington would describe 1948 as "the last year of the Thirties." Truman's victory, Wallace's humiliation, a second Republican resurgence after 1948, the corrosive impact of McCarthyism, and debilitating ideological warfare within organized labor all contributed to narrowing the boundaries of national political discourse for at least a generation. In one small-scale example of the postelection score-settling inside organized labor, Marvin Miller was abruptly dismissed from his position with the Machinists union. The ostensible reason given by superiors was that the IAM membership now faced widespread job reductions that could no longer be delayed and that dictated comparable staff contractions. Marvin, however, suspected ulterior political motives in his release. Neither he nor his wife had tried to conceal their support of Wallace, and he surmised that his Progressive affiliation had made him persona non grata to his pro-Truman bosses at the IAM's headquarters.[17]

Miller managed to land a position as a regional organizer for the United Auto Workers, but even there his new superiors intimated that his appointment would likely be temporary. Just how short term it was became abundantly clear in mere months. Once again the quick axe seemed more consistent with post-election revenge against pro-Wallace dissidents than to any complaint with his job performance. At the same time that the UAW was carrying out its own internal retribution against leftist dissidents, it was battling the IAM for recruits inside the large aircraft plants and their smaller parts factories. In the midst of this recruiting war, Miller was summoned before Autoworkers regional director Charles Kerrigan and grilled over his prior support for Wallace as well as the ALP. Miller replied truthfully, and was sacked. After the firing he concluded that a former Machinist colleague turned competitor had passed on the knowledge of his electoral activities to Kerrigan, which then had led to his dismissal.[18]

It was not surprising that after the 1948 election the more conservative AFL would seek to purge itself of its comparatively smaller numbers of dissidents. But as demonstrated by such individual examples as the UAW's firing of Miller, a similar crackdown was also under way inside CIO affiliates despite its more militant heritage. The CIO's chief, Philip Murray, had always hated Communism, but for the sake of internal harmony in the past he had tolerated pro-Soviet members and even affiliate officers so long as they did not openly defy the national leadership in matters of political strategy. But for Murray the 1948

Wallace campaign's backing from CIO leftists had amounted to direct insubordination. In his annual addresses before the 1948 and 1949 CIO conventions, Murray had assailed the federation's left-wing faction with open contempt and ominous threats. At the 1949 gathering, with Murray's blessing, the CIO endorsed disciplinary procedures that accepted circumstantial evidence of Communist Party loyalty (such as a dissident's public endorsement of "pro-Soviet" positions) as sufficient proof of actual affiliation to justify expulsion of an affiliate's officers or even the affiliate itself from the federation. According to the subsequent findings of a report compiled by the CIO regulars, under this new standard fully twelve of the federation's thirty-five member unions—the largest being the United Electrical Workers—merited removal.[19]

As labor's blood feud proceeded, the ostracized Marvin Miller now turned to employment in the ranks of municipal government and managed to land a job in the city's Office of the Housing Expediter as a compliance official. Technically it was a federal post, since in response to the phasing-out of local rent control the national government had stepped in to temporarily take charge of Gotham's program. New York's housing stock remained inadequate some four years past war's end, and as a result the need to restrain a surge in residential rental prices had persisted. Miller's new position brought only modest pay and little prospect of advancement, especially in view of shifting national political winds that at any time could trigger a sudden pullout of the federal government from the rent-control program. Adding to his financial as well as professional anxieties was also the fact that in October—even before his wife's run for the State Assembly had concluded in defeat—she had become pregnant with their second child.[20]

On July 25, 1949, the couple welcomed the new offspring—a baby girl they named Susan Toni. The event provided an occasion of joy in what was otherwise a demoralizing time. Since Marvin's graduation from NYU over a decade earlier, he had held a dozen different jobs, and he and Terry had bounced from New York to Washington and back again, then between Washington and Philadelphia, and finally back to his native city. They had cast their political lot with the ALP and the Wallace campaign only to see their efforts meet not just defeat but economic retaliation. As the new decade loomed, Marvin faced anew the imperative to secure a stable career for his own sake and for that of his family. He still clung to his political convictions, but now was forced to confront the humbling need to restrain his expression of them save at home and in the presence of select friends.[21]

In February 1950, Miller's fortunes suddenly turned. From a former War Labor Board colleague named Otis Brubaker he was tipped off to a promising new opening at the United Steelworkers of America (USWA). Since his wartime work with Miller at the WLB, Brubaker had been hired by president Philip Murray to run his union's Research Department. Otis now wanted Marvin to join him as his assistant. Given the USWA's vast membership and clout, Miller knew that the Steelworkers position could provide his family with a financial security it had not known. Employment with the powerful union meant office work in the Pittsburgh headquarters of the nation's second-largest such institution, where he would serve at the wishes of arguably organized labor's most politically connected leader. Proving himself in that post could in turn lead to greater opportunities to shape Steelworker bargaining policy, political strategy, and, through both of these channels, the wider union movement.[22]

Philip Murray's commitment to the betterment of working people had never been in question, even from his adversaries within the CIO. The son of Irish Catholics and immigrants twice over, first to the mines of Blantyre—where he had been born—and then to Pennsylvania's coal districts, Murray was often willing to shelve ideological purity for the sake of membership betterment. If he had a guiding philosophy, it was a blend of Catholic social justice and gut-level understanding of a worker's basic economic needs. Back when he first had led SWOC's pioneering representation drives against Big Steel, his approach had been encapsulated in his asking and then answering the question, "What does the SWOC want by organizing Steel?" With a burr that thickened when in the company of workingmen, he had stated emphatically, "The aim is to have a home for every worker, food on the table, carpet on the floor, pictures on the wall, and music in the home. That is what we want!"[23]

From Murray's perspective, it had been precisely to secure and protect such goals that he had steered his Steelworkers and the CIO federation on the path of full partnership—even to the point of subordination—with the Democratic Party. To guard organized labor against any loss of its hard-won power and legitimacy in a cold war America, he had shown himself zealous in his efforts to drive out not merely openly Communist unions and officers but those as well who, merely in supporting Henry Wallace, had displayed organizational disloyalty and had jeopardized the political alliance upon which labor's postwar fortunes relied. Ironically, it was now Marvin Miller—former Wallace backer, delegate to the 1948 Progressive convention, and husband of an ALP state-legislative candidate—who was seeking a job whose filling required Philip Murray's direct blessing.[24]

Given how desperately Miller needed that position at Steelworker headquarters, he agonized over how frank he should be about his past political affiliations and activities. Would refusing to volunteer such details, declining to answer direct questions about them if asked, or lying about them all be betrayals of his integrity? Did Murray already know of his political past, and would he use Miller's upcoming interview as a test of his loyalty? And if, one way or another, he told Murray the truth, would he be endangering not merely his own job prospects but endangering Brubaker, given that his friend had gone out on a limb to recommend him? More immediately than at any time so far in his life, the competing pressures of principle and of family well-being tugged at him from opposing directions. It was in microcosm the same type of dilemma that many Americans, whether in Hollywood, government, academia, or the labor movement, were already confronting or would confront in an era of Joe McCarthy.

After intense bouts of soul-searching with Terry, Miller opted for a middle path that fell short of either an open confession or a betrayal of past loyalties. He would not volunteer the details of his 1948 political activity, but if Murray asked he would answer honestly despite the potential consequences. When Miller and his prospective supervisor Brubaker arrived for the crucial interview, it turned out to be a surprisingly awkward Philip Murray who fumbled to make conversation with the young man less than half his age. Given Miller's own nervousness—the reason for which Murray appeared blessedly unaware—he similarly volunteered few words. After twenty minutes of painful silences occasionally punctuated by single sentences, Murray abruptly volunteered his judgment that Miller seemed well qualified. "Some unions don't consider the research department to be all that important, but I don't feel that way. I think a staff economist is a very responsible position, and I want you to understand that." A relieved Miller immediately concurred.[25]

Once more, silence descended upon the room with the threesome resembling, as Miller later recalled, "strangers in a stuck elevator." Again it fell upon Murray to break through the quiet, and he did so with the question Marvin had prayed for: "When can you come to work?" The dazed applicant paused to gather his frazzled wits, then managed to utter that he would need to provide notice to his current employer first and secure lodgings in the Steel City. "I guess," Miller continued while silently calculating prospective dates on the fly, "I can start in a few weeks." Checking his own desk calendar, Murray then curtly responded in a manner that indicated that the session was about to wrap up: "March first okay?" "Fine," Miller answered. The three men stood up and shook hands, then parted ways.[26]

In a career marked by moments of chance and even irony, Marvin Miller's interview with Philip Murray was the most critical occasion in his professional life. Without the opportunity offered by the Steelworkers, in a cold war era marked by blacklisting and intolerance of left-wing politics, Miller likely never would have succeeded in reviving his career in the union movement. Without his subsequent successes at the USWA that his initial hiring made possible, a decade and a half later he would have never been considered a viable candidate to head any union—even a pathetic excuse of one claiming to represent major-league ballplayers. It was the choicest irony that instead of Marvin Miller's postwar political and professional disappointments having destroyed what was left of his career in the labor movement, they had instead set the stage for its revival on a different, more promising, track.

Six

Technician

The United Steelworkers of America that Marvin Miller joined in February 1950 shared a status with the United Auto Workers as one of the two flagship organizations of the American union movement. By the early 1950s it claimed more than one million members in more than twenty-three hundred locals, including not just workers in basic steel but also aluminum, can manufacture, iron ore, nonferrous metals, fabrication, and locomotive making. The USWA even counted among its ranks the makers of Shenango pottery and—ironic in light of Marvin Miller's eventual career path—Louisville Slugger bats. Geographically, the union covered a wide swath as well, with locals blanketing not just the United States and Canada but Puerto Rico, Mexico, and Venezuela.

Although his starting pay with the Steelworkers lagged that of his old Machinists salary, Miller's opportunity represented an advance in every other respect. From previous discussions with Otis Brubaker, Miller knew that his Research Department post was neither short-term nor make-work. It offered much greater economic stability and advancement prospects at the moment his growing family needed them most. Because he would be working in the union's Pittsburgh national headquarters rather than in a regional office, he would also be in direct proximity to the highest-ranking officials of a labor organization widely respected for its clout in both the collective-bargaining and political spheres.[1]

The USWA had come a long way since the formative years of the Depression. As head of both the USWA and the CIO, Philip Murray held sway within Democratic circles second to no one in organized labor. Reflecting his dual role as union president and Washington powerbroker, Murray maintained offices in both the Steel City and the nation's capital. His USWA empire contained multiple layers of locals, district offices, functional departments, and national boards and officers. Whereas his union's first contract had been but a few pages long, by the fifties USWA pacts numbered in the hundreds of pages and covered not merely basic representation rights and wage scales but an ever-expanding array of other benefits, job schedules, shop-floor protections, and arbitration procedures. Because SWOC's initial battles against U.S. Steel that had led to the first contract in 1937 and formal recognition, grievance machinery, seniority rights, and paid vacations, the Steelworkers in the years since had added holiday premiums and reporting-time pay in 1941; the union's largest hourly wage increase at 18½ cents in 1946; job classification, rating, and severance pay in 1947; and most recently in 1949 a pension plan and sickness and accident benefits.[2]

In the USWA's rented Pittsburgh offices that spanned multiple floors of the downtown Commonwealth Building, a talented aggregation of men with varied histories gave the union arguably the deepest "bench" of any current labor organization. As Miller would soon discover, Steelworker officialdom was in particular a contrasting but effective merger of Irish "politicians" and Jewish "technicians." The former mainly constituted the union's public face, the latter a major share of the brainpower that generated the union's positions. Whatever the differences of ethnicity or of religious background, the majority of them—with Miller a quiet exception—had either championed or at least backed the efforts at the Steelworkers and elsewhere to expel Communist and pro-Soviet unionists from labor's ranks. With the union's early struggle for survival and labor's postwar turmoil over political orthodoxy now both in the rearview mirror, the USWA focused upon continuing its pragmatic advances in the economic security of its membership, one increasingly middle-class in outlook and material aspiration.[3]

At the literal "top of the tower" sat Philip Murray. Although deceptively shy, he ruled the fifteenth, or Executive, floor as an unquestioned autocrat. Next to his suite were the offices of vice president Jim Thimmes, secretary-treasurer and heir-apparent David McDonald, and general counsel Arthur Goldberg. Murray's subordinates respected and even loved their aging patriarch, but few save perhaps McDonald—his former personal secretary and "adopted son" of sorts—could claim to truly know him. In an example of the USWA chief's rigid formality from early in Miller's tenure, when Elmer Maloy of the Wage Inequity Department ventured upstairs to complain tongue-in-cheek that his floor had not yet gotten air conditioning, his boss quickly took him to task: "Don't you even know how to proceed? What kind of trade unionist are you?" Taking his boss' blunt critique to heart, Maloy promptly assembled a grievance committee, presented a formal petition, and in two weeks had his air conditioning.[4]

Undergirding the Steelworkers' top rank was the collection of department heads and staff dubbed the "technicians." Like Miller, many of them had arrived relatively recently as the union had mushroomed in reach and organizational complexity. Prominent among them was Otis Brubaker, Miller's former WLB colleague and now superior as the union's research director. To those who occupied "cabinet" posts of similar rank and knocked heads with Brubaker, the "self-appointed conscience of the Steelworkers" as some sardonically called him, Miller's boss frequently gave off a sense of ideological rigidity and a personality more comfortable in the company of statistics than with people. No one doubted, however, his credentials or his commitment. Another second-tier Steelworker official was Ben Fischer, the gruff former Long Islander and one-time head of Michigan's Socialist Party who had migrated to the Aluminum Workers of America (AWA) as its research director—where he had helped rid that union of Communists—and then as the Steelworkers associate director of its same department once the USWA absorbed the AWA. It was in fact Fischer's promotion to head of the Steelworkers' Contract and Arbitration Division that had enabled both Brubaker's ascent and with it Miller's opening. Fischer reigned as the USWA's unquestioned expert on contract language and workplace arbitration procedures and within a short time had established himself as an indispensable member of Steelworker collective-bargaining teams.[5]

The most powerful of all the USWA "technicians" at the time of Miller's arrival, however, was but thirty-seven years old and had held his post at the union for barely a year. Arthur Goldberg, Lee Pressman's replacement as general counsel to both the USWA and CIO and the Steelworkers' policy driving-force and "shadow president" during the 1950s, was like Miller a descendant of eastern European Jews, in Goldberg's case from the Ukraine. Born and raised in Chicago, he had worked his way through Northwestern Law School and after graduation had started his own labor-law firm in 1933. When years later the CIO's ideological rifts split the labor federation, as a visible leader of its anti-Communist faction, victory had propelled him to greater heights. A key figure in designing organized labor's postwar relations with both the federal government and the business community, social-democrat Goldberg fought management attempts to regain lost prewar prerogatives but did not challenge the companies' continued control of such fundamental matters as capital investment and plant-location decisions. Instead, he stressed the goal of full-employment through the pursuit of Keynesian macroeconomic policies and pushed for the expansion of private benefit programs to fill the gaps within America's social-welfare system.[6]

Whatever the differences of background or opinion that existed among the USWA hierarchy, the "Steelworker way" of the 1950s emphasized the need for officers and staff to close ranks once the union's positions had been determined. These included unquestioning acceptance of USWA support for both Truman and Eisenhower cold war foreign policy, and it also meant safeguarding existing members' economic security over the pursuit of more radical aims or 1930s-style open class warfare. After years of struggle, both sides in the steel industry's collective-bargaining relationship had come to fundamentally accept each other's legitimacy. The USWA's national office conducted primary negotiations with U.S. Steel, while the USWA's district directors purportedly carried on parallel talks with the lesser firms. In truth, the district officials largely bided their time until the "big boys" had settled and then rubber-stamped similar deals, with local adjustments. Each collective bargaining round began about sixty days prior to the particular strike deadline, and real give-and-take usually waited until the last eight to ten days. Although steel strikes still took place every few years and each confrontation inevitably landed in Washington, each side accepted as a given that the other's basic survival was not at stake and that whatever short-term loss of wages, production, and revenues would be quickly made up.[7]

Despite the lingering image of militancy generated by the periodic shutdowns and government interventions, USWA officialdom's fighting spirit often seemed more directed at Walter Reuther's UAW, the Steelworkers' chief labor rival, than at Big Steel. The mutual antagonism only grew worse after Murray's death in late 1952, which triggered a struggle for the CIO succession between Reuther and McDonald. Steelworker aides took their cues from their leader—a man critics labeled as a "tuxedo unionist" for his Hollywood looks and lavish lifestyle—and attempted to cast doubt on Reuther's squeaky-clean image as a workingman's unionist who peeled his own breakfast oranges. But despite its bitterness, the intramural rivalry served American workers well, as gains scored by one union invariably spurred the competitive zeal of the other and thereby raised the bar for the labor movement generally. Within months of Miller's joining the Steelworkers, to take but one example, the UAW announced the attainment of a new five-year pact with the major car makers that included the pioneering "annual improvement factor"—a system of wage boosts tied not to the cost of living alone but also to company productivity gains—which in the 1950s often proved more generous.[8]

The increasingly sophisticated negotiations conducted by Big Labor logically translated into greater responsibilities for union research departments. At the

Steelworkers, that meant that the Research Department staff of Brubaker, Miller, three to six junior aides, and a handful of secretaries fielded an array of requests from higher up for industry-trend data and other facts for speeches and government testimony, field-organizer materials, and collective-bargaining packets. Ironically, because of the generous protections provided to USWA secretaries by their separate contract, these support personnel worked only 32½ hours per week while superiors Brubaker and Miller frequently toiled longer weekdays and even weekends. Reflecting the union's need to assert mastery over its far-flung network of divisions, departments, offices, and contracts, Miller's first major assignment at the union was the data compilation for the first of what would become an annual series of USWA organizational directories.[9]

A second assignment was soon dropped on Miller's plate. To gather and distill detailed up-to-date information on companies' policies, records of compliance with active agreements, and prospective bargaining stances, USWA officials regularly called upon the Research Department to draft the questionnaires they then submitted to their management adversaries with the objective of smoking out the facts. Such probing by each side was another postwar byproduct of federal labor law, with its more elaborate reporting requirements. But the gambits also helped the USWA proactively to identify weaknesses in management's negotiating posture and gave the union early warning of planned unilateral industry actions involving automation, production adjustments, plant relocations, and other capital-investment shifts. Both sides' discoveries then could trigger new grievances, which meant yet more union research to buttress USWA complaints and ward off those of management.[10]

Miller's mounting workload left him little time for complaint, but it was evident both to him and to his wife that Pittsburgh—even with its virtues—would never replace New York in their hearts. The family had settled into a "garden community" within the Brookline neighborhood of South Hills, which was but fifteen minutes' distance by car to Marvin's downtown office. The Steel City was in the midst of a civic-improvement renaissance that eventually included constructions of the Gateway Center, a new municipal airport, a new civic arena, and new corporate headquarters for both Alcoa and U.S. Steel. Medical researchers were conducting gamma-globulin vaccine experiments for polio, the pediatrician Dr. Benjamin Spock had chosen to make the city his professional home, and Pittsburgh's civic fathers had adopted such enlightened public policies as a fair employment ordinance and fluoridation of the water supply. Probably most significant to the local residents, a partnership between the Mellon family and Democratic mayor David Lawrence had led to an overdue push to impose "smoke control" over the metropolis's long-polluted skies. In his early years at the Steelworkers, Miller would find it necessary to take an extra dress shirt to work and change into it by noon because of the soot. But by the late 1950s the city's air had improved so much that Miller traded in an older Ford sedan for a shiny new 1957 hardtop convertible.[11]

Despite the Steel City's improvements, however, in other respects Pittsburgh would remain a kind of "Siberia" for the Millers, as Marvin later described it. The extreme weather they endured in their first winter there, which piled snow up to their windows, underscored the symbolism. More significant, though, was that despite the class-conscious persona projected by Pittsburgh, the city still seemed ideologically rigid. Local examples of McCarthy-style attacks on civil liberties, sporadic incidents of police harassment toward leftist demonstrators, and the anti-Red antics of local jurist Michael Musmanno and Matthew ("I Was a Communist") Cvetic garnered front-page newspaper headlines, prompting free-lance journalist Terry to offer her own satirical commentaries about them to the *Nation* and the *New Republic*.[12]

Philip Murray's death in 1952—an event observers insisted only partly in jest stemmed from a broken heart at the election of Republican Dwight Eisenhower—would lead to still more responsibilities for Miller. Although Murray's successor David McDonald was not actually a dilettante, the growing complexity of collective-bargaining issues before the union and its new president's readiness to delegate to his technicians meant for Miller even longer days, but the promise of a greater role in Steelworker policy. In 1953, McDonald abandoned the formality of having the USWA's Pittsburgh national office and district director-led negotiating teams conduct parallel negotiations. Now all talks would be centralized in Pittsburgh, and all panels would be headed, at least in name, by McDonald personally. Relegating the district directors to the rank of "assistant chairmen" on their respective teams, McDonald assembled a core bargaining group that in addition to himself included his vice president, secretary-treasurer, counsel, and one or two more staffers. Big Steel in turn replaced its outdated separate panels with a similar four-person negotiating committee consisting of U.S. Steel's head of labor relations, his deputy, and the labor-policy chiefs of Bethlehem and Republic Steel.[13]

Given the constant flow of demands from top officers for data and assessments of management proposals, and from district directors requiring prompt notice of any potential local complications emanating from the national contracts being negotiated, as the Research Department's "answer man," Miller now frequently became a direct participant at the bargaining table. Personality issues also played a key role in the assignments. Years before, David McDonald had opposed Otis Brubaker's hiring only to be overruled by Philip Murray, and the animosity between the president and the research director had never evaporated. As for Ben Fischer, whose expertise otherwise made him a logical addition to virtually any USWA bargaining panel, he found it hard to get along with the prickly Brubaker for his own reasons. In contrast, Miller's good working relationship with his boss, his prior experience at regional contract negotiations with the Machinists, and his low-key personality allowed him to mesh better with his bargaining colleagues.[14]

Miller's growing role on Steelworker negotiating committees not only gave him up-close insight into the personalities of his colleagues, it also provided him the chance to take the measure of those on the other side of the table. Among the revelations, he learned that, as a group, industry executives were no more monolithic or immune from factionalism than his side. He discovered that while a Big Steel team might include such open reactionaries as Republic Steel's vice president for labor relations Harold "Lefty" Lamb—a man who as a teen had eagerly joined the Hitler Youth—the Alcoa bargaining panel represented a company that sponsored Edward R. Murrow's CBS news show *See It Now* and to Miller's surprise occasionally endorsed the journalist's anti-McCarthy views.[15]

Although Miller's duties now extended well beyond those of a researcher, his title and rank continued to trail. As if his plate was not already full enough, the union's need for effective spokesmen to fulfill its public-relations demands led to still another category of assignments. Miller's ability to process factual information quickly, to think on his feet, and to deliver clear expositions of USWA positions with a minimal need to refer to notes led his superiors to steer more of their public-appearance appointments his way. Positive response to his performances then led to still more such opportunities, including presentations to industrial research and arbitration associations, participation in college-sponsored seminars, broadcast interviews, and appearances on local public-affairs shows.[16]

While Miller accommodated his expanding schedule, his wife gamely reconciled her primary role in raising their young daughter with her own need for outside avenues. In addition to a nursery and a lunch service, the local YMCA offered guest speakers and twelve-week "Ladies Day Out" classes on such varied subjects as oil painting, drawing, ceramics, hat decoration, current events, human relations, and sports. Because of the Millers' longstanding love of athletics and Terry's insistence that the children similarly enjoy year-round access to sports facilities, she spearheaded formation of a local committee that successfully petitioned Mayor Lawrence to expand the neighborhood park schedule beyond its previous four summer months. For his part, Marvin, who had never played tennis despite his mother's past example, now took up the game and embraced it with characteristic zeal. In less than a year he was skilled enough to win local amateur tournaments, bringing home new trophies that joined his Brighton Beach handball prizes on the family mantlepiece.[17]

As Miller strove to climb the Steelworker version of the corporate ladder, his home life was similarly evolving into a mix of middle-class consumerism and resilient leftist idealism. After being without a television the first few years, Marvin then bought his family a Dumont, from which aired such varied fare as *The Ed Sullivan Show, Alfred Hitchcock Presents, Playhouse 90, Ernie Kovacs, Sid Caesar, The Honeymooners,* and even the anti-Red thriller *I Led Three Lives.* Marvin and Terry indulged son Peter's boyhood obsessions with Hopalong Cassidy and Davy Crockett by appropriately outfitting him. Having started out in the Steel City with a humpbacked 1948 Ford, the family moved up to a 1954 Fairlane and then the 1957 convertible. Miller delighted in packing up his family for cruises around the city, often capping off the rides with treats at the nearby Eat 'n' Park. At the same time, however, as antifascist products of the 1930s and the World War II generation, the Millers refused to abandon their bedrock convictions. If Marvin's job required him to exercise circumspection at work, he and Terry could be freer in expressing their opinions in front of their children. Marvin's nightly reading from the newspaper at the dinner table was an interactive event marked by biting commentary on current events. He also insisted upon maintaining a personal quirk of his—consuming the paper from back to front because of his insistence that the "kept press" buried the "real" news in the back pages. For insurgent reportage and opinion, the Millers supplemented mainstream reading with *I.F. Stone's Weekly, The Nation,* and occasionally the *New Republic,* although the latter drew from them the scornful moniker of the "New Republican."[18]

As parents, Marvin and Terry were similarly determined to utilize the television medium in the service of what today would be called "teachable moments." For example, Peter Miller marveled at his father's seemingly uncanny ability to predict the endings of television dramas. On one such occasion after Miller had accurately forecast the conclusion of a Hitchcock episode, his son insisted that he must have seen it before. Marvin then explained to Peter that if a viewer recognized the standard plot formulas, one could usually anticipate an episode's twists and turns. In the real world, too, Miller continued, if you knew the basic self-interests and the relative strength of each side involved in a confrontation—whether a labor-management battle or a crisis between nations—you could usually predict not just each side's actions but their consequences as well.

As with their supervision of television watching, in their musical instruction the Millers took to heart the cautionary title of a favorite song from *South Pacific,* "You've Got to Be Carefully Taught." As Marvin would later state with a coarse pride, "I think my whole life, and Terry's whole life certainly, one of the values I think we gave the kids was that racism and religious and national and ethnic differences were for the birds and that hatred built on that was bull———." Besides classical symphonies and show tunes, the Miller home echoed with the sounds of Pete Seeger and Woody Guthrie 78s and of such labor standards as "Solidarity Forever," "Union Maid," and "I Dreamed I Saw Joe Hill Last Night."[19]

Even the Millers' summer-camp choices reflected their determination to make social consciousness compatible with fun. A favorite family venue was Camp Tamiment, originally founded as a recreational facility for socialist-leaning families by New York's Rand School of Social Science. When the camp in the Poconos had first opened, the facility had advertised itself as "the largest summer school and camp for workers in the world." But by the 1950s, Tamiment's educational mission had largely gone, leaving behind a more conventional retreat with a menu of outdoor recreation and high-level entertainment for an increasingly mainstream clientele. The camp's biggest attraction now was its Playhouse, which served as a training ground and creative outlet for such actors and comedians as Danny Kaye and Imogene Coca.[20]

Although the Millers' first home in the Steel City served adequately, by mid-decade Marvin and his family had outgrown it. Marvin's expanded portfolio had fed his yearning for a promotion, and that in turn argued for relocation to a better residential neighborhood, though his proletarian identity caused guilt pangs. One factor in overcoming any hesitancy was that Peter had experienced occasional anti-Semitism at his neighborhood school, including a Catholic classmate tossing the epithet "Kike" at him. What definitively sealed the parents' decision to move the family, however, was when the son came home from school one day and abruptly demanded that his parents buy him a leather jacket like those worn by his friends. Parental visions of Peter's pending juvenile delinquency clashed with Marvin's sense of betrayal at the thought of selling out for a tonier neighborhood. In the end, however, the Millers opted for the children's sake for the exodus to Squirrel Hill.[21]

The move meant an even shorter work commute for Marvin, and a home life in a three-story house with leafy expanses of green, broad avenues, and convenient access to streetcars, bakeries, and places of worship. Most appealing to Miller, however, was the proximity to three separate parks—Frick, Schenley, and Highland—with well-maintained tennis courts that he could test out regularly with Otis Brubaker. As a birthday present, Terry even gave him his own center-court net, allowing him to begin his personal season even before the city brought out its cords on Memorial Day weekend each year. An added benefit of Miller's tennis-playing addiction in his new neighborhood was also the social introduction it gave him to the area's racially mixed and upwardly mobile population, from jazz musicians to white-collar professionals.[22]

Miller had forged a comfortable, secure life for himself and his family. But the longer he toiled at Steelworker headquarters the more it seemed that his career had hit an invisible ceiling. In an odd parallel, the same could be said of his union itself and the firms whose workers it represented. During the first half of the 1950s, steel industry labor-management confrontations had arisen out of the companies' short-sighted profit-milking without serious investment in modernization. Industry executives jacked up prices and then blamed the union for the higher production costs and the dips in demand that their actions triggered. World War II temporarily had crippled the U.S. industry's foreign rivals' competitive position, but for more than a decade afterward, American companies had continued to behave as if that advantage would last forever. With this smug certainty in their hegemony shared by complacent traditionalists in the USWA as well—especially within the ranks of the district directors—both sides lethargically persisted in their ritualistic confrontations.[23]

It was beyond dispute that steel's labor-management relationship had produced gains for the membership in the form of paid holidays, union-shop protections, elimination of wage differentials in iron ore and between regions, Sunday premium pay, jury duty compensation, and supplemental unemployment benefits (SUBs). But as the emergence of SUBs as a central bargaining issue in 1956 had hinted at, the American steel industry was now starting to hemorrhage jobs. Boosted at first by postwar Marshall Plan aid, rebuilt modern factories in Germany and Japan now reemerged as serious competitors. As technicians such as Miller, who followed the trends, clearly recognized even if some of their bosses did not, the stop-and-start character of the U.S. industry's negotiations and the periodic recessions of the Eisenhower years aggravated the steel economy's cyclical volatility as firms failed to prepare for a more uncertain future. What the times now called for were creative joint approaches to reduce the disruptions resulting from the collective-bargaining relationship, ameliorate the hardship to workers of recessions or strikes, prepare the membership for the likely long-term slowdown in steel employment, and facilitate the industry's competitiveness by incentivizing worker cooperation.[24]

Spurred by the technicians' research, what the Steelworkers union was groping toward was an economic-security policy for its membership that would sustain incomes in good times and bad while facilitating the American steel industry's long-term survival via improved productivity. But instituting a "guaranteed-annual-wage" system—one that coordinated the allocation of regular workers' schedules with those of temporary replacements and the wages of each with government unemployment compensation, private supplemental benefits, vacation time and pay, sickness and accident benefits, retiree pensions, and incentive plans and productivity bonuses—required massive rethinking and ongoing labor-management cooperation that, ironically, the USWA could probably only achieve through a collective-bargaining showdown. And did the Steelworkers union itself have both the requisite foresight and the solidarity to push through such forward-thinking changes? Prior to the 1956 collective-bargaining round, David McDonald had floated inside the union the idea of a thirty-two-hour week in basic steel as a means of spreading work and thus guaranteeing a broader-based economic security for his membership, only in the face of intense criticism to retreat in favor of alternatives for allocating work while maintaining USWA members' prior incomes.[25]

Borrowing upon the pioneering early work of Murray Latimer at the Railroad Retirement Board, the Steelworkers' Research Department turned to the idea of negotiated private supplementary benefits that would augment government unemployment payments in times of job cutbacks and wage contractions. But Miller and his fellow technicians recognized that a more comprehensive economic-security system was needed. Other concepts they considered included those of adjusting full-time employees' schedules on a weekly or monthly basis and coordinating the timing of cutbacks with deployment of a replacement pool of substitute workers. The replacements would enjoy comparable yearly incomes as the full-time employees through SUB contributions and federal unemployment compensation. (By the 1960s, the adoption for regular employees of the standard thirteen-week paid vacation every five years, combined with maintaining a short-term-replacement pool that received supplemental benefits to boost their incomes, eventually became the steel industry's preferred solution.) The technicians similarly began to work on innovative schemes for calculating productivity savings, with the aim of workers sharing the measurable dollar efficiencies through bonus payments on top of base-wage and cost-of-living raises.[26]

In 1959 Big Steel's long-gestating crisis finally reached its head. Triggering a Steelworker walkout was management's abrupt demand for repeal of paragraph

2b of the industry basic contract. Paragraph 2b, which had been first negotiated by Lee Pressman back in 1947 in his last triumph as USWA counsel, required the companies to empirically justify any unilateral changes in their production processes, including any alterations of crew sizes and job classifications or introduction of new technology. Firms could still initiate such changes, but they would then be subject to grievance procedures and the possibility of reversal if the predicted productivity gains could not be proven. As with previous steel showdowns, the impasse found its way to Washington, but the imposition of an eighty-day cooling-off period failed to break the ongoing stalemate.[27]

By the fall of 1959, however, splits began to emerge within management's ranks. In October Kaiser Steel broke with its larger competitors and reached a separate deal with the USWA that included a 22½-cent hourly-wage boost over two years, a joint study panel to study company work rules, and—most significant—creation of a new joint group called the Kaiser Long-Range Sharing Committee. Consisting of three industry and union representatives each and a trio of outside experts, the Kaiser Committee was tasked with crafting a long-term plan for the sharing of productivity savings. But despite the Kaiser pact and USWA deals with Detroit Steel and Granite City Steel, the industry's top firms continued to hold out. With neither side budging on 2b, the union proposed it be assigned to its own joint study committee. While pressure continued to build on both sides, the companies now felt it more. In past strikes Big Steel had been able to initiate production speedups and to stockpile material in advance, then count on their customers re-upping with it despite the higher postsettlement prices. But by 1959 the new reality of foreign competition meant that those same purchasers of American steel were no longer supplicants of the U.S. firms.[28]

While the 1959 steel impasse tested the stamina of USWA negotiators and staffs, new agreements also were being bargained with Alcoa and can-manufacture companies. For Miller personally—engaged in all three sets of negotiations—the strain was almost unbearable. It was not just the incessant travel between Pittsburgh and the various bargaining sites, or the pay suspensions he and his colleagues endured in solidarity with the membership. It was also the building frustration that despite his sacrifices he was on a professional treadmill, running faster just to remain in place. His exasperation reached a head one Friday that December. Marvin and Ben Fischer were flying home from the nation's capital late in the day after another fruitless week of round-the-clock talks called by Vice President Richard Nixon and Labor Secretary James Mitchell. Upon landing in Pittsburgh, they were greeted by an abrupt summons from Arthur Goldberg to return immediately to Washington. Uncharacteristically, Miller flatly refused to fly back until Monday. He then approached Fischer, who had become the sounding board for his discontent, and confidentially unveiled a reshuffling proposal. No longer wanting to stay as Otis Brubaker's understudy, Miller proposed coming to work for Fischer as his deputy in a new USWA Aluminum Division. [29]

Miller soldiered on without an immediate response, and the union successfully concluded its aluminum and can negotiations at year's end. The larger struggle with Big Steel, though, continued to drag on. With visions of lost contracts and terminated jobs now weighing heavily upon both parties, a deal was finally reached on January 4, 1960. Although the basic-steel pact included a 3½–3¾ percent annual pay-and-benefit increase and the establishment of a noncontributory insurance plan, its most significant elements were the creation of the 2b joint-study committee and a new ongoing joint panel to be called the Human Relations Research Committee. The HRRC would have broad latitude to confront issues of mutual concern in the periods between active negotiations. Though it would not serve as an official bargaining committee, it would try to resolve potentially contentious matters in advance prior to each new bargaining round.[30]

Once the steel talks had concluded, Miller and Fischer marched together to see David McDonald and address Marvin's professional unhappiness. Fischer did not want the added responsibility of running a new department, and instead he recommended Miller to head up the proposed new aluminum subdivision. McDonald concurred with Fischer's fears of becoming overloaded and diverted from his current responsibilities. But the Steelworker president favored a different set of assignments for Miller—ones that would carry a significant promotion with them. If he was willing to take on multiple tasks, he would be named as lead USWA representative on the new Human Relations Research Committee, as well as to a similar role on the 2b study group. On top of those appointments, he would also be called upon to become the primary USWA technician, serving under Arthur Goldberg, on the Kaiser Long-Range Sharing Plan panel. Commensurate with these expanded responsibilities, effective in April Miller would be elevated to the ranks of chief economist and assistant to the president of the Steelworkers.[31] After a decade of toiling in the shadows within a powerful union bureaucracy, Marvin Miller finally would be a central player. Designated first among equals among the technicians, he would now have his chance to make his mark.

Seven

A House Divided

In the words of colleague Ben Fischer, by April 1960 Marvin Miller had reached the "big time" at the Steelworkers. Besides newly holding the titles of chief economist and assistant to the president, Miller was now in the inner circle of USWA leaders, along with Fischer, Arthur Goldberg, and pension-and-insurance specialist John Tomayko, who spearheaded the union's collective-bargaining efforts. His salary climbed to $16,000, trailing only that of David McDonald at $50,000 and the USWA district directors at $20,000 each. There was but one melancholy note to the timing of his ascent. His father, Alex, had passed away in February, just two months before Marvin's promotion was scheduled to take effect. For a man who since childhood had been driven to prove himself in the eyes of others, none more than his father, Miller was deprived of the opportunity to share the pride Alex undoubtedly would have felt.[1]

Miller's plethora of new responsibilities left him little time to grieve. First on the agenda were his duties on the Work Rules ("2b") Committee. While the USWA's McDonald and his opposite-number Conrad Cooper of U.S. Steel jointly chaired the panel, it was Miller and his industry counterpart who served as the group's "joint coordinators" and actually oversaw the panel's day-to-day business. Given the union's desire to maintain the status quo, the 2b committee's rapid demise itself became another feather in Miller's cap. He employed multiple working groups and public hearings to undermine the companies' arguments against 2b. Miller deliberately summoned local plant managers and foremen in the knowledge that their bosses hated such testimony, not least because it showed that many of the shop-floor rules that executives complained about had actually been adopted at their request, or at least with the consent of their site managers. The defensive magnates first chose to defer, and then cancelled outright, the remaining hearings. Within less than a year the industry quietly abandoned its crusade for 2b "reform."[2]

The demise of the 2b panel left Miller free to focus upon the considerably more challenging issues facing the Human Relations Research Committee and the Kaiser Long-Range Sharing Plan group. Pre-HRRC mechanisms to address longer-term industry challenges between regular bargaining rounds, most notably the Continuous Study Program, had seldom been activated. When previous joint panels had been formed, they had been in the fashion of single-issue working groups similar to the now-defunct 2b committee. By contrast, HRRC was designed to operate continuously with a broad mandate. The USWA's representation consisted of Miller and the union's top-tier officers, joined by a comparable delegation from Big Steel. The panel's overall mandate called upon members to work cooperatively to rationalize and standardize industry shop-floor practices and personnel policies with the goals of mutual benefit and reduced strife. HRRC's initial agenda was quite conventional, including issues of seniority practices, the contracting-out of plant work, crew sizes, interplant transfers, coordination of work schedules and vacation time, and nondiscrimination policies.[3]

To increase the Human Relations Committee's chances of success, what it needed more than anything was hands-on leadership competent at managing staff resources, having a mastery of industry complexities, and skilled at delegating inquiries to subcommittees in a manner that facilitated mutual trust and thus gave the policy recommendations that followed greater weight. Full-committee sessions, where subgroup reports were taken up and proposals debated—placed a further premium on the leaders' facility at promoting "reasonable discussion" instead of confrontation. Miller's meticulously organized yet low-key style proved particularly well suited to the task. At his urging the panel established initial working groups on seniority, grievance procedures and arbitration, economic guides and statistics, medical care, job classification, and incentive programs. In HRRC's first two years, from January 1960 to 1962, it and its subgroups would hold two hundred working sessions.[4]

In similar fashion Miller quickly rose to prominence on the Kaiser Long-Range Sharing Plan committee. Initially designated as Arthur Goldberg's right-hand technician on the panel, Miller assumed the leadership of the union side once Goldberg left the Steelworkers for the Kennedy administration. One notable difference between the Kaiser group and either the 2b and HRRC panels was that it included not just USWA and company appointees but outside representation as well. Dr. George W. Taylor, a labor advisor to every U.S. president since Hoover and a faculty member at the Wharton School of Business, served as the overall chairman of the committee. David Cole, the former head of the Federal Mediation and Conciliation Service, occupied a second seat on the panel, while Harvard University professor and professional arbitrator John Dunlop rounded out the outside membership. But while Taylor generally acted as the Kaiser committee's spokesperson, Cole headed the subcommittee on unresolved grievances, and Dunlop offered general expertise, it was Miller, assisted by USWA colleagues David Feller and Frank Pollara, who with Kaiser-counterpart Ralph Vaughn provided the main inspiration for an innovative productivity-sharing scheme.[5]

In designing Kaiser's novel approach, a major hurdle to the calculation of efficiency savings—and from them the additional benefits to be dispersed to workers—was the complexity of the company's existing incentive-pay programs. By the early 1960s, the menu of incentives at Kaiser (and elsewhere) had expanded to an extent that in some cases less-skilled men were earning more than their skilled-craft coworkers. Any new scheme to supplement employee wages by productivity bonuses would have to confront these imbalances if it hoped to produce a more generous yet fairer compensation system. The productivity bonuses would have to be phased in as the old incentives were eased out, without antagonizing those who had benefitted from the existing regime. A second and even more fundamental issue facing Miller and his colleagues was how to operationally define productivity improvement in mutually acceptable, measurable ways. Both sides accepted the premise that old-fashioned cost-cutting represented an obvious form of efficiency improvement. But gains could also result from retraining workers, reforming the recruitment process, and eliminating "negative incentives" that encouraged workers to obstruct changes out of false perceptions of self-interest.[6]

Once again Miller demonstrated the endurance, the detailed grasp of shop-floor operations, and a talent for fostering cooperation that propelled the effort. The full Kaiser panel held a dozen meetings in its first two years and subcommittees convened hundreds of working sessions. Miller cited the time-consuming nature of the Kaiser group's work in defending his de facto leadership, pointing out later, "How could David McDonald have found the time to meet over two hundred times with Kaiser to work out that agreement?" But while the workload was enormous, the Kaiser family's hospitality made the task more than bearable. Patriarch Henry Kaiser, whose "liberty ships" had carried America's

Steelworkers' president David McDonald and Miller
(Kaiser Steel /Tamiment Library, NYU)

arsenal of democracy to the battlefronts of World War II, had long since retired from active management of the family enterprises in favor of son Edgar and had turned his attention to the civic betterment of his adopted Honolulu. But he lent his luxurious island estate for sharing committee annual meetings, actively participated in sessions, then hosted lavish nighttime entertainments complete with orchestra, dancing, and jaunts on his catamaran. On one occasion David McDonald, who otherwise rarely missed a good party, could not attend because of illness, and the Millers became the focus of Kaiser's hospitality into the wee hours of the morning.[7]

After two years' hard work, by early 1962 the Kaiser group was nearing the goal of designing a landmark productivity-sharing system. From the start the committee had proceeded with the understanding that while it had the power to draft a guiding blueprint, formal adoption would require it to be incorporated within the company's overall USWA contract and ratified by both sides. In the panel's final draft, individual-worker participation was left optional. Nonetheless, two-thirds of the company's six-thousand-member workforce would eventually switch over to the new plan. Participating workers would receive monthly bonuses of just under one-third of Kaiser's before-tax productivity savings. The company would keep the remaining two-thirds share, both to supplement its profits and to meet corporate tax obligations.[8]

Just as the Kaiser panel neared the finish line on its draft proposal, USWA basic-contract negotiations resumed with Big Steel. As part of both sides' push to reach a new deal without another damaging stoppage, leading up to the new bargaining round the HRRC met daily to narrow the scope of disputed issues. Contract talks ensued on February 14, 1962, with the thirteen-week paid vacation and the establishment of a permanent worker-replacement pool at the forefront of the union's agenda. In less than two months the parties agreed to an interim pact containing employee savings and vacation plans, pension improvements, and enhanced seniority and work-week protections. At the same time, the contract called for only a 2½ percent annual increase in base pay and no boost in the first year of the deal. As for the thirteen-week vacation and replacement-labor-pool, the two sides agreed to task the HRRC with producing recommendations by May 1, 1963. In a decision that would prove objectionable to many union district directors, the two sides' national negotiating teams arbitrarily agreed that if they proved satisfied with the recommendations from Miller's HRRC, they would not have to conduct a second ratification vote but could automatically place them into effect. If the deadlock could not be resolved by the HRRC, standard collective bargaining would again try to resolve the differences by reopening the 1962 pact.[9]

Because of Big Steel's consent to an interim contract and the delegation of remaining issues to the HRRC, the USWA's top leadership now turned to concluding its basic-contract talks with Kaiser. As with the previous round, Kaiser chose not to drag matters out by waiting for more powerful rivals to reach terms but instead wrapped up a separate deal, including both the thirteen-week vacation and the worker-replacement pool, with the union by December 1962. Shortly after Christmas, Miller traveled to Kaiser's Fontana, California, plant to head up the nine days of worker briefings in preparation for the ratification vote. By the time Miller had finished the briefings—which included four-hour sessions three times a day with every department and shift—he estimated that he had spoken to fully 97 percent of Kaiser's union workers. As one who had not risen from inside the mills, he dealt with initial shop-floor grumbling and "who is this guy?" skepticism. Complicating his efforts, the plant's management had been marked by internal factionalism for years, and several supervisors attempted to undercut Edgar Kaiser's endorsement of the pact. But Miller's patience in explaining the plan's nuances ultimately paid off. Kaiser workers ratified the new contract, including the Long-Range Sharing Plan, by more than a three-to-one margin.[10]

When the Kaiser productivity-savings payouts began the next year, they soon made the company's employees the best-paid steelworkers in America. It was not the innovative distribution of efficiency gains alone but also the pact's income and employment-security provisions that made the Kaiser plan revolutionary for its time. The *Detroit Free Press* reported that by the close of the plan's first reporting period at the end of April 1963, the average bonus awarded to participating workers came to an extra $80 per month over and above their regular pay at a time when the *total* average weekly pay of U.S. manufacturing employees was still less than $100. Kaiser job-security provisions also guaranteed that if a worker's employment was terminated for reasons other than normal market fluctuations, the idled man was entitled to join a reserve labor pool and have his pay continued. Not only did Fontana's workers profit handsomely, so too did the company—not least from four years of guaranteed labor peace. By April 1966, Kaiser workers were garnering an additional boost of $1,550 over and above base wages while the total average national pay stood at but $6,000.[11]

Because the 1962 Kaiser negotiations, followed as they had been by those with the Continental and American Can companies and Alcoa, had resulted in the adoption of extended vacations and replacement pools, pressure mounted anew upon Big Steel to adopt the same without first resorting to a reopening of its 1962 interim pact. The companies' controversial decision to hike steel prices in the past year had put them squarely on the defensive, and with the aid of public pressure the HRRC worked feverishly to complete a draft proposal that would, as Miller put it, "get a large chunk of replacement [income] but for manageable cost." Without a contract reopening or a strike, on June 29, 1963, the USWA and the major steel firms announced agreement on an amended contract that phased in thirteen-week vacations for up to half of the full-time workforce over five years, coordinated the vacations with rehiring of laid-off and part-time workers, boosted industry hospital-insurance coverage from 120 days to a full year, and upped the membership's weekly sickness and accident payouts and life-insurance benefits.[12]

It was a remarkable result, achieved cooperatively. Along with his prior role in shepherding through the Kaiser plan, Marvin Miller's HRRC pact with Big Steel now elevated him to the status of a rising star in the field of labor relations. It was 1960s-style "peaceful coexistence" in the labor field, orchestrated by the private sector's version of the "best and brightest." Desirous to highlight this trend, that summer John F. Kennedy reconstituted the President's Advisory Committee on Labor-Management Policy and named Miller as one of its members. The panel's mandate called for examining and promoting new ways of improving the collective-bargaining process, with the aims of minimizing the frequency and duration of disruptions that could harm the national economy. The twelve-person body, consisting of six representatives each from labor and business serving under the auspices of the president and FMCS head William Simkin, had been originally authorized by the Taft-Hartley Act, only to lie dormant since 1950.[13]

Ironically, despite the public perception of Miller as an advocate of labor-management cooperation, he had never abandoned his belief in the need for periodic and even disruptive collective-bargaining showdowns. Ever convinced of the fundamentally adversarial nature of labor-management relations, he was not nearly as much an exemplar of the Kennedy's administration's faith in industrial cooperation as it thought. Although Miller also privately opposed many of the administration's cold war foreign policies, when the president personally welcomed his newly appointed panelists to the White House, Miller was impressed by Kennedy's air of sophistication, easy facility with the names and backgrounds of his guests, and his better grasp of the nuances of current labor issues than most politicians. After Kennedy's shocking assassination just five months later, successor Lyndon Johnson quickly reappointed Miller and the other members of the presidential advisory panel.[14]

During Miller's time on the national advisory committee, presentations to the group highlighted purported examples of creative cooperation from both sides of the labor-management divide. To his eyes, however, some of them instead demonstrated how, in the increasingly complex arena of industrial relations, old-line unionists could be tricked into making bad deals. One of the saddest examples to him personally involved a longtime labor hero, radical longshoreman Harry Bridges. An attorney for the employer association that had recently struck a deal with Bridges's dockworkers described the new contract at length and hailed it as an example of both sides' willingness to embrace modernization. But as one well versed in the trade-offs involved in automation and related productivity issues—in the case of Bridges's membership, containerization and the mechanized handling of ship cargoes—Miller observed with dismay that the agreement had only protected the union-security guarantees of the current membership and not those of future hires.[15]

Miller's renown now also translated into a busy travel schedule of speaking engagements around the country. While he enjoyed the elevated profile, his family soldiered on at home. Terry, who had received her master's degree from Pitt in 1958, had followed it up with a doctorate in clinical psychology three years later. Supported by a Ford Foundation grant to the Squirrel Hill school district, she had then joined the Pittsburgh educational system's Mental Health Team—a group that promoted classroom acceptance and academic success of "unconventional" children of varied backgrounds and achievement levels. Carnegie Tech hired her as an assistant professor, and she took on the role of consultant to the city's school-to-college orientation program for underprivileged children. As for the Millers' own children, daughter Susan had started high school, and Peter—who had embraced pacifism and antipoverty work through his participation in American Friends Service Committee camps—had enrolled at Columbia University and was flourishing in sociology courses offered by luminaries Steven Marcus and Daniel Bell.[16]

The Millers' enhanced professional status also meant more frequent social entertaining at their Squirrel Hill home. Whether via dinner parties, cocktail receptions, or casual bridge nights, Marvin and Terry played host to colleagues, protégés, and accomplished acquaintances outside their own fields. Cookie Thomas, the spouse of a Steelworker aide Marvin had mentored since 1952, would later insist that, in her opinion and that of her husband, Miller possessed the necessary qualities, including the intellect, capacity for reflection, and self-control, that would have made an admirable president—of the United States. While Marvin played a more low-key role at social occasions, more often listening rather than initiating or leading discussions, the bold Terry delighted in her self-appointed role as provocateur, injecting controversial topics and playing "devil's advocate" for views she often opposed in order to enliven the conversation.[17]

By early 1965 Miller had added yet another professional accomplishment to his list. Working with USWA staff and representatives of the Alan Wood Steel Company—a maverick firm that, like Kaiser, had managed to avoid strikes since 1946—he designed an even more sophisticated productivity-sharing scheme than the previous effort at Fontana. Learning from the earlier difficulties encountered there, Alan Wood's Joint Economic Expansion Plan, or JEEP, retained its preexisting incentives for longer, thereby providing workers an easier transition. At first, Alan Wood's productivity bonuses applied only to the 60 percent of company employees not drawing traditional incentives. As at Kaiser, the worker/company split of savings was one-third to two-thirds, with the allocations coming from company pretax revenues. The plan also promised that any adverse differential between an employee's previous bonus and his new version would be reimbursed. Employees would also still be entitled to the cost-savings bonuses even when, owing to unrelated factors, the productivity savings did not immediately translate into higher company profits.[18]

Because Alan Wood's cost savings proved easier to determine and greater than those of Kaiser, the plan's bonuses were even more generous. Additionally, the company joined in adopting thirteen-week vacations (every five years) and the employee reserve pool. Because the work week was kept at thirty-eight hours instead of the thirty-two-hour standard in the larger steel firms, Alan Wood's income-maintenance provisions held at 95 percent of its workers' prior pay levels in the event they were bumped down to lower-level jobs. Even if an employee was laid off completely, if he claimed ten years or more seniority he would still draw 85 percent of his previous full-time wages (compared to a 60 percent level throughout most of basic steel) for an unlimited duration thanks to SUBs, and younger employees would receive the same generous income percentage for a full two years after layoff. USWA president David McDonald justifiably lauded the pact as a shining example of his union's modern "total job security" agenda.[19]

Nonetheless, Miller was soon found defending his unconventional deal to skeptical secretary-treasurer I.W. Abel, the USWA's Wage Policy Committee, and the district directors. They attacked the pact primarily for having bargained just an initial two-cent base-wage hourly increase. Looming behind the specific criticism was a leadership split that had long been brewing within Steelworker ranks. An internal rebellion against McDonald by Abel had "grown like topsy," in Miller's own words, in the aftermath of the 1963 Big Steel pact. An additional source of the rift grew out of sharp differences in social background and operating style between the two men. McDonald had not come up from the shop floor, though his father had been a mill worker. With his Hollywood looks, his wedge of bodyguards, and his ostentatious profile that included a lavish D.C. hotel suite, to critics McDonald was the very embodiment of a "tuxedo unionist." No matter how often he recited the words, "I was born with a union spoon in my mouth" at annual USWA conventions, grumbling rivals remained unconvinced.[20]

Despite the USWA president's efforts to reward even opponents with high-ranking positions, perhaps in the hopes of buying them off, internal dissatisfaction had continued to mount as the technicians' role within the union had expanded. Hints of anti-Semitism from the dissident faction suggested further, cruder motivations behind the hostility. Before 1961, owing to the skillful assistance of his "shadow president" Arthur Goldberg, McDonald had been able to contain the smoldering discontent. But after Goldberg's departure to become secretary of labor, no other individual had proven capable of filling those large shoes. Lawyers David Feller and Elliot Bredhof had tried, with Feller assuming the bulk of Goldberg's official legal duties. But the increasingly emboldened district directors had never come to view either man with the same degree of awe and fear that they had considered Goldberg.[21]

Providing the essential rank-and-file backing for a successful challenge to McDonald was the growing segment of the union's Canadian membership and younger workers dissatisfied with the modest basic-wage gains of recent pacts. In the "glory days" of Philip Murray and in his successor's early years, annual wage increases in basic steel had averaged 8 percent. But the 1960s deals—which had featured a greater bargaining role by the technicians—had accepted smaller base increases in exchange for greater long-term economic security. Younger men, with their inherent tendency to discount the prospect of layoffs, debilitating illness, or accident, tended to prioritize the size of their immediate raises over provisions for longer-run income stabilization. But even the older membership, unless it was regularly and effectively educated in the virtues of the recent pacts, was itself prone by habit to measure a contract's merit by the traditional standard of hourly-wage growth rather than the often-confusing provisions crafted by experts.[22]

For the first time since joining the USWA, Miller now weighed running for a union office himself—that of USWA secretary-treasurer on the incumbent's slate. Part of the fleeting appeal to him of making a campaign was the enduring, albeit quixotic, dream of eventually becoming the Steelworkers' president and using it to spearhead the eventual emergence of a European-style labor party in America. Fearing the danger of long-term damage to the Steelworkers if its internal strife persisted, having good relations with leaders in each of the rival factions, and convinced of his personal ability to win the trust of the rank-and-file, Marvin floated his idea to Terry. She was adamantly opposed, going so far as to cite a fear that he might be assassinated. And even if his family was willing to accept the risks to his career and perhaps even his life, how could he raise the necessary funds without bankrupting his family, since direct application of union funds for such purposes was prohibited? After weighing the pros and cons, Miller soon shelved further thoughts of a candidacy.[23]

It was a bitter election, with the two contenders for the presidency giving and receiving no quarter. Challenger Abel, who had started as a foundry man and then SWOC organizer, district director, and ultimately USWA secretary-treasurer, relentlessly blasted McDonald as a "crown prince" surrounded by a "palace guard." Abel supporters distributed photographs of McDonald from a White House black-tie dinner to illustrate the "tuxedo unionist" charge. Incumbent McDonald countered by labeling his adversary a "sell-out artist."

Despite assurances from Abel that he would not drag the ostensibly apolitical technicians into the union's leadership fracas, his campaign disseminated leaflets containing crude anti-Semitic slurs directed at the trio of Feller, Fischer, and Miller. An angry Marvin then confronted the secretary-treasurer and successfully won the withdrawal of the offensive material.[24]

Complicating the Steelworkers' internal disarray was that the union's next round of basic-steel bargaining was looming. Early negotiating sessions went on as scheduled as the election campaign raged, with the two highest-ranking men on the Steelworkers' side of the table refusing even to speak to each other. Given the uncertainty of the electoral outcome, management representatives did not know with whom to hammer out a deal. On February 9, 1965, the bitter presidential contest produced a narrow victory for Abel. McDonald had carried a slight majority of his U.S. membership, but lopsided support for his rival from the Canadian locals had resulted in a narrow Abel margin of 2 percent—fewer than ten thousand votes out of a half-million total. Given the tally's closeness, speculation ran rampant on whether McDonald would formally challenge the initial count. While the lame duck weighed his options, the union managed to secure a four-month temporary extension of the existing steel contract.[25]

As McDonald vacillated and Miller and other staffers pondered their fate, Abel issued pronouncements reflecting a man with no doubt of his victory. The presumptive president hinted that he would adopt a "tougher" bargaining posture that reemphasized traditional priorities, and that he would also call for a diminished role for, or even the elimination of, the HRRC. In a gesture for postelection unity, Abel did not demand the immediate removal of his defeated rival from the union's bargaining team, but he diluted its pro-McDonald representation by appointing his own additional loyalists. He also reassured Miller that the latter would retain his posts as presidential assistant and member of the basic-steel negotiating committee. Other colleagues were not so fortunate. Besides the defeated McDonald, his vice presidential running mate Howard Hague, and his secretary-treasurer candidate Al Whitehouse, associate general counsel David Feller was forced to resign shortly after the election. So too initially did Ben Fischer, only like Miller to be talked into staying by the new president-elect. Ironically, the new regime's determination to employ long-moribund mandatory-retirement rules in order to clean out remaining McDonald loyalists cost Abel-backer Otis Brubaker his position. Some three months after the election, McDonald finally decided not to challenge the verdict, sold his home in Pittsburgh, and moved to Palm Springs, California, for a comfortable retirement.[26]

Amid the turmoil the resumed steel talks went forward at a snail's pace. As the June 1965 deadline neared, President Lyndon Johnson vigorously intervened. The administration was in the early stages of its massive military buildup in Vietnam, and the last thing Johnson wanted at that moment was a steel strike. After federal mediation at lower levels failed, the president then summoned the two sides to the White House for eight days and nights of what Miller later described as "ball busting." Each team received the full "Johnson treatment"— including a flight on Air Force One, transfers by helicopter from Andrews Air Force Base to the White House lawn, and a chauffeured limousine hop of 150 yards to the entrance. After an animated pep talk from their impatient host, the rival negotiators were escorted to a half-submerged room deep within the Old Executive Office Building where the air conditioning had "broken down." When lunchtime arrived, the two sides were served stale, soggy sandwiches. On day five of the talks, LBJ showed up in midafternoon to personally upbraid his captive audience. Requesting a separate meeting with the union reps, Johnson employed a guilt trip with clear references to Vietnam, without success.[27]

After a full week in the EOB sauna, the two sides crept close to an agreement. In anticipation of a possible breakdown of talks, however, the companies had already issued orders that their furnaces be banked. Now, to the sheer frustration of the steel executives, as soon as news of an agreement reached the Oval Office, LBJ summoned the parties for what amounted to a stall until he could make his own announcement of the deal with maximum television coverage. All the while the industry leaders sat, fuming in the knowledge that every lost second they endured before revoking their prior shutdown order meant the further loss of company revenue. With Cooper and Abel both visibly fidgeting, Johnson finally issued his statement at 6 P.M.—and then further detained the unhappy bargainers for photographs. Only after that did he speed through his goodbyes and rush out the door for his awaiting transportation to his Texas ranch.[28]

Aluminum and can negotiations still remained to be concluded. Being just as involved in them, an exhausted Miller was increasingly irritable from the cumulative effect of two years of joint-study meetings, bargaining rounds, and office strife. Dick Moss, a talented attorney who had joined Ben Fischer's contract-arbitration section five years before, was a regular partner in the can-company talks. When the latest round hit an unexpected last-minute snag just an hour from the strike deadline, the Steelworker team adjourned to the sanctuary of a nearby watering hole. Over the years, colleagues had noticed that Miller's choice of lunchtime cocktail revealed his mood. A Tom Collins meant that he was in good spirits, a martini signaled frustration with a particular matter, and

Old Grand-Dad bourbon equaled big trouble—and this was a bourbon occasion. Over their drinks, each person revealed his personal dream for an alternative career. Moss volunteered tongue-in-cheek that he had fantasized of being either the Pope or the commissioner of baseball. The frazzled Miller, incapable at the moment of letting go of his frustration, countered that he would rather have the opportunity to be commissioner of the Internal Revenue Service, so that he could use his office to exact as much pain upon his adversaries on the other side as possible.[29]

Miller at least had his assurances from Abel that he would not suffer a loss of responsibility or prestige at the new regime's hands. Although the president-elect did follow through on dismantling the HRRC, Miller retained the leadership of successor single-issue panels as the coordinator of a "Department of Joint Studies." He also kept his rank as Abel's assistant—although his degree of access shrank. Newly ascendant officers such as vice president Joseph Molony did seek out his opinion on proposed changes to the union's organizational structure and bargaining agenda. Privately, however, Miller railed at the new leadership, scribbling angrily on his note pad, "See the great settlements. . . . 21 cents, 22 cents—three years!" "Vacation in Vegas for the chosen few . . . Abel?" He pointedly cited the case of a Jewish USWA district official who had been arbitrarily docked two days' pay and then seen his complaint brushed aside by the union's new leadership. And despite Abel's personal reassurances to the contrary, loyalists to the new order with accompanying expectations of advance were still angling to supplant him. Ben Fischer insisted to Miller that he remained indispensable to the union despite the recent leadership shuffle and would continue to "rule the roost." But in private Fischer had his doubts about his friend's willingness to play the necessary games. "Marvin is not basically a politician," he noted. "He's relatively orthodox and relatively absolute in his view of the world." Conceding the precariousness of Miller's perch, he added, "You couldn't just think of Marvin and Abe. It was a palace-politics situation and you had to look at where you fit in."[30]

The nervous Miller now privately solicited outside job offers, utilizing the contacts he had accumulated over his career. One proposal came from the Carnegie Endowment for International Peace, which had received a grant for a multiyear study examining the potential efficacy of collective-bargaining techniques in the international-relations arena. If he accepted, Miller would become the project's director. He travelled to New York for an interview, but despite the allure of returning home, the position seemed to be too much a "loosely structured academic exercise." More tempting was a rival offer from

Harvard University. Having accepted an invitation from his former Kaiser-committee colleague John Dunlop to speak to the latter's graduate seminar, over drinks Miller received a verbal offer of a visiting professorship. The position would run one to three years, with a higher salary than his Steelworker pay and portable pension benefits. His work year would be just eight and a half months, only a modest amount of writing would be required, and he could sign up for as much or little graduate-level teaching as he chose. Aware of Miller's passion for tennis, Dunlop even pointed out that new year-round campus courts had been built. After almost accepting the offer on the spot, Miller suppressed the impulse and went home to consider.[31]

Before he could give a formal response to Harvard, however, a third opportunity—riskier but with a unique allure—presented itself. In early December, he traveled to San Francisco for his annual Kaiser Committee sessions. As he rode down the hotel elevator to join the other panelists, the compartment abruptly stopped and chairman George Taylor stepped in. As they descended together, Taylor, a Philadelphia native and faculty member at the University of Pennsylvania's Wharton School, asked Miller if he had ever heard of Robin Roberts. As a lifelong baseball fan, Marvin certainly had heard of the famous pitcher, a six-time twenty-game winner who after fourteen seasons with the Phillies had recently been unceremoniously dealt to Baltimore and then Houston. Taylor related that the hurler was heading a committee seeking someone to revive the players' organization; someone who would be adept at dealing with management, understood contracts, and was especially conversant with pension plans. Roberts had asked Taylor for suggestions, and the latter had immediately thought of Miller. (What Taylor did not let on was that Miller had not been the first person he had approached about the job. Lane Kirkland, the assistant to and eventual successor to George Meany as leader of the AFL-CIO, had been probed about the position and had turned down the idea.) When his companion now asked if he was interested, Marvin hesitated. Then he remembered Roberts's heroic performance in a losing cause against Joe DiMaggio's Yankees in the 1950 World Series and thought to himself, "What the hell. It can't hurt to find out more about it." He then answered, "Sounds interesting . . . I'll certainly talk to him."[32]

As the elevator door opened and the two men exited to their meeting, the Wharton professor mentioned that he would contact Roberts to relay word of Miller's possible interest. Within an hour, Taylor had set up a pre-Christmas meeting in Cleveland in two weeks for Miller with the pitcher and the other members of the search committee. Upon Marvin's return to Pittsburgh, he weighed his options with his family. Should he pursue any of the outside offers or remain with the Steelworkers? Son Peter, himself an Ivy Leaguer, weighed in for the Harvard post. But his father retained doubts about a university position. He was, to be sure, weary of long hours and union intrigue, but was he ready yet for the relative quiet of an academic life? And other similar opportunities could very well pop up again. But another chance to lead major-league ballplayers almost certainly would never come his way. If he succeeded in raising their stature and securing greater rights and incomes for them, it would be a truly noteworthy feat. And for the first time in his life, opting to lead the players would give him the chance finally to head his own union.[33] Two weeks later, Marvin Miller found himself across the table from a trio of famous athletes, being interviewed for the opportunity to change his and their professional lives—and with them the industry of baseball—forever.

Part Two

Baseball Revolutionary
(1966–1985)

"A specter is haunting the capitals of
sport—the specter of unionism."
—Robert Lipsyte, *New York Times*,
January 18, 1968

Eight

A Fresh Start

Shortly before Christmas of 1965, forty-eight-year-old Marvin Miller was seated in the office of Cleveland pension-fund actuary John Gabel. He was interviewing for the position of executive director of a union so weak it barely merited the label. The Major League Baseball Players Association (MLBPA) was the successor to a player-representation system consisting of team representatives and a league-wide player delegate from each of the two circuits. Major-league owners had granted it in 1946 along with a minimal pension program after having crushed a unionization threat from the American Baseball Guild. Eight years later the players had incorporated as the MLBPA, but in most respects their organization remained a company union. Across two decades the major-league minimum salary had risen by only a thousand dollars to $6,000. Ensuring the ballplayers' low pay—only five stars had ever reached the $100,000 mark—was a reserve system that technically bound a player to his club for one additional year after his contract expired, but that the owners interpreted as empowering them to renew the indenture indefinitely.[1]

At the time the major leaguers had relabeled their association in the 1950s, they had hired J. Norman Lewis as their counsel and had sought pension improvements. After just five years, the owners had forced him out. Under successor Robert Cannon, a Milwaukee circuit court judge and son of a 1920s player rights' advocate, the MLBPA had fallen back into lethargy. The widespread speculation was that Cannon's refusal to rock the boat stemmed from a desire to be baseball's commissioner. By the end of 1965, the organization's assets consisted of $5,700 in dues and a beat-up file cabinet in the Biltmore Hotel office of agent Frank Scott.[2]

Some players were losing patience with Cannon's company-union ways. Their desire to create a new top post and staff it with a professional negotiator demonstrated a dawning recognition that their industry was entering a new era of big television money. Robin Roberts and Jim Bunning in particular grasped that unless the players retained an effective leader, their cut of an expanding revenue pie—in particular that share made available for their pension—would be forfeited to management greed. For baseball's long-underpaid athletes, the pensions they qualified for after five years of major-league service were a modest yet essential floor of economic security later in life. By the end of 1965 the pension fund was accruing $1.6 million a year. Active players contributed $344 annually into the commissioner's Central Fund, and owners chipped in 60 percent of All-Star Game and World Series broadcasting fees and 95 percent of All-Star gate receipts. Roberts and Bunning already suspected that in the clubs' prior negotiations with the television networks, the owners' had deliberately low-balled their estimated return from these sources to lessen their pension contributions.[3]

Even before coming to Cleveland, Miller had been urged by friends to remove his name from consideration. If he obtained the MLBPA leadership post, he would be trading away an established job at one of the nation's most powerful unions for leadership of a band of athletes ignorant in the ways of collective bargaining. But viewed from the opposite angle, taking over leadership of an organization presently so powerless also meant it would be hard to fail. Miller already had become sympathetic to the ballplayers' need for guidance, and harbored no illusions about what he would be walking into. As he later recalled, "The beginning was absolutely the worst because to the hard-line owners of that day, unionism was treason. . . . For very wealthy people who owned franchises, baseball was a respite of the tensions and problems elsewhere; here you could control everything: no unions, a reserve clause that made the players prisoners, no grievance procedure, no salary arbitration, no nothing." In lacking any real system of employment rights, the players seemed to him, "the most exploited group of workers I had ever seen—more exploited than the grape pickers of Cesar Chavez." Given how low a rung the players currently occupied, even if Miller failed to turn things around at the MLBPA, his reputation within the union movement would still likely enable him to return to a more traditional post.[4]

Miller was not the search committee's sole candidate for executive director, much less the favorite. Despite the rumblings from certain player activists,

Robert Cannon was seen as the "inside" choice. One member of the search panel, Pittsburgh hurler Bob Friend, was so committed to the current MLBPA counsel that he did not even bother to show up to Miller's interview, leaving the trio of Roberts, Bunning, and Milwaukee Braves outfielder Harvey Kuenn to conduct the interview. Bunning had his own favorite in the person of Detroit attorney Tom Costello, who had handled some of the pitcher's personal legal matters. Retired Cleveland right-hander and 1950s player-activist Bob Feller was also campaigning for the job. Other possible choices included former Tiger slugger Hank Greenberg and, in a clear demonstration of the players' naiveté, San Francisco Giants vice president Chub Feeney.[5]

By the time the interview had entered a third hour, Miller had already concluded that Roberts was the search panel's key figure. Bunning seemed preoccupied with such grievances as substandard field conditions and clubhouse facilities, outdated travel accommodations, and the playing season's length—which had been expanded from 154 to 162 games with no commensurate boost in player benefits. Kuenn sat in stony silence. The interviewers did reveal to the candidate that after a similar session with Judge Cannon, the "incumbent" had gone to the owners and extracted a promise from them to restore $150,000 from All-Star Game coffers for the new executive director's salary and expenses. Miller concealed his dismay at the arrangement, despite recognizing it as a likely violation of Taft-Hartley provisions against company unions and a subtraction from moneys otherwise subject to the pension plan. Only later would Miller discover an even more egregious example of the players' deference to management. Unknown to him, the search committee had provided Commissioner William "Spike" Eckert with the MLBPA's preliminary list of candidates for scrutiny.[6]

During the interview Roberts repeated the stereotypical fear of cigar-chomping, mob-linked union officials and "goon squads" in behalf of an idea he now floated—a "two-headed" leadership structure for the association. Under the scheme, Miller, were he to be selected, would be paired with a "safer" partner who would be the MLBPA's general counsel. The specific individual Roberts had in mind was former Vice President Richard Nixon. Miller internally recoiled at the thought of teaming up with the former Red-baiter, and he remembered an incident during the 1959 steel talks that had underscored Nixon's crudeness. On that occasion, the vice president had embarrassed himself in front of Arthur Goldberg by wishing the USWA lead negotiator a "Happy Ka-noo-kah." Goldberg had laughed off the apparently unintentional slight, attributing it to Nixon's ignorance of Jewish culture. Miller then endeavored to shoot down Roberts's trial balloon, knowing full well that in so doing he might be dooming his own prospects. He described the proposed coleader as an owners' man with no background representing workers and who "wouldn't know the difference between a pension plan and a pitcher's mound." He added that Nixon would not likely be available anyway, since he was preparing the groundwork for a 1968 presidential run. Drawing upon the divisive impact of factionalism at the Steelworkers, Miller went on to argue that given the Players Association's tiny staff and membership, any top-level conflicts could not be overcome through a professional union bureaucracy and would be disastrous. A far better course, he advised, was to have the executive director select his own man as the players' counsel.[7]

Miller quickly recognized that his opinion had not been welcome to Roberts. Upon returning to Pittsburgh, he told his family they should "forget about going back to New York." But his yearning for the job remained strong enough that he wrote back to Roberts a week later to put a favorable spin on the interview. "I am impressed," he soothingly stated, "with the virtually perfect fit between your needs and my skills." Once more, he emphasized his professional and personal qualifications. He also took pains, up to the edge of misleading his audience, to downplay committee fears that a Players Association led by him would seek out confrontation. Years later Robin Roberts would insist that Miller had even promised that he would never initiate a strike. While this was an overstatement of Miller's actual words, it was true that he had offered a more nuanced reassurance. "It is especially important," he had said, "that harmonious relationships prevail without any sacrifice of player interests."[8]

As for the main focus of Miller's letter—his emphasis upon his track record and range of practical experience—it was amply justified. Whether the search committee recognized it yet, Miller's decades of experience would prove essential to the Players Association's ultimate success. In a fledgling union of fewer than 650 players, coaches, managers, and trainers and without a staff, the man they chose to lead them would necessarily have to shoulder most of the load. Absent a sudden stroke of luck, however, it seemed unlikely that Miller would get the chance to demonstrate his suitability. Fortunately for him, the front-runner proceeded to erode his advantage of incumbency through arrogance and greed. Following the search committee's recommendation of Cannon, a January player reps' meeting—with Commissioner Eckert and aide Lee MacPhail present—had seconded the endorsement. Although the initial round of rep voting gave Cannon a plurality but not a majority, a second ballot had produced the judge's "unanimous" selection. While attending a National Academy of Arbitrators meeting in Puerto Rico, Miller had received the disappointing news by phone from Robin Roberts's wife. Just ten days later, however, Cannon's inevitable ascent unraveled. The nominee rejected the representatives' request that he locate his office in New York rather than Milwaukee, even dismissing a compromise suggestion of Chicago. He then tried to hold up the association for more money by demanding to be paid not only a $50,000 salary but the dollar value of his judicial pension as well. Cannon's high-handedness eventually turned off even loyalist Bob Friend, whose sympathy for the judge's opposition to relocating to New York also waned when the pitcher received word that he was being traded to the Yankees without a say in the matter.[9]

The humbled search committee now turned to Miller. At first, pride kept him from accepting the panel's renewed courtship. After a Robin Roberts intercession by phone and a similar mea culpa from Friend, the satisfied candidate responded, "If the players elect me, I'll accept the job." Again, however, not just Frank Scott but management figure MacPhail and even Judge Cannon were invited to the MLBPA reps' revote in early March. Even at this late date, if Commissioner Eckert or his aides had bothered to thoroughly investigate Miller's background and then objected to his selection on the basis of the candidate's leftist past, they could easily have killed his selection. But Eckert, the former military procurement officer scornfully labeled the "unknown soldier" by baseball scribes, only urged discretion and did not veto Miller outright but extended a vague offer of cooperation.[10]

With his voice barely audible over the clubhouse din, Minnesota rep Bob Allison phoned with the news that his colleagues had endorsed putting Miller's name before the full membership. Only then did the executive director nominee realize that he had never given notice to his USWA superiors. How would Abel react? By the next morning—a Sunday—sports pages across the country were running with the story. Congratulations poured in, with many callers ignorant of the fact that the player rank-and-file still had to approve the nomination. With the pending spring-training balloting in mind, Robin Roberts now urged Miller to shave off his trademark mustache in keeping with club facial-hair bans and to demonstrate visually that he was not some shadowy underworld figure. Irritated at the suggestion, Miller pointed out that many of those attending baseball games sported their own mustaches, beards, and long hair. "Robbie, this is 1966," he declared. "I'm not going to shave a mustache I've had since I was seventeen because of some management hang-up."[11]

That evening, in part to escape the tide of well-wishes, the Millers privately celebrated at a local restaurant. Early the next morning, Marvin sought out his union president to belatedly explain his pursuit of another job, only to discover that Abel was fishing in South America and would return only as far as Miami before switching planes for the upcoming Kaiser Committee meetings in California. In the meantime, Miller prepared for his clubhouse campaign visits by distributing a favorable *New York Times* article to club player reps entitled, "Creative Labor Man Goes to Bat for Ballplayers." He flew to Ft. Lauderdale to finalize the team-meeting schedule, and then continued to Miami for a rendezvous with his current boss. Booking a seat next to Abel on the West Coast flight, Miller briefed him on his prospective baseball job, conceding, "There's an awful lot about this I don't understand." Nonetheless, when Abel labeled such a move as "crazy," Miller politely disagreed, insisting that he would "kick himself" later if he did not give it a fair shot.[12]

Upon landing in Los Angeles, Miller found that he had far more than Abel's skepticism left to overcome. One day before a scheduled meeting with Angels players and coaches in Palm Springs, an article in that morning's *Herald-Examiner* entitled, "We Don't Want Any Labor Boss in Baseball" quoted team rep Buck Rodgers and veteran Jimmy Piersall attacking his nomination. Following Kaiser Committee morning sessions, the blindsided Miller separated himself from colleagues and spent his lunchtime alone with his thoughts. As he went over a list of the quoted players, he guessed correctly that Judge Cannon was behind the smear campaign. Most revealing was a line from the anti-Miller petition cited in the newspaper article that called for an executive director with legal experience and someone "the owners can respect." As he sat in the hotel courtyard, I. W. Abel ventured over to offer his support. His dazed listener admitted to confusion at the situation, volunteering, "I don't understand any of this." Sensing that a trap awaited his subordinate, Abel repeated his advice to Miller not to be "a fool" and to withdraw his name. But when the latter expressed his continuing determination to press ahead, the Steelworkers president generously extended him the option of returning to the USWA should the new job not work out.[13]

The next morning, as he rode to Palm Springs in a rented car, Miller's thoughts turned to the unfair attacks from players who had never ever met him. With typical sardonic humor, he counted up his adversaries and found they came up short of a full All-Star team. When he arrived, however, he discovered that no reservation had been made for him and that there were no lodging vacancies within a forty-mile radius. At his USWA driver's suggestion, he took a chance and rang up his former boss—and local resident—David McDonald. Even though the two men had not spoken for a year, despite being on his way out the door to a dinner party the ex-president invited his surprise visitor to stay at his house overnight and offered the use of his wife's car for the next day. After several more hours restlessly reviewing his planned remarks to the Angels, Miller finally adjourned to bed.[14]

Early the next morning, an angry Miller confronted Rodgers at a premeeting breakfast. The nervous rep admitted that Judge Cannon had filled his head and those of teammates with visions of union racketeers and thugs. Reinforcing the concerns had been recent press quotes from the Teamsters' Jimmy Hoffa suggesting that his own union was considering organizing professional athletes—remarks seized upon by National League president Warren Giles and Eckert public-relations man Joe Reichler. Immediately after his tense meeting with Rodgers, Miller's session in the Angels clubhouse ensued. Having anticipated a give-and-take session like those of his past Kaiser briefings, Miller found his new audience by turns indifferent and hostile. After twenty minutes of remarks from scribbled notes, the nominee opened the floor to questions. Deafening silence fell over the room. The scrambling Miller turned to the subject of the pension, pointing out that, because of its failure to keep up with inflation, the assembled were worse off now than when the plan had started. Upon that sobering news, a few eyebrows finally raised. Miller concluded the meeting with both a personal plea to his listeners to become active in their association and a declaration that its aims would be determined by them and not by him.[15]

One of the few questions posed to him—from the skeptical Piersall—spoke to the athletes' widely shared trepidation over what union membership meant: "Are you going to have the ballplayers go out on strike?" Despite the ongoing story of the 1966 joint holdout of Dodger pitching stars Sandy Koufax and Don Drysdale over their demands for multiyear pacts containing big salary increases, most of their contemporaries still found it hard to draw the parallel between two individuals' coordinated refusal to work and a strike. Mindful of needing to walk a verbal tightrope before the anxious players, Miller pointed out that under the strict legal definition of a union as the elected, collective representative of an employee group, the Players Association *already* was one. It was the organizational expression of a legitimate adversarial relationship in which its existence served as a necessary "restraint on what an employer can otherwise do." Strikes resembled individual holdouts but in behalf of shared aims and with the greater leverage that came with numbers. Though strikes constituted a "last resort," they were appropriate when the cause justified it and when the decision for it had been democratically decided. Miller emphasized from the start that if the players expected his own relationship with the owners to be one in which industry officialdom always liked him, they would be disappointed, and if they saw such a relationship emerging it meant that he was not doing his job for them.[16]

The three remaining Cactus League visits in Arizona, with the San Francisco Giants, Chicago Cubs, and Cleveland Indians, went equally badly or worse. After the Giants' session, the club's inebriated, but at least hospitable, owner Horace Stoneham arranged for Miller to meet one of his baseball idols, Willie Mays. But the team public-relations man tried to embarrass the nominee in front of reporters by hoping to stump him on his knowledge of the 1930s Brooklyn Dodgers. Miller turned the tables and forced his inquisitor's retreat by success-fully reciting the roster of his boyhood heroes down to the backup catcher. The next meeting, with the Cubs and their hostile rep Larry Jackson, also proved an uphill battle to capture and maintain player attention. The most openly hostile reception, though, came during Miller's Cleveland clubhouse session. Manager Birdie Tebbetts constantly interrupted him, even floating the accusation, "How can the players be sure you're not a Communist?" Startled, Miller replied, "A what?" Tebbetts continued on, "Have you ever been investigated by the FBI?" Ironically, the Cleveland manager's barbs, though not based on any personal knowledge, pointed to the most vulnerable spot in his background—not the ridiculous assertions of mob ties but his genuine past identification with left-wing labor politics. Given the crude and unsubstantiated form of Tebbetts's attacks, however, Miller was able to easily deflect them, pointedly noting that unlike the Indians' manager, he had actually been the subject of a mandatory FBI background check as a prior member of a presidential panel. When the man-ager nonetheless continued with his barrage of interruptions, an exasperated Miller ended the duel by declaring, "It's clear that all you want to do is sabotage the meeting . . . now let the players have their meeting back!"[17]

Early returns from the four western "precincts" indicated trouble. As had been the case at the candidate's squad appearances, the subsequent voting had been crashed by their managers. Frank Scott reviewed the tallies first and, hoping not to demoralize Miller, opted not to share the results with him until the Florida squads had been given the chance to meet him and cast ballots. The Angels' tally had been 25–6 against him, while the Giants had voted 27–0 in opposition with one player abstention—possibly Mays. The Cubs had recorded a narrower 18–10 negative result, but the Indians' repudiation had been by a depressingly resounding 32–1. The Cactus League total of 102–17 against Miller pointed to a landslide rejection if it repeated in the Grapefruit League. Recognizing the need to improve his presentation beforehand, Miller dispatched Terry to do additional research that included reading maverick owner Bill Veeck's autobiography and Simon Rottenberg's 1956 study of the player market, while he tied up loose ends at Steelworker headquarters.

Miller's Florida backers, led by the now-supportive Robin Roberts, were all too aware of the Cactus League debacle and were determined not to permit a repeat. First up, though, was the squad Miller thought would be the most likely to give him a hard time—the New York Yankees. "Rooting for them," he reasoned, "was like rooting for U.S. Steel." But soon it became clear that a change had set in. Giving evidence that the eastern reps had done their due diligence, not only were the players running the meetings but they were prepared to interact positively with Miller. During the first of his new briefings, Miller broached the matter of baseball's reserve clause and volunteered his personal opinion that the prior court rulings supporting it had been in error. With characteristic brashness, pitcher Jim Bouton immediately challenged him, arguing, "Without the reserve clause, wouldn't the wealthiest teams get all the stars?" The nominee quickly turned the question back upon its author, noting that under the reserve system one franchise alone had won thirty league pennants and twenty World Series over a forty-five-year span. The grinning Bouton provided Miller with his exclamation point—"You mean the Yankees!"[18]

Baseball management kept up its campaign of spying and harassment. After the Yankee session, Joe Reichler pulled Bouton aside to warn him to be "very, very, *very* careful about this guy Miller." Outside the clubhouse, Reichler similarly offered the "friendly advice" to the candidate that "in order to be elected it's going to be very important to have the owners on your side," and toward that end Miller should actively socialize with them. His listener pointedly replied that while he would not refuse to join an individual owner for a drink, both as a matter of propriety and as a newcomer "I don't think that courting them is my job." Reichler continued to press Miller on the point, insisting that he at least pay a call upon John Galbreath, even though the Pirates owner and pension-committee chairman had already warned his players at the team's off-season cookout not to vote for a "labor boss" who would ruin the game.[19]

The rest of Miller's Grapefruit League tour unfolded as a blur of rental cars, motels, and clubhouse faces. At Miller's before-session meal in Orlando with rep Bob Allison and the Twins' tight-fisted owner Calvin Griffith, the latter poked uneasily at his food until his guest reassured him that he would have neither time nor inclination to inject himself in individual players' contract talks. When Miller arrived in Cocoa Beach to meet the Houston squad, Robin Roberts relayed the welcome news that his soundings indicated a membership warming to the candidacy. Following the last of the squad meetings in West Palm Beach, Miller returned to Pittsburgh to await his prospective constituents' verdict. The final tally would soon be known, because eighteen of the twenty squads had already voted by the time he had concluded his presentations, and the results from the remainder were expected in a day or two.[20]

The next morning—coinciding with Opening Day of the 1966 regular season—Frank Scott called to deliver the good news. It had been a landslide after all, but one in Miller's favor. In Florida he had carried the day by a resounding 472–34 margin. Five clubs had unanimously voted for him and three others had recorded but one negative tally each. Even the eastern squad with the largest number of "no" votes cast, the Boston Red Sox, had registered but six. Miller drew particular satisfaction that two "hometown" teams of his—the Dodgers and Pirates—had backed him without exception. Even with the earlier Cactus League totals included, his overall victory margin came to an impressive 489 to 136. Most remarkably, even a majority of the union's nonplayer members had voted for him. Just two days short of his forty-ninth birthday, Marvin Miller was now the duly elected executive director of the MLBPA.[21]

Congratulations again poured in, with the first one coming from David Mc-Donald. The most colorful response, though, came from Miller's Uncle Sid. The young Marvin's one-time ballpark companion now offered his grown nephew two bits of advice: first, "give those baseball bosses Hell," and second—befitting the experience of a one-time Jersey contractor—hire a bodyguard in view of the powerful enemies he now claimed. The day after Miller's birthday, Steelworker colleague Dick Moss bounded into the office and insisted upon treating him to the Pirates' home-opener. As the pair passed through the turnstiles, the ticket-taker remarked to the players' chief that, given his new status, the day's contest might be the last he would ever have to pay for. Determined to be a model of rectitude, however, Miller privately resolved not to accept even the most modest tokens from those who would now be his adversaries. Despite the vow, Miller would eventually accept a handful of Opening Day invitations, usually as a guest of one of the New York teams.[22]

Despite his overwhelming victory, Miller's election marked just the opening round in management efforts to force him out. Mere days after the season opener, Jim Bunning called him to relay that Robert Cannon—still the MLBPA's counsel in name—wanted to discuss the details of Miller's contract. When the two met over dinner, it immediately became clear that Cannon's draft was a trap. It set the start date of Miller's employment not at July 1, 1966—as he and the player reps had verbally agreed upon—but January 1, 1967, well after the expiration of the current pension pact and thus effectively preventing him from representing the membership in negotiations over a new one. Cannon also had set the length of the contract at just two years, ignoring Miller's insistence upon a five-year agreement. The proposal did include the prior understandings regarding the executive director's pay and expenses, set at $50,000 and $20,000 respectively. But the expense-account provisions also constituted a potential landmine, considering that they failed to spell out the proper procedures for reimbursements while empowering union reps to fire him for mere accusation of public ridicule or moral turpitude upon just three days' notice. A sarcastic Miller pointedly asked Cannon if he had ever heard of "innocent until proven guilty," and he pressed for alternative language that would mandate his submitting detailed individual expense and reimbursement reports, prohibit expense advances, and include a good-conduct clause identical to that contained in the players' own contracts.[23]

While Cannon's machinations delayed the official start of Miller's MLBPA duties, the owners dropped another shoe. Having questionably subsidized the Players Association for two years from their pension contributions to the commissioner's Central Fund, and having promised to fork over $150,000 in salary and expenses for the new MLBPA executive director when they had assumed it would be Cannon, the clubs now suddenly "discovered" that such subsidization of the union violated Taft-Hartley. Lee MacPhail then argued that the MLBPA should not extend a contract to its new leader until it secured its own separate funding for the position. One silver lining for Miller in this "squeeze play," however, was that in acknowledging Taft-Hartley's applicability in the matter, management had de facto conceded that baseball was a business engaged in interstate commerce and that the Players Association was a union as defined under federal law.[24]

By June, Commissioner Eckert had offered to hold an "unprecedented" meeting of the owners' Executive Council with Cannon and the MLBPA reps to discuss both the pension and union finances. But conspicuously absent from the list of invitees was Miller, on the stale pretext that his executive director contract had not been finalized. The owners apparently intended to keep him—unable to relinquish his Pittsburgh home or line up new housing in New York without an employment contract—in perpetual limbo while they continued to dictate terms to a headless union. Anticipating that the owners' decision to drop their subsidization would be publicly announced at the scheduled June 6 "D-Day" session, Miller successfully prevailed upon Eckert to let him attend, in exchange for offering the commissioner a "helpful suggestion"—one intended to test his fairness and at the same time possibly drive a wedge between Eckert and his owners.[25]

Miller proposed that at the same time the industry withdrew its subsidization of union expenses, the clubs should pair the announcement with another eliminating the past requirement that players contribute personally to their pension plan. Making the pension "non-contributory" would save each association member $344 annually, an amount that could then be converted into a dues check-off. Although Miller would still posture for months against the owners for financially pulling the rug out from under the union, because it served to rally his membership, privately he knew that whether legal or not, continued management underwriting of the union would have hung like a sword of Damocles over the players. And with a dollar-for-dollar conversion of the membership's pension contributions into union dues, the players could now pocket the additional $50 in dues payments they had previously been making. If Eckert presented the idea ad hoc at the meeting, the owners might well be caught flatfooted and put on the spot to either endorse or stonewall the idea. If, as he expected, they chose the latter, the union's solidarity would strengthen from fresh outrage at their refusal.[26]

One risk in Miller's gambit, however, was that even if the owners agreed to convert players' pension contributions into union dues, the check-offs could only begin with a new salary year in spring 1967. In the meantime the MLBPA would still confront an owner-generated financial crisis for three-quarters of a year with no apparent means of paying the new executive director. When the two sides met, as expected the clubs pressed ahead with their plans to defund the Players Association. Management lawyer Paul Porter in turn slammed the door on a rival financing suggestion from the union to declare an appropriate portion of All-Star Game receipts as directly belonging to the players. Under such a scheme, the owners would either name the union as a formal cosponsor of the midseason classic or pay the membership collectively up front for individuals' participation with the union and then convert the group payment into dues.[27]

The owners, however, had no desire to help Miller's organization survive a financial crisis they had intentionally orchestrated. Adding insult to injury, industry lawyers incredulously claimed that they had simply "failed to focus" previously on the legality of the clubs' union subsidization and refused to admit that their belated "discovery" had been prompted by the players' choice of an executive director the owners opposed. Further provoking the player reps in attendance, pension-chairman Galbreath did not bother to show up. Management figures present in turn adopted the posture of grandees accustomed to receiving supplicants but not responding to their entreaties. When Miller demanded late in the session that the owners at least come up with a formal reply to the union's suggestions "as expeditiously as possible," Eckert only offered more excuses. At the end of the unproductive six-hour marathon, White Sox rep Eddie

Fisher erupted that it had been a "complete waste of time." Coincidentally or not, six days later the hurler was traded to the Baltimore Orioles.[28]

Immediately after the meeting, Miller rallied his troops in a nearby conference room to emphasize what had actually been accomplished. To begin with, the players had forced the unprecedented in-season meeting session and his presence at it. They had gotten the clubs to admit that their previous subsidization of the union had been illegal. The timing of the withdrawal of financial support had also revealed the owners' fear of the players' potential, and instead of their obstinacy causing the union to fold, it had actually bolstered its solidarity. He promised them that he would report to work with or without a contract on July 1. To prove the point, once the reps' meeting broke up, Miller joined his wife on a house-hunting expedition in Manhattan. Spying a "For Rent" sign in the first-floor window of a Greenwich Village apartment, the couple entered and promptly slapped down a deposit.

With the All-Star break already near, Miller had originally intended to use the time to pore over the union's records still stored in Frank Scott's office. Word that the clubs intended to disclose details of their new television contracts at their July All-Star meetings quickly squashed that idea. Given the direct relevance of higher network fees to the upcoming negotiations over management pension contributions, Miller flew uninvited to Chicago to crash the gathering. Among the magnates present for the television-deal announcement were Eckert; league presidents Giles and Cronin; owners Bob Carpenter, Gabe Paul, and Walter O'Malley; and a pompous National League assistant counsel by the name of Bowie Kuhn. When Miller confronted O'Malley in the hotel lobby, to the union leader's surprise, the Los Angeles owner seemed pleased to see him. The reason was that O'Malley had talked recently with Dodger fan David McDonald, who had reassured the nervous patriarch that his former Steelworker subordinate was no "socialist." Curious—and slightly apprehensive—about what else his old boss had said, Miller inquired, "How'd that come up?" O'Malley related that according to McDonald many trade unionists lacked a proper understanding of or sympathy toward the profit motive, but he had been assured that Miller understood "why we're in business . . . for profit." Miller tactfully concurred with his own comment that "when it comes to collective bargaining, bankrupt is a dirty word."[29]

Despite O'Malley's individual pleasantries, it soon became clear that a month's time had not altered the owners' insistence that nothing had changed. Kuhn proclaimed as settled fact that, beginning in April 1967, a new pension deal would raise clubs' annual contribution amounts to $4 million—up substantially from the previous $1.6 million but less than that suggested by the majors' traditional 60/40 (60 percent to the pension, 40 percent kept by the clubs) division of All-Star and World Series broadcast fees. When Miller pressed for details of the television contract, Kuhn admitted that the owners unilaterally had scrapped the percentage formula and thereby shorted the pension $200,000. And despite the absence of any collective bargaining on the subject, the commissioner had nonetheless scheduled a press briefing for that afternoon to announce the television and pension figures. Only after Miller pulled Eckert aside and pointed out the owners' vulnerability to charges of federal labor-law violations if he went ahead did the commissioner hastily summon his lawyers and then call off the media session.[30]

Miller had planned to fly directly from Chicago to St. Louis, the site of the All-Star Game, to brief his board on the troubling developments. Owing to an airline strike, though, he was instead forced to endure a steamy bus ride to his destination. Gathering with the reps one day before the midseason classic, he briefed them on the owners' unilateral decision to drop 60/40. Making the best of this fait accompli, Miller explained that any guaranteed ratio in past pacts had never been binding past the expiration date of a particular pension contract. Each subsequent pact had still required formal renewal of it or any other provisions. In any event, because the owners had hoarded the details of their previous television contracts, there had never been any way for the players to confirm that they had actually received the purported 60 percent. Consequently, securing a specific dollar figure rather than an unverifiable revenue percentage in new negotiations would actually carry greater certainty that the players were getting the amounts specified.[31]

Here too, management's blatant betrayal of what players had seen as a long-standing precedent only strengthened the reps' solidarity behind Miller. Rather than blaming him for the clubs' retrenchment, they saw the unfolding confrontation as yet another sign that under Miller they were finally starting to be taken seriously. Because of the reaction, Miller now felt it safe to broach the issue of his employment contract. He emphasized that not only had he sold his Pittsburgh home, his wife had resigned from her salaried position at Carnegie-Mellon. While he reaffirmed that his commitment was unshakeable, he noted that his many years in trade unionism had driven home the fundamental principle of "No contract, no work." Having already violated that maxim for three months, he now asked his assembled reps to formally ratify his terms. With players Johnny Edwards and Buck Rodgers as cosigners and Bob Locker, Don Lock, and Roy McMillan his witnesses, the MLBPA finally made official Miller's status as the organization's leader.[32]

During that same All-Star break, three separate incidents underscored to the new executive director his members' need of his professional expertise. Starting on the mound for the National League was the brilliant lefthander from Brooklyn, Sandy Koufax, a man Miller already admired not just for his ability but also the nerve he had shown in his joint holdout with Don Drysdale. By the time Koufax departed the game after five innings, the thermometer still stood at a brutal 104 degrees. Choosing to similarly adjourn to the NL clubhouse to escape the heat, Miller encountered the hurler engaged in his customary yet gruesome routine of immersing his horribly swollen elbow in ice. Koufax's spectacular career would in fact end following that year's World Series. The next morning, while Miller waited for his flight back to New York, American League president Joe Cronin invited him for drinks in the terminal bar. When the intercom announced boarding for Miller's flight, the industry executive left him with a pointed warning: "Young man . . . the players come and go, but the owners stay on forever." Once the warned Miller had boarded his plane, and as it had taxied down the runway, Los Angeles' famous base-stealer Maury Wills abruptly plopped down into the adjacent empty seat. At first Wills was hesitant to speak, but as the flight continued, the player poured out a litany of problems black major-leaguers still faced despite the passage of civil rights legislation, including the continued scarcity of integrated housing and public accommodations in Florida's spring-training towns. As their long conversation ended as the plane touched down, Wills left Miller with words both encouraging and challenging: "The black and Latino ballplayers are especially eager to support this union. . . . Discrimination is not dead."[33]

As Wills's confessional suggested, increasingly players were coming around to trust their new executive director enough to approach him with their particular concerns. Cincinnati's Johnny Edwards, initially a critic, now called Miller to seek his help in denying local press accounts that had identified him with antiunion sentiments. Whether or not the statements within Jim Enright's anti-MLBPA article in the *Sporting News* were accurate or not—and in this instance the union chief tended to believe Edwards, given that Miller's election had dashed the particular reporter's hopes of becoming Judge Cannon's public relations man—it was in any event good internal politics for Miller to issue a public denunciation of the article rather take up the matter in private. It was the first of many such spats Miller would have with the traditional baseball press, which soon learned that the players' new leader brooked no coverage he deemed inaccurate or harmful to Players Association unity.[34]

As Miller's first season at the MLBPA neared its end, two organizational issues remained unresolved. Given the many demands upon him and the obvious unsuitability of Robert Cannon going forward, Miller needed a qualified, trustworthy counsel. He already had someone in mind. Dick Moss, the thirty-five-year-old Harvard Law graduate and former Pennsylvania assistant attorney general, had actually first sought the MLBPA legal post in the late 1950s before having joined the Steelworkers. Since 1960 he had worked first in Ben Fischer's arbitration section and then as the union's associate general counsel. Besides his impressive résumé, Moss was also a huge baseball fan. As Fischer had once joked, "If there was a conflict between watching a baseball game and negotiating a contract, you never knew which he has going to do." But despite his wish to offer Moss the job promptly, Miller was obligated to carry out a pledge to Robin Roberts—meeting with Richard Nixon—before he could make a recommendation to his reps.[35]

After seeking and getting the board's reassurance that he was not obligated to actually make an offer to Nixon, Miller went to see the former vice president at his 5th Avenue apartment. A man still of durable proletarian convictions, the executive director was rendered momentarily speechless at being greeted at the door by a butler, who then escorted him to his waiting host. Determined not to be the one to initiate discussion of the counsel post, Miller exchanged awkward banter with Nixon on the current baseball season. Suddenly—and to Miller's profound relief—his host signaled that he was ready to wrap up what had proven merely a courtesy call. Volunteering that "I am on very good terms with the owners," Nixon only extended a vague willingness to help when possible through his management contacts. Avoiding uttering the words running through his head—"I bet you are"—Miller gave a polite thank-you and escaped unscathed.[36]

The other unresolved problem remained the union's finances. Miller was increasingly confident the players would approve the dues check-off, but scheduling conflicts during the playing season made it impossible to arrange team briefings and a formal membership vote before September. In the meantime, the dues authorization form—including a limited-duration clause allowing players to opt out—had yet to be drafted, leaving the union in financial peril. Examination of Frank Scott's records, however, had revealed that the union at one time had negotiated a group-licensing deal for player cards on the backs of Wheaties cereal boxes. Additionally, some players held individual agreements with Topps in which they received a $5 signing fee for a five-year pact plus $125 for each year the player lasted in the majors. In turn the company retained exclusive rights to use these players' images on baseball cards sold alone or with such confectionary products as bubble gum. Miller initially hoped to strike a quick group-licensing deal with Topps, or barring that, at least persuade the company to raise its fees to the level of the players' proposed dues payments. But Topps executive Joel Shorin rejected the overture, bluntly stating, "I don't see any muscle in your position."[37]

With Dick Moss also already providing unofficial legal advice, Miller and Frank Scott jointly drafted a waiver document for each player that granted the union the authority to negotiate a group-licensing deal, with its annual benefits to be equally distributed among the membership. In order to hold any player harmless should he personally have the opportunity to strike a more lucrative deal, the form also allowed the player to sign with another company if the union's group licensee refused to match the rival suitor's offer. Scott then went to work bartering with Coca-Cola for the rights to display player likenesses inside bottle caps. The two-year pact he successfully concluded in the fall immediately generated $60,000 and the same the next season—sufficient revenue to tide the union over until its dues check-off could take effect. When baseball officialdom found out about the MLPBA licensing deal, it tried to torpedo it by denying the players the right to display club insignias on their images, but Coke and the union retaliated by simply having the logos airbrushed from the photos employed.[38]

With similar petulance, the clubs also tried to stonewall Miller's push to negotiate a player-pension boost greater than the summer's premature $4 million figure. Until he had secured his licensing deal with Coca-Cola, Miller had held little leverage. The clubs were determined to wait out the union until the old pension pact expired at year's end and then unilaterally impose the earlier figure. But now the union possessed the resources to sustain the fight, and in November an unexpected gift—a product of the owners' past greed and ignorance of state pension law—fell into Miller's lap. The New York State Department of Insurance reported discovery of a clear violation of pension law dating back to 1962, when the major-league clubs, after having accidently contributed more money to the pension fund than had been required, had secretly—and illegally—withdrawn the sum of $167,440.[39]

Armed with the legal hammer, Miller demanded the owners make good their prior theft through boosting the new contribution amount by the $200,000 necessary to bring it in line with the old 60/40 formula, in exchange for the union's consent to hold management harmless for the legal transgression and saving the owners at least that much in penalties and interest. During the final stage of the "negotiation," the owners' pension committee and Miller's team were sequestered in separate rooms of the Biltmore Hotel. Walter O'Malley played dealmaker, with Bowie Kuhn serving as his errand-boy. Under the agreement the two sides struck in December, the owners came halfway toward the union's figure by increasing their annual contribution to $4.1 million, an amount that would result in a doubling of a current players' eventual monthly retirement and disability payments. Retired ten-year veterans would now get $500 a month upon reaching age fifty, and $1,300 a month if they deferred payments until sixty-five. While a handful of past MLBPA—most notably Bob Feller and Allie Reynolds—criticized the pact for abandoning the strict 60/40 formula, the vast majority of the active membership was pleased with the outcome.[40]

By the end of 1966, the players' Executive Board had also ratified Dick Moss as the union's counsel, and all but six of the MLBPA's members had authorized the dues check-off from their pay. Only two of these holdouts were even players, as opposed to managers, coaches, and trainers. As for the implementation, after Bowie Kuhn stalled a quick agreement by offering a "poison pill" allowing owners the right to suspend dues withholding for any reason after just thirty-days' notice, Miller's personal intercession with Walter O'Malley magically lifted the roadblock. It had been but one year since Miller's unpromising initial interview with the players' search committee. Yet with all the subsequent twists and turns, the new executive director with remarkable speed had jump-started his union. He had successfully sidestepped the landmines the owners had placed in his way to secure for his members a major pension boost, while also freeing them from the burden of future contributions. More important than the tangible gains, however, his insistence that the owners show respect to him and to his men had started the process of instilling the collective pride and solidarity that would be necessary for the much bigger battles to come.

Nine

Securing the Basics

Thanks to Marvin Miller's leadership, by the beginning of 1967 the Major League Baseball Players Association was already on a much more solid footing. Not only did the union finally have professional leadership, its finances were more reliable and safe from management manipulation. Reflecting its improved position, the Players Association moved out of its earlier improvised accommodations to a thirty-eighth-floor suite—one story above famed architect Philip Johnson—in the Seagram's Building. Concerned to maintain a modest image, despite his new digs Miller refused to wear monogrammed shirts, rode the subway to work, and presided over a Spartan staff of counsel Moss and two secretaries. From his desk he toiled ten-hour days, chain-smoking Marlboros. Years later, former player–turned union official Mark Belanger pondered the breadth of Miller's duties in the early days and wondered aloud, "How did you and Dick do all this?"[1]

Miller's standing with his membership had also risen sharply in a short time. The year before, the *Kansas City Star*'s Joe McGuff had opined to Athletics player rep Wes Stock that if he and his colleagues were willing to accept confrontation as the price to secure their rights, Miller was their man. As the executive director settled into the now-familiar routine of team visits in the spring of 1967, he was invited to private player parties of men who in just the past year had qualified for the benefit plan through sixty days' big-league service or the pension by having finishing five seasons. Because of the newly won benefit increases secured by the union, these fresh eligibles had obvious reason to be happy. In marked contrast, Miller's spring-training encounter with the legendary Joe DiMaggio only

The executive director in his office (source unknown/Tamiment Library, NYU)

left the executive director depressed. The Yankee Clipper had been hired by his old team as a part-time hitting instructor and came to spring training donning worn-out pinstripes because the club had refused to pay for a new uniform. The all-time great addressed "Mr. Miller" with an awkward deference and lamented that as an old-timer he could only qualify for the union's latest pension boost if he came out of retirement to take a full-time big-league job. When DiMaggio virtually begged for Miller's help in securing a new uniform, his stunned listener quickly replied, "Sure, Mr. DiMaggio . . . I'll see what I can do."[2]

Another sign of Miller's initial success in earning credibility with the player force was that the label "players' union" was rapidly losing its negative connotation, although, in a sign of professional pride, some still preferred "Players Association." Reflecting the executive director's growing confidence in his men's loyalty, to underscore the importance of strict compliance by both sides to their contract stipulations, he blocked the Baltimore Orioles players' demand for additional bonuses for postgame interviews. Insisting upon reciprocal compliance with agreements from the clubs, Miller returned a check addressed to the MLBPA for more than $1,000 from White Sox magnate Arthur Allyn on the grounds that the payment violated the requirement that union dues be directly withdrawn from the salaries of team coaches and players alike.[3]

Baseball scribes were already noting how Miller and his partner Moss complemented yet contrasted with each other. Compared to his boss, the union counsel was more extroverted and openly mischievous. The press sometimes interpreted their interplay as a "good cop/bad cop" routine, but it was not that simple. Moss's more polished background and lawyer's training combined to shape the counsel's approach toward management as that of a competitor facing off against a rival in a sporting contest, albeit with serious stakes. Miller projected a lower-key, no-nonsense persona that unless directly provoked was at first less overtly abrasive. But beneath his matter-of-fact surface, he carried the class-conscious intensity of a man molded by the ideological struggles of his younger days and by his longer history in the union movement. When his anger was unleashed, he could become a caustic and even vengeful adversary.

Armed with Moss's labor-law expertise, Miller in 1967 planned to focus upon clearly establishing in contract form big-league players' rights and obligations— the fundamentals of workplace rules, minimum wages, scheduling and safety issues, and grievance procedures that constituted the core of modern-day labor contracts. Much of what he sought at first seemed tedious and unnecessary to fans and to the baseball press alike, but, as a labor veteran, Miller understood how crucial they were to the pursuit of greater future goals. Cautioning his own membership against impatience with the push for what seemed at first glance a mundane agenda, he counseled them to "swing for the singles," assuring that "the home runs will come." At the top of the list of "singles" sought was a higher big-league minimum salary, which by 1967 still only stood at $7,000, a thousand dollars less than an average U.S. worker's pay.[4]

Starting in January, Miller pressed the owners to negotiate a minimum-salary increase to $12,000. When he, Moss, and the union's league reps Steve Hamilton and Jim Pagliaroni showed up for their initial session of the year with management, however, they found their opposites as unwilling to treat with them as ever. No owners or general managers were present. Instead, AL president Cronin, the NL's Giles, the latter's legal advisor Bowie Kuhn, and several staff came to listen but not deal. As Jim Bouton later commented regarding their recalcitrance, "If they'd have just said, 'We'll raise the minimum salary to $10,000, then raise it $1,000 a year for the next twenty years. . . . Then we'll throw in an annual cost-of-living increase on the meal money,' the union would have lost all its momentum." But not only did the industry representatives refuse to make a counteroffer, they denied the union access to the salary data that provided the starting point for any such negotiation. Nor were they willing to address the players' workplace complaints, which included split day-night doubleheaders and dual tilts on days after night games, arduous travel schedules, the length of the regular season, and outdated language that still presumed in-season travel by train rather than airplane.[5]

Miller considered immediately filing an NLRB complaint to force the release of the industry's pay figures. But wanting to avoid further delays and seeing in the owners' recalcitrance an opportunity to capitalize again on players' indignation, he instead requested his men to confidentially volunteer their individual salary figures to the union. Based upon the submissions, Miller was able to calculate the mean pay at $19,000 and the median at $17,000. Thirty-five of the new season's rookies, not having yet been on big-league rosters as late as June 1 of a season, were only entitled to a "sub-minimum" wage of $6,000. Fully one-third of the player force earned $10,000 or less. Even with the union's promise of secrecy, members quickly discerned by "reading between the lines" that club general managers had frequently lied to them. Los Angeles first baseman Ron Fairly, who had been assured by his bosses that he was the fourth-highest-paid Dodger, discovered that he actually ranked only eighth.[6]

Armed with his own salary numbers, Miller reiterated his demand for a joint session with management that included actual club executives. In the meantime, the owners had finally recognized the threat posed by the MLBPA as serious enough to require their own labor-relations panel—forerunner to the eventual Player Relations Committee—of Orioles general manager Harry Dalton, the Mets' Bing Devine, the Senators' George Selkirk, and the Dodgers' Buzzie Bavasi. Nonetheless, they also refused to meet union representatives directly, instead dispatching Cronin, Kuhn, AL attorney Sandy Hadden, and NL secretary Fred Fleig. As Moss described it, the clubs' refusal to directly bargain resembled "a scene from the Thirties in the mid-Sixties." Kuhn even blamed Miller for "misunderstanding" whether team officers would attend, insisting that a letter notifying the executive director of their intention not to show up had been sent out while Miller had been out traveling to the player camps. After another month passed without the clubs agreeing to schedule a bargaining session, the union chief called upon the most reasonable man on the other side, Yankees owner Mike Burke, to intervene. At a meeting of the commissioner's Executive Council of club owners and league presidents, Burke advocated reasonableness. "Marvin Miller is here, like it or not," he proclaimed. "If he were the Devil himself, you'd have to deal with him," he noted, adding, "The Alka-Seltzer tablet is in the water." But Burke's pleas fell on deaf ears after Bowie Kuhn reassured the assembled that he could "handle" Miller alone.[7]

Few claims ever proved more false. With his irate player reps solidly behind him, Miller now turned up the heat. One form it took was the floating of a trial balloon of a single giant union of professional athletes representing all of the major sports. The year before, following the 1966 NFL-AFL merger, player activist and Cleveland Browns' defensive back Bernie Parrish had asked Miller to review pro football's pension plan. The executive director then had relayed the bad news that for the NFL's players their deal was scarcely worth the paper it was written on, containing language allowing the owners to unilaterally cancel it at any time. Prompted by the encouragement offered by the Teamsters' Jim Gibbons, Parrish then had recontacted Miller to promote the idea of an all-sports union. Two well-publicized meetings did follow between pro athletes Buck Rodgers (baseball), Bobby Orr (hockey), Parrish, Mike Pyle, Jack Kemp (football), and Oscar Robertson (basketball) with Miller, NBA Players Association leader Larry Fleisher, the NHL performers' Alan Eagelson, and the NFL players' Creighton Miller. Given the weakness of the other unions and the instinctive rivalry between the different camps, the MLBPA head concluded that unification would deliver little for his men.[8]

Once speculation of an all-sports union faded, Miller employed new tactical moves. He had hoped for a quick agreement on a new minimum salary followed by separate talks on other basic-contract issues, only to see the clubs demolish those expectations. In late June, management offered only a $1,500 boost in the major-league minimum—leading Dick Moss to covertly suggest to catcher Tim McCarver at a bargaining session that he throw up on the table in reply. An angry Miller now piled everything the union sought in an omnibus Basic Agreement at once into the bargaining round, including proposals on the minimum salary; scheduling rules; the season's length; an independent grievance process; recognition of the Players Association as major leaguers' sole bargaining representative; one-year percentage limits on salary cuts; moving compensation for traded players; boosts in spring training and regular-season travel, lodgings, and meal payments; guaranteed first-class hotel and airplane accommodations; an equal voice in playing-rule changes; negotiations over the language and interpretation of the reserve clause; and much more. Miller gambled that when confronted by this flood tide of demands, the owners would be forced to get serious about negotiating or risk NLRB sanctions for failure to bargain in good faith.[9]

Utilizing the time provided through management's continued stalling, Miller pressed forward with the ongoing task of educating his membership, with the goal of forging an engaged, "bottom-up" union. As he explained repeatedly to his men, baseball was an industry like any other and not an institution somehow exempt from labor laws. Though he maintained a realism bordering on pessimism that occasionally led him to be overly skeptical of his players' resolve, Miller believed in constantly teaching the players about their power to change their daily realities if they grounded their efforts in the reasonable context of safeguarding their employment rights. Emphasizing the union's democratic nature, he consistently encouraged his men to assume an active role in formulating their agenda. But for the players to be effective in defining and then pursuing the goals they set for themselves, what mattered was their *informed* involvement, followed by unwavering solidarity once bargaining positions had been democratically decided.

It was a striking irony that the executive director was convinced no one—not even baseball management—was beyond his ability to teach, and not surprisingly owners often rankled at what they viewed as arrogance in his lecturing them on their business and its shortcomings. Nonetheless, whether during bargaining sessions or clubhouse meetings, Miller almost always disdained emotional outbursts or crude verbal arm-twisting. Instead, as Peter described his father's technique, the key to his success both at rallying the players and infuriating the owners was his talent for laying out a coherent vision of the shape of things to come: a modern labor-management relationship in baseball in which the two sides confronted each other vigorously but as equals, rather than a paternalistic order in which clubs treated their on-field employees as dependents. Within such a transformed setting, he repeatedly insisted to his membership, if they simply stood united there was nothing reasonable they could not win. "Together," he regularly intoned, "you are irreplaceable. . . . You *are* the game."[10]

Not all of Miller's educational methods panned out. An in-season newsletter intended to keep players regularly informed about the union flopped, because too many performers lacked either the time or the inclination to read it regularly. The ill-fated newsletter did accomplish one thing, however: provide the union clear proof that the owners were monitoring its communications. When Dick Moss deliberately misidentified the second newsletter as "Number Three" to test the presence of management curiosity, baseball officialdom fell into the trap by inquiring on the whereabouts of the "missing" issue. In any event, Miller—recognizing the superior value of face-to-face contact and verbal communication with his membership—kept his phone number openly listed and encouraged MLBPA reps and the grassroots membership alike to call him directly or drop by the association's offices. The latter was actually quite practical, given that every AL and NL team came to New York for games at least three times per season.[11]

The heart of Miller's communications approach, however, was his group sessions with individual teams or even larger player aggregations. Whether addressing his Executive Board of team and league player representatives or a spring-training squad, he was soft-spoken, well-organized, and methodical. Giving every man who wished to the chance to speak his mind, he still managed to steer discussions in a Socratic fashion, asking speakers, "Now is this what you mean?" He would then often follow up with, "If it is, this is what's likely to happen." As Jim Bouton recalled, Miller regularly came across as "the least gung-ho of anyone in the room." While better-informed members sometimes found the repetition tedious, at the end of each meeting none of them could say that they had not been given ample opportunity to understand and discuss the issues. Miller also encouraged rank-and-file players to sit in on union bargaining sessions to further their education and to train them as a next generation of reps. Attendance by grassroots members also provided the MLBPA bargaining team with a "gallery"—a fact not lost on irritated opponents on the other side of the table.[12]

Many owners would persist in depicting Miller as a Svengali who duped and manipulated his ignorant wards into unthinking militancy. The depiction badly mischaracterized the executive director, and it also dangerously underestimated the attitudinal changes independently occurring in the player force. By comparison to their counterparts of earlier decades, major leaguers had become more skeptical and less submissive. Minority performers in particular had come to the majors during a new national era marked by confrontations with paternalistic segregationists claiming to be the guardians of cherished tradition. Within the white majority of the player force, a growing share no longer hailed from teenage sandlots or rural ball fields but colleges, where the slogan, "Question authority!" had taken on greater currency in the Vietnam War era. At the same time, even the new generation of college-educated ballplayers had not been the "big men on campus" that football and basketball stars were, and their subsequent apprenticeships in the minors had reinforced a "school-of-hard-knocks" unity with those of humbler backgrounds. Though not "working class" in the fashion of Depression-era players, they were savvier toward the workings of contemporary society and more socially conscious of its flaws. A number of them brought not just educational perspective but real-world experience in modern finance with them into their baseball lives. Joe Torre, to take one example, claimed both working-class Brooklyn roots and a brief Wall Street apprenticeship not unlike that of his leader. Jim Bunning, though he lobbied his executive director to utter aloud the word "shit" just for shock effect, was no rube either. Bunning would later insist that the players' only real deficiency at the time Miller joined them was that "we lacked direction, and that's what Marvin gave us."[13]

Miller's principles and his players' embrace of them could be seen in the union's revised constitution and bylaws the reps approved at the All-Star break. The document included an antidiscrimination clause that guaranteed all members an equal voice "regardless of race, creed, color, or nationality." The new charter formally recognized and defined the executive director and counsel posts, made clear that league-wide representatives did not have to be team delegates, designated the former as the organization's treasurers with responsibility for overseeing annual audits with strict accounting standards, and authorized the Executive Board of reps to administer the MLBPA's affairs, subject to the approval of the rank and file, including the authority to drop an individual member from the union with "proper cause."[14]

In contrast to Miller's rank and file, who under his tutelage were becoming both savvier and more unified, the owners were in equal parts overwhelmed and overconfident. U.S. Steel executive and management consultant Bruce Johnston insisted that it was not that Miller was somehow uniquely talented, claiming more than a bit too broadly that "you could have found ten thousand guys like him." But Miller and Moss were veterans of the Steelworkers organization who had been "turned loose on an industry that was, in terms of labor relations, naïve and illiterate." The baseball owners by comparison were a "loose amalgam of highly individualistic entrepreneurs . . . the worst people in the world to deal with labor" and "impatient, egocentric, and exasperating to represent." Even the club owners' competitiveness—the characteristic that drove them to buy teams in the first place and to chase pennants—contributed to a tendency to break into quarreling factions at crucial junctures. It was a weakness Johnson likened to opening "borders to a Panzer Division," and one Miller would repeatedly exploit.[15]

Belatedly, the owners perceived their own need for a professional labor negotiator. Bowie Kuhn contacted Harvard professor James Healy for advice, and when he informed the consultant of the identity of the leader of the Players Association, the response was blunt—"Bowie, you need lots of help." Management expanded its Player Relations Committee by adding two general managers from each circuit, and more importantly they replaced Cronin as lead negotiator with the experienced, street-smart New Yorker John Gaherin. Before heeding major-league baseball's call, Gaherin had been labor-relations chief for the Eastern Conference of Carriers, a consortium of northeastern railroads; vice president for labor relations at American Airlines; and head of the Publishers Association of New York (the bargaining arm of Gotham's major newspapers). Insisting that he preferred working with and against true professionals, Miller publicly welcomed the Gaherin hire as a sign the clubs were finally serious about hammering out a Basic Agreement. He had already been tipped off to the owners' choice by the former chair of the War Labor Board's New York regional office,

Ted Kheel, when the two had traveled together to an upstate labor-management seminar. Kheel had himself been approached by baseball officials for advice and been the source of the Gaherin recommendation. In a pointed gesture to his new opponent, at their first meeting Miller presented Gaherin with a *Sports Illustrated* series of articles that described Dodger general manager Buzzie Bavasi's admitted salary flimflamming of his players.[16]

Following Gaherin's hire, progress ensued on many Basic Agreement side issues, but it remained frustrating to Miller that the restructured PRC still took no direct bargaining role. But despite the potential for communications glitches on the management side because of its self-imposed detachment from the talks, by late summer the two sides had narrowed the gap on the minimum salary, with the clubs inching up to $10,000 and the players still holding out for $12,000. Spring-training and regular-season meal allowances had been agreed upon, and management had boosted its "Murphy money" offer (the term for spring-training player expense payments) to $40 a week. The parties had agreed in principle to giving the Players Association a say in scheduling approval, requiring management to give "just cause" for player disciplinary actions, guaranteeing first-class air travel and accommodations and stadium parking, and extending performers' salaries during periods of required National Guard or reserve duty. The owners rejected the union's calls for an increased spring room allowance, reimbursement for off-season moving expenses, a role in industry broadcast negotiations, $150 bonuses for participation in exhibition tilts, guaranteed college scholarships, a joint licensing program, and management cooperation in cracking down on the commercial exploitation of player's names and images. As for the issue of the maximum salary cut, the union still sought a 10 percent limit in any single year, while the clubs insisted on 20 percent. Recognizing early on the futility of haggling for the moment over the season's length or the reserve system, the two sides had already agreed to delegate them to study committees resembling those Miller had utilized at the Steelworkers.[17]

One fundamental issue remained that Miller refused to similarly defer— that of creating an independent grievance procedure to resolve disputes over noncompliance with or differences of interpretation over either collective-bargaining pacts or an individual player's standard contract. Building upon the experiences of the War Labor Board in which Miller had served, impartial grievance arbitration had become standard procedure throughout postwar U.S. industry—with no small boost from the Steelworkers and the UAW. Outside arbitration offered workers a formal means to challenge arbitrary firing, unilateral management changes to work conditions, and safety violations.

In a series of critical rulings, especially those of the *Lincoln Mills* (1957) and *Steelworkers Trilogy* (1960) cases, the federal judiciary in turn had upheld independent arbitrators' immunity from judicial second-guessing save in cases of incapacity or malfeasance.[18]

In contrast to most of American industry, however, baseball's authority to adjudicate contract grievances still lay with the owners' man, the commissioner—and the maintenance of this outdated and unprofessional system had led to incompetent record keeping of decisions rendered and overt pro-club bias. In a current set of examples, Kansas City's Charles O. Finley had first suspended and fined pitcher Lew Krausse for purported rowdiness on a team flight, only to abruptly lift the suspension after just four days; then released slugger Ken Harrelson for having criticized the owner's interference in the Krausse matter; then fired manager Alvin Dark; and finally docked club player rep Jack Aker over a dubious curfew violation. Miller demanded that each of the affected players receive a hearing before the commissioner, and he additionally filed an unfair-practices charge with the NLRB, which he dropped after forcing an all-night session with Eckert, Finley, the owner's lawyer (and future Supreme Court justice) John Paul Stevens, and Dick Moss. But Miller was under no illusion that under the existing format, players' grievances could ever receive an impartial hearing.[19]

Undercutting Miller on the issue, unfortunately, was a small-scale insurrection from dissidents within his ranks. The Giants' Tom Haller and the Cubs' Randy Hundley, two traditionalists on the MLBPA Executive Board, complained to the press that they had not been consulted beforehand about Miller's NLRB filing. Hundley went further, however, asserting, "We feel that such matters should be settled with baseball without going to the NLRB like a labor union." Moving to shore up the solidarity of his reps, Miller eventually secured a statement from them that claimed the dissenters' comments had stemmed from an innocent misunderstanding and that now declared they all concurred with their leader's actions. The underlying message Miller drew, however, was that despite his progress with his reps on the issues, he was not at that point at which the Players Association could "go to the mat" over grievance arbitration.[20]

On the other side of the table, owners' fury at what they saw as a blatant lack of respect and decorum from the union—a situation they directly blamed on Miller—had reached the boiling point. As weekly bargaining sessions failed to break the logjams over the minimum salary and outside arbitration, management participants fumed at player antagonists noisily scribbling and passing notes during their presentations, Miller's insistence upon using the term "workers" to characterize his men, and the disruption of meetings by rank-and-file players with extraneous concerns. Union participant Joe Torre, however, sensed a deeper underlying reason for the other side's anxiety: "You could just feel the attitude from the other side of the table—'We're afraid to open the door a crack because it just may crash in on us.'"[21]

In late November the long-simmering ill will erupted. With the owners having scheduled their end-of-season meetings in Mexico City, the union Executive Board did the same in hopes of forcing a joint session. A mix-up over whether an invitation to do so had been extended to the players then led to ownership issuing a blunt *no*. On hearing the news, player rep Milt Pappas exploded, "Let's go tell them [the owners] to f— themselves." Dueling press conferences followed, and in a show of defiance the union board voted to extend Miller's contract through 1970 and raised his salary $5,000. The reps also threatened further undefined "specific action" in the spring if no contract agreement had been reached. The scope of possible MLBPA retaliation included a NLRB refusal-to-bargain complaint, a player boycott of signing individual contracts, or a full-scale strike. At a union press opportunity, Jim Bunning made one thing unmistakably clear: "Marvin Miller will be around for a long time!"[22]

Firebrands within management seemed just as eager to fight. During Gaherin's presentation to owners on the state of the stalled talks, Atlanta Braves hardliner Paul Richards and St. Louis's Gussie Busch openly disparaged their negotiator's recommendation to accept outside arbitration of routine grievances despite his insistence that "sooner or later we'll have to do this, and we have to start in some form." Pointing to the clubs' clumsy efforts to claim the commissioner's independence from them—including keeping him from that same meeting, Gaherin added, "You can't have him in the middle of every grievance that comes along. . . . You're dealing with a real union now, and they won't be shy about filing them." Walter O'Malley then fired back, "Tell that Jewish boy [Miller] to go on back to Brooklyn." At management's press conference, Cronin, Kuhn, and Mike Burke tried to lower the temperature by excusing the latest conflagration on a "breakdown in communications." But an apparently intoxicated Richards crashed the briefing to blast Miller as both a liar and an "outsider." The executive director's initial reaction to the outburst was to draft retaliation in the form of a letter, addressed to all Braves players, in which he called the attacks "unreasonable," mockingly urged Richards to seek "some kind of internal release," and added low blows on his antagonist's poor performance as a general manager. Upon further review, however, Miller shelved his reply.[23]

The wisdom of Miller's choice of restraint soon became clearer. Despite its mounting frustration with the union, the industry was not prepared to call its bluff regarding the threat of "specific action." Some clubs did retaliate against those team reps who had openly voiced their defiance. Within weeks, Jim Bunning had been traded to the Pirates. But despite the Mexico City blow-up, by mid-December the two sides had resumed negotiations. In a signal that Gaherin was determined not to sabotage a pending deal, when Miller introduced Mrs. Elston Howard (wife of the Yankees' veteran catcher) to make an extraneous plea at a bargaining session for higher spring-training allowances to minority players, the PRC negotiator calmly asked if the suggestion carried the union's endorsement. Miller replied that it was "a" but not "the" position and that the issue could be discussed later "as we go along." When AL president Cronin fumed afterward about the unscheduled appearance, Gaherin correctly predicted to him that "we'll never hear from them on this one again."[24]

Each side now began to express optimism—though the owners publicly displayed a greater enthusiasm. Though Bowie Kuhn suggested an agreement was near, Dick Moss countered that "we are pretty far apart yet," but he conceded the two sides were now "a little closer." Just after New Year's Day, John Gaherin again signaled his willingness to compromise. "Baseball is not Neanderthal," he observed. "Yesterday died with the sunset." After a final gambit from Miller proposing federal mediation on the grievance-arbitration and minimum-salary issues—an intervention that required both sides' consent and accordingly was summarily rejected by the owners—the Players Association and the PRC concluded a pact on February 19, 1968.[25]

The two-year Basic Agreement of 1968 was the first of its kind in the history of baseball. It went far beyond incorporating the preexisting pension deal, the dues check-off, and the standard player's contract to lay out an entirely new player-management relationship. Article VII even required that the owners provide formal notice of any planned playing-rule changes no later than the preceding off-season, and such alterations with the potential to affect player pay and benefits would require union consent—in effect, a 2b-style protection against unilateral changes to the players' worksite rules. The minimum salary immediately rose to $10,000, and individual pay cuts were capped at 20 percent. Joint study committees were assigned the issues of the playing season and the reserve clause, with reports due at the end of 1969. Absent from the pact, however—and Miller's biggest disappointment—was an independent grievance-arbitration system. Although more precise procedures for filing and hearing grievances were included in Article IV, for now the commissioner still retained the final say.[26]

Still, Miller and his membership had stood toe to toe with the industry and had won major gains. Reflecting the union's confidence, it now prepared to launch a first "specific action" that spring—but not at the clubs. Instead the target was Topps, over the still-unsatisfactory relationship between the players and the company over the licensing fees paid for major leaguers' likenesses. The distribution of the $60,000 from the Coca-Cola deal at spring training in the form of hundred-dollar checks per man was another potent reminder that the Players Association's collective strength could produce real gains. Now Miller urged his rank and file, including those with expiring individual Topps contracts, to implement a unionwide boycott. For those with longstanding relationships with the card company it meant the potential loss of up to $600 over the next five years. But if the players were willing to show to Joel Shorin the "muscle" behind their position, they could garner much more. Trusting in their leader, en masse they rejected signing new deals.[27]

The union's boycott was not its only means of putting the squeeze on Topps. Ever since the successful bottle-cap deal with Coke, Miller had pursued similar opportunities. Exploiting a loophole within Topps' monopolistic contracts, Miller struck competing deals with "non-confectionary" companies, including one with Kellogg's for 3-D player likenesses and a Milk Duds agreement to display player pictures on candy boxes. Administering this spate of new group agreements, handling individual player complaints against abuse by the licensing companies, and combating pirated merchandise, however, proved too time consuming for Miller to balance with his many other duties. Accordingly, he contracted out the handling of similar future deals to a professional marketing agency, the Weston Merchandising Corporation.[28]

The Players Association's newfound aggressiveness in licensing deals did not escape the industry's notice. Having already rejected Miller's overtures for cooperative ventures in the recent Basic Agreement talks, the owners instead created their own separate operation, dubbed the Major League Baseball Promotions Corporation. But cooperation or at least peaceful coexistence in the merchandising area only made sense, given that the union was now official gatekeeper to the players, and the owners controlled the use of team logos. But while baseball's promotions-panel chairman Mike Burke sincerely sought to reconcile the two parties, Bowie Kuhn—assigned to work through the legal issues with Miller—effectively torpedoed the effort through bad faith. Stanley Weston—the union's agent—was already suspicious of the competing firm the owners had retained. Miller's discussions with Kuhn then reached the point at which each side had to demonstrate trust to each other by revealing the details of their separate pacts. As part of the arrangement, Kuhn promised that he would not reveal the terms of Weston's pacts to the owners' firm, but in less than a month, Miller discovered that they been leaked. When confronted with the obvious breach of confidentiality, Kuhn weakly offered, "These things happen." Despite having had no complicity in the bad faith, Mike Burke personally apologized to Miller, but the talks still collapsed.[29]

Having relinquished direct responsibility for recruiting new licensing deals, Miller now focused upon ensuring strict management compliance with the new Basic Agreement. That meant the aggressive use of the existing, however inadequate, grievance process to hold Commissioner Eckert's feet to the fire. During the Mexico City Executive Board meetings with his reps, he had urged them to write down every possible example of unacceptable work conditions, down to insufficient clubhouse electrical outlets, as a basis for possible grievances. If a flood of filings exasperated Eckert, it might serve to hasten management's eventual acceptance of outside arbitrators. Having rebuffed Arthur Allyn's previous attempt to separate managers' and coaches' method of paying dues from that of their players, Miller now accused the White Sox owner of going further still and pressuring the nonplayer employees into withdrawing from union membership. He ominously warned those employees—and by inference any other "free riders" benefitting from MLBPA-negotiated gains—that "the next generation of ballplayers might not want to cut the manager or coaches in on a World Series share if they are considered part of management."[30]

Formal disputes over player contract rights and reciprocal obligations now proliferated. One grievance involved Boston pitcher Jim Lonborg, who had been injured in an off-season skiing accident. Despite no specific prohibition on such activity in his contract, the Red Sox had placed him on the club's "restricted list," which enabled it to withhold pay, insurance coverage, and service time toward the pension. After the union filed its challenge, the club hastily reversed itself by reassigning Lonborg to the disabled list and restoring his benefits. In similar fashion, the Baltimore Orioles fined outfielder Curt Blefary for playing in charitable basketball exhibitions and initially refusing to stop despite orders. In that instance, however, the union and its player lost their case. Even so, angry Orioles officialdom retaliated against the MLBPA by abruptly ending the team's longstanding policy of providing tax consultation to its players, blaming the Players Association for its action by purportedly having already shattering the club's prior harmonious relationship with its men.[31]

Miller's side continued to press ahead and won the next series of grievances with management, involving the players' guarantees of first-class air travel and hotel accommodations. In the first of these—an airplane dispute—the union took on Cincinnati general manager Bob Howsam for having bumped

Reds players from first-class seats in favor of reporters, broadcasters, and team coaches. The Players Association's subsequent victory, however, was again followed by an act of management retaliation—the trading of player rep Milt Pappas to the Cubs. The next confrontation—over substandard road lodgings—involved visiting AL teams Cleveland and Chicago, which had been forced to stay at the archaic Hotel Baltimore. The shabby accommodations led the Indians, for their part, to book lodgings elsewhere for a later series, and caused the White Sox organization to join the union in bringing a complaint to Commissioner Eckert. After his decision in the plaintiff's favor, the White Sox also switched reservations to a different hotel for their remaining visits against the Orioles.

The most volatile set-to in 1968 between Miller and club management over Basic Agreement rights, however, stemmed from a game between the Braves and Mets played in wet conditions. The visiting New Yorkers and their player rep afterward criticized the umpiring crew chief and the host team for ignoring player safety concerns. When Miller filed a formal complaint to NL president Giles and had a copy delivered to the Braves' Paul Richards, the latter predictably erupted. Writing to the union chief that the matter was "none of your business," the GM insisted that in forty-two years in baseball he had "never seen a baseball player hurt on a wet infield." He then closed with the salvo, "I would appreciate it very much if in the future you take me off your [mailing] list and refrain from giving me advice regarding baseball players." Miller immediately fired back in kind. "Mr. Richards," Miller wrote, "You are mistaken on all accounts. . . . First, the health and safety of the players is very much my business and the business of the Players Association. Your opinion to the contrary is irrelevant and of no interest." He continued, "Your appalling lack of awareness of injuries to players on a wet field in the last 42 years is equally irrelevant. The fact is that such injuries have occurred." The executive director then ended with his own parting shot: "You are in error in assuming that I have offered you advice. My letter . . . was addressed to the league president. A carbon copy was sent to you for reasons of courtesy."[32]

When seen against the backdrop of the national tumult of 1968, Marvin Miller's squabbles with baseball management were innocent child's play compared to the grim procession of the assassinations of Martin Luther King and Robert Kennedy, urban race riots, violence at the Democratic National Convention, and the ongoing Vietnam conflict. But in that turbulent season, unknown to his membership, Miller's own spouse had been involved in a bitter public controversy in New York. Over the decades the city had become ever more racially segregated, but even in predominantly minority districts whites still dominated local education bureaucracies and teacher ranks. In response, blacks and Latinos had increasingly demanded greater diversity and "community control," but such demands threatened the employment of existing teachers in Albert Shanker's United Federation of Teachers. When ten instructors were fired in Brooklyn in May to make room for minority replacements, Shanker—ironically like Miller a descendant of Russian Jews from the Lower East Side—filed suit and eventually launched a series of citywide strikes that paralyzed the school system. But in marked contrast, Terry Miller, as director of a Great Society team-teaching project on Harlem's West Side training black apprentices, unequivocally supported the other side. Frustrated with her school's halfhearted support for the affirmative-action program, Terry and her two main assistants in late May staged a fiery press conference at their storefront office at which they announced their resignations and accused the district of racism.[33]

Terry Miller did manage to land on her feet, securing jobs as a clinical psychologist and an adjunct teacher for area colleges. While she aimed her professional energies in a new direction, her husband maintained his focus upon his own immediate tasks at hand. It was now time to turn the screws tighter on Topps to force a more generous licensing pact. The pressure from the union's boycott of individual contracts took all season to bear fruit, but the company finally caved. Serious bargaining commenced in September, and after one last delay triggered by the heart-attack death of Joel Shorin's attorney, the deal was done. Beginning in 1969, each union member would receive a yearly check of $250, plus an 8 percent royalty on Topps' cumulative card-sale revenue up to $4 million and 10 percent for its returns above that figure. In the first year alone, the new pact generated the union $320,000—more than $500 per member—compared to the $100 per player from the earlier Coca-Cola deal. Even more significant for the membership's future prospects, the contract included provisions that gave players the right to grant other companies use of their likenesses within specified size parameters. By the late 1980s, the union's share from the combined earnings of five different card companies would reach an astounding $50 million.[34]

Thanks to Miller's leadership, the players had built a solid foundation of workplace rights and monetary gains in a remarkably short time. With the pension deal soon to expire, a new campaign loomed. But it would take place absent one high-ranking, albeit ineffectual, figure. By the 1968 winter meetings, the attending owners were ready to cast aside Spike Eckert. Fans were grumbling not just at the industry's insensitive responses to the King and Kennedy tragedies but about boring games and anemic offenses. Batting averages had plunged, and major-league attendance had followed suit by fully two million fans each of the last two seasons. But the choice of a replacement had become entangled in squabbles over expansion, disagreements over offense-minded rules changes, and disagreements over the new commissioner's powers. In previous times of unchallenged paternalism, having a figurehead at the top of the organizational chart had been not only acceptable but desirable to the magnates. But now a handful of "Young Turks" wanted to make the commissioner an actual CEO, and the man they backed was Mike Burke. Traditionalists, on the other hand, opposed a major overhaul and backed Chub Feeney to succeed the departing Eckert. After two more months of deadlock, the clubs eventually came together behind a choice whose kingmaker was none other than the powerful Walter O'Malley—Bowie Kuhn.[35]

Even with their new commissioner, however, the owners faced the disconcerting reality that, primarily owing to one man, their business had changed from a paternal paradise to an adversarial battlefield. Instead of their on-field employees continuing in docile acquiescence, increasingly they now behaved as if they agreed with their leader that they were the game. The Kuhn selection would also mark the start of nearly a decade-and-a-half of struggle between the players' leader and the industry counterpart he did not respect. To put it mildly, Bowie Kuhn's ascendancy was not destined to signal the "beginning of a beautiful friendship" with one Marvin Miller.

Ten

Taking On the Plantation

Despite major-league baseball's late-sixties attendance slump, the industry's long-term prospects remained reasonably bright. The industry's total broadcast revenues had risen to more than $30 million, and increasingly they—not gate receipts—represented the sport's economic future. Expansion by four teams delivered an extra $20 million entry-fee bonanza to the other NL franchises and $11.2 million to the AL clubs. Despite this money infusion—or rather perhaps because of it—the owners entered a new round of pension negotiations with Marvin Miller's MLBPA showing even greater combativeness. At the clubs' December meetings they fired an early salvo, declaring that they would suspend players' pay not just for off-field accidents but even on-field injuries unless the latter had been certified both by the club doctor and the league president. Miller quickly denounced the owners' unilateral announcement as a "vicious anti-player action."[1]

As far back as the 1968 All-Star break, Miller had tried to jump-start talks on the next pension deal. The clubs had refused, claiming that conducting negotiations during the season would "distract" their players. The frustrated executive director replied that just like other Americans, his membership was already coping with more serious "distractions" such as the Vietnam War. By September Miller and his Executive Board were already weighing the options of a player individual-contract boycott or a spring-training strike to force serious bargaining before the old pact's March expiration. Performers' failure to report would cripple the clubs' exhibition-season revenue, and a boycott of individual deals would pave the way for a challenge of the owners' interpretation of the reserve clause via a massive assertion of free agency after the 1969 season. Miller's own reading of the Standard Player's Contract convinced him that a team could retain an unsigned performer for no more than one additional, postcontract year. Like their baseball brethren, professional basketball owners had asserted a more expansive meaning of their player-reserve clause, but Rick Barry's 1967 lawsuit had generated a federal judicial ruling freeing him after just a lone option year. With one-year pacts still the norm in baseball, a group challenge of the reserve clause would consequently include virtually the entire player force.[2]

Although pension talks formally began in late October 1968, the PRC still continued to stall. The union proposed a 44 percent increase in the clubs' yearly contributions to $5.9 million—slightly over the percentage growth in industry revenue from the new television contract—along with a reduction in the number of big-league seasons required for pension eligibility to four, and a retroactive application of the new service-time and benefit levels for qualifying veterans of 1959 forward. Miller calculated that, under the current five-year eligibility standard, nearly three-fifths of the player population failed to qualify. Reducing the standard even one year would cut the number excluded by half. Under the expiring pact, each club's annual contribution came to $205,000, adding up to the industry-wide total of $4.1 million. But with franchise expansion expected to generate a 20 percent increase in the MLBPA membership and a similar upsurge in the ranks of future pensioners, an annual increase to management's total contributions of even a million dollars would only barely sustain the existing benefit level. Nonetheless, the PRC offered that very figure, and making matters worse, the owners continued to refuse any direct formal linkage between contribution levels and national television revenues, much less a guaranteed percentage of the latter. They also rejected the union's proposals for retroactive improvements and easing eligibility, while at the same time asserted the unilateral right to terminate the pension entirely once a new pact expired.[3]

Once more the two sides held winter meetings side by side—this time in San Francisco—and once more the owners stiffed Miller and his reps. The fresh insult only reinforced the union's determination to move forward with its planned mass holdout. After voting in favor of the boycott, the Executive Board launched a phone-a-thon in which each rep polled his teammates on both the clubs' offer and the proposed boycott. After five frenzied hours, the board reassembled and reported that the rank and file had rejected the PRC's offer 461 to 6 and had endorsed the player holdout without a single dissenting vote. Even the legendary Mickey Mantle, who had planned in any event to retire before the start of the season, volunteered to hold back his formal announcement so that his name could be included among those taking part in the boycott.[4]

January brought resumed bargaining, but no movement. A lingering complication remained the vacant commissioner's chair. When Bowie's Kuhn's selection at last became official in early February, Miller extended polite congratulations by phone and then in person at the MLBPA suite. A union press release extended the organization's willingness to "play a constructive role in efforts to modernize baseball's structure." But with the PRC still refusing to compromise, at Miller's call the players staged a "pep rally" at the Biltmore Hotel. The executive director had expected the majority of the reps to appear, but to his delight 130 additional members showed up to demonstrate solidarity with their leaders, including Joe Torre in his trademark turtleneck shirt, Detroit's Al Kaline in a business suit, and Dick Allen in a dashiki.[5]

The acid test of player solidarity with Miller's boycott strategy, however, came in mid-February—the moment when pitchers and catchers normally reported to spring training. To encourage them to defy the union's directive, the clubs sent each player a packet full of hostile press clippings from home-town sports-writers. Angels' owner Gene Autry went so far as to threaten to shut down his club for good and return to a singing career for what he deemed his players' ingratitude. The oft-quotable Paul Richards lashed out again at Miller, labeling him a "communist" and a "four-flushing mustachioed union organizer." Under the pressure, a trickle of players—many with high hopes for their teams in the upcoming season or hailing from clubs with longstanding reputations for cozy owner paternalism—deserted the union. The list included the Red Sox's Russ Nixon, the Orioles' Jim Palmer and Pete Rickert, and the Reds' Clay Carroll. Despite having even attended the MLBPA's New York pep rally at its expense, Mets catcher Jerry Grote also bailed. Battery-mate Tom Seaver also chose to report, although at least he delayed his arrival in camp until the mandatory March 1 deadline for all players. Others, including Boston's former AL Most Valuable Player Carl Yastrzemski, openly waffled in the press. Scrambling to keep the initiative, Miller blasted management obstinacy with remarkably personal language, comparing the clubs' attitude to "an old father who can't seem to understand that his young boy has turned out to be a man." After denying a scurrilous rumor that he intended to continue getting his own salary during the boycott, the executive director instructed each team rep to organize regional telephone networks to keep the far-flung membership updated and unified.[6]

Despite these efforts, nineteen Baltimore players showed up to work following intense lobbying from the Orioles' Jerry Hoffberger. What had been as yet a trickle of defectors now threatened to become a flood. Reflecting his PRC bosses' confidence, John Gaherin resubmitted management's previous proposal unmodified and called it his side's "last, best" offer. In private, owners boasted that they now had Marvin Miller "by the balls." But two factors then intervened to change the dynamic. One was NBC's nervousness at the possibility of no regular-season baseball or at best a diluted product with replacement players. Having anted up big-league prices, it was not about to idly accept "minor-league" games. Accordingly, it threatened legal action to recapture its rights fees. The other was the presence now of a new image-conscious commissioner determined to get the "interim" tag removed from his title. Recoiling at the thought of his reign starting with both an industry shutdown *and* the loss of a national television contract, Bowie Kuhn conveyed his demand for a pension settlement to the PRC's Bing Devine, who then informed negotiator Gaherin. When the latter suddenly requested that the two sides return to the bargaining table, Miller correctly sensed that his adversaries had blinked. At the next session, Gaherin suddenly upped his offer to $5.3 million annually. Details remained to be hammered out, but by the end of February—just in time for camps to open on schedule—the two sides reached a deal.[7]

The new pact actually ended up boosting the clubs' contributions to $5.45 million—or halfway between each side's earlier positions. Miller failed to get an explicit restatement of the 60/40 commitment, or even the clubs' acceptance in principle to linkage with television revenue growth, but he did win reduction of the service-time requirement to four years, its application to veterans as far back as the pension's birth year of 1947, and the retroactive application of the benefit levels to post-1959 ballplayers. The contribution hike provided full coverage to the union's expanding membership and a $10 rise in monthly benefits for each year of an individual's big-league service. In reviewing the battle, Miller regretted that fifty of his members had broken ranks to re-sign, and he wondered whether the final package might have been even stronger with something closer to perfect solidarity. But he reminded himself on the other hand that if the impasse had lasted beyond March 1, many more players likely would have defected, forcing a significantly worse deal or even the union's disintegration. Given Miller's pride, it grated upon him that the union owed some debt to Bowie Kuhn for the outcome—a fact he did manage to acknowledge later in his autobiography when he termed the commissioner's intervention his "finest hours." But the standing ovations he now received from the membership at his annual spring-training visits helped soothe the sting of having to share credit for the deal.[8]

One example demonstrated the importance of what Miller's pension victory meant not just for current performers but former stars. The Atlanta Braves in a publicity stunt had hired impoverished Negro League legend Satchel Paige as a pitching instructor. When Miller visited the team that spring, the old ace asked if the executive director could help him establish his eligibility for the pension. The major stumbling block was the former pitcher's inability to provide reliable documentation of his age. When Miller asked if there were any surviving baptism records, Paige indicated that they had been burned in a church fire. Armed only with old press accounts of the hurler's mound performances and the age projections he made from them, the union chief succeeded in persuading the pension's administrators to accept Paige's eligibility and with it the now-higher benefits.[9]

Burned out from the pension showdown, Miller took a brief break and renewed himself in his usual ways—voracious reading (with Kurt Vonnegut novels his latest passion) and tennis. His competitive fire still burned at bright as ever, in spite of his more than fifty years of age. Enrolling in a spring Adirondack Mountains tournament, he dispatched an opponent half his years in straight sets on his way to the resort championship. But all too soon work called him back. Evidence was again mounting that clubs were exacting revenge upon those performers seen as the ringleaders of the recent boycott. Paul Richards threatened to dock Joe Torre the maximum 20 percent and then traded him to St. Louis. Clubs also were refusing to adjust upcoming postseason pay levels to reflect that 1969 would be the first year of expanded playoffs, including new League Championship series prior to the World Series. Although management was willing to extend postseason pay to players on an additional sixth team in each circuit (meaning three out of the six clubs in each of four divisions rather than five of ten squads in each league), World Series participant shares would remain capped at $15,000 per winner and $10,000 per loser despite the extra round of play. On each divisional runner-up (equivalent to third- and fourth-place league teams under the old format), squad members would each receive just $1,200—a figure less than what their equivalent had earned the year before. Demanding World Series boosts to $25,500 and $17,000, Miller filed a grievance but was pessimistic of its outcome, given the commissioner's final say.[10]

In other ongoing conflicts involving enforcement of Basic Agreement rights, the Players Association's leader was still adamant about holding management to its obligations despite the lack of an outside grievance process. When the Mets scheduled an additional May exhibition at West Point against a U.S. Army squad in excess of the yearly number allowed, Miller took the heat and challenged, forcing the game's cancellation. Mets brass, having ignored his suggestion to avoid Basic Agreement limits by having no individual player appear in more than three exhibition tilts, lamented, "We send boys over to Vietnam to fight for our country but a little man like Marvin Miller can sit in his office and tell a ball club it can't play a game to entertain 3,500 cadets at our military academy. The grand old game is now being run by a bunch of shop stewards and a union boss."[11]

Repressing the urge to fire back publicly, Miller turned his attention to the two study groups created by the 1968 contract. Of the pair, the one dealing with the reserve issue held the larger significance. Even though the signing boycott had already been lifted, during spring training pitcher Al Downing had threatened to play out 1969 without a contract and then test the owners' definition of the reserve clause. Miller had bluntly told the hurler he stood no chance of winning before the commissioner, and that the Yankees still held "the whip hand" and could simply release him given his poor previous season. Eventually Downing had re-signed with New York, only to be traded to Oakland. Having run joint-study panels while at the Steelworkers, Miller respected their potential for narrowing labor-management differences. But although the two committees were obliged to submit their reports by year's end in 1969, initial sessions did not convene until that same spring. Miller, Moss, and Jim Bunning made up the union's side of the reserve panel, while management was represented by a five-person team led by Gaherin. Industry reps pressed to get the Players Association on the record that its objections to the reserve clause's traditional interpretation were purely monetary—a concession that if made would have allowed management to assert that collective bargaining alone could address the reserve clause's impact without having to eliminate it. Miller refused to take the bait and insisted that just as much at stake was a player's chance to perform rather than sit, and his right as a human being to be treated as employees of other industries rather than as a piece of property to be involuntarily kept, traded, or sold. Citing the example of backup catcher Bob Barton, who in four seasons had played in only four games but was prevented from seeking a better opportunity with another club, Miller argued that such performers deserved the leverage of free agency to force current employers not only to bargain in good faith but to give players the chance to pursue careers elsewhere.[12]

The industry's representatives then refused to attend a follow-up session for two months. Ultimately, about the only thing accomplished by the study panel from the union's point of view—though it was not insignificant—was the opportunity it gave Miller to invite rank-and-file members to the remaining meetings to further their education on the reserve clause. The MLBPA generated comparative data showing how other major professional sports featured more flexible reserve systems. Management countered with the constant claim of baseball's uniqueness, including its costly minor-league apprenticeships. With chutzpah the industry even argued that in defending the reserve clause it was generously sparing players the inevitable depression in salaries that would result from wholesale free agency. The claim prompted Miller's retort that looking out for the interests of the players was *his* job and not theirs. After another such session, he was inspired to covertly scribble a mock advertisement directed at potential baseball investors in which he cited baseball's fan appeal, its negligible material costs, municipalities "eager to serve your needs" through stadiums and tax breaks, an "ample supply" of skilled workmen drawing less than fifteen percent of total revenues, profits from broadcasting fees alone sufficient to meet those costs "thrice over," monopolistic practices sheltered by a federal antitrust exemption, and the assurance of generous capital gains given the average franchise's 50 percent jump in value the past few years. Miller's satirical missive concluded, "How can you resist? OWN YOUR OWN LABOR SUPPLY—ENJOY THE FINEST TAX SHELTER IN THE NATION."[13]

When the reserve panel reached its deadline, the two sides filed dueling reports. The union's draft bore Miller's distinct ideological imprint, with even Immanuel Kant cited. "Freedom is independent of the compulsory will of another," it maintained, "and . . . it is the one sole, original inborn right belonging to every man in virtue of his humanity." The document continued, "There is . . . an innate quality belonging to every man which consists in his right to be independent of being bound by others to anything more than that to which he may reciprocally bind them." Miller then moved on to quote from the 1949 opinion of federal judge Jerome Frank in Danny Gardella's previous unsuccessful challenge to the reserve clause and its enforcement via a blacklist. The jurist had penned, "It is of no moment that they [ballplayers] are well paid; only the totalitarian-minded will believe that high pay excuses virtual slavery."[14]

Thoughts of "well-paid slaves" were increasingly on Miller's mind at the time he cited those words. In November he had been jolted from his chair by a phone call from St. Louis center fielder Curt Flood. Flood had been traded after the season to the Philadelphia Phillies, an organization with a longstanding racist reputation and one far from the community in which he had already established various outside enterprises. Miller did not really know Flood, though the latter had occasionally dropped in at the MLBPA headquarters during road trips and had backed the spring boycott. But after having consulted lawyer Allan Zerman, Flood now informed the executive director that he intend not to report to his new club and would challenge the reserve clause in federal court. Back in 1922, in response to a lawsuit against Organized Baseball from owners of the defunct Federal League, the Supreme Court had declared that professional baseball was not an interstate-commerce activity subject to antitrust restraint. In the process it had also extended its specific blessing to the reserve clause, stating that its presence in individual playing contracts was "intended to protect the rights of clubs . . . to retain the services of sufficient players." Despite his characteristic displays of pessimism, Miller was not above taking on great odds. Terry delighted in poking fun at her husband by calling him "J. C." or "Don Quixote." But taking on baseball's antitrust exemption and reserve system in court, given prior defeats and the usual judicial fealty to stare decisis, seemed a fool's errand. Citing the earlier verdicts, Miller candidly told Flood he "wouldn't bet the farm" on his chances.[15]

Nevertheless, Miller invited the ballplayer and his lawyer to a Summit Hotel breakfast meeting on November 25. With much greater detail than before, Miller restated the daunting legal obstacles and added that even if the player succeeded, his current $90,000 salary and the Phillies' own pending six-figure offer meant he was unlikely to be awarded damages. The latter was significant given that a case could be expected to drag on for two to three years before resolution, over which time the idled Flood's playing skills would erode. In pursuing the lawsuit, he would likely be ending his playing career and sacrificing future big-league coaching or scouting prospects. Even Flood's outside businesses—already on shaky footing—would be threatened if he defied his hometown Cardinals and refused the trade. Miller also made it clear that if the outfielder began a challenge only to settle out of court, it would cause irreparable damage to the union's own aim of ending the reserve system.[16]

Miller then interrogated Flood about any personal skeletons. While admitting to a brother with a criminal history, he concealed other matters that the executive director would only find out about much later—including alcohol problems, a gossiped relationship with an older white business manager, IRS problems, and the disturbing truth that the oil portraits that bore his name as artist had actually been painted by an anonymous Burbank accomplice. While exercising tact in attorney Zerman's presence, Miller suggested that Flood also would need to retain high-powered representation given that his reserve clause challenge would need to go all the way to the Supreme Court. In reply, the outfielder requested the union's financial backing. Wishing to stay noncommittal for the moment, Miller asked his guests to mull over the matter for two more weeks before making a final decision. In early December, Flood phoned and reiterated his determination to press ahead. Miller again summoned him to New York for a final discussion. After their second get-together at the Miller's Greenwich Village apartment, followed by dinner at a nearby restaurant, Miller decided to back the Flood action.[17]

But would the union concur with its executive director? Pending were the Executive Board winter meetings in San Juan. Complicating an open consideration of the matter, there was Bowie Kuhn's desire to crash MLBPA sessions. Miller had come to tolerate and even enjoy his verbal sparring with the commissioner, who at least had a sense of humor and displayed less of his characteristic pomposity once he had consumed an initial martini. But despite Kuhn's occasional strays from self-importance, his "commissioneritis"—a "disease" Miller characterized as one in which, despite his employers, a baseball chief executive somehow conceived himself to be an impartial leader—had only grown worse from the praise received for his role in ending the pension dispute. During previous visits to union Executive Board meetings, Kuhn's resort to paternalistic rhetoric and his refusal to give straight answers to reps' pointed questions had led them to view him on such occasions as little more than a mole. After pressing the commissioner to reveal his intended topics at their forthcoming meeting, Miller reluctantly agreed to let him appear before the board but did not let on about Flood's scheduled appearance for the day before.[18]

On December 13, Flood landed in Puerto Rico. Before the outfielder's presentation, Miller huddled with him to coordinate their remarks and then preceded him to describe the proposed lawsuit and reassure his board that he had properly briefed the prospective litigant on the risks. Miller then recommended that the reps back Flood by agreeing to pay his legal fees and related travel expenses in exchange for the union choosing the litigant's lead attorney. It then fell to Flood to close the sale by reassuring his audience of his sincerity. With Miller as the moderator, Executive Board members grilled their petitioner for over an hour. Had he allowed himself to be blinded with militancy because of his race? Was he in it just for the money? Would he see the case all the way through? Flood passionately defended himself and his cause, then left the room.

When the players then asked Miller for his own opinion, he stressed to them that the issue of involuntary servitude raised by the litigation affected them all, and that they therefore had a fundamental stake in choosing Flood's lawyer. He also reassured them that in the view of Dick Moss, even if the Phillies relinquished their claim upon Flood and released him, the suit would not be jeopardized. Miller added that as long as the case remained active, no similar litigation would be taken on by the union. Finally, he emphasized the fundamental point that even if Flood won, the end result for them would likely not be universal freedom for the membership—an outcome many players actually feared for the insecurity it would create and for the potential oversaturation of the free-agent market—but a new round of collective bargaining to create a mutually acceptable modification of the reserve system. When asked whether in the slim chance Flood won damages he would reimburse the union, Miller left the room to find out and returned with the assurance. The Executive Board then voted 25–0 to endorse the decision.[19]

Miller already knew who he wanted as Flood's lead attorney—his old Steelworker superior Arthur Goldberg. Ten days before the union winter meetings, he had sounded out the distinguished lawyer, now a partner in the firm of Paul, Weiss, Goldberg, Rifkind, Wharton & Garrison. Not only was Goldberg a logical choice for prestige reasons, he had argued the illegality of professional basketball's reserve clause in behalf of client George Mikan back in 1946–1947. One potential snag was that the New York press was rife with rumors that Democratic heavy-hitters were recruiting him to oppose incumbent Nelson Rockefeller for governor. After first pulling Miller's leg with a "not if, but when" quip about the possible candidacy, Goldberg reassured him he had no intention of running for office that year. Five days later he publicly issued the same guarantee. He even offered to take the Flood case pro bono, asking only that the union reimburse subordinates for any related fees and expenses. Of this additional coup, Miller remarked, "Arthur Goldberg for expenses. . . . That was like Sandy Koufax pitching for pass-the-hat."[20]

The day after Flood's appearance before the union reps, Bowie Kuhn arrived for his own session. The courteous reception he received was even more of a charade than usual, considering no one in the union hierarchy wanted to reveal the imminent reserve clause challenge. Ironically, given the owners' past obstinacy in the matter, the commissioner began by voicing his disappointment at the players' choice of a different city from that of the owners for their meetings, and he reiterated his past demand that they open up their sessions to the press. With justification Miller suspected the gambit was merely an effort by management to gain early tips as to the MLBPA agenda for the coming year. The commissioner then asked for the union's endorsement of his decrees for fan All-Star balloting and the requirement of protective flaps on batting helmets, and encouraged the ballplayers' voluntary participation in USO trips to Vietnam. In response Miller pointedly noted that the union had not been consulted about either one of Kuhn's edicts, and he added that the players' decision to meet at a separate site had only been reached after years of prior snubs. After the usual safety and season-length questions from reps, which Kuhn as ever evaded, each side expressed hopes for early completion of a new Basic Agreement. The commissioner then departed, every bit as much in the dark as before about the union's plans.[21]

Curt Flood and Arthur J. Goldberg (source unknown/
Tamiment Library, NYU)

The MLBPA's media allies were not similarly excluded. The Millers invited *New York Times* columnist Leonard Koppett to dinner, at which he was given a heads-up on the pending lawsuit in return for his promise to sit on the story, until receiving clearance to publish. Shortly before Christmas, Miller and Moss drafted Flood's formal letter of notification to Commissioner Kuhn and Phillies general manager John Quinn, ran the document by Goldberg for fine-tuning, and then secured the player's own approval. Reflecting an almost cavalier air of defiance, Miller and Moss jokingly considered an opening line of "I'm free, black, and thirty-one," but immediately substituted formalistic wording that had the unfortunate side effect of betraying the outsiders' role in drafting Flood's letter. Kuhn's lawyers would subsequently take note of lines that would not have been expected from the petitioner, such as, "after twelve years in the major leagues,

I do not feel that I am a piece of property to be bought and sold irrespective of my wishes" and the description of the reserve clause as "inconsistent with the laws of the United States and of the several States."[22]

Flood's notification letter was dispatched on Christmas Eve. By the twenty-ninth, and with the litigant having received no official reply, Miller issued a memorandum to his rank and file revealing the suit and endorsing the Executive Board's decision to back it. The next morning the *Times* and *Post* both contained articles on Flood's intention to sue baseball and the union's retention of Goldberg as the plaintiff's attorney. Only then did Kuhn phone the player and read him directly an advance copy of his reply, which was carried by the press on New Year's Eve morning. Columnist Red Smith paraphrased the commissioner's letter as smugly declaring, "Run along, sonny, you bother me." Four days hence, Flood and Miller appeared together for a Howard Cosell segment on ABC's *Wide World of Sports*. Pressed by the abrasive Cosell about the outfielder's high salary, Flood countered that "A well-paid slave is still a slave." Miller in turn discounted the importance of public sympathy to winning the lawsuit, but then seemed to contradict himself with the words, "If people think slavery is all right as long as the money's OK, then maybe we won't."[23]

In mid-January, Flood's legal team filed its lawsuit in New York federal district court requesting an injunction against the player's trade to Philadelphia and asking for $1 million in damages. Under prevailing law, however, if he won he could receive three times that amount. Miller nonetheless continued to caution him not to expect any such bonanza. Industry lawyers, already galled at the Flood team's characterization of its client as a "slave," grew even more furious when served papers at a collective-bargaining session. NL counsel Lou Hoynes blasted Miller for the "bad-faith" gesture that jeopardized the Basic Agreement talks, but the executive director rejected Hoynes's characterization and observed that if the owners were ready to negotiate a modification of the reserve clause, the lawsuit would disappear. The league presidents then issued a joint statement rejecting the "slavery" tag and predicting industry chaos if the reserve clause was struck down. Miller again rejected the arguments as "phony."[24]

As demonstrated by the back and forth, despite Miller's show of indifference to public opinion, both sides were working overtime to influence media coverage. In New York, the union had several sympathetic voices, including Koppett, Smith, and Robert Lipsyte of the *Times;* Milton Gross of the *Post;* Gene Ward of the *Daily News;* and broadcasters Cosell and ex-NFL star Kyle Rote. Outside Gotham, Miller could count on positive coverage from the *Chicago Sun-Times'* Jerome Holtzman. On the other side, however, the *Daily News'* Dick Young was a relentless assailant of the union, and across the country the overwhelming majority of columnists and home-town reporters embraced the owners' perspective. So too did a handful of promanagement players within the MLBPA. Boston star Carl Yastrzemski publicly criticized the union leadership for failing to poll the rank and file before the decision to back Flood. Miller struck back with a seven-page memo to the full membership that cited Yaz's lukewarm support of the Players Association in previous battles and pointedly noted the similarity between the dissident's call for a membership poll and one from AL president Cronin.[25]

A bigger problem for the Flood case in the court of public opinion, however, was the silence emanating from fellow African American stars such as Hank Aaron, Willie Mays, and Ernie Banks. But the most disruptive, and unexpected, blow to the suit came two months later, when, contrary to earlier assurances, Arthur Goldberg declared his candidacy for governor of New York. Caught flat-footed by the announcement while visiting Grapefruit League squads, Miller phoned from Sarasota and demanded an explanation. A defensive Goldberg explained that he had been under intense pressure from party leaders and liberal groups alike to make the race, and insisted that associate Jay Topkis could handle the pretrial preparation and courtroom arguments. Supporting Goldberg's faith in Topkis's command of the case was the fact that as a law student the associate had written an in-depth study of the Gardella case that had been published in the *Yale Law Journal* under the title, "Monopoly in Professional Sports."[26]

The Flood lawsuit continued to hover over the negotiations for a new Basic Agreement. Despite the old pact's expiration, the owners were in absolutely no hurry to cut a deal. Although Miller complained about the absence of progress on the previous pacts' joint-study issues, the union's main objective remained a different item also left unresolved by the last contract—outside grievance arbitration. As for the reserve clause, the PRC's determination not to change a single word or punctuation mark was obvious, especially while the reserve system remained in litigation. When Jim Bouton mockingly proposed that the owners accept a reserve system in which performers could test the market when they reached the age of sixty-five, management's Lou Carroll refused to discuss even that, insisting, "Next time you'll want it reduced to fifty-five." For his part, Miller justified the union's emphasis on impartial grievance arbitration as not just essential to the protection of members' contractual rights generally, but as a foot in the door toward striking down the owners' version of the reserve clause. If a player could play out his option year and then seek an outside arbitrator's ruling on whether his club's hold on him had thus expired—as the Players Association claimed—he would then have won "free agency" rights to entertain bids from any other clubs for his services. In the event of such a victory, the owners then would be forced to negotiate a less-restrictive reserve system or risk virtually all their talent each off-season to the vagaries of an open marketplace.[27]

Besides outside grievance arbitration, Miller also wanted an immediate minimum-salary boost to $12,000 with raises over the following two seasons to $13,500, a 30 percent limit on pay cuts over any two consecutive years, extension of player severance pay to sixty days, and—driving a stake in the heart of the owners' old paternalism—industry recognition of players' rights to be represented by their own agents in individual contract negotiations. As in the prior Basic Agreement, Miller was demanding a comprehensive pact that, as John Gaherin later described admiringly, "applied to the least and the most." What he sought, in the mold of past Steelworkers pacts, was another deal that moved the ball forward in multiple mutually reinforcing ways. And as before, relatively quick progress on secondary issues was followed by gridlock on the central matter of contention. Given his own familiarity with outside grievance processes in other businesses, John Gaherin actually agreed with Miller on the wisdom and the inevitability of the commissioner relinquishing his arbitrator role in all but rare cases that directly threatened the sport's integrity. He also realized that unlike in 1968, Miller was not going to yield on the subject. The industry's negotiator told his bosses bluntly, "Marvin wouldn't accept Christ Almighty as an arbitrator if he didn't think he was a neutral." To neither side's surprise, the union membership voted down the PRC's proposal, which lacked an outside arbitration process, by a resounding 505–89 margin. Miller then again issued veiled threats that if no deal had been reached by the start of the regular season, MLBPA "concerted action" would almost certainly follow.[28]

In contrast to the previous year's pension fight, this time the primary obstacle to compromise on the central issue was not the PRC but Bowie Kuhn. Over the past year the relationship between the commissioner and Miller had steadily deteriorated, and the current dispute directly involved the circumscribing of the commissioner's authority. In a reversal of roles, it was now some owners— failing to foresee what the acceptance of outside grievance arbitration might ultimately produce—who cheered the come-uppance of a commissioner whose prior intervention had torpedoed their hard-line pension stance. While Kuhn drew upon a cadre of advisors—in particular Lou Hoynes and Sandy Hadden— the ultimate influence on his stance was the man who had made him "king," Walter O'Malley. If the Dodger titan could be made to see that a regular-season interruption could be avoided only by compromising on grievance arbitration, and if Kuhn in turn could be convinced that giving up some power was not a betrayal of the legacy of Judge Landis, then Gaherin and Miller could quickly reach a deal.[29]

Following a particularly long, unproductive bargaining session in Florida, the participants adjourned to Miller's hotel room. Standing with the executive director and counsel Moss on the suite's balcony, Gaherin pitched a compromise. Insisting "with Lou's help I can deliver Bowie," the PRC negotiator proposed that "nuts and bolts" cases be resolved through outside arbitration, while "the son of God [Kuhn]" would retain the final say in grievances involving such subjects as gambling and game fixing that fundamentally threatened public confidence in the sport. Well aware that the devil lay in the details, Miller stubbornly refused to immediately commit to the proposal, but Moss was visibly intrigued. The next morning at breakfast, Gaherin and Lou Hoynes pursued a similar tack with the commissioner. By month's end talks had advanced sufficiently that Miller agreed to suspend consideration of "concerted action."[30]

Weeks of bargaining remained, but by late May the two sides finally came together. Overwhelming union ratification by a 541–54 margin quickly followed. The new Basic Agreement, a three-year pact with the monetary provisions retroactive to the season's start, sidestepped the two sides' "differing views" on the reserve clause. The MLBPA agreed not to file any grievance challenging the owner's interpretation as long as the Flood case remained in litigation or to reopen the contract early to seek rewording of the reserve clause. Post-*Flood*, however, the union made no such assurances. Instead of the reserve clause, the centerpiece of the 1970 Basic Agreement was the initiation of independent grievance arbitration of disputes involving contract interpretation by tripartite panels similar to the kind Miller had presided over in his wartime days. The triumvirate would consist of union and industry representatives, chaired by an outside professional arbitrator acceptable to both sides from the American Arbitration Association. Almost immediately the new system paid dividends for Miller's members. On June 23, arbitration chair and swing voter David Cole sided with the union in the long-running dispute over 1969 playoff shares, retroactively awarding raises to LCS and World Series participants and $82,000 additionally to divisional runners-up.[31]

By the time the Basic Agreement talks successfully concluded, hearings in the Flood lawsuit had already begun before Judge Ben Irving Cooper. In the weeks leading up to opening arguments, Cooper had rejected ploys from the respective sides to enjoin Flood's trade or have the suit dismissed. Across thirteen weeks of proceedings in the federal courthouse on Foley Square, Miller sat alongside Flood and lawyers Goldberg, Topkis, Zerman, and Moss facing the court reporter and the judge. To his left were nine industry attorneys, with Kuhn and his league presidents one row back. Miller's main capacity was that of a witness, fielding softball questions from Flood's side and parrying his adversaries' cross-examinations. Though he personally acquitted himself well enough, on balance the district trial did not go well for Flood. The plaintiff's nervousness on the stand, Goldberg's tardiness and lack of preparation, and Judge Cooper's apparent bias all took their toll. Miller's testimony specifically focused on the owners' refusal to negotiate reserve system changes—a fact buttressing Flood's justification for judicial intervention—and his conversations leading up to the union's decision to join the lawsuit. When pressed under oath by Sandy Hadden, Miller was forced to concede that on many issues besides the reserve clause the clubs had shown their willingness to bargain. Before the trial's August conclusion, Miller took the stand a third time to rebut John Gaherin's assertions of industry good faith.[32]

Besides his personal testimony, Miller was also involved in the selection of other witnesses. Those called eventually included author and ex-pitcher Jim Brosnan, Hall-of-Fame slugger Hank Greenberg, colorful former-owner Bill Veeck, and integration-pioneer Jackie Robinson. The cast conspicuously did not include any current players, underscoring the difficulty of asking players to testify midseason and risk club retaliation. As for Robinson, Miller was aware of the Brooklyn star's 1958 House subcommittee testimony in which he had seemingly endorsed the reserve system. In his Flood appearance on the stand, however, Robinson praised the current litigant as a "courageous young man" and attributed his own contradictory past statements regarding the reserve clause to being "young and ignorant at the time. . . . I know differently now and I won't hesitate to say so." As for Veeck, after a lengthy mealtime questioning in which drinks flowed freely and the former owner regaled his audience, the executive director emerged satisfied that the maverick would prove a useful witness. On the appointed day, Veeck arrived at court holding a trademark lit cigarette, and Goldberg was forced to point out the courtroom smoking ban and absence of ashtrays. Unfazed, Veeck proceeded to put out his smoke on his artificial leg and took his seat.[33]

Years later, Miller admitted that in a case so unevenly presented by the plaintiff's side, his own biggest fault was in not insisting that current ballplayers attend the hearings to show solidarity with Flood. He acknowledged members' fears and scheduling conflicts, but he was right to chastise himself for not at least pressing the more "bulletproof" stars, "For God's sake, this is a colleague of yours!" Nonetheless, given the court's predisposition, it almost certainly made no difference to the outcome. On August 12, Cooper ruled against Flood. Attempting to put a positive spin on this initial defeat, Miller maintained that it reflected the usual tendency of lower courts to defer to the Supreme Court rather than lead in overturning longstanding precedent.[34]

Flood's lawyers then filed an appeal, while their client abruptly left the country for Denmark. In October the Phillies offered to trade their idled performer to Bob Short's Washington Senators. In a meeting convened by Arthur Goldberg in his New York apartment, Flood, Short, Miller, and Moss collectively attempted to draft a new playing contract that would not sabotage the legal case. Fearing that the Supreme Court would point to an active contract as reason to declare Flood's claim moot, Miller pressed the outfielder not to sign any new deal specifically containing a reserve clause. Goldberg, for his part, had prepared a two-page memo outlining his suggested modifications to Short's original offer, including the insertion of no-cut and no-trade clauses, automatic free agency at the pact's end in two years, and explicit concurrence by both sides in the ongoing litigation that the Senators contract did not prejudice the lawsuit. Short proved willing to accept Goldberg's suggestions and extended Flood the offer of a hefty $100,000 salary, but at one point in the conversation he awkwardly made reference to his prospective employee as "the boy." When Miller peered sideways to see if Flood had caught the unintended slur, the latter responded with a smile and a wink.[35]

Revealingly, the commissioner rejected all of the proposed contract modifications except the language regarding Flood's appeal—a sign of the owners' overwhelming confidence in the judicial outcome. Rejecting Miller's renewed pleas not to agree to a contract without all of the protections proposed by his legal team, Flood signed the contract. The Senators sweetened their offer by boosting the annual salary to $110,000, starting payments in November rather than waiting until the beginning of the 1971 season, and guaranteeing Flood full salary for the year even if he only lasted to June 15. Within days the Phillies agreed to the proposed trade, receiving in return a major-leaguer and two prospects. Flood reiterated to Miller his continued commitment to the lawsuit, saying of his return to baseball, "I wouldn't do this if I weren't in a financial bind." But news of the trade armed critics such as Dick Young, who had ridiculed the litigation as the "Dred Flood case," with fresh ammunition. At the union's winter meetings, some reps also voiced frustration. Despite his own growing doubts, Miller optimistically reassured both that the plaintiff's return to the field would not cripple the legal appeal and that he remained "very much in Flood's corner."[36]

Despite the disappointments with the Flood litigation, at year's end Miller could look back with pride at the support of his men and the grudging respect of the owners. Fifty-six of Miller's players now earned more than $50,000 per year, up from nine at that level just five years before. The Executive Board raised his own pay to $65,000 with $5,000 additional boosts each of the next two seasons. And not just among players, the money tide Miller had triggered was lifting other industry employee boats. Reflecting how rising player salaries exerted pressure to boost manager pay to buttress their authority, the latter salaries now climbed to a range between $30,000 and $75,000. Subordinate coaches now earned what a typical player had received just a few years back. As industry pay increased and Miller's union continued to earn respect, the commissioner grew more resentful. When Kuhn summoned Jim Bouton, author of a racy tell-all memoir called *Ball Four,* in an attempt to have the player self-censor his book, the pitcher arrived accompanied by not just his editor but Miller and Moss. By the end of the session in Kuhn's Fifth Avenue office—described as decorated in "Early American Authority" with U.S. flags and presidential portraits—the player still refused to retract any passages or to cast blame on ghostwriter Leonard Shecter.[37]

Throughout the baseball industry other employee groups were taking notice. Puerto Rican players had formed their own union and had threatened a strike of the 1969–1970 winter-league season, demanding higher pay and per diems. At their All-Star Game, Marvin Miller was invited to throw out the first pitch and was presented with a plaque thanking him for "his outstanding contributions to the welfare and power of the [playing] family." To the south, the Confederation of Workers announced its intention to organize Mexican League players and other national professional athletes after passage of new national laws that recognized the reserve system but barred sales of players without their permission and guaranteed men 25 percent of their purchase prices plus an extra 5 percent for each year of tenure. And U.S. major-league umpires—whose NL segment had been organized since 1963 but not its AL brethren—were also on the march. Back in late 1968, Miller had quietly solicited the AFL-CIO's help in filing an amicus brief supporting fired AL umpire activists Al Salerno and Bill Valentine. Although the two arbiters lost their NLRB case, a Major League Umpires Association covering the "men in blue" of both circuits then struck the first game of the 1970 League Championship Series. Although the league presidents refused to agree to a basic agreement similar to the one Miller had secured his players, they reluctantly agreed to boost LCS umpires' pay from $2,500 to $3,000 per man and World Series stipends from $6,500 to $7,500.[38]

The business of professional baseball was turning upside down. Montreal Expos president John McHale acknowledged Marvin Miller's central role, admitting, "He's done so much for the players he can take a vacation for the next five years—and he'll still be ahead of us." Other magnates openly cursed the MLBPA chief. Bowie Kuhn wrangled a last invitation to a union Executive Board meeting in December 1970, but after first being made to cool his heels only to draw perfunctory questions from reps, he never again sought to crash the sessions. The next spring, prefaced by run-ins with Miller over allowances to players lodging outside the team hotel and compensation for a demoted performer's travel expenses, San Diego general manager Buzzie Bavasi erupted at his adversary. Perhaps also still stinging from having been pushed out of the Dodger organization to make room for Walter O'Malley's son Peter, Bavasi lashed out at an innocent remark with the words, "Do that again and I'll knock you on your fanny." Other club officials privately referred to Miller as "that gimpy-armed Jew bastard." Displaying slightly more erudition, the Phillies' Bob Carpenter called him a "plebeian socialist." Claiming to delight in the slurs as vindication, Miller carried out his annual visits of the spring camps and even found time for drop-in piano playing at local watering holes.[39]

With the Flood appeal headed for the court of appeals and with Arthur Goldberg having lost badly in his gubernatorial race, Miller now expected his old colleague to devote more attention to the case. Goldberg had left New York to open a new practice in the nation's capital, fortuitously placing him in close proximity to the suit's likely eventual destination of the U.S. Supreme Court. That presumption became fact in April, when the appeals panel also rejected Flood's arguments. Later the same month, the outfielder, who had quit the Senators barely two weeks into the regular season and left for Majorca, telephoned Miller of his retirement decision but gave no reasons other than that "the situation had deteriorated." In truth, he was washed up. Later that fall the executive director was informed by Goldberg that the Supreme Court had agreed to hear the case in its 1972 spring term. Flood then wrote the union to request payment of $10,000 in early severance. Under the most recent pension pact, future beneficiaries could withdraw $1,000 for each year of big-league service, up to a maximum $10,000, so long as they repaid it with interest, before the date they began to draw their regular pension. With Miller absent from his office when the request arrived, Dick Moss delivered the bad news that Flood was ineligible for early severance until a full year's passage since the April 27, 1971 start of his retirement.[40]

Because he was precluded under the existing Basic Agreement from sponsoring a grievance-arbitration challenge to the reserve clause as long as Flood's case remained alive, Miller was helpless to aid active players such as Baltimore pitcher Dave Leonhard being harmed by it. A journeyman hurler buried behind the Orioles' starting rotation yet unable to migrate to another team, Leonhard described his dilemma to his executive director: "I have the option of quitting the game, and like Curt [Flood] I can't afford to do so." Miller continued to take on other battles that season, however. Rebuffed in the last pension talks when he had demanded explicit linkage between industry television-revenue levels and owner contributions, he now filed an NLRB action intended to at least force the clubs to share the specifics of their NBC pact. In order to avoid a likely adverse ruling, the owners yielded in November and the union withdrew its unfair-labor-practices charge.[41]

Miller's most surprising victory that campaign, however, was his successful defense of troubled Angels slugger Alex Johnson—the very first grievance heard under the new arbitration system that involved a minority player. Johnson, the AL's 1970 batting champion, had since exhibited increasingly erratic behavior, leading his club to fine him twenty-five separate times. When the Angels had been unable to trade him by the June 15 deadline, it had suspended him for thirty days and sent him back to his native Detroit without pay. Commissioner Kuhn then made matters worse for him by unilaterally shifting him from the suspended to the "restricted" list—a form of unpaid indefinite suspension Miller publicly compared to government "jailing political dissidents." In a landmark filing, the union asserted that Johnson suffered from a diagnosed emotional illness and that just as with a physical injury, he did not deserve denial of pay and service time. Arbitrator Lewis Gill cast the deciding vote in Johnson's favor, although his judgment to uphold the Angels' original fines led to a Miller dissent.[42]

Miller now entertained at least fleeting thoughts of a career change. Back in the spring he had jokingly told a reporter he could be "bought off" if the owners would only agree to modify the reserve clause, reduce the season, and accept a shared control of television revenue. Among his continuing irritations were the slings and arrows thrown at him and his union by their critics in the press. Miller and the Executive Board solicited presentations from a half dozen public relations firms. That same fall, in another indication that he was giving at least some consideration to ending his MLBPA tenure, Miller retained an agent to investigate the possibility of a book deal with publisher Athenaeum. Wistfully he confessed to good friend Jerome Holtzman the allure of a college post in a warm climate where he could freely indulge his passion for tennis while contributing the occasional article on labor issues.[43]

Adding to Miller's introspection was a family emergency. Son Peter had earned his master's degree at Berkeley but as a result had become eligible for the military draft. Persuading Selective Service of his pacifist convictions, the younger Miller had fulfilled his obligation as a customer-complaint officer in the environmental section of San Francisco's public health department and had then reenrolled in school to pursue his doctorate. While walking along Bancroft Way between home and class, he was struck by a car that had lurched over the street curb, mangling the tendons and muscles in one leg. Doctors judged that infection in the affected tissues required an amputation. Both Miller parents felt their son's anguish deeply, but Marvin was particularly haunted given his own struggles to overcome physical handicap and his grandfather's death from similar circumstances years before. The sympathetic Bill Veeck volunteered the backstory of his own leg injury while in the Marines, and the subsequent fruitless efforts to save his limb. Noting the progress made in prosthetics since then, he confidentially suggested it might be best that Peter accept amputation rather than submit himself to additional painful and possibly fruitless surgeries. But with his son resolute to save his leg at all costs, Miller kept Veeck's advice to himself.[44] Shelving any further thoughts of alternative employment for the time being, he instead refocused on the task immediately at hand.

Eleven

Earning Respect

As 1971 wound down, Marvin Miller steeled himself for the next round of pension negotiations. Given the emotions stirred by his son's injury and painful rehabilitation, the last thing he wanted was another protracted showdown—and he did not expect one. In the three years since the last deal, the value of both club contributions and member benefits had eroded from inflation, and the price of players' health care had jumped a half-million dollars. Accordingly, the MLBPA proposal called for a 17 percent annual boost in clubs' payments to $6.5 million and a similar adjustment to the health-care fund. To make the proposal more palatable to management, Miller pointed out that the pension fund currently claimed a $800,000 surplus relative to liabilities and that therefore no new revenues were needed from the clubs to address the benefit-erosion problem. At first, the PRC's Gaherin likewise did not signal a looming confrontation either. Although he did not frame his counteroffer as a formal proposal, the owners' man floated the similar idea of injecting $500,000 in surplus into the health-care plan.[1]

But what Miller failed to recognize was the sheer depth of resentment he and his union now inspired in a key bloc of hard-liners—venom that drove these owners into overreacting despite the modest numbers involved. If the union's chief had fully understood the burning intensity of the hatred toward him, he might well have reconsidered his choice to tweak the magnates over the recent $70 million television pact. Angry executives resented what they saw as public grandstanding in Miller's suggestion that they give the union all their broadcast revenue for player salaries and benefits in exchange for management keeping all other income. Both sides were well aware that baseball's immediate economic future lay much more in a growing broadcast revenue stream than in old-style gate receipts. Nor did the clubs take kindly to Miller's continued jabs at their tax shelters and subsidies, which he had highlighted at a Brookings Institution seminar early in the New Year.[2]

Nevertheless, though in the first weeks of 1972 progress in the pension talks was modest, it seemed no different than usual. Miller was actually more concerned at the clubs' hesitancy to finalize individual contracts, a delay they attributed to uncertainty over the applicability of the Nixon administration's wage controls. The union chief was already well into his spring-training rounds when—as he was preparing for a meeting with White Sox players—he was notified of the clubs' sudden outright declaration of war. Having already spoken to six teams, Miller now learned with alarm that Gaherin had retracted the earlier $500,000 offer and was determined to oppose any health-coverage boost over $400,000. The PRC's negotiator also insisted that his bosses would not agree to more than $372,000 in additional contributions to address the pension benefit-erosion problem. Miller scrambled to arrange fresh briefings with the clubs he had already met, reworked his White Sox presentation, and then traveled to his remaining seventeen Florida and Cactus League camps in the remaining twenty-three days before the regular season's start. His message was the same— the owners clearly meant to force a life-or-death showdown, and therefore the membership would need to give its blessing to the Executive Board to authorize a strike if necessary, with March 31 the drop-dead date for the reps' decision.[3]

To the PRC's hard-liners, the fundamental issue was not so much the dollar amount of a pension boost than reversing their erosion of control over their industry. As press mouthpiece Dick Young put it, "To the owners, the enemy is not the players, whom the owners regard merely as . . . misled ingrates. . . . The enemy is Marvin Miller." He concluded, "It is not over a few more thousand dollars . . . it is over the principle of who will run their baseball business, they, the Lords, or this man Miller." The PRC now contained such dead-enders as the Reds' Francis Dale (publisher of the *Cincinnati Enquirer* and subsequently treasurer of CREEP, Richard Nixon's 1972 campaign organization), Calvin Griffith of Minnesota, and Pittsburgh's Dan Galbreath.[4]

By the time Miller finished his briefings and the votes were tallied from the twenty-four squads, the strike-authorization vote came to an overwhelming 663–10. Eight dissenters hailed from just two teams, the Boston Red Sox and Los Angeles Dodgers. John Gaherin discounted the vote's significance, claiming that any labor leader worth his salt could orchestrate a similar result upon demand. And in private, Miller himself was not sanguine over the huge margin of approval. When matters reached a head, would players who had never before been asked to carry out a regular-season strike stay firm? Because if the union went forward with its planned action, it would be not only the first of its kind in the history of baseball, but also more broadly in the annals of American professional sport.[5]

Still befuddled at the owners' determination for war over what he considered "peanuts," Miller accepted an invitation to the type of management-sponsored social event he usually shunned—Walter O'Malley's St. Patrick's Day bash in Vero Beach. When he arrived, Miller quietly noted with disapproval that while ex-players Sandy Koufax and Roy Campanella had been flown in for the occasion, no current squad members had been invited. The soiree was a gaudy spectacle of green, from the décor and the attendees' leprechaun hats to the emerald-dyed water, beer, and Scotch. When Miller and Dick Moss managed a private moment with the Dodger patriarch and his son and heir-apparent Peter O'Malley, the executive director's freely expressed concern over the pending confrontation was brushed aside by his host. "Don't worry," the elder O'Malley asserted, "We'll resolve this." He then cryptically added, "A lot can happen in two weeks." O'Malley then tried unsuccessfully to pump Miller for the names of the few Los Angeles players who had voted against the strike authorization. To the union chief's surprise, O'Malley stated that his motive was not to reward but rather to punish them for an action he deemed deleterious to team morale. True to his principles, O'Malley eventually jettisoned the four players, two—including player-rep Wes Parker—by trade, the others through retirement.[6]

In marked contrast to his role in the 1969 pension talks, the commissioner this time was determined to remain a spectator, to the point that a sportswriter eventually quipped of the showdown, "This would never have happened if Bowie Kuhn were alive." On March 22 the PRC instructed Gaherin to hold fast to its latest, uncompromising position. As the strategy session broke up, its participants agreed among themselves not to issue provocative statements that might undermine public support or fire up the players. Within minutes, Gussie Busch shattered the facade of reasonableness and erupted before the assembled reporters: "We're not going to give them [the players] another goddamn cent. If they want to strike, let 'em!" The Cardinals owner's diatribe thus provided Miller with bulletin-board material just when he needed it most.[7]

As the strike deadline neared, each side tried to call the other's bluff. On the twenty-ninth Miller proposed—and the owners immediately rejected—binding

Miller, Dick Moss, and Terry at Walter O'Malley's St. Patrick's party
(source unknown/Tamiment Library, NYU)

arbitration by an outsider chosen from a list of candidates to be nominated by President Nixon, former President Johnson, or former Chief Justice Warren. Huddling in Scottsdale before the next day's scheduled Executive Board meeting in Dallas and possible strike vote, Miller and Moss privately concurred that the union would have to execute a graceful fold. In both men's view the membership was simply not yet ready for such a showdown, and the union lacked an adequate strike fund or an effective cross-country and international communications setup. The executive director observed ominously, "You only get one chance at a first strike, and if you don't win that one, you have lost the union."[8]

With the stylistic assistance of Terry Miller, the MLBPA leaders drafted a resolution of retreat for presentation to the reps. The union would lift the immediate strike threat and continue bargaining. If by season's end no agreement had been reached, they would propose the talks be folded into those on the next Basic Agreement. If the owners refused to accept that idea, the union would pursue a political long shot of congressional intervention. The trio pointedly nicknamed their document "the Sacco-Vanzetti statement," after the famous anarchist pair who, while awaiting their execution for robbery and murder, had composed public letters attributing their fate to their adversaries' abuse of power. On the flight to Love Field for the meeting with the reps, however, Miller began to sense that perhaps he had underestimated his men's resolve. Seated directly behind him were Oakland A's delegate Chuck Dobson and team alternate Reggie Jackson, and unexpectedly both men were voicing defiance.

At the four-hour meeting of the thirty-first, Miller counseled caution to a now-surprisingly fired-up audience. He warned them, "With all due respect, you've never done this before—it won't be a picnic." But the reps refused to be dissuaded. Jackson launched into a profanity-laced tirade and demanded the strike. Spontaneously, as if from Odets's *Waiting for Lefty*, the assembled began to chant in rising volume, "Strike! Strike! Strike!" as Miller quietly slipped his surrender document back into his pocket. Alone among the forty-eight reps and alternates in refusing to endorse the work stoppage was Wes Parker. The squads' remaining exhibition games would now be cancelled and the strike would continue for as long as required. The executive director and his counsel both took themselves off the payroll for the duration, and they now hastily drew up a press release the opposite of the one they had drafted just the night before.[9]

Officers and players alike scrambled to book flights to homes near and far. Unable to secure a direct plane to New York, the Millers managed to book a connection through Baltimore. During the flight's second leg, New York Knicks basketball players strolled up the aisle one by one to offer their support. Upon landing in Gotham, one of them, forward Bill Bradley, even volunteered to contribute a public letter refuting columnist Dick Young's latest attacks. The executive director's return to New York, however, would be brief. With owner Francis Dale and his press allies attacking the Reds' players over the strike, rep Jim Merritt requested his leader's presence at a squad meeting for April 5—formerly the date of the club home opener against Pittsburgh. At the urging of Pittsburgh star Roberto Clemente, Miller also conducted a session with the visiting team, although the Pirates' demeanor indicated no bucking-up was needed.[10]

While Miller shored up union solidarity, management tried to exploit any cracks in the players' morale. Phillies owner Bob Carpenter verbally arm-twisted union reps Tom Harmon and Tim McCarver, and similar efforts by Baltimore's Jerry Hoffberger prompted rep Brooks Robinson to organize a countermeeting at his home with Miller and twenty-one teammates. One of the most respected player leaders, Minnesota's Jim Perry, kept his fellow Twins solid by securing free lodging for his younger teammates with veteran players and by arranging bus transportation to and from high-school ball fields for informal workouts. The loyalty of the reps in general proved so strong that even on the Dodgers, when the well-paid Maury Wills publicly threatened to lead a band of thirteen dissenters back for the home opener, Wes Parker set aside his misgivings over the strike to squelch the rebellion.[11]

Still, the sporadic demonstrations of player wavering threatened to embolden the owners further. In a dramatic gambit intended both to cement solidarity and display his reps' unshakeable defiance, Miller scheduled a pep rally for the backroom of the Four Seasons restaurant. The session's highlight was the legendary Willie Mays's strike endorsement. Mays had been thrust into unexpected duty as the Giants' rep because of the club's having shipped off predecessors Hal Lanier and Gaylord Perry. Despite his management's willingness for retaliation and his shrinking career window, the veteran star pledged unwavering backing for the union. While other clubs followed the Giants' lead and publicly demonized their own striking stars, it was Miller who became the primary focus of industry scorn. Reds' general manager Bob Howsam claimed, "There would be no strike if it were not for Marvin Miller," and went on to argue, "Baseball is not the steel industry, and he [Miller] can't use the tactics of a steel negotiator." Paul Richards in turn insisted that the owners "simply aren't going to let Marvin Miller run over them anymore," and concluded with a typically over-the-top comment: "Tojo and Hirohito couldn't stop baseball, but Marvin Miller did."[12]

By the end of the strike's first week, despite the public bluster, cracks were starting to show in the clubs' solidarity. Ironically, John Gaherin was partly to blame by having brought in pension expert John Able, who had proceeded to explain to the owners the logic of Miller's original $800,000 accruals-transfer idea. When the still-unmoved Gussie Busch called upon the majors' wealthier clubs to pony up $1 million to shore up their weaker brethren, Walter O'Malley now fired back that the loss of regular-season games was costing his organization by itself that amount each week. In response to a nervous Calvin Griffith, Gaherin offered his own judgment that if the owners intended to break the union, they would have to hold firm until at least May 1. Further demoralized at the projection, the former fire-breather could only meekly utter in reply, "What will the press do to us?" As the PRC negotiator would later recall of the situation, "Marvin had it all going for him. Everybody wanted to shoot [him], but nobody wanted to pull the trigger." It was now Oakland's hawkish Charley Finley—a militant but also a man who had made millions selling medical insurance and understood how benefit plans worked—who provided colleagues the necessary fig leaf for a retreat. He now insisted—dubiously—that prior to Able's presentation "few" owners had actually grasped the existence of the pension-fund surplus, even though Miller had raised it as the basis for the MLBPA's bargaining position from the start.[13]

On April 8 Gaherin indicated that the owners had abandoned their previously rigid stance, proposing to split the difference with the union by raising the owners' contribution an extra $400,000, with the additional money coming from the pension fund's surplus. Three clubs then defied earlier PRC strictures and opened their workout facilities to striking players. Within three days Gaherin had restored his original health-insurance offer and was endorsing automatic cost-of-living pension adjustments. Once the clubs' abrupt reversal took place, the only remaining obstacles to a deal were those the strike itself had generated—whether or not cancelled games would be made up and whether strikers would be granted back pay and service credit for the lost time. Informally, Miller suggested to Gaherin that in a gesture to win back fans, the two sides could reschedule cancelled tilts while charging no admission and donating concessions money to charity. When the clubs bluntly rejected that idea, Miller returned to a stance the union had taken since April 10—that while the clubs would not need to make up lost games or restore players' back salary, they would have to grant service credit. On April 13 the PRC yielded, the two sides agreed to short-term pension and health-insurance pacts that would carry forward to the year's end, and the next pension round was merged with the upcoming 1973 Basic Agreement negotiations.[14]

The day after the announcement of the interim pension settlement, Miller indulged himself with a fifty-fifth birthday celebration that lasted into the night. The major-league season belatedly began the next afternoon. In St. Louis only 7,808 fans showed up, many apparently to boo union activist Joe Torre. In Baltimore, former World Series hero Brooks Robinson drew similar scorn. But in truth, had the clubs not delayed a deal for three extra days only to ultimately accept Miller's terms, nearly half of the strike's losses of games and revenues could have been avoided. As it were, a total of eighty-six regular-season games—more than seven per club—had been cancelled. Because of the unequal number of cancellations across teams, some squads played as few as 153 contests, others as many as 156. The difference would prove decisive in Boston's losing the AL East pennant to Detroit by a half-game. Overall the industry lost an estimated $5.2 million, while the players sacrificed a cumulative $600,000 in salary.[15]

Individuals on both sides continued to gripe even after the return to work. Gussie Busch drew a union grievance for attempting the retaliatory economy of cancelling his players' single-room road accommodations, and a self-absorbed Pete Rose insisted, "If there's another strike . . . the Players Association won't get my support." But Miller knew that he and his union had won a historic victory. Not only had the MLBPA secured a half-million-dollar boost to the player health and pension funds, the membership had gone through a trial by fire and had emerged triumphant. Having forced a showdown unnecessarily, the owners had been dealt a major defeat. Johnson Spink acknowledged in the *Sporting News* that Miller had emerged as "the most powerful man in baseball," and the *New York Times'* Leonard Koppett offered his own postscript:

> PLAYERS: We want higher pensions.
> OWNERS: We won't give you one damn cent for that.
> PLAYERS: You don't have to—the money is already there. Just let us use it.
> OWNERS: It would be imprudent.
> PLAYERS: We did it before, and anyway, we won't play unless we can have some of it.
> OWNERS: Okay.[16]

Miller's own postmortem projected surface modesty but also heralded the dawn of a new day. Professing the hope that the owners would quickly turn from bitterness, he insisted that the outcome had been in the best interests of all. "A relationship between a superior and an inferior is not a good one," he maintained, "even if the relationship is peaceful. A relationship between equals is a far better relationship, even if it is stormy." Despite the charitable public words, though, his personal correspondence vacillated between additional examples of extending the olive branch and fiery defenses of himself and his union. To Buzzie Bavasi, who had lost a private bet with catcher Bob Barton that Miller would continue to receive his salary during the strike, the executive director now needled him to settle up with the player. In another missive, Miller took the Reds' Dale sharply to task for having his newspaper propagate "an appalling amount of misinformation" during the strike—included a Dick Forbes column that had compared management considerations of compromise with Neville Chamberlain's appeasement of Hitler. Not surprisingly given his Jewish roots and antifascist bona fides, the union chief retorted sharply, "It was as if General Motors, in order to propagandize its position in a dispute, screamed at the public that its employees turned out defective automobiles—and then wondered why the sale of Chevrolets, Pontiacs, etc., fell off." Miller similarly chastised the Pirates' Dan Galbreath for having allowed a "small minority" to hijack the pension talks and seek to dictate a deal rather than bargain in good faith.[17]

Toward those few open dissenters in his own ranks, Miller showed a pragmatic, forgiving side. To Wes Parker he was generous with his praise for the "great integrity and distinction" that the dissident rep had shown during the strike. But in his replies to hostile fans, whose correspondence Miller insisted upon reading even though it infuriated him as uninformed, he showed a strikingly thin skin. In one such reply to a disapproving clergyman, Miller's rejoinder began unsparingly, "Your knowledge of economic problems is on a par with my knowledge of the Presbyterian ministry—absolute zero." Of greater concern to him in the strike's aftermath than fan feelings, however, was the disturbing continued pattern of clubs exacting revenge against their union reps. From October 1971 through the following spring, sixteen of twenty-four team delegates had been expelled from their organizations through trade, sale, or release. Three more had resigned their posts under duress to avoid a similar fate.[18]

It was clearly no time for him to let down his guard. The need for continued vigilance in behalf of members' contract rights led Miller, for example, to file a grievance against the Montreal Expos for unilaterally rescheduling a strike-postponed double-header as split contests on the same day. The controversy triggered yet another back-and-forth between the executive director and *Sporting News* editor Spink. Miller also limited his outside speaking commitments to a single Harvard symposium and rebuffed new overtures for the rights to his life story. To baseball writer and friend Jerome Holtzman he again admitted to a yearning for even a brief Cape Cod vacation. The opportunity would have to await one more event, however—the Supreme Court ruling on Curt Flood's antitrust challenge to the reserve clause.[19]

On June 19, 1972, the justices delivered their long-anticipated verdict. In a five-to-three decision they found against Flood. The majority opinion, penned by Justice Harry Blackmun, was long in tributes to the national pastime and to stare decisis but short on internal consistency. Six of the panel's eight participating justices (Nixon appointee Lewis Powell had recused himself because of possession of Busch stock) even admitted that if the issue of an antitrust exemption for baseball had come to them fresh they would not have supported the claim. According to Bob Woodward's later account in *The Brethren*, the final majority vote owed to Chief Justice Warren Burger's desire to give his fellow Minnesotan the chance to author a major ruling—a consideration that would have been rendered moot anyway a year later by Blackmun's landmark *Roe v. Wade* abortion decision. When it appeared the Court might deadlock four to four—still representing a defeat for Flood but one that would not have necessitated the preparation of a majority opinion—Burger reportedly switched his vote to the opposing side. With all three participating Nixon appointees thus ultimately siding with the industry, Miller was additionally left to ponder what the fate of the lawsuit might have been if brought earlier before a Court with the likes of Hugo Black or John Harlan. He also was forced to painfully admit that Arthur Goldberg had again harmed Flood's chances—this time through a poor performance during oral arguments.[20]

Immediately after the Court's decision was released, Miller phoned Flood with the bad news. Despite his inherent skepticism and his earlier open doubts about the case, it was the executive director who was now the more disconsolate of the two. In an exchange of letters with Jay Topkis regarding the union's remaining $75,000 balance on its $100,000 legal fees, Miller similarly found the attorney consoling him and expressing gratitude for his support in the litigation. As Topkis bravely put it, "The only bad thing about the case from my point of view was losing it—everything else aside, Mrs. Lincoln, how was the show?" Miller managed his own brave face before the press, emphasizing the Court's call to both sides to resolve their disagreement on the reserve clause through collective bargaining as a helpful prod. Privately, John Gaherin too was expressing similar sentiments to his bosses. Cautioning them against gloating, he reiterated, "Fellas, this is the 20th Century. You can't get anybody, drunk or sober, to agree that once a fella goes to work for the A&P, he has to work for the A&P the rest of his life!"[21]

Now that the *Flood* case's conclusion had lifted the hold upon other player challenges, Miller searched for someone else willing to lead the gambit of serving out a postcontract option year and then filing a grievance seeking free agency. Attention on both sides fell on one particular man—twenty-one-year-old St. Louis catcher Ted Simmons. In his first full big-league season in 1971 he had batted over .300 and had prompted his club to shift Joe Torre to third base. Older Cardinal players saw the youthful Simmons, nicknamed "Simba" for his flowing locks, as something of a flake, but they respected his talent and his loyalty to teammates. Having earned but $14,000 and with the club citing government wage policy in offering him only an increase to the low $20,000s, Simmons now demanded $35,000. MLBPA veteran Torre immediately contacted Miller to suggest his young teammate as a reserve clause test candidate and personally attested to his reliability. Given St. Louis's need to restore the faith of its fan base by keeping its best talent on the field, the club was likely to be hesitant to assert Major League Rule 3C—which according to clubs' reading gave them the right to bar an unsigned player from playing—both from fear of public outcry and another union grievance.[22]

With the Cardinals choosing to play their young catcher despite his lack of an active contract, by midseason of 1972 Simmons's performance had earned him a spot on the All-Star team. Despite his obvious value, the Cardinals were unable to deal the holdout hitter to another organization, in part because no other club wanted to become the new object of a reserve clause case. With industry lawyers and Gaherin both pleading with St. Louis to come to terms with its catcher, general manager Bing Devine ponied up in a meeting in an Atlanta hotel room during the All-Star break. The Cardinals offered Simmons a two-year pact at $30,000 for the current season and $45,000 the next. The apologetic player then phoned Miller to inform him of his decision to sign, since the deal met his previously stated demands. The executive director could not blame the catcher, considering he had not caved before an unfair offer. The outcome even offered the union valuable evidence of the market value of a young star. But the bottom line remained that a grievance hearing testing the length of the reserve clause would now have to wait another year.[23]

Miller's push to win his membership the right to determine its value in an open marketplace now shifted to the bargaining table. In early Basic Agreement talks that fall, the owners signaled a new preference for not forcing another disastrous showdown. A more temperate executive, Milwaukee's Ed Fitzgerald, had assumed the chairmanship of the PRC, the panel's size had been cut from an unwieldy ten to a streamlined six, and the threshold for ratification of a new pact had been reduced from a concurrent majority of clubs in each league to an overall majority of major-league organizations. With Fitzgerald's blessing, Gaherin probed the union's receptiveness toward alternatives to a massive reserve clause overhaul that would nonetheless offer players continued salary growth and at least one opportunity in their careers to change clubs. But Gaherin and Fitzgerald still faced the problem of a hard-line segment of ownership who viewed the *Flood* result as proof no compromise was needed. This group still believed that the federal courts would always step in and save the day, even in the event of an adverse grievance-arbitration ruling. Occupying a key middle ground between industry's more moderate and militant owners were Commissioner Kuhn and patron Walter O'Malley, who could be relied upon to loyally support PRC tests of union resolve up to, but not beyond, the point at which regular-season games and revenues were threatened. Kuhn still insisted on portraying himself as baseball's impartial steward, but contradicting the pose were his covert meetings in the PRC office before and after each bargaining session, after which to Miller's scorn he would then parrot the owners' positions.[24]

The union promptly tested the clubs' willingness to negotiate a modified reserve clause. In September, Miller proposed that big-league performers enjoy free-agency rights at least once over their careers. Men with three years' big-league experience but earning less than the average player salary would be eligible to test the market, as would five-year men earning below 150 percent of the mean. Seven-, twelve-, and seventeen-year veterans would be allowed to enter free agency regardless of their pay. For weeks the owners' only counterproposal was to suggest another joint-study committee. On November 29 Commissioner Kuhn finally emerged from the shadows to publicly tout a plan. In his proposal a five-year veteran making less than $30,000 would qualify for free agency, as would eight-year men earning under $40,000. Ten-year players regardless of pay would have the right to veto trades but would not gain outright freedom. Miller was furious at the plan's deceptive penury. Only five of his current members would qualify immediately for free agency, and the clubs could simply cancel out the monetary impact by cutting reserve rosters by two per team—a loss of forty-eight union jobs. Accordingly, Miller blasted "rank amateur" Kuhn for acting as if he was the de facto "coordinator" of the PRC and for making "fraudulent" statements that violated the two sides' pledge not to negotiate in the media.[25]

Miller had been holding out for a reserve system that would guarantee universal free agency for players at the end of a specific length of service. Now, however, he recognized that such a direct addressing of the reserve clause would not be achievable in the current round. Because of the heightened attention both sides now were placing upon the reserve clause, past bitter subjects such as the pension and the minimum salary ironically took on a routine status. The owners wanted to avoid another pension squabble, and on the minimum salary they were already offering to boost levels to $15,000 by the last year of a new pact in 1975. The union countered with a call for a first contract-year minimum of $15,500 and a $17,500 figure by the pact's last season. Holding no realistic hope of negotiating an immediate alternative to the existing reserve system, Miller instead turned to an indirect substitute—outside salary arbitration. Pay arbitration in cases in which individual owners and players could not agree upon financial terms could mirror the existing grievance-arbitration structure and could enable a fairer salary system for men with as little as two years' big-league service. Once again, John Gaherin had already suggested the same idea to his bosses as a way to reduce the number of spring holdouts and also possibly defer the union's assault on the reserve clause.[26]

Through the winter, owners privately wrangled over whether to offer pay arbitration. As late as New Year's Day 1973, Commissioner Kuhn remained insistent that his earlier proposals represented the limits of the industry's flexibility. But he conspicuously left open the door of negotiation a crack by suggesting that the clubs' main objection to outside salary arbitration was their fear that such adjudicators, ignorant of industry realities, would just reflexively "split the difference" between opposing bids and thus encourage players' agents to make outrageous proposals. Four days later Miller admitted publicly that talks in the "whole Reserve System area" were irrevocably bogged down and that he was shifting his focus to salary arbitration. In truth, he viewed outside pay arbitration as essential regardless of whether the reserve clause was modified to allow limited free agency. He also suspected that in the event both processes were instituted, the clubs would collude to "fix" any free-agent marketplace. If they did, however, the existence of salary arbitration would still provide players greater salary leverage than they currently possessed. As the union position now stated, "Given the [owners'] absolute power over players, salary arbitration is a must."[27]

Miller also had a logical counterargument to the claim that outside pay arbitration would invariably lead to "split-the-difference" awards. During his time at the Steelworkers he had examined other unions' systems of pay resolution and had taken particular note of those of the Amalgamated Streetcar and Railway Employees. In its municipal pacts the transit union had effectively employed "final-offer," or "either-or," arbitration. According to this method, an outside arbiter or a deciding vote on a three-member panel had to select one side's or the other's final bid as his verdict. The system effectively forced both parties to submit responsible offers or risk defeat. Dropping the MLBPA's by now routine demand for a shortened season and offering to accept another one-year joint-study committee on the reserve clause, Miller now pressed for industry to accept "final-offer" for unsigned big leaguers with at least two years' experience.[28]

In early February the owners made a counterproposal that reiterated their call for a three-year study committee on the reserve clause but embraced salary arbitration for unsigned veterans with three years or more tenure. One snag in the industry's offer, however, was the insistence that performers only be allowed to utilize the process every other year—a system the union logically suspected would lead to clubs "yo-yoing" players with alternating years of arbitration-induced raises and 20 percent pay cuts. When the two sides resumed direct negotiations in midmonth, however, it soon became clear that the ice had been broken. At the end of February 1973, a new Basic Agreement was reached. It did not include the goal Miller had initially sought—the modification of the reserve clause—but it also did not contain any prohibition of a union grievance test.[29]

Rather than a new reserve system, the 1973 Basic Agreement's centerpiece was the establishment of salary arbitration for unsigned players with two or more years' big-league service. The union and the clubs agreed to select a pool of salary arbitrators from lists provided by the American Arbitration Association, with a different individual assigned to each specific case. The clubs would be required to provide the MLBPA with comprehensive individual-level salary data for dissemination to agents—which also effectively guaranteed that big-league performers would no longer be kept in the dark on their comparative standing. Applicants' claims would be filed in the first ten days of February, with the arbitrators required to hold hearings within a week and to issue their verdicts within seventy-two hours. In addition to salary arbitration, the new pact also provided ten-year veterans with five years' continuous service with their current teams the right to nullify trades—a right Curt Flood would have qualified for had it existed at the time. Five-year men now could also contest demotions to the minors and instead receive an outright release from their clubs.[30]

The new Basic Agreement also extended the players' progress on a host of other fronts. The minimum salary immediately jumped to $15,000 and would reach $16,000 in 1975. World Series winner shares were boosted to a guaranteed minimum $20,000. Pension benefits for ten-year veterans who chose to start collecting at age fifty leaped $110 to $710 a month and rose to $1,813 for those with initial payments at age sixty-five. Five-year men's monthly pension installments starting at age sixty-five rose to $919. Players' eligibility for college scholarships was now extended to two years beyond the end of playing careers. Across the board the membership won higher preseason and road meal allowances, spring-training "Murphy money," and supplemental allowances; guaranteed single rooms on the road; bans of road double-headers on "getaway" days; and the power to approve or deny the rescheduling of postponed contests.[31]

Once more Miller's union had won impressive gains, and the sporting press took notice. Columnist Phil Pepe predicted that baseball's salary-arbitration system would be forever known as "Marvin's Law." The grudging Furman Bisher in the *Sporting News* concurred, writing of the players' chief, "His is the loudest voice in a game he invaded." Another reporter even suggested that given Miller's success at the bargaining table, he should attempt the same for such largely invisible employees as traveling club secretaries, publicity directors, and equipment men, who were not part of the players' pension. As a testament to Miller's power, when Houston manager Leo Durocher attempted to undermine a union briefing session on the new pact, first by forcing players to rise at 5:00 A.M. for a 165-mile ride to the meeting and then by having coaches hit fungoes into the assembled men—Miller's threat to hold up the ratification vote in re-taliation resulted in an NL fine of $250 on the skipper. Kansas City owner Ewing Kauffman subsequently invited the union's leader to the Royals' home opener. By the end of the season even Buzzie Bavasi was joking to his antagonist, "I feel slighted. . . . During the past year you and I have had no correspondence re player grievances." With his own tongue similarly planted in cheek, Miller replied, "We would not slight you under any circumstances. The only remedy I can suggest is that you confess to any and all violations of the Basic Agreement during the 1973 season, so that we can take appropriate action."[32]

Not all in Miller's life was as light-hearted. He continued to worry over the health of his son, who that spring had endured another one of many operations on his leg. He also continued to receive a steady stream of hostile fan letters at-tacking his members for refusing to sign autographs or in general being "greedy and grasping." Replying to one such diatribe from a junior-high principal, he blasted its author's "shoddy thinking" and counseled the man to "educate thy-self." During the 1973 season he also filed fresh arbitration grievances against nine different AL clubs that had tried to cut their active rosters to less than twenty-five men on the excuse they needed fewer pitchers given the league's new designated-hitter rule. And to Detroit general manager Jim Campbell, who had sounded off against a handful of Tigers players for taking part in an in-season charity softball game sponsored by the Muscular Dystrophy Fund, Miller fired back that their teammates, manager, and coaches had taken part in a nonchar-ity golf tournament without drawing similar criticism.[33]

Miller's biggest official disappointment that season, however, was that none of his men managed to provide a new grievance-arbitration test of the reserve clause. At the start of the campaign, five men had still not signed contracts—pitcher Stan Bahnsen, catcher Dick Billings, infielders Mike Andrews and Jerry Kenney, and outfielder Rick Reichardt. Diminishing the odds that any of them would be able to hold out for the entire season, however, was that none were marquee stars with the leverage to demand hefty contracts yet be too valuable to their respective teams to bench or release. Therefore it came as no surprise that by season's end all the potential candidates but one had inked new pacts, while lone holdout Kenney had been let go by his organization.

In the absence of a viable reserve clause challenge, Miller's main use of the grievance-arbitration system was once more the defense of rank-and-file players against arbitrary club discipline. On these matters he remained obsessively vigilant, befitting a man with his own memories of firings and blacklisting for reasons unrelated to performance. The most publicized case of 1973 involved

Cincinnati outfielder Bobby Tolan. Tolan had initially triggered run-ins with the club and general manager Bob Howsam—a man Miller unsparingly described as "a character out of Dickens"—by defying organization strictures against long hair, sideburns, moustaches, or beards. Near the end of the campaign an especially nasty confrontation ensued between the player and Reds official Sheldon Bender, which led to the latter's calling Tolan a "bastard" and threatening his wife. When the outfielder then refused to take part in pregame batting practice, the club suspended him for insubordination and "divisiveness." As Miller saw it, the imbroglio had been provoked by a combination of the club's outdated standards and the provocation by a representative of management. Not denying that Tolan had violated team rules, the Players Association still argued that the regulations and the clubs' behavior had been excessive and justified lifting Tolan's fine and suspension. Howsam did not help his organization's position at the grievance hearing by claiming that his efforts to reach Tolan to inform him of his reinstatement had failed because the outfielder had been "shacking up with a white woman." Although the arbitrator declined to order a formal apology as the union demanded, he did lift Tolan's penalties, and Cincinnati proceeded to trade the "troublemaker" to San Diego.[34]

Unfortunately for Miller, not all abuses of players lent themselves to intervention via the grievance-arbitration system. In an odd postscript to his aborted free agency, infielder Mike Andrews—who had been released by the White Sox and snatched up by Charley Finley's A's—subsequently committed two errors in a World Series game and was then abruptly dropped from Oakland's playoff roster for his transgressions. Finley incredibly insisted that the player was not being punished but was "disabled." A skeptical Bowie Kuhn then blocked Oakland's effort to fill Andrews's vacated spot for the remainder of the Series. Miller expressed sympathy at Andrews's plight but ruefully admitted, "There are certain things we simply can't cover in our Basic Agreement. . . . If the owner is vindictive . . . he can really ruin a guy." In December, longtime Cubs star Ron Santo—a "10/5 man" with the right to veto trades—blocked his being dispatched to the California Angels. His club responded by threatening to impose a 20 percent salary cut and demote him to the bench if he did not withdraw the objection. As an unsigned player, Santo had the right to appeal his pay impasse before an arbitrator, but neither he nor the union could prevent his enforced idleness. The frustrated Santo eventually gave in and was traded away. Miller related the case in testimony criticizing Congress for not having removed the industry's antitrust exemption, and he equated the "scandalous" inaction—which he attributed to District hopes of a major-league team—to Watergate.[35]

During the off-season of 1973–1974, however, the eyes of most baseball observers were on the inaugural round of salary arbitration. Despite Basic Agreement requirements, Miller had been forced to threaten NLRB action to get the clubs to release their salary data, and only rumors of a pending prounion ruling had prompted them to do so just before the start of hearings. Of all the clubs that had been unable to reach preemptive agreements with their unsigned players, the one with the greatest number of cases was Charley Finley's A's. Fully nine Oakland players—testament to the owner's deserved reputation for penury—went to arbitration. Miller personally had been witness to Finley's eccentricities. Once he had run into him in New York as both entered a seafood restaurant, Finley personally bearing his own fresh catch still in its fish paper for his meal. Thus it came as no surprise that at the salary hearings Finley was at his theatrical best, or worst, assuming the self-appointed role of a southern lawyer out of a Hollywood movie. Unfortunately, he managed to frequently contradict himself. On one day he argued against starter Ken Holtzman's claim on the grounds that his win totals were inflated by the A's fine bullpen, and the next he insisted that closer Rollie Fingers had overstated his value because of the excellence of such starters as Holtzman.[36]

Not surprisingly both Oakland pitchers won their cases, as did reliever Darold Knowles and third baseman Sal Bando. On the other hand, outfielder Joe Rudi and catcher/first baseman Gene Tenace lost their salary hearings. But the greatest public attention focused upon outfielder Reggie Jackson, who after being advised by Miller not to settle with the club at a low-ball figure was demanding a hefty $135,000. After two days' delay because of Jackson's agent's fear of flying, the slugger prevailed. When it was all done, both sides professed satisfaction with the industry's first joint experiment in outside pay arbitration. Total payrolls rose by 12 percent on average over the previous year, about double the previous year's rate. Twenty-five of fifty-four salary cases had been settled in advance of hearings, and of the remaining twenty-nine, management had won sixteen and the players thirteen. Though Finley's A's had "lost" an extra $87,000 in 1974 pay to his five winning players, a more typical team "score" was recorded by the Baltimore Orioles, who won two out of three hearings and ended up with a net $28,000 in higher payroll.[37]

Across the country from the unknowing Marvin Miller, son Peter had found himself literally next door to a dramatic story—the kidnapping of celebrity-heiress Patty Hearst. In marked contrast, Miller himself enjoyed a more relaxed preseason than normal, fitting in three sets of tennis a day between his spring-training visits and receiving individual instruction from a club pro. Once the regular season began, he even found himself voicing rare endorsement of a Bowie Kuhn action. With Hank Aaron on the verge of shattering Babe Ruth's career home-run record, Braves management clearly wanted the event to take place in front of a home crowd. But sitting Aaron down for the season-opening road series at the Reds would harm the visitors' chances of victory as well as deprive paying Cincinnati fans the opportunity to see the slugger in action. When Kuhn overruled the Braves' decision to sit Aaron and ordered the club to play its star against the Reds, Miller refused to question the ruling, agreeing that the matter seemed "definitely to concern the ethics of baseball" and thus "fell within the Commissioner's management prerogatives."[38]

The executive director had not declared a complete armistice with baseball management, for example taking on McDonald's magnate and Padres owner Ray Kroc for using his team's public address system to blast his squad's "stupid ball playing." But it was indication both of his temporary freedom from any ongoing negotiations and his itch for combat that he considered demanding an All-Star-break appearance before the owners in behalf of nonunion minor leaguers, whose individual contracts and pay could be nullified whenever they were demoted to a lower classification. On the whole, however, the season promised to play out peacefully for both Miller and his adversaries—unless a player finally succeeded in completing an option season unsigned and provided the union with a reserve clause test. But once again the playing campaign passed by without any performers "going the distance." At the start of the regular campaign seven MLBPA members remained unsigned, with the biggest names being Yankees' reliever Sparky Lyle and the maverick Bobby Tolan. But just two weeks before the regular season's end, New York locked up Lyle with a two-year pact. In the case of Tolan, who was seeking a raise that would boost his pay to six figures, it was John Gaherin—who privately disparaged the player as being incapable of "writing his name twice and spelling it the same"—who pleaded with Padres officials to meet the demand and make the case disappear. Just before a grievance case could be initiated, Ray Kroc ponied up a two-year deal at $100,000 per season and even threw in an interest-free loan for a home purchase in San Diego. Once again Miller could not fault the performer for accepting, but he had hoped differently given the union's stalwart defense of Tolan the previous year.[39]

That fall Miller found himself on the receiving end in a different controversy, pitting his membership against that of the umpires. Earlier in the season the union had secretly conducted a rating survey of the men in blue, with the umpires given summary grades ranging from poor to excellent. Although the Players Association had intended the results to remain confidential, reporters had pried them loose by season's end, leading the Major League Umpires Association and individual umpires to publicly denounce their player-union coworkers. But by the time the 1974 World Series had begun, the teapot tempest with the umpires was already overshadowed by a much bigger story. The fall classic would be the last of Oakland's run of three straight championships. A key to the dynasty was star right-hander Jim "Catfish" Hunter. Back in the spring, Hunter had agreed to a two-year pact with the A's paying $100,000 per campaign. To reduce his tax obligations, Hunter and attorney J. Carlton Cherry had stipulated that Finley pay half of the pitcher's annual salary in the form of an insurance-annuity contribution—a stratagem made possible because of the first Basic Agreement Marvin Miller had secured back in 1968. Whether stemming from cash-flow problems or a desire to claim the entire $100,000 as payroll for tax purposes, Finley failed to make the annuity payment. After repeated efforts to force compliance, Hunter's lawyer in September informed the union of the A's contract violation.[40]

Miller and his counsel Dick Moss immediately grasped the magnitude of the blunder. Finley had blatantly broken Hunter's deal and, if a grievance arbitrator reached the same conclusion, the explicit remedy stated in every performer's playing contract was its nullification and the granting of free agency. Moss then sent Finley the required formal ten-days' notice of violation under Section 7(a) of the Uniform Player's Contract. When the Oakland owner still failed to make good on his obligation within the ten-day window provided under baseball law, the union stated Catfish Hunter's contract to be null and void effective October 4, 1974. As the controversy continued to boil throughout the World Series, Finley foolishly continued to shrug it off as a simple misunderstanding. Under intense pressure from AL President Lee MacPhail and the PRC, who both recognized the peril that the Oakland magnate did not, Finley belatedly offered Hunter a $50,000 personal check to make the matter go away. The offer was equally too little and too late, given the expired deadline of the annuity payment and the practical matter that if Hunter accepted the check he, and not Finley, would be liable for the taxes owed.[41]

Once the World Series had ended in victory for Hunter and his teammates over the Dodgers, Miller and Moss jointly informed John Gaherin that the union was filing a formal grievance in behalf of the hurler. Miller was confident in Hunter's prospects of freedom, but he was thrown an unexpected curve when he learned a day before the hearing that the pitcher had hired Jerry Kapstein as an agent. To put it mildly, Miller held Kapstein in low professional regard.

The executive director bluntly ordered the unwelcome interloper to keep his mouth shut both at the grievance hearing and before the press. Nevertheless, after Hunter's first day before veteran arbitrator Peter Seitz, "someone" on the player's team confided to reporter Frank Dolson the opinion that Seitz would not grant the pitcher free agency. The assertion almost certainly had come from Kapstein, who had expressed similar uninformed opinions to Miller before the session. To Miller's satisfaction, attorney Cherry then notified Kapstein that his client would no longer require the agent's services.[42]

Kapstein's prophecy proved dead wrong. Arbitrator Seitz had tipped his hand on his likely verdict immediately after Finley's floundering testimony of the first day, whispering to Gaherin, "John, you know your client's a liar." On December 13, 1974, after the panel cast its predictable, two-to-one verdict, Seitz started to read his lengthy majority opinion ordering Finley to make the delinquent annuity payment while voiding Hunter's Oakland contract. At first, unfortunately, Seitz's public statement failed to make clear that by nullifying the pitcher's current pact the decision effectively made Hunter a free agent. Sensing that any ambiguity might give the clubs ammunition for their almost certain appeal, Miller quickly requested a short recess and huddled with Seitz. After the break, the arbitrator resumed reading his decision and included new wording making explicit Catfish Hunter's free agency.[43]

Baseball officialdom desperately scrambled to block the Hunter ruling, but without avail. Comparing the severity of Oakland's punishment with "a life sentence to a pickpocket," Bowie Kuhn ordered the other clubs not to extend contract offers to the pitcher. Miller retaliated that the central issue involved in the Hunter grievance did not fall within the commissioner's post-1970 intervention grounds, and accordingly he charged Kuhn with violating language in effect since that same Basic Agreement that barred collusive behavior on the part of either side to impede individual salary negotiations. On December 18 Kuhn backed down, and a parallel effort by Finley to overturn the Seitz decision through judicial appeal subsequently was rejected by the California Supreme Court.[44]

While Marvin and Terry Miller celebrated their thirty-fifth wedding anniversary, a different type of courtship now played out on Catfish Hunter's North Carolina farm. Miller had urged the pitcher not to jump at his first good offer and to reject any deal that did not at least double his salary. Within days of Kuhn's surrender, every major-league club except the A's and its Bay Area neighbor the Giants had made bids over the phone. Soon, team officials were hopping flights to see Hunter in person. The eventual winners in the Hunter sweepstakes were the New York Yankees. George Steinbrenner—head of a partnership group that had purchased the Yankees in early 1973 at a bargain-basement price of $10 million—now offered Hunter more than 35 percent that amount in total salary—$3.75 million spread out over five years, and dispatched the pitcher's original scout Clyde Kluttz to seal the deal. The Yankee pact also contained a $1 million signing bonus, a life-insurance policy in the same amount, $500,000 in additional deferred money, $50,000 in scholarships for Hunter's children, and $200,000 in attorney fees to Cherry.[45]

Weary but giddy, Catfish Hunter signed his new pact on New Year's Eve. For Marvin Miller, the scenario that had led to the Hunter deal had not been what he would have predicted. But because of his diligence, negotiation after negotiation, in erecting the structure of basic contractual and procedural rights for his members, and because of the combination of arrogance and ineptitude of a single owner, his players now knew just what they could expect for their services in a free and open marketplace. The Hunter signing had thrown the door wide open for some other now-enlightened performer to see to the end a grievance that directly challenged the owners' claim of a perpetual reserve. As the new year of 1975 dawned, the odds of that now happening had just improved dramatically.

Twelve

Emancipation

Despite the impressive gains recorded by Marvin Miller's MLBPA, in 1975 base-ball remained the only major professional sport in America that lacked a version of free agency for its performers. To be sure, in such cases as the NFL—where the "Rozelle rule" authorized the league's commissioner to determine compensation in the form of a player of "equal status" from the team signing a free agent—the right existed more in theory than fact. Every spring training since 1967, Miller had reiterated to his membership that according to his reading of the Uniform Player's Contract, paragraph 10(a), a club could only renew an un-signed performer's services "for a period of one year on the same terms" save a unilateral pay cut of 20 percent. Under the 1973 Basic Agreement, the union could not seek either direct modification or elimination of the reserve language via negotiation until the pact expired at the end of 1975. But nothing prevented the union from testing management's *interpretation* of the 10(a) language through grievance arbitration, so long as the litigating player remained unsigned through the end of his option year. Given the bonanza Catfish Hunter had just reaped as a result of his free agency from a successful grievance, it finally seemed likely that a new season would produce a direct reserve clause test.[1]

It was therefore no surprise that the 1975 season unfolded as prelude to a reserve-clause showdown. For Miller the year started in typical fashion, with him defending individual members from press attacks and arbitrary club discipline. In St. Petersburg, despite the fact local authorities had dropped the charges, an indecent-exposure accusation against Mets outfielder Cleon Jones led his organization to fine him $2,000 and pressure him into a humiliating public confession. Miller scathingly condemned the degrading spectacle. By August, the executive director was once more in his annual scrap with the *Sporting News'* Johnson Spink, this time over the editor's attacks on the salary-arbitration system. Defending the idea that a player could unilaterally demand a hearing but an owner could not similarly scuttle one, Miller retorted to Spink, "If you are hung up on 'one-way streets,' where is your editorial urging that a player should have the right to renew his contract for one additional year by simply notifying a club that he is doing so?"[2]

Providing a backdrop to Miller's renewed call to reform the reserve system was a strike that summer by the NFLPA, with the football union trumpeting the slogan, "Players demand freedom!" Miller observed the football players' action from the sidelines with interest, but he considered NFLPA leader Ed Garvey at best an inept amateur. Three years earlier in response to a CBS reporter, the executive director had indirectly slammed the football union by insisting that in contrast to its counterpart the MLBPA was "not in the nature of a joke." Given Miller's leftist roots, he viewed Garvey's postwar service as a CIA mole inside the pro-Communist World Federation of Trade Unionists as additional reason for contempt. He was hardly surprised, then, when barely three weeks into the strike 108 NFLPA players had already defected, with the number jumping to 250 just a week later. When the NFL owners on August 10 threatened to cancel further negotiations until the union dropped the "freedom issue," Garvey called a halt the next day.[3]

In major-league baseball, nine men had begun the 1975 regular season without an active contract. By summer, that list had been pared to just two. One of the remaining men, veteran pitcher Dave McNally, had actually already decided to retire back in June and had returned to his Ford dealership in Billings, Montana. Although under management's interpretation of the reserve clause the rights to a voluntarily retired or "inactive" player remained indefinitely with his last club, McNally's choice to cease playing apparently rendered moot his filing for free agency after the season. That seemingly left only Andy Messersmith. An Anaheim native and All-American at Cal-Berkeley, after four major-league seasons with the Angels he had been traded to the Dodgers, where he had blossomed into a star. Already a twenty-game winner twice over, by 1975 Messersmith was seeking the security of a multiyear contract with a trade-approval clause, but he soon had become embroiled in acrimonious negotiations with club executive Al Campanis. Relations between the two had deteriorated so much that Messersmith now insisted on conducting further dealings directly with Peter O'Malley.[4]

Andy Messersmith and Dave McNally (National Baseball Hall of
Fame Library, Cooperstown, N.Y.)

That season Messersmith enjoyed another outstanding year, but the Dodgers
fell far back in the pennant chase. Miller contacted the unsigned pitcher and the
two men exchanged information, with the union chief briefing the player on his
potential reserve clause–challenger status and the grievance-arbitration process,
and the hurler updating his leader on the stalled contract talks. Although the club
was offering Messersmith $115,000 for the next year, it blamed "organizational
philosophy" for its refusal to consider a multiyear deal or a no-trade clause. But
once the season concluded, Los Angeles abruptly made a retroactive offer of
$135,000 for the just-ended campaign plus three additional years at $150,000,
$170,000, and $220,000. Behind the sweetened new offer was John Gaherin, who
had insisted no owners allow a reserve clause case to reach grievance arbitration
or the courts. "Marvin can afford to lose a hundred times," he implored, "as long
as he wins once." Supported by PRC leader Ed Fitzgerald, Gaherin wanted to entice Miller back to the bargaining table with an offer of limited free agency for
the union's long-term vets. A ten-year threshold—perhaps as short as eight—he
thought might be enticing to the executive director and his membership.[5]

With the backing of NL president Feeney and a hard-line PRC majority, however, Dodger management refused to yield on the single issue of a no-trade

clause. League lawyers, still confident they would always win in court even if they lost before an arbitrator, backed them up. The aging Walter O'Malley then personally appealed to his pitcher's loyalty to his teammates and excused his inflexibility by insisting that both Feeney and the PRC had threatened retribution against the club if he defied them. Given O'Malley's power inside the baseball hierarchy, Miller for one did not buy the hand wringing. But he also found it equally hard to believe that any owner would be so foolish as to risk an arbitration loss on the reserve clause for the sake of any nonmonetary contract clause. He therefore decided that he needed a second litigant as insurance against the likelihood Messersmith might be bought off at the last minute.[6]

Revisiting the original list of 1975 nonsignees, Miller and Dick Moss kept returning to Dave McNally. The former four-time Baltimore twenty-game winner, as it happened, was still bitter at Montreal—his most recent employer—and owner John McHale. The previous off-season the Expos' magnate had promised the left-hander a two-year pact at $115,000 per season if he waived his "10/5" rights and allowed the Orioles to trade him. On the basis of his prospective owner's seemingly sincere offer, McNally had allowed himself to be moved, only to receive just a one-year offer from Montreal at $5,000 less. In addition to McNally's fury with McHale, Miller thought, the hurler also brought with him an additional plus as a plaintiff—that he had always been a loyal union activist, even serving at one time as Orioles team rep. To the executive director's relief, McNally required no special lobbying to persuade him to join in the litigation. "If you need me," he unhesitatingly replied, "I'm willing to help."[7]

Word quickly reached the PRC of McNally's reemergence in the reserve-clause challenge. Gaherin pleaded to McHale to fly to Montana, "get the bastard [McNally] drunk," and sign him. Following the Players Association's filing of formal notice to the affected clubs, league officials, and the commissioner, the Expos' owner tried just that. Over drinks in a Billings bar McHale offered McNally an immediate, nonrefundable $25,000 bonus if he would simply sign a contract carrying a $125,000 salary that would be paid in full if he merely remained in the organization until the start of next season. To his credit the pitcher refused to cooperate in the charade. He reported to Miller his remaining firm in the face of McHale's offer, citing as his reason that the club "wasn't honest with me last year." Given his intent ultimately to stay retired, he added that as a matter of integrity, "it wouldn't be right to take the money." Ironically, the failure of McHale's mission now relieved the pressure upon the Dodgers to strike a preemptive deal with Andy Messersmith. With at least one reserve clause case certain to be filed, the clubs then sought an injunction from federal judge

John Oliver. He rejected the owners' petition but agreed to hear any subsequent appeal that might result from the pending grievance-arbitration case.[8]

Baseball's top management now weighed two other steps of dubious legality intended to scuttle the union's case. Having inexplicably consented to Peter Seitz's 1974 appointment as the industry's grievance arbitrator given his support of a 1969 California court decision granting free agency to basketball's Rick Barry, the clubs had already compounded the earlier mistake by not unilaterally firing him immediately after the Hunter decision, as was their right under the Basic Agreement. But only now—after the Messersmith-McNally grievances had already been filed—the owners debated axing him. Miller, for his part, knew well that any such effort to fire Seitz after he had been assigned the cases would almost certainly be overturned by the courts. If such tactics were legitimized, the precedent would encourage routine firings of arbitrators in other industries, effectively destroying the grievance process altogether.[9]

Despite the gambit's dubious legality, ex-lawyer Kuhn forced two separate PRC votes on it, only to lose both times by a 6–1 margin. Only Montreal's McHale stood with him while the rest of the owners continued to place their faith in their lawyers and in Gaherin's counsel that "better the devil you know [Seitz] than the one you don't." The other last-ditch option considered then also required a "convenient" interpretation of baseball law. It called for Kuhn to claim his "best-interests-of-baseball" powers as justification for seizing the matter outright from the arbitrator and adjudicating it himself. When he proposed the second scenario to Gaherin, however, the latter argued against it on grounds it would poison upcoming Basic Agreement talks and provoke an eventual regular-season strike in 1976. Given the warning, the commissioner reluctantly opted against preempting Seitz.[10]

Shortly before Thanksgiving the Messersmith-McNally hearings began. They lasted three days, generating fully 842 pages of transcripts. Serving as the owners' chief advocate was the NL lawyer Lou Hoynes, who urged that the plaintiff's claims be rejected on both procedural and substantive grounds. The former argument was not likely to meet with Seitz's approval, because it questioned his authority to hear any case involving the reserve clause. In his second line of attack, Hoynes maintained that the language of 10(a) could not be interpreted in isolation from the multitudes of industry rules, policies, and precedents that together constituted the perpetual reserve system. If 10(a)'s traditional understanding was overturned, Hoynes warned, it would trigger mass chaos and cause baseball irreparable harm. On the hearings' second day, Commissioner Kuhn echoed these sentiments, only to be carved up in cross-examination by

Dick Moss. Nonetheless, Hoynes reiterated in his closing plea that Seitz uphold the status quo lest the baseball world be "turned upside down."[11]

In marked contrast to management, the union kept its focus on the actual language of paragraph 10(a). Moss noted that the wording differed in no meaningful way from the player contracts of other sports, including—in an obvious jog to Seitz's memory—the NBA, which held the reserve to be just a single-year option. Calling witnesses such as Jim Bouton—who read from the stand pertinent passages from *Ball Four*—the union also succeeded in turning owners' past statements on the issue against them. Most damning was a newspaper quote from Minnesota's Calvin Griffith in early 1974 in which he referred to holdout slugger Tony Oliva as a player the club would lose to another team if he played out his *one-year* reserve season. When the hearings then concluded, the two sides adjourned to their corners for nearly a month. In the interim Seitz dispatched an eight-page letter to both sides urging them to preempt a ruling by negotiating a solution. Keeping the threat of a player strike alive, Miller indicated a willingness to deal only if an acceptable agreement was reached by the start of spring training. For his part, having read the "tea leaves" of Seitz's request as a warning for his side to compromise or face the consequences, Gaherin similarly advocated negotiation to his bosses, but without avail.[12]

In the later description of Peter Seitz—a seventy-year-old academic type with a penchant for historical or literary allusions—the owners resembled no one more than "the French barons in the Twelfth Century" in their "stubborn and stupid" refusal to bargain a solution. Carrying the visage of a condemned man, Gaherin conveyed the clubs' rejection of negotiations to the arbitrator and told him to "turn the crank." On December 23, 1975, Seitz did just that. With Miller in concurrence, the arbitrator read aloud his finding in the 2–1 decision that granted free agency to Andy Messersmith and Dave McNally. The language of the reserve clause, the chairman declared, did limit a club's hold on an unsigned player to one year. Having waited out their option season, the two plaintiffs were now freed from their former teams. With the ink still wet on the panel's signatures, as soon as Seitz finished his presentation, Gaherin handed him a note informing him he had just been fired, adding, "I'm sorry, Peter."[13]

News of the decision raced through the press and the owner fraternity. Upon hearing the verdict at a holiday party, a stunned Calvin Griffith blurted out, "Oh, shit!" When asked for the reasoning behind his decision, the now-unemployed Seitz insisted that he was not a "new Abraham Lincoln freeing the slaves" but merely a person who "as a lawyer and an elderly arbitrator" had done his job in interpreting the player contract's language. As he had tried after the Hunter ruling, Commissioner Kuhn now issued a ban on club bids on the new free agents while the industry petitioned Judge Oliver for salvation. Miller and Moss countered by recruiting a local labor-law attorney well-acquainted with Oliver's Kansas City court to help block management's appeal—a young man with a brusque demeanor by the name of Donald Fehr. On February 4, 1976, District Judge Oliver upheld the Seitz ruling, and barely more than a month later the Eighth Circuit Court of Appeals followed suit. Especially meaningful for USWA veterans Miller and Dick Moss was that both decisions were anchored in the precedents established in the 1960 *Steelworkers Trilogy* rulings.[14]

So long as the Messersmith-McNally matter had remained in legal dispute, the owners had adamantly refused to negotiate any modification of the reserve clause. Despite realizing that, Miller had still laid out union bargaining proposals on the subject and on other Basic Agreement and pension issues as early as the 1975 All-Star break. Citing the clubs' fresh four-year World Series and All-Star Game broadcast deal, with its reported $5.3 million hike in rights fees, at that time he had called for a $3-million boost in the owners' annual pension contributions to roughly $9.5 million and a $3,500 raise in the minimum salary to $19,000. Subsequent industry poverty claims had then once more led him to demand documentation and to cite federal labor law that entitled the union to see industry financial records whenever it asserted an "inability to pay." To escape a pro-union NLRB judgment, Gaherin had been forced to retract his bosses' claims of penury. But the PRC still had insisted that the union's proposals would cost baseball an extra $10 million per year, and it had countered the union's demands with its own for give-backs that according to Miller would "turn the clock back twenty years." He publicly blamed a "hard-bitten minority" led by Finley and Howsam for the insulting counteroffer, which included elimination of cost-of-living adjustments for players' expense reimbursements, expansion in the number of exhibition games, reductions of team rosters, cuts to injured players' wages, the abolition of termination pay for released players, jettisoning both the "10/5" rule and the right of five-year men to contest demotions, language rendering Hunter-style contract voiding impossible in the future, elimination of limits on pay cuts, and the restoration of clubs' unilateral power to schedule day-night doubleheaders after night games.[15]

Behind this rhetorical back-and-forth, however, the central issue remained revising the reserve system. Signaling their intent to play hardball by locking players out of spring training and possibly even the regular season, the owners in November had given formal notice of termination of the Basic Agreement as well as its pension contracts. Miller had responded by affirming the union's support for playing the spring training tilts, but pointedly he had refused to make similar reassurances regarding the regular season. With the industry seemingly bent upon a "scorched earth" strategy unless the courts reversed the Seitz ruling, the union's obvious countermove had been to advise its members without 1976 contracts to stay unsigned, setting the stage for a free-agent flood after the coming season. To Miller privately this seemed a wiser strategy than a strike, especially if the owners chose to lift their lockout threat but continued to refuse any compromise on the reserve system. As in 1972, the pessimist in him questioned his men's staying power through a regular-season stoppage, for he still feared that many players did not fully grasp the immense stakes involved in the battle.[16]

Privately most owners, given their craving for stability, did not want to call the union's bluff and thereby risk massive free-agent losses. One of the few who did not shirk from the prospect, however, was Charley Finley, who expected to lose his stars anyway if the Seitz ruling stood. "Make 'em all free agents," he bellowed, predicting that the oversupply of talent would actually drive the market down. Miller feared Finley might well be right. Although as a staunch civil libertarian Miller embraced a player's unfettered choice of an employer in the abstract—"How do you turn down freedom?"—the economist inside him favored a limited reserve that gave the majority of big-leaguers a chance to change bosses at least once and preferably twice. Similar debates had arisen inside the Executive Board, with a libertarian minority of Mike Marshall and Jerry Reuss advocating unrestricted free agency and the majority favoring an integrated system that offered generous minimum salaries to entry-level players, salary arbitration for two-year men up to a negotiated free-agency threshold, and access to the open market for older veterans. They reasoned that limiting the yearly supply of free agents would result in more generous offers to each eligible individual, and that the contracts they garnered would peg player values more generally, thereby resulting in higher arbitration awards for the younger performers as well. In short, a well-thought-out modification of the reserve system, rather than its total elimination, would lift all boats.[17]

But what was the optimal service threshold for free agency? To paraphrase Goldilocks, how many years were "just right?" How high the bar was set would not only determine the proportion of the membership that achieved free agency at all, but also their chance to repeat. In his initial discussions with his reps at the 1975 All-Star break, Miller had suggested free agency after five years' professional tenure in the minors and the majors combined plus one additional option year. To make the proposal palatable to management and to prevent oversaturation of the market, he linked the proposal to a limit on the number of men any team could lose in any given year. He even declined to rule out nonmonetary compensation such as extra draft picks for teams that lost free agents. By the time 1976 dawned, the union's best confidential assumption was that when combined with an escalating minimum salary and the existence of salary arbitration, a free-agency eligibility standard of six big-league seasons, followed by a second "bite of the apple" after ten years' tenure, would maximize the membership's earnings. It was all speculation, for as Miller later conceded, "No one knew what the magic figure was." But such a standard would likely mean "first-bite" candidates would be men in their late twenties or early thirties— their prime—and thus in position to command top dollar. Younger players were being asked to postpone an early chance at freedom in favor of salary growth through arbitration, while the segment of the player force that managed to last six years to initial free agency stood a chance to earn freedom a second time when ten-year men.[18]

While the union awaited the start of actual bargaining and secretly pondered different free-agency scenarios, the PRC held fast behind a much more limited freedom while hoping vainly that the courts would render any greater compromise moot. Negotiator Gaherin's offer proposed restricting first-time free agency to ten-year veterans (nine contracted seasons plus an option year) whose teams had failed to extend offers of at least $30,000, with the number of suitors for each candidate restricted to eight clubs. As Reds catcher Johnny Bench pointedly noted, only 4 percent of current big leaguers would qualify under a ten-year threshold. Nevertheless, maverick Mike Marshall declared the offer a "big advance," forcing Miller privately to set him straight on the need for solidarity. Once the union rejected the owners' scheme, the clubs launched their lockout of Grapefruit and Cactus League camps for all but nonroster players. Miller then reiterated his advice to his unsigned men not to ink new pacts, and followed the gambit with the bluff of a rival circuit.[19]

Despite having earlier directed harsh language at Bowie Kuhn—whose criticism of the union had provoked Miller to claim the commissioner did not "know his ass from his elbow"—the executive director now called upon Kuhn to stop the lockout. Privately Miller was growing more worried about his members' resolve. One of the reps, Tom Seaver, had organized player workouts near spring training sites in contravention of the leadership's urgings. Workouts did keep teammates together and arguably made it easier for the union to communicate with them, but at the same time it lessened management concern that the longer its lockout the lengthier the subsequent delay in starting the regular season owing to players' need for reconditioning. In truth, both sides were scrambling to maintain solidarity. When White Sox owner Bill Veeck—allowed back into the fraternity after a long hiatus—publicly expressed his hopes for a compromise, a PRC fine threat quickly silenced him. Jim Palmer in turn defied Miller's "don't sign" edict and inked a multiyear pact with the Orioles. Reporters collected "let's play ball" quotes from antsy stars, causing Miller to explain again to his men that such expressions of impatience only encouraged owner stonewalling and served to delay a reasonable deal. Miller even received a phone call from an Astros player begging the union to yield to club demands and permit him to return to work. Not long after, however, he discovered that the ballplayer's entreaty had been delivered in the presence of club general manager Tal Smith. Smith's resort to such a tactic led Miller to threaten a grievance, forcing John Gaherin to order the Astros' executive to cease and desist.[20]

The union's hand grew significantly stronger with news of the appellate-court rejection of the owners' legal appeal, followed by their decision not to take the matter to the Supreme Court. When Miller contacted a happy Andy Messersmith, however, the hurler's follow-up question spoke volumes: "Great . . . so what do I do now?" Would the owners now make a better offer at the bargaining table? Would other clubs now make bids for the free-agent pitcher? Would the commissioner now change his mind and put a halt to the lockout? The PRC's most recent proposal had demanded that the 1976 free agents be treated no differently than those in subsequent years—in other words only nine-year men would be eligible even at the end of the current year and with a maximum of eight suitors apiece. Compensation in the form of both cash and a major-league player would be owed by teams that signed free agents to those losing them. A club that inked a player would have to pay its opposite number three times the amount of the new signee's most recent salary up to a $300,000 maximum, *plus* $5,000 multiplied by his new team's per-game attendance, *plus* still more money if the player ranked at the top of one or more of fourteen performance categories. The monetary compensation alone for a free agent changing organizations could add up to as much as $520,000. The PRC proposal also barred any team from signing a second free agent in the same year until all other major-league organizations had inked one, a third signee until competitors had signed two, and so on.[21]

Miller constantly emphasized to his men that "free agency with compensation is not free agency." But Gaherin was having some success in peeling away dissident players from support of the union stance. Partly for such internal reasons, while Miller rejected the PRC proposal, he did express a willingness to consider various service-time thresholds, higher compensation for clubs that lost free agents, and a cap on the number of teams eligible to bid on any individual performer. The union's formal counterproposal now called for free agency for six-year big-league veterans or players with nine seasons of total professional experience, and modest monetary compensation to teams that lost men, with the dollar amount shrinking with each year of a free agent's seniority. The two sides then agreed to conduct a joint meeting in a Tampa airport-hotel auditorium, but the session only produced name calling, with Reds' GM Howsam and his star Johnny Bench the featured combatants.[22]

Less than a week after the owners' court challenge had fizzled, rumors surfaced that the Braves, Angels, and possibly several other teams intended to bid for Andy Messersmith. Gaherin now made what he termed the PRC's "final" offer. It formally recognized the Messersmith-McNally precedent and granted free agency over the next two seasons to any big-leaguer who played out his option, but it suspended salary arbitration over the same period and called for its eventual elimination. After the two-year interval, it proposed limiting free agency to once per career for veterans with at least eight years' service time, with the pact not including specific anticollusion language. The PRC demanded union acceptance of the proposal by April 1. In the MLBPA's Executive Board session that followed, five reps supported acceptance but seventeen remained with Miller in opposition. Notifying Gaherin of the reps' rejection, the executive director declared, "If it is take it or leave it, they will leave it."[23]

Despite the reps' vote, Gaherin remained convinced that if the clubs stayed with their lockout strategy, the union would be pressing Miller by the end of April to fold. Once the players felt the full pain of lost incomes, mounting bills, and IRS obligations, he reasoned, the Players Association membership would force its leaders to accept industry's terms. Miller insisted that the owners were deluding themselves in that belief and consequently costing themselves millions in regular-season revenue when the players had indicated their willingness to return to work without a contract. But if Gaherin was right and either the union's reps or the rank and file did suddenly order Miller to cave, the executive director insisted that he would simply refuse and turn the face-off into a referendum on his leadership. If management was determined to make the current impasse a test of which side would blink first, Miller was determined that it would not be him.[24]

As had been the case on multiple previous occasions, it was management that ultimately cracked—in the person of Bowie Kuhn. Having never shared the PRC's enthusiasm for a lockout if it extended to the regular season, the commissioner once more found himself under intense pressure from the television networks and from key big-market owners—not just the Dodgers' O'Malley but Yankee newcomer George Steinbrenner as well—to preempt that scenario. From backchannel communications with pitcher Jim Kaat, Kuhn was convinced that the longer the lockout continued the more furious the players would become, making the successful conclusion of any deal all the more problematic. On March 17, the commissioner announced his decision to order reopening of spring camps. Furious at Kuhn's unilateral action, Gaherin and Ed Fitzgerald predicted that the players would never again take a management lockout threat seriously. The relieved Miller reciprocated Kuhn's edict by lifting his prior recommendation to members not to sign new individual contracts.[25]

With the leverage provided by the lockout gone, for a month and a half the PRC floundered to formulate a plan B. In the meantime Miller approached the Dodgers' Al Campanis and prevailed upon him to have his team's physician squash a "damaged-goods" whispering campaign designed to discourage bids on Andy Messersmith. In early April Steinbrenner's Yankees nearly signed the hurler, only to have Kuhn void the contract when it was disclosed that Messersmith's agent had agreed to the offer without either his client's direct knowledge or signature. The bizarre twist enabled flamboyant superstation-mogul Ted Turner to sweep in and sign the star to a $1.75 million multiyear pact with Atlanta. A fresh set of contract problems then surfaced when the union reviewed the deal and discovered Messersmith had signed away his right to repeat free agency via a "right of first refusal" clause. Citing Basic Agreement language that barred players from voluntarily forfeiting their due-process rights, Miller persuaded NL president Feeney to have the offending clause stricken from the contract.[26]

Miller's earlier fear that a huge inaugural class of free agents would cause the value of each to plummet subsided as more teams inked option-year stars to lucrative preemptive deals. By April 20 the number of potential free agents had already shrunk to seventy-six. The remaining list still contained such luminaries as Tom Seaver and Reggie Jackson. The Twins stood to lose up to twelve men, while Charley Finley's A's were staring at the likely departure of all their high-profile stars. With no bargaining sessions on tap for a month, Miller visited his squads to update them on the negotiation's player-benefit issues and to exhort them to stay solid. Speaking from notes scribbled on cards, he told them, "I am not on one side, management on the other, and players in the middle—we are together. . . . If a player doesn't understand that it is management's job to screw him—but in a manner that is not obvious—then that player will have to learn it the hard way. I work for you—and that is fundamental." Defending the union's free-agency stance, he insisted that "99 percent of our time has been spent dealing with owner demands for player concessions." He reiterated his plea that the men exercise caution in their public comments, noting that "free speech is everyone's right" but that they needed to be "aware of its effects—and possibility of misinterpretation."[27]

By May 22 Miller had visited twenty-two big-league teams, and only one player out of five hundred had openly expressed support for the owners' proposal. Despite the union's demonstration of unity, the executive director still frowned upon either an in-season strike or a postseason boycott to squeeze the owners further. One signal that the talks were entering a crucial phase now came from John Gaherin, who suggested each side "get rid of the lawyers" and scale down their bargaining teams. Miller agreed on the condition that he could keep right-hand-man Dick Moss. The pared-down sides then resumed daily bargaining at the Biltmore Hotel. Both sides were briefly diverted, however, by the antics of Charley Finley. Facing the prospect of his roster being dismantled, and seeking to cash in by moving his talent on his terms, Finley by then had already traded Reggie Jackson and Ken Holtzman to Baltimore for pitcher Mike Torrez and outfielder Don Baylor. But five other lame-duck A's stars remained—Rudi, Fingers, Tenace, Blue, and Bando—and the June 15 trade deadline loomed. Preferring to receive cash rather than inferior replacements as his leverage evaporated, Finley sold Rudi and Fingers to Boston and Blue to the Yankees for a total of $3.5 million.[28]

To the owner's dismay, Kuhn then unilaterally voided the sales, citing as his imperatives maintaining the integrity of the pennant races and protecting Oakland's fans. In truth, the commissioner was also doing O'Malley's bidding, for the Dodger patriarch resented efforts by potential rivals to stockpile Finley's talent while Los Angeles tried to maintain its payroll line. O'Malley also reasoned—and thus so did Kuhn—that if the commissioner's action was upheld in court, it could serve as precedent for future interventions to block free-agent signings. Miller feared that the latter was Kuhn's purpose, and it hardened his determination that the Basic Agreement under negotiation must include specific language barring any such interference. The executive director reasoned that if creating a precedent to nullify the free-agent marketplace was not Kuhn's focus, then all he was doing by voiding Finley's deals was vindictively preventing an owner who had tried to depose him the previous year from reaping the proceeds of his stars' sales. At a hearing attended by Miller and the direct parties to the deals, Kuhn reiterated his determination to block the transactions, leading Finley to call the commissioner a "village idiot" and then sue him unsuccessfully for $10 million. Miller's sharp criticism of Kuhn at the meeting drew rare praise from the maverick owner, who proclaimed to his unlikely new ally, "Where have you been all my life?"[29]

The Kuhn-Finley controversy brought to the forefront of the ongoing negotiations the issue of language preventing a commissioner from intervening in the free-agent market. It now joined two other bones of contention as final obstacles to a deal: whether or not the number of 1976 free agents should be capped and what service-time threshold should apply to future eligibles after the first year of free agency. With AL president Lee MacPhail acting as management draftsman, as the All-Star break neared, the two sides inched closer to a deal. Gaherin agreed to abandon the owners' demand to apply the same service-time requirement to the current year's crop as upon future claimants, and to Miller's amazement he also dropped the insistence on expensive compensation for teams losing talent. The two sides then agreed to a lower level of recompense in the form of an amateur draft pick from the signing organization. Gaherin even offered to lower the free-agency threshold in subsequent years to seven big-league seasons, and Miller raised his counterproposal from two years' tenure to four. In actuality, the union and its leader were setting the stage for achieving their preferred threshold by making it appear to be a concession. Miller and his reps had already privately examined the options and concluded that a five-year eligibility standard was actually preferable to four. If forced to choose between four- and six-year thresholds, they would opt for the latter as long as five-year men could still force trades and rule out undesirable suitors.[30]

When the owners then offered a six-year service requirement for free agency, union rep Phil Garner remembered that those on his side of the table struggled "not to grin and you're trying to say, 'Oh, Christ, this is going to kill us. Meanwhile, inside you're going, 'Yes! Yes! Yes!'" What still remained to be overcome, however, was Kuhn's opposition to any neutering of his power in the free-agency arena. As Gaherin put it bluntly, "The big political nut was Bowie's nuts." The PRC bargainer shuttled back and forth between Kuhn and the negotiators, and on July 12 a deal was concluded. The union Executive Board, convening at the All Star Game's Philadelphia host, the Bellevue-Stratford Hotel, approved the pact by a 23–1 margin, with only libertarian Mike Marshall dissenting. Upon completion of the balloting, Miller celebrated the fresh triumph with his wife and wartime-era friends of theirs in the City of Brotherly Love. Ironically, the Millers and the rest of the Bellevue-Stratford's All-Star guest list would barely escape being caught up in a medical tragedy. Mere weeks later, a mysterious ailment would sweep through an American Legion convention, causing several deaths and adding a new term to the lexicon: Legionnaire's disease.[31]

By August the full MLBPA membership had given overwhelming endorsement to the new pact. Gaherin faced a tougher sell, but after intense lobbying and with the assistance of MacPhail and Feeney, a narrower 17–7 victory margin was secured. The 1976 Basic Agreement boosted each club's annual pension contribution by $2 million and raised the minimum salary to $19,000 in 1976–1977 and $21,000 by 1978–1979. But it was the new free-agency system that understandably drew the greatest attention. All unsigned players who had played out their options in 1976 would now be released from their former clubs. In November teams would conduct a draft to assign bidding rights to specific men, with teams from each league picking alternatively from last place to first. Up to a dozen clubs could bid for the same player, and they along with the performer's prior team would constitute his suitors. Each organization that lost a free agent would receive compensation from the club signing the same player in the form of a selection in the following June's amateur draft. After 1976, free agency would be limited to those big-league performers with six years' accumulated service who had played out their option season. Once someone had availed of free agency, he could not do so again for another five seasons. Five-year men under contract could demand to be traded and designate as many as six clubs to which they could refuse to be dealt. If by the March following their fifth season their current teams had failed to trade them, they too became free agents. If a five-year man successfully exercised his trade option, however, he could not reassert that right until three more seasons had passed.[32]

In contract language that would prove especially significant a decade later, the Basic Agreement also contained an explicit ban on collusion by either side to violate the integrity of the free-agent marketplace. Ironically, in the 1976 negotiations the clubs proved as eager for the clause as the Players Association, remembering as they did the joint Koufax-Drysdale holdout of 1966 and fearing that either the union or players' agents with disproportionate numbers of clients would coordinate individual negotiations to maximize the overall take. Whether the comments represented face-saving or conviction, Lee MacPhail now declared that baseball's new free-agency process gave the industry "the best reserve system in sports." Commissioner Kuhn even extended nemesis Miller credit for having been "constructive" by not demanding "full Seitz," or unlimited free agency. Gaherin concurred, observing of his opposite number years later, "Marvin wasn't an anarchist."[33]

If industry spokesmen thought that kind words would soften Miller's zeal, however, his testimony to the House Select Committee on Professional Sports that same month dispelled such illusions. Miller blasted the commissioner for his voiding of the Finley sales, cautioned against similar mischief in the upcoming round of free-agent bidding, and demanded Congress act to lift the industry's antitrust exemption. Having initially reached agreement in the rough form of a memorandum of understanding rather than in formal contractual language, Miller and Moss also found themselves engaged up to the eve of the free-agent draft hammering out the precise wording. With both sides haggling over virtually every line, the delay led to another union-sponsored NLRB filing. Miller fired still another shot across management's bow in the form of an arbitration grievance citing the leagues' obligation to secure MLBPA permission before employing the designated hitter in the upcoming World Series. On one key matter, however, the two sides managed to agree—the choice of career arbitrator Alexander Porter to replace the fired Peter Seitz.[34]

By the draft's November deadline, twenty-two players remained eligible for free agency. Over seventeen rounds, thirteen men were picked by the maximum number of clubs, while only Cincinnati refused to take part entirely. By nightfall Boston had struck first, signing Minnesota reliever Bill Campbell to five years and a cumulative $1 million. Former A's Gene Tenace and Rollie Fingers ended up in San Diego, inking five- and six-year deals at a combined grand total of nearly $3.5 million. Gene Autry landed Don Baylor and Joe Rudi respectively for $1.6 million over six seasons and $2 million over five campaigns. Despite the age of thirty-two-year-old shortstop Bert Campaneris, Texas still shelled out one million dollars over five years for him. Starter Wayne Garland attracted an astounding *ten*-year deal from lowly Cleveland. But by far the greatest hoopla attended the courtship of the flamboyant Reggie Jackson. After being "hustled like a broad," as he put it, Jackson was signed by George Steinbrenner's Yankees for a reported $3 million over five seasons. Given the sudden proliferation of six-figure salaries, the outfielder posed the question freshly in the minds of many within baseball: "Do you think there will ever be a million-dollar ballplayer?"[35]

It was indeed a whole new world for the ballplayer, and for an industry whose relationship with its employees had been turned upside down. In little more than a decade Marvin Miller and the union he had saved from obscurity had erected an edifice of on-field player rights and financial gains that was the envy of virtually all Americans. The new free-agency system, taken together with the raises in minimum salaries and the outside arbitration enjoyed by baseball's two- to five-year men, boosted the major-league average in 1977 roughly 50 percent to

Miller briefing Phillies and Red Sox players at spring training 1977
(Barton Silverman/*New York Times*/Redux)

more than $76,000. Even with 1970s "stagflation" the membership's real wages rose nearly 40 percent. Nor was the salary jump a one-year phenomenon that quickly leveled off. In 1978 major-league pay would climb another 31 percent and by 1979 it would reach an average of $113,558—already more than double the major-league mean in the last year before free agency.[36]

Despite the owners' fears that free agency would usher in a new era of vagabond performers and diminished fan identification, the system in fact would not trigger wholesale migration. In the previous quarter-century under the old reserve system, the average yearly number of players lost by a club to its rivals had been 4.7. Now the figure actually fell slightly. What free agency did create—as Miller had intended—was leverage for the player and his agent in negotiations with his current team. Although the vast majority of eligibles of 1976–1978 who pursued the entire process to become free agents switched teams, far more men instead chose to ink preemptive deals, often lucrative multiyear pacts, with their old clubs. By the start of the new decade, nearly 40 percent of major-leaguers would possess the greater security of multiyear pacts, compared to just *one* such performer—Catfish Hunter—in 1975.[37]

Free-agent contracts in turn now set the standard in pay and contract length for salary-arbitration eligibles. Owners had initially imagined that the factor of seniority would dominate in arbitration rulings. But beginning with the 1975 award of $114,500 to young Atlanta star Ralph Garr, verdicts shattered that expectation. What turned out to matter most were not how many years a big-leaguer had played but how his statistical performance in the season just concluded compared with others at his position, and how much they were earning. The consequence, as in the free-agent marketplace, was a tendency for teams to avoid arbitration by locking up young performers to multiyear deals. In the minority of cases in which an arbitration hearing could not be avoided, the clubs actually won a majority of them. But because of the nature of best-offer arbitration, management "wins" still usually carried substantial pay raises. Even grievance arbitration, usually viewed as a means of protecting player workplace rights, buttressed the new salary structure by preventing owners from imposing subterranean salary cuts. In 1979, for example, the Braves would try to slash third-baseman Bob Horner's incentive-laden contract sixfold by claiming that such reductions to payments beyond base wages were not subject to the 20 percent maximum. A successful union grievance, however, would restore the Atlanta slugger's money.

The Horner case amply illustrated the linkage between formalized player rights and the attainment of financial security—a nexus that, because of his prior experience at the Steelworkers, Marvin Miller understood far better than his adversaries, the media, or the public. From the start he had carefully laid a foundation for the fullest measure of both protections *and* benefits. By the late 1970s, and based upon a negotiated formula of guaranteed minimums for the first three LCS games and the first four World Series tilts each year, individual shares to those on championship and runner-up squads rose to more than $28,000 and $22,000 respectively. LCS losers split the higher of a $160,000 pool or 25 percent of the gate, and divisional second- and third-place teams divided $128,000 or 9.5 percent and $32,000 or 2.5 percent. Players now enjoyed an owner-paid college scholarship plan, and the union's group-licensing income had climbed to $700,000. In a delicious irony for Miller, when Fleer sued the Topps monopoly in 1978 and named the union as a codefendant, the plaintiff's eventual victory actually produced a proliferation of separate card-company deals that generated the MLBPA $50 million per year within another decade.[38]

Among the other rights and privileges MLBPA members now enjoyed were protection from in-season job cuts through guaranteed twenty-five-man pre-September and postseason rosters and forty-man September squads; pay continuation during National Guard and military reserve obligations; free stadium parking; cost-of-living–adjusted spring training reimbursements; regular-season lodgings and meals; and mandatory first-class air travel. Major-leaguers did not have to report until March 1 each season, and married men with as little as sixty-days' big-league tenure and single men with three years' service could lodge outside the team's facilities. If an individual became disabled from a playing injury, he continued to draw meal allowances, housing, and salary, minus any government workman's compensation benefits. All-Star Game selectees were entitled to free travel to and from the classic and accommodations for them and their spouses or guests. Clubs could not "deport" demoted players to minor leagues outside the United States or Canada against their will, and if a performer was released or traded, his old club was required to provide him first-class air travel and moving expenses as well as lump-sum payments from $300 to $1,200 depending upon the number of time zones crossed. If a player was released in the exhibition season, he still drew thirty days' severance pay, and if he lasted into the regular season he won an entire year's sum.

The workplace rights and "shift rules" that now protected major-leaguers on the job were equally impressive. Association locals had the right in spring training to conduct meetings of guaranteed ninety-minute duration with ten days' notice. Clauses barring either management or union discrimination on the basis of race, religion, or creed were now standard in individual contracts and in the MLBPA constitution. Players claimed the power to negotiate the length of their season, and no performer could be forced to play winter ball without his permission. Big-leaguers could only be required to participate in two in-season exhibitions a year, and they were protected against split day-night doubleheaders and one-day road trips. Night games before doubleheader days, individual tilts before "getaway" days if the traveling team faced more than a 1½ -hour trip, and day games before 1 P.M. save for up to six mutually recognized holidays were likewise barred.

To protect his members' health and safety on the job, Miller had even seen to the establishment of a permanent joint-advisory committee that met at least once a year to make recommendations and could be called into session by any individual member. As for the clubs' traditional disciplinary prerogatives, teams could still initially hand out fines as before, but these or any other penalties were now subject to union grievances. In any event, such fines from management increasingly paled in comparison to the wages of those they tried to sanction. When in 1977 major-league umpires tried similarly to maintain longstanding powers to impose fines for on-field infractions, Miller demanded an automatic arbitrator review of every such case before any penalties could be administered. When the umpires complained, the executive director was unmoved, stating that if they did not like it they could move to Communist China.[39]

In provisions hearkening back to Steelworker 2(b) rights, Miller's efforts had even won his men a foot in the door toward the shared control of playing and scoring rules that directly impacted their on-field productivity and thus their pay. And in an unprecedented show of aggressiveness, under Miller the MLBPA even regularly demanded a say in franchise relocations, expansion decisions, and negotiation of national broadcasting rights. Absent winning union participation in the exercise of these traditionally management prerogatives, the Players Association asserted the right to reopen any existing collective-bargaining agreement upon ten days' advance notice to address the material impact of such industry decisions upon the membership.[40]

Taking stock of a decade of remarkable—and remarkably rapid—gains, the nearly sixty-year-old Miller was still driven by an undimmed class-consciousness and a natural competitiveness to strive for still more progress on the minimum salary, scheduling and safety issues, and above all in the strange new world of free agency, the oversight of an agent profession riddled with abuses. Despite his advancing age he was determined to press ahead on these and other matters before making way for a successor. But though he did not yet grasp it, from this point he and his union would find themselves in the less inspiring yet necessary position of playing defense, rather than offense. It was a testament to how far he had brought the Players Association—but also because of it how much more was now at risk from an industry stinging from its repeated humiliations.

Thirteen

Holding the Line

After more than a decade at the helm of the Players Association, Marvin Miller was by 1977 arguably the most recognizable labor leader in America. As he briskly strode the forty-five-minute walk to his office from the $40,000-a-year Upper East Side apartment he now called home, he found himself the frequent object of comments from fellow pedestrians offering their opinions on the national pastime. In recognition of his efforts on the membership's behalf, his union had voted him raises placing his compensation package at nearly $200,000 and setting up an $185,000 retirement annuity that put his pension on par with theirs. As an indication of the grudging respect that even those on the other side of the baseball labor-management divide held toward him, an anonymous Mets official suggested that when Miller retired as MLBPA leader, he should switch sides and become commissioner to "help even things up." But with the union's successes now came fresh challenges. The material progress that the players had achieved in so short a time now threatened to distort their perspective and undermine their solidarity. Though stars savored lucrative multiyear contracts, their inexperience in handling their newfound wealth fed dangerous tendencies to self-indulgence and greater vulnerability to predators.[1]

One source of such problems was the uneven quality of player agents. As early as the winter of 1976–1977 Miller had given voice to his frustrations at the often unprofessional behavior of these personal representatives, revealing in the process his special contempt of Jerry Kapstein. In one free-agency year alone Kapstein had raked in more money for just a few days' work than any single client of his had earned for an entire season. Demonstrating ignorance or coziness toward management, the agent had also agreed to contracts for stars Carlton Fisk, Fred Lynn, and Rick Burleson that had contained "right-of-first-refusal" clauses negating their repeat free-agency rights. Miller had then been forced to intervene to prevent the unwitting trio from handing away hard-won rights the union had secured for them.[2]

Some reporters attributed Miller's outrage toward agent malfeasance to personal jealousy that his players might be finding alternate recipients of their appreciation. Whether this held true or not—and Miller did come across as unduly sensitive to the affection shown some agents by their clients—he was still justified in his criticism of the agent profession. Employment as a representative of a major-leaguer only required that you declare yourself one. No experience even as a theatrical or Hollywood agent was necessary. In some cases representatives charged rates approaching 10 percent for doing nothing more than taking credit for a beginner's minimum salary. Other fly-by-night operators exacted percentages of clients' off-field incomes as well as their baseball wages, or tried to entice players into self-interested investment schemes. Some representatives charged tax-preparation fees far above standard rates, only to fail to file returns and thereby make their clients vulnerable to IRS prosecution. Still other agents not only maintained close relationships with clubs but actually received pay from them.[3]

Despite the agent profession's glaring shortcomings, however, Miller had little success in rallying the membership behind reform. The union did offer training classes and briefings to educate agents on the details of its collective-bargaining agreements, but few of them bothered to attend. At a January 1977 news conference, Miller and Dick Moss jointly blasted Kapstein and those like him who in their judgment were "ripping off" clients. But the rank and file turned a deaf ear to their pleas to establish strict agent-licensing requirements. In the short run, all that Miller gained from his campaign was a ban on the clubs' practice of making end runs around players by making direct payments to agents. It would be more than a decade later, after Miller's departure and during the collusion scandal of the late 1980s, that the Players Association would finally adopt an agent-certification program.[4]

If Miller's members now enjoyed something close to full market value for the first time, the heightened stakes of their performances and the greater opportunities for self-indulgence also led to the growing abuse of both performance-related and recreational drugs. Alongside baseball's traditional scourge of alcoholism, the use of amphetamines, or "uppers," by players had become so commonplace that jars full of pep pills were readily accessible inside clubhouses. Miller personally was skeptical of the substances' actual value to performers, suspecting that the energy boosts claimed were more in players' imaginations than in their bodies. But he opted to look the other way, reasoning that if neither the grassroots membership nor the reps viewed the matter as serious, he would not give it such visibility that it could provide the owners with public-relations ammunition against the union.[5]

As for the issue of ballplayers' indulgence in recreational drugs, Bowie Kuhn had launched a largely meaningless drug-education campaign in 1971 and in 1978 had supplemented it with an alcohol-information drive featuring recovering alcoholic and former Dodger-great Don Newcombe. But until the late 1970s baseball had largely avoided the NFL's embarrassments over marijuana, cocaine, and even heroin use. Once more Miller drew the conclusion that because the membership did not perceive the use of illegal recreational drugs as a major problem, he would not publicly indicate otherwise. He reasoned that on this subject as much as any other, it was up to the players to set the union's agenda. Indicative of an acute sensitivity dating back to the McCarthy era to anything smacking of witch-hunts or invasions of privacy of belief or behavior, Miller adamantly insisted that it was not the job of a union to police its members' off-field lives.[6]

Viewed from any angle, by the late 1970s Miller's MLBPA had achieved more than anyone could have imagined just a few short years back. Not surprisingly such a speedy attainment by big-league ballplayers of their wildest material dreams encouraged them to think more in terms of defending existing gains than striking out in fresh directions. Because their executive director justifiably remained unconvinced that the owners had accepted the industry's changed power balance and the end of its unchallenged paternalism, he did little to challenge his members' "conservative" thinking. The rank and file had little interest, for example, in expanding their organization's reach to encompass minor leaguers, merging with nonplayer employee groups in professional baseball, or affiliating with the professional athletes of other sports. Baseball's minor leaguers clearly needed a comparable form of representation, making less than $2,500 per month at the Triple-A level and less than $600 at entry levels. To be fair, little reciprocal interest was shown by the minor leaguers themselves, whether because of youthful naiveté, the belief in and reality of geographic and upward mobility that inhibited solidarity, or the dream of achieving deferred financial bonanzas once in the majors. In 1978 the MLBPA did survey major-league coaches and trainers to probe interest in union representation beyond the pension, but the idea went nowhere. Instead the players' union remained what it had become thanks in large measure to Marvin Miller—an AFL-style craft union representing top-line baseball performers and focused upon securing and protecting their jobs, wages, benefits, and due-process rights. Its visibility and clout meant that its actions were not irrelevant to the professional lives of other athletes, but its influence remained primarily in its example.[7]

In major-league baseball's revamped labor economy, the Players Association had suddenly switched and become the conservator of the system, while management now constituted the "bomb-thrower." As both sides looked to their next round of combat, the battle now would include a new participant at Miller's side. Dick Moss, the union's legal tactician since 1967, stepped down to quickly establish his own lucrative agent practice. The departure stung Miller even though he shared Moss's contempt for the existing state of the agent profession and the conviction that its quality be upgraded. But despite his colleague's insistence that he had not decided to become an agent before opting to leave the union, Miller did not believe Moss, and uncharitably implied that by leaving for greener pastures the former counsel was failing to demonstrate the willingness to sacrifice of a true trade unionist. When Moss was subsequently quoted in an article stating, "When I won the free agent [Messersmith-McNally] case," a resentful Miller responded by letter to a third party with bitterness, "A man risks damaging his vertebra twisting around in that fashion to pat himself on the back." Highlighting the roles of Curt Flood, other lawyers, the MLBPA membership and reps, and "even a small contribution by the writer which had a little something to do with reforming the reserve rules," he added sardonically, "Perhaps my memory is playing tricks."[8]

Taking Moss's place now beside Miller was a much younger man—Don Fehr. Fehr had earned his spurs by successfully thwarting the owners' court challenge of the Seitz decision. When Miller and Moss had jointly reviewed candidate applications for the latter's successor, it was to Fehr they kept returning, not just because of his already demonstrated competence and capacity for hard work, but—just as important—his commitment to the union's philosophy. On the negative side, Fehr's relative greenness—he was not yet thirty years old—and taciturn personality in comparison to the gregarious Moss meant that at least in the short run, Miller would have to shoulder a greater share of the role of the Players Association's public face.[9]

For their part, the owners had also retained a new representative, choosing to jettison their negotiator of a decade John Gaherin in favor of a more confrontational alternative. What the clubs desperately wanted, ironically, was their own Marvin Miller—a professional who would be a pit bull at the bargaining table yet effective in dealing with the media. To the players' executive director, however, the industry's decision to fire Gaherin was a disturbing omen, and the word of his successor made it more so. As Miller would relate to Gaherin after both of them had retired, "on balance" he had enjoyed his time representing the players. However—and only partly in praise of his one-time adversary— Miller drew a sharp distinction between the "pre-1978" and "post-1978" periods, explaining, "The characteristics of the earlier period include professionalism and integrity. The latter period would not fare that well using the same criteria." A primary reason for his assessment was Ray Grebey.[10]

C. Raymond Grebey—Gaherin's successor as PRC negotiator—was selected by the owners out of a trio of finalists generated by an executive-search firm. Ironically, he was not seen by his prospective bosses as the most aggressively antiunion of the lot. That distinction belonged to Jack Donlon, who was subsequently retained by the NFL and would ruthlessly wage labor war on players through the 1980s. But baseball's choice, formerly the number-two man in labor relations at General Electric, came from a company with its own hardball philosophy, one forged by the infamous Lemuel Boulware. A Kenyon College product who sought to project the casual cultivation of an academic don down to his pipe and tweed jacket, Grebey seemed the right adversary to a man who had beaten the owners repeatedly and then rubbed their noses in it. As Lou Hoynes recalled, "He [Grebey] was intelligent, subtle, and sophisticated. . . . We thought he'd be a good match for Marvin." But Grebey's appearance did not hide a streak of arrogance toward those with whom he dealt, whether on his side or the opposition—a characteristic that would eventually poison his relationship not just with Miller but his own bosses. As one example of the negotiator's hubris, writer Lee Lowenfish later recalled a 1980 comment in which Grebey insulted the MLBPA membership by asserting, "You know, the players don't really have any long-term interest in the game. They are really like long-distance truck drivers."[11]

From the start the relationship between Marvin Miller and Ray Grebey would go badly even for one structured to be adversarial. Union research into the new antagonist revealed a man with a reputation not just for bare-knuckle tactics but bad faith and a loathing for surprises. MLBPA activist Mark Belanger relayed his mother's direct memories of Grebey's divisive role in a 102-day standoff in 1969 at her GE plant in Pittsfield, Massachusetts. When the departing John Gaherin, acting as chaperon, introduced his successor to Miller, the newcomer pompously pronounced, "My door is always open." After surreptitiously glancing sideways to see Gaherin unsuccessfully suppressing a laugh, Miller replied with tongue firmly in cheek, "That's good, because *my* door is always open, too. . . . We'll talk to each other with our doors open." In front of the media, Grebey initially offered kind words, insisting of the executive director, "I like the guy." Describing his new adversary as "a tough SOB," the owners' new man still maintained that Miller was the kind of opponent he could still "have a drink with" after a tough bargaining session.[12]

As discouraging an omen for labor peace as the Grebey hire was the departure of Walter O'Malley, the former Dodger owner and NL power broker now dying of throat cancer. Without his influence over Commissioner Kuhn, owner hardliners had one fewer obstacle to maintaining uncompromising stances. Led by Calvin Griffith, Bob Howsam, Gussie Busch, Boston's Haywood Sullivan, and Detroit's Jim Campbell, management officials issued dire predictions of a financial train-wreck unless free-agency spending was checked. It was true that some low-payroll organizations, most notably the A's and Twins, were suffering competitive woes. But relative to inflation, major-league baseball ticket prices were lower than in the early 1970s, and fans were attending in greater numbers. While the average player salary had risen from under $45,000 to over $113,000 in just four years, gate receipts had climbed 60 percent and television revenue a whopping 355 percent since the start of the decade. AL franchise expansion by two teams had generated rivals even more cash in the form of entry fees. Competitive on-field balance was actually better with free agency. Big-league profits had risen by $10 million in less than five years and the sale price of a single franchise had reached $13 million. With player salaries but 28 percent of club revenues, a rational basis for concern still seemed lacking.[13]

What lay at the heart of owner angst was not verifiable economic or competitive crisis, but rather the collapse of what had been their paternal control of their industry. That lack of prior dominance was on sharp display in baseball's new labor economics, but not just there. Illustrative of the broader erosion of management's prerogatives was the spring 1979 duel of memos between Chub Feeney and Miller over the NL's planned regulation of player observance of the national anthem. The proposed new strictures called for performers and coaches alike to "stand at attention, feet together, head steady, facing the flag with cap in right hand placed over the heart and left arm extended downward along the left pants leg." Relishing the chance to tweak management over even such a minor matter, Miller replied, "As with many regulations and directions, the omission of exceptions can lead to problems of administration and enforcement." Perhaps thinking of his own infirmity, he then cited scenarios in which a temporary or permanent physical restriction could cause a violation. Miller concluded by offering the friendly advice, "How about trying a second draft?"[14]

While small-scale skirmishes came and went, the union and the PRC geared up for what both sides anticipated as a bitter showdown over the infant free-agency system. The owners voted to amass a $3.5 million strike fund through a 2 percent withdrawal from the previous year's gate receipts and secured strike insurance from Lloyds of London that would pay the clubs a total of $1 million per day in the event of a regular-season stoppage of more than two weeks. At Grebey's insistence, the owners also self-imposed a "gag rule" with fines up to a half-million dollars assessed to those who undermined solidarity by "pissing at each other in public." As part of the union's own mobilization, Miller had persuaded his Executive Board to set aside $1 million from licensing revenues as an emergency fund. As he told the membership during his spring 1979 squad tour, "The frontal attack I anticipate from the owners will be in the area of the reserve rules—to get them back as close as possible to where they were prior to the 1976 Agreement—prior to the Messersmith-McNally arbitration decision." He added, "I think we can expect them [the owners] to put their emphasis on demanding that the Club which a free agent leaves must receive large compensation from the Club which signs that player." Ending with a rhetorical call to arms, he proclaimed, "We *cannot* put players into a position of being ransomed—we cannot require players to ransom their own bodies—their own talent."[15]

Firm confirmation of Miller's fears came only after the season, at a sit-down over drinks with Bowie Kuhn at the 21 Club. The commissioner had sought out the opportunity to lobby the union chief in advance of Basic Agreement talks, and he now used the clubs' claims of looming payroll crisis to emphasize the industry's "need" for a bargaining victory. To Miller it smacked of an inappropriate request that he "throw" the upcoming negotiations. In his own recollection of the conversation, Kuhn quoted the executive director as having bluntly responded, "Over my dead body." Miller, who prided himself on his verbal self-control, denied having employed the coarse phrasing but admitted to the substance of his reply. The union would not accept givebacks, especially not on a free-agency system the players had struggled to achieve and whose purported harm had not been shown. In one respect Kuhn's message had gotten through, however. The owners were prepared to go to war over free agency. Miller related the exchange to Don Fehr and then added, "We're in for a hell of a fight."[16]

In late October the PRC delivered the expected notice of intent to terminate the Basic Agreement at the end of 1979. Miller eyed the pending showdown as probably his last before retirement, and as such he was all the more determined

Bowie Kuhn and Miller (source unknown/
Tamiment Library, NYU)

not to yield an inch. Despite Grebey's history at GE, the union chief did not believe that the owners' extreme militancy stemmed primarily from their new negotiator's arm twisting but rather from their accumulated frustrations at the hands of the players. As for industry assertions of hardship, he refused to grant them any credence whatsoever, sarcastically equating them with claims from the Flat Earth Society. Whatever factors had inspired the clubs' militancy, an additional contributing element was the fact that in the broader economic arena, in marked contrast to major-league baseball, the power of organized labor was eroding. If the players managed to prevail this time, they would be bucking a national trend of union bargaining losses and givebacks that included the UAW's forfeiture of $642 million in benefits after the Chrysler bankruptcy and bailout.[17]

As the year-end deadline approached, Miller laid out the players' demands. They included lowering free-agency eligibility to four years' service, a pension boost proportionate to the owners' new $47.5 million annual television deal, a minimum-salary hike to $40,000 with automatic cost-of-living adjustments, and elimination of the five-year waiting period for repeat free agency. Grebey's more radical counterproposals included the scrapping of salary arbitration, a demand for a pay scale upon players with less than six years' tenure, and increased direct compensation for clubs losing free agents in the form of replacement major-leaguers from signing teams. On its face the proposed salary scale for younger performers was a rollback, because it called for a cap on first-year men's pay of $25,200 and a maximum of $187,900 for a sixth-year player. Miller pointed out that Boston slugger Jim Rice already earned $700,000 despite not having yet reached free-agent eligibility. Were the owners seriously suggesting that Rice endure a pay cut? Given the union's certain rejection of the salary-scale and pay-arbitration proposals, Grebey then demanded modifications to the arbitration system requiring seniority to be factored into pay awards. Hoping to peel away rookies' support for the union, Grebey also offered to grant pension eligibility to anyone with any big-league experience at all and to boost minimum salaries to $25,000 in the first two years and $28,500 over the last two of a proposed four-year Basic Agreement deal.[18]

Remaining the core of the PRC agenda, however, was the owners' demand for "meaningful compensation" directly from teams that signed free agents to those that lost them. In management's scheme, any club losing a "ranking" free agent—one drafted by the maximum of eight suitors—would be assured compensation in the form of a major-leaguer from the signing team. Also, each club that inked a free agent could only "protect" fifteen players on its twenty-five-man active roster. Grebey disavowed any intention of gutting free agency, and he urged the skeptical player reps to "Trust me." He insisted that under the plan only seven free agents each in 1978 and 1979 would have required direct player compensation, and only three more in 1980. Miller was openly dismissive of his opposite-number's claims. To him it defied credibility that poverty-pleading owners would demand this particular boost in free-agent compensation only to assert a negligible impact. He noted that under the existing system, which provided compensation in the form of amateur draft picks, only twenty of 149 first- and second-round June draftees from the past three years had yet reached the majors. As a result, the current compensation had not created a meaningful drag on free-agent offers. But if a club thinking of bidding on a free agent suddenly faced the loss of an established player, such a greater penalty would effectively convert free agency into a trade and seriously deter offers. Not above resorting to extreme language to express his disdain at the PRC proposal, Miller alluded to the ongoing crisis with Iran to describe it as a form of management "taking hostages."[19]

As expected, the MLBPA Executive Board then set a strike date for April 1, 1980. In response the PRC dropped the salary-scale trial balloon. But the industry persisted in poor-mouthing despite the risk such statements posed of triggering an NLRB complaint. In one instance, Grebey personally appeared on *60 Minutes* to insist that twenty-one of the twenty-six clubs were losing money. By the end of March, the two sides had agreed to nonbinding arbitration by FMCS deputy director Kenneth Moffett, and Miller accordingly offered to lift the union's strike threat for the time being if the owners agreed to bargain in good faith all outstanding matters save for the issue of free-agent compensation. The latter issue would be pushed down the road via creation of a two-year joint-study committee. When the PRC rejected his offer, Miller and his reps endorsed "shock therapy," in the form of a strike limited to the remaining spring games. If no agreement had been reached by May 22, however, the players would reinitiate a walkout beginning the next day. The rank and file then approved the revised deadline by a 967–1 vote, with only the Twins' Jerry Terrell in opposition.[20]

With each side digging in, bargaining now devolved into dueling press conferences. Yielding to the reality that nothing would happen until the revised strike deadline was imminent, mediator Moffett proposed that negotiating sessions be suspended until May 6. When they resumed, the PRC still refused to move off its demand for direct player compensation. Although Grebey agreed to add performance measures as additional criteria in determining which players were "Type-A" free agents, the performance minimum proposed was so low that half of each year's free-agent crop would have met the standard. A furious Miller scolded, "They started out giving us Rod Carew and Vida Blue as examples. . . . Now their eleventh-hour proposal includes hitters with .222 averages and pitchers with earned-run averages over six!" The union response demanded a far more selective performance threshold for players requiring the higher compensation and an "indirect" method of recompense from a big-league–wide pool of players left over after teams had shielded virtually all of their active rosters.[21]

As the strike deadline neared, the union sought to project unshakeable resolve. The Yankees' Rudy May insisted that the membership's support for Miller was unwavering given what he had accomplished for them, claiming, "There's going to be a whole generation of ballplayers' sons who grew up with the middle name Marvin." Kansas City Royals star George Brett warned potential scabs that they would be "ducking pitches" the rest of their careers if they broke ranks. Privately, Miller was concerned. Reports indicated that as many as thirteen Boston players were balking. Adding to his uncertainty, the current MLBPA membership included a generation of performers who had not been around during the union's 1972 strike. When Miller asked Fehr for his opinion on whether the membership would endure an extended stoppage, his subordinate hesitated before replying in the affirmative. Miller's reaction gave voice to his own doubts: "We'd better be right."[22]

On May 18 Moffett suspended the talks again for twenty-four hours. Behind the scenes, management unity had finally begun to crack. Mavericks Edward Bennett Williams of Baltimore, Texas's Eddie Chiles, and New York's Steinbrenner were lobbying Commissioner Kuhn to intervene and forestall a strike. Kuhn declined, but he did expand the PRC delegation and personally attended the next bargaining session. When the May 22 deadline arrived, the owners tried a final bluff. Grebey and company arrived an hour late for the 10 A.M. session, then Chub Feeney blasted Miller over the news that Dodger players had been instructed not to board the team airplane for their next series. After the executive director explained that such directives were standard procedure for carrying out a strike on schedule, he turned to Fehr, issued his trademark audible sigh, and whispered, "They never believe it." When the parties returned after lunch, it soon became clear that the PRC's posture had changed. Both sides jettisoned their lawyers and note takers and relocated first to Grebey's room via freight elevator and then Moffett's suite to throw off the press. Behind a closed bedroom door, Miller and Grebey sketched out a one-year interim deal while the mediator and the remaining others played cards in the next room.[23]

Two stopgap pacts called for raises in the minimum salary to $35,000 by 1984 and pension contributions of $15.5 million. Free-agent compensation was assigned to a joint-study committee, with a final report due at year's end. If no subsequent agreement was reached by February 19, 1981, the owners would have the unilateral power to impose their latest bargaining proposal, which, unless contested by the union, would take effect with the winter 1981–1982 free-agent class. That would mean a requirement of direct compensation from teams inking a Type-A free agent—now being defined as a player in the top third among hitters or pitchers—in the form of players not among the signing teams' fifteen top men. To sign a Type-B free agent—one ranking between the top third and top half of major leaguers—a club could shield its top eighteen roster members. To prevent the PRC scheme from taking effect, the union would need to declare its formal objection by March 1, 1981, to be followed by a strike no later than June 1 to force a negotiated alternative.[24]

The MLBPA rank and file ratified the pension agreement by 749–11 and did likewise with the stopgap Basic Agreement by a slightly narrower 619–22. Miller insisted that the one-year deferment of the owners' compensation proposal was no victory for either side, pointing out that it guaranteed the winter 1980–1981 class would still operate under the old system. But Grebey insisted on describing the interim deal as a union giveback and wasted no time issuing a press release to that effect. Commissioner Kuhn showed scarcely more restraint, appearing on *Today* to take credit for having saved the season. A defensive Miller lashed out at Grebey's victory claims as "horribly inaccurate." Behind the scenes, Miller and Fehr reassured themselves with the thought that the industry's gloating would further fire up reps who already loathed Grebey from personal experience at the bargaining table. At a fiftieth birthday party for Ken Moffett hosted by Ed Williams and attended by Orioles rep Doug DeCinces, the latter made the point by handing the mediator a T-shirt mocking a familiar Grebey line, "Trust Me."[25]

The rest of 1980 largely served as a prelude to a renewed showdown, although unrelated controversies occasionally erupted. Late in the season, airport authorities in Toronto found small quantities of marijuana, hashish, and cocaine in the luggage of pitcher Ferguson Jenkins. Once the story broke, Kuhn ordered Jenkins to his office and demanded a sworn confession, which on counsel's advice, the Canadian refused to provide. The commissioner then suspended him, and the union filed a grievance seeking to overturn the ruling. Miller even suggested that the drugs had been planted in Jenkins's bags considering the items had been sitting unattended for hours before being searched by airport security. On September 22, arbitrator Raymond Goetz sided with the union and reversed the suspension. Jenkins was subsequently found guilty in a Canadian court, only to have the trial judge then void his conviction.[26]

While Miller and Grebey prepared for round two over meaningful compensation, the joint-study committee met and—as expected—accomplished nothing. Dueling reports followed, with the union's version drafted by Don Fehr discounting the whole idea that players were assets to be brokered rather than free actors entitled to pursue optimal employment without strings attached. The majors' big-spending clubs then engaged in a final binge of free-agent signing before the imposition of the PRC's compensation formula. Five out of fourteen men garnered offers of more than a half-million dollars per year, topped by Dave Winfield's astounding ten-year pact with the Yankees. Revealing his new owner's expectations, however, the contract did not guarantee the $1.4 million for 1981 in the event of a strike. Having extended the lordly sum, with typical chutzpah Steinbrenner dared Miller to lead his membership out. "Marvin always wants three or four owners to bolt," he blustered. "It won't happen this time." The union chief fired back that if the Yankee magnate believed so strongly in the principle of compensation to rivals for lost talent, he should have offered something to San Diego for having swiped Winfield. Perhaps, Miller sarcastically suggested, Steinbrenner should have offered the Padres a front-line starter or, better still, one of his racehorses.[27]

Big-league clubs had already amassed a $15 million pool to assist their weaker organizations in the event of a player walkout. The $1 million in strike insurance would also kick in at 153 total games lost—slightly under two weeks into a stoppage—and would compensate clubs for their losses up to a maximum of five hundred more games, or approximately forty days of the season. The union possessed a strike fund too, but its membership would still endure a major salary hit save for the few with guaranteed contracts. After thirty days of going through collective-bargaining motions, the owners announced imposition of the PRC free-agent compensation plan effective February 19. In turn, the Players Association fulfilled the spring exhibition schedule but set a regular-season strike date for May 29. By now bad blood thoroughly permeated the bargaining environment. Players dressed in jeans and T-shirts crashed bargaining sessions not just to listen but also—with Miller's apparent blessing—to get under Ray Grebey's skin. Miller did the same by scheduling a bargaining session for the day of Grebey's son's Kenyon graduation. In turn, fully aware that it grated upon his opposite number, Grebey pointedly addressed Miller with the condescending nickname "Marv." On several occasions furious player reps privately expressed their wish for just five minutes alone with the PRC negotiator in a dark room.[28]

Guaranteeing that there would be no last-minute rescue this time, Bowie Kuhn not only refused to intervene but accused the union of having become "prisoners" of Miller's ego. In the process of insulting Miller, however, Kuhn provided him a fresh opening. Claiming that three big-league clubs—Baltimore, Atlanta, and the Chicago Cubs—had lost money ranging from $53,000 to $1 million in 1980, the commissioner imprudently asserted that more teams would join them in the red "unless we find oil under second base." Jumping on the poverty claims, Miller filed another "inability to pay" grievance with the NLRB and demanded on its basis that the clubs open their books. If the owners refused and the NLRB then upheld the union's filing, then Miller could seek an injunction to block imposition of the PRC free-agent-compensation scheme. Dangling a carrot as he brandished his stick, Miller reiterated the MLBPA's willingness to accept "indirect" compensation in the form of players picked from a big-league pool of men on forty-man reserve rosters but not active squads.[29]

At first it appeared the union's gambit might succeed. NLRB general counsel William Lubbers sided with the MLBPA and went to federal court seeking the injunction just twenty-four hours before the strike deadline. When Milwaukee general manager Harry Dalton publicly criticized both sides for having allowed the talks to degenerate into a "macho test of wills" and suggested the union might compromise, the comments drew a $50,000 fine. Informed of the owners' punishment, Miller quipped, "I had always realized the truth had a price, but I never realized it was that expensive." Although the NLRB's pursuit of an injunction before federal judge Henry Werker caused a two-week postponement of the strike date, it did not produce the union's desired outcome. On June 10, Judge Werker rejected the request. Two days later, the strike began. Risking PRC wrath, Ed Williams helped his stranded Orioles arrange flights home. Industry directives, however, immediately banned the use of ballpark facilities and halted pay to all striking performers save those with guaranteed contracts.[30]

In solidarity with their membership, Miller and Fehr refused their own pay. In contrast management personnel continued to receive full salaries, with Bowie Kuhn keeping his $200,000. Maverick owners again maneuvered to coax the commissioner's intervention, but to no avail. George Steinbrenner even recruited umpire-union chief Richie Phillips for back-channel phone calls to Miller's home. After one such missive, the irritated Terry Miller suggested to Phillips that the Yankee magnate have the guts to meet her husband at the Players Association offices, but "the Boss" cowered at the prospect of PRC discovery. The executive director's wife then pointedly retorted that Steinbrenner stood to lose far more than the amount of any fine if he refused to grow a backbone. Following more secret entreaties, the two principals agreed for Phillips to arrange a clandestine meeting between them. The umpires' chief set up a lunchtime rendezvous at the Hyatt Regency Hotel in a suite registered under his name. At the meeting Miller pressed the idea of a pooled monetary fund from which teams losing free agents would be compensated. The Yankee mogul admitted mounting owner suspicions of Grebey duplicity toward them, implying that the PRC negotiator's descriptions of union positions had been deliberately inaccurate in order to keep the clubs behind him. At the end of the session, each man exited separately to avoid press detection. That same evening Miller learned to his surprise and amusement that within minutes after their respective departures, matchmaker Phillips had gone into an adjoining room to collect his briefcase, only to barely escape being drenched when the ceiling suddenly collapsed from a water-main break. The outside hallway had then quickly filled with startled guests seeking to discover the source of the clamor.[31]

Despite the behind-the-scenes drama, the dissidents' efforts failed, with Kuhn personally dressing down Eddie Chiles for his machinations, and the influential Lee MacPhail torpedoing the pooled-money compensation Miller had suggested to Steinbrenner. The owners' Executive Council then gave Grebey a fresh vote of confidence. Although Williams pressed on anyway, the chastened Steinbrenner muttered, "Soon they'll be sending Chiles and me to Lower Slobbovea." As for their more militant colleagues, a PRC member later revealed that at the time the players' strike had commenced, owner bets on its duration had only included a top estimate of five days. Supporting hard-liners' confidence was the salary hit the players were taking—ranging from $181 per day for those at the minimum to Dave Winfield's $7,777. Hawks also pointed to the pressure the strikers would feel from losing their annual pension contributions because of cancellation of the All-Star Game. After just two hours' negotiation in the strike's first week, mediator Moffett cancelled talks scheduled for June 24 and described the impasse as the most bizarre in his twenty-two years as a professional troubleshooter. A major factor in the impasse was that just a single issue remained on the table— a reality that rendered impossible the tradeoffs usually essential to completing a deal. Irate fans flooded Miller with vitriolic letters. In one particularly nasty example, an enraged correspondent wrote, "You're an a—hole if there ever was one. You're letting these g—damn ballplayers get too g—damn much money. Their [sic] ruining the game of baseball. . . . Wise up you jerk!"[32]

Growing tired and irascible from the lack of progress and determined to undercut owner claims that he was the problem, Miller abruptly removed himself and left the bargaining-table responsibilities temporarily to Fehr and the reps. From outside the talks, he again floated the threat of a rival, player-run league in 1982. He then rejoined the negotiations on July 1 after member grumbling over his prior withdrawal. By July 4, more than 250 games had been lost. The union had also been forced to react to management gambits of minor-league games at Shea Stadium and in Cleveland with calls to prospective participants not to cross picket lines. When Yale president A. Bartlett Giamatti delivered a "plague-on-both-your-houses" critique of the impasse in the *New York Times* and self-righteously demanded that the adversaries set aside their "squalid little squabbles," a furious Miller fired back. Rejecting Giamatti's basic assertion that baseball's current labor relations had made "a mess" of the national pastime, he accused his target of willingly lending his voice to "a strike breaking effort." Miller would never forgive Giamatti's attack on himself and the union, refusing all subsequent overtures for a bury-the-hatchet lunch.[33]

Behind the scenes, the Orioles' Ed Williams finally managed to recruit the eight votes necessary to force a full-scale owners meeting for July 9, but Grebey loyalists managed to convert the session into a pep rally. Nevertheless, sufficient doubts had now arisen regarding their negotiator's level of honesty that Lou

Hoynes now provided separate bargaining updates. Owners' misgivings toward Grebey then escalated when it was disclosed that he had withheld from them the details of a Moffett proposal for pooled player compensation. Because, as an impartial intermediary, Moffett could not order his suggestion to be presented to either side's membership without the blessing of its negotiator, the onus had laid squarely with Grebey. Convinced that the mediator's offer had originated with Miller, however, the PRC's bargainer-in-chief had brazenly kept his constituents in the dark. Sensing the rising dissension and hoping to capitalize on it, Miller now urged that Moffett be granted binding-arbitration authority to impose the pooled-compensation plan. Doing so, however, required the consent of both sides' bargainers, however, which Grebey refused to give.[34]

The All-Star Game now became the strike's next casualty. By July 12 the number of lost regular-season games approached four hundred. Because the umpires' contract had guaranteed them forty-five-days' pay in the event of a 1980 stoppage but only thirty-days' worth in 1981, their salaries now also halted. Hoping to peel off groups of players from the strike, Grebey offered selective enticements, including a proposal to make twelve-year veterans soon to seek free agency—including stars Reggie Jackson, Don Baylor, Johnny Bench, and Joe and Phil Niekro—exempt from signee direct-compensation requirements. A similar offer was extended to repeat free agents. Grebey even tried to lure dissenters with suggestions that clubs might be willing to extend more players long-term pacts, rendering the recipients of such largesse less likely candidates for free agency and thereby reducing their stake in the current dispute.[35]

The PRC, however, continued to struggle with its own solidarity. Once more D.C. insider Ed Williams weighed in, lobbying Secretary of Labor Raymond Donovan to intervene. After holding separate meetings with Grebey and Miller, Donovan flew to New York to personally impress the need for progress upon his listeners and then summoned the parties to the capital. He only succeeded, however, in getting the antagonists to stop exchanging salvoes in the media. For Miller, his agreement to this cease-fire proved a rare tactical error. Without the access provided through regular media conferences and press releases, his ability to keep his membership updated and its unity strong suffered. On July 22 the *Los Angeles Times* reported that Dodger second-baseman Davey Lopes had called the stalled talks a "circus" and demanded to return to work. Boston pitcher Dennis Eckersley was similarly quoted as saying, "Screw the strike, let's play ball!" Pressured by worried reps, Miller reluctantly agreed to suspend bargaining long enough to convene regional union meetings to plug the holes. According to reporter John Helyar, one team rep who years later still insisted upon anonymity maintained, "I believe ownership didn't know how close they were to causing huge cracks." Whether or not the claim was accurate, the public discontent from union members and Miller's sudden scheduling of rallies led Ed Williams to wonder whether the executive director had "lost control of his union."[36]

The 1981 strike had reached its crucial juncture. If the union proved to not be on the verge of crumbling, pressure would immediately shift back upon management. For in the absence of a deal by August 1, there would no longer be time for a playing schedule with the necessary minimum of one hundred games to legitimate postseason participants. The bulk of the industry's television revenue, coming as it did from network rights to the playoffs and World Series, would be put at serious risk. Last but not least, the clubs' strike fund would run out after the first week of August. At the union's Los Angeles regional meeting, under pressure Lopes recanted his prior criticism. The Chicago-area MLBPA session produced more demonstrations of resolve. As word spread of the union's apparent hardening, rumors of growing leaks within management again surfaced. Among the gossip was that Grebey was to be demoted or removed entirely from the negotiations. De facto confirmation reached Miller in the form of a behind-the-scenes overture from Lee MacPhail. For months the management veteran had been "drafting and doodling" potential compromise formulas based on the concept of pooled-player compensation. Now, while continuing to deflect calls from AL "doves" for binding outside arbitration, MacPhail revealed his newly central role in the talks.[37]

On day fifty of the strike MacPhail convened a private meeting with Grebey, Miller, and Fehr at his AL office with the purpose of "making a settlement." Miller rejected a last-ditch gambit for direct free-agent compensation and pressed for nothing short of victory on the union's two unshakeable demands—the limited player-pool compensation formula for teams losing top free agents and the awarding of back service-time to his striking men. Within forty-eight hours the sides reached agreement. At a joint announcement the exhausted Miller, without needing much prompting from his reps, studiously avoided shaking hands with Grebey. Mark Belanger pulled Lee MacPhail aside and delivered a stern admonition "never to let this happen again." It had been an unnecessary war—and one that had ultimately resulted in a deal that could have been achieved at least as far back as the spring.[38]

Under the new Basic Agreement, the non–free agency provisions of the 1980 interim deal were extended through 1984. On the fractious issue of free-agent compensation, the new arrangement permitted each major-league club to protect twenty-four men, leaving the rest of their forty-man rosters eligible for a pool from which teams that lost Type-A free agents—of whom there could be no more than nine a year, drawn from the statistical top 20 percent of big-leaguers—could select replacements. A club opting not to take part at all in the process in a given year could exempt an additional two men from the replacement pool. Up to but not more than five organizations could exempt themselves over the entire length of the Basic Agreement and in return protect their full forty-man rosters. The union agreed to drop its NLRB action, and the membership received full credit for service time over the period of the strike.[39]

The players' work stoppage had cost more than seven hundred big-league games—over a third of the schedule—along with $72 million in club revenues and $50 million in strike insurance. The players had sacrificed $30 million in wages, with individual hits ranging from $11,000 to Dave Winfield's $390,000 and an average loss of $52,000. Miller bluntly called the just-concluded confrontation an "exercise in terminal stupidity." Responding to Gussie Busch's fruitless efforts to defeat the contract through such arguments as, "If nothing else it will show that the ownership of baseball is not insane," the scornful Miller retorted, "That is something." For their part, the players overwhelmingly ratified the new deal by a 627–37 margin. A split season followed, producing playoffs that matched up each half's winners. The arrangement left the Cincinnati Reds, with baseball's best record over the entire year, on the sidelines, as well as the NL East's best such club—Busch's St. Louis Cardinals.[40]

Compared to the 1976 Basic Agreement's free-agency system, the 1981 deal did mark a modest retreat by the union. But when compared with the owners' original goal of gutting the free-agency system entirely, it was a crucial victory for Miller. The union had taken management's best shot and had stood firm, and in so doing had preserved the heart of earlier gains and maintained its credibility. When viewed amid the new decade's increasingly rightward tilt and erosion of labor's national strength, the MLBPA's achievement was the more exceptional. While the Reagan administration was firing striking air-traffic controllers and destroying their PATCO union, all that baseball's spokesman Barry Rona could summon up in endorsement of his industry's new contract was that it was "better than nothing." To Marvin Miller, it was his union's "finest hour."[41]

It was also intended to be his "last hurrah" as Players Association leader. The Executive Board gratefully reimbursed him for his strike sacrifices and boosted his compensation to nearly $166,000 in salary and a $37,000 expense account. The actions made Miller the third-highest-paid labor leader in America, trailing only the Teamsters' Roy Williams and the Airline Pilots Association's John O'Donnell. The players even extended him and his wife a one-month all-expenses-paid

A weary Miller at his desk (source unknown/Tamiment Library, NYU)

vacation at a place of their choosing. If anyone questioned whether he had earned such rewards, all that was needed was a reminder that while his own pay had risen fourfold since 1966, the membership's average income had jumped fifteen times over to a figure of $240,000 for the upcoming season. Having intended to quit after a successful negotiation in 1980, only to be forced by circumstances to stay an extra year, the sixty-four-year-old Miller was badly in need of a rest. His wife Terry had already retired, turning her energies to volunteering at New York's International Center—an organization offering cultural outreach to spouses of foreign executives in the Big Apple. She had also mastered Japanese—not solely because of her new avocation. Son Peter had met a young woman from Japan during consulting work for Honda and Toyota and had married her, and the couple was preparing to move to the Land of the Rising Sun.[42]

As accurately described by columnist Joe Durso, Marvin Miller had "rewritten" the history of baseball. He had built a remarkable labor organization that was the first of its kind in professional sports, and he had seen it through its greatest

test to date. With justified pride Miller pointed out to a reporter, "The Players Association has no provision for compulsory membership—none. But every player in the major leagues belongs. I kind of doubt you'd find that to be true in any other organization." Having erected his own living monument, he planned to spend the last year of his leadership in preparation to hand it off to another man. And in contrast to antagonists Kuhn and Grebey, he would be leaving on his own terms. At the end of his seven-year term in late 1982, Kuhn would lose an owner no-confidence vote and then be forced to remain in lame-duck status until the delayed arrival of successor Peter Ueberroth. Grebey's stay in baseball would prove even shorter, with the clubs terminating him at the end of 1983.[43]

As Miller prepared to hand over the reins of his union, he knew that it was not perfect. But in his image it was tough and honest, and it had avoided the corruption that had plagued all too many labor organizations. He had helped win something resembling real economic freedom as well as material gains for his membership, and he had transformed the labor economics of baseball in a way that offered players the kind of security he had fought for previously in the nation's steel mills. His public posture had unapologetically been adversarial, but by his reckoning he had achieved his goals without crippling the national pastime. Perhaps the contemporary fan viewed his men with less reverence than in a bygone era. But Miller had never put much stock in such illusions. While others might still prefer to see baseball as just a game, to him it was an industry that for far too long had relied upon exploitation of its performers. It was not that way any longer. With his mission seemingly accomplished, he looked ahead to a life in retirement of travel, occasional public pronouncements, the warm glow of tributes, and a good rest. It would not turn out quite that way.

Fourteen

Flunking Retirement

Marvin Miller's daily routine altered little in his last year at the helm of the Players Association. He was determined not to convey any sign of slacking that might embolden his adversaries, and he was driven by his desire to preserve the legacy of a fighting organization that would endure after he left. He continued to battle any efforts to undermine the free-agency system, and he pressed his demand for a coequal union role in baseball's television negotiations. When the Angels' Buzzie Bavasi declared his wish to compensate the Yankees with a return player for signing Reggie Jackson, the vigilant executive director confronted him and pointed out that such a "trade" for Jackson was expressly banned "since he's already a free agent." Rumors of owner collusion to stop bids on players in the 1981–1982 off-season led him to fire off a fresh NLRB complaint. In his scheduled appearance before Congress, Miller repeated his call for repealing the industry's antitrust exemption. As a testament to his clout, NBC Sports' Ken Schanzer arranged a confidential luncheon with him before the network began a new round of bargaining over rights fees. Miller was happy to oblige, seeing in the overture an opportunity to end-run the owners and lay groundwork for a substantial boost in television money for the pension.[1]

Besides his goals for the membership, Miller was equally determined to safeguard his own reputation for posterity. If the players' union and the changes it had brought were monuments on which he refused to permit backsliding, he also wanted his role in shaping them similarly to be unchallenged by his contemporaries and by history. Determined to confront any real or imagined public slights in his final season, once more he locked horns with the *Sporting News*' Furman Bisher. Author Jane Leavy approached him about a biography, and publishers Macmillan and Norton each solicited a ghostwritten memoir. He also lent his cooperation to his cousin Malvin Wald for a Hollywood documentary pilot, "The Big Business of Sports: Athletes in Union Suits," with actor Joseph Campanella as the narrator. When the venture collapsed, Miller was left with a $3000 stipend for his service as a technical advisor.[2]

His most important professional responsibility in 1982 was to ensure a smooth leadership transition for the MLBPA. To Miller that meant selection of a successor who would share his philosophy and vigorously defend the union's hard-won prerogatives and monetary gains. Given the unique insight he possessed in what it took to be an effective executive director, and the stakes of getting the choice right, there was no excuse for failure—but fail he did. Whether out of sheer weariness, the belief that being "too" hands-on would show a lack of faith in the Executive Board, or the understandable if selfish disinterest of one on his way out, he failed to take charge of the process or to spell out sufficiently the range of attributes the job demanded. Yet another part of the problem was that there was no obvious "insider" candidate. For all of Don Fehr's intelligence and commitment, his media skills and his personal relationship with the rank and file needed more refining. Dick Moss, who had been more of a natural in those areas, had departed the union five years earlier and was comfortably ensconced in his agent practice.[3]

Instead of Miller playing the lead role, a screening committee consisting of former and current players Mark Belanger, Ted Simmons, Doug DeCinces, Phil Garner, and Steve Rogers solicited nominations. Miller relayed the names of a handful of possibilities that came to his attention, but in general the search panel approached him only in ad hoc fashion to sound out his reaction to specific candidates. One search-committee member even repeated Robin Roberts's earlier naiveté and floated Richard Nixon's name again. As 1982 unfolded and the search process drifted, Miller was belatedly forced to recruit additional candidates. The list he generated included an international union vice president, the counsel for a New York symphony musicians' organization, and a Steelworker wage-policy advisor from Ohio who had failed to gain higher USWA office. All three of the supplementary candidates, however, "fell flat" in their interviews with the search committee.[4]

From early on in the process, the name of one person had appealed most to the players—Kenneth Moffett. The mediator nominally met Miller's bottom line that his successor possess trade-union roots. Moffett's father and grandfather had both been union miners in the Harrisburg coalfields, and after his graduation from the University of Maryland he had held a staff position in the United Mine Workers' Baltimore office before shifting to the mediation field. Having been near the top of the Federal Mediation and Conciliation Service as its deputy director and having been its designated representative in the Players Association's recent collective-bargaining showdown with the owners, he had won the enthusiastic backing of Orioles activists DeCinces and Belanger. When the union had started its executive director search, Moffett had at first disavowed interest, but once it had become clear to him that the Reagan administration belatedly planned to replace him, he had relayed a change of heart to the committee.[5]

While the screening panel continued to drift toward a choice of Moffett, Miller rejected entreaties of his own from new suitors. Among those sounding out his postbaseball interest in more collective bargaining were a wide array of groups that included the Northeast Conference of Rabbis, Belmont Park and Albany thoroughbred jockeys, General Motors dealer/distributors, airline hostesses, and even Playboy bunnies. But at sixty-five he remained too tired for the time being to give more than casual consideration to another union executive job. Still, had he really prepared himself emotionally for life outside the labor arena in general or the Players Association in particular? He had convinced himself he was ready to move on—but others who knew him well were not so certain. Once the Executive Board finalized the Moffett choice, Miller arranged a get-acquainted cocktail party for Moffett and a session with the board at its 1982 winter meeting. But the words Moffett uttered had the immediate effect of setting his predecessor's teeth on edge—both for what had been said and what had not. Projecting the approach of a mediator accustomed to brokering opposing sides rather than uncompromisingly advocating in behalf of one of them, the new leader astonished Miller with the statement, "No one ever wins a strike." Not only was the statement inaccurate on its face in view of the Players Association's recent history, the outgoing Miller took it as a show of disrespect. Deeply concerned but not yet ready to show it, the now ex-leader consoled himself with a tennis workout followed by a drink at the hotel pool. Indulging himself in a note of self-pity, he mused that in the transition to another leader he had at least been spared the obligatory gift of a pocket watch.[6]

To the *New York Times*' Murray Chass, Moffett claimed to have "stood in awe of Marvin for twenty years." When asked about his change from mediator to advocate, he emphasized his commitment to the players and pointed out that while several colleagues had eagerly leaped over to management positions, he had been the first to "go to labor." Despite the reassurances, Miller was unconvinced, and in his diminished role as a consultant he was clearly a fish out of water. When Ben Fischer came to New York for a visit, he could see that his old colleague had not come to terms with the change in his life. He urged Miller to create greater distance from his former employers. "Get a suitcase or some box," he pointedly advised, "and get your stuff out." But for the former executive director there was always a dutiful excuse for not following his friend's counsel. Yet the more he continued to drop in at the MLBPA's offices, the more frustrated Miller became. As he saw it, his successor was not showing the appropriate dedication by refusing for months to relocate and by wasting Fridays and Mondays commuting to and from Washington. Moffett had also immediately brought in his own personal aides while keeping Don Fehr at arm's length. Having viewed Miller's efforts to brief him on various union subjects as meddling, Moffett had traveled from a personal vacation directly to the spring-training camps without bothering to 'touch base" with his predecessor.[7]

Matters "hit the fan" when Moffett publicly praised the industry's new five-year billion-dollar television deal with NBC and ABC. To Miller, such overt pleasure at the unilaterally negotiated bargain effectively undercut the union's longstanding demand for participation in such talks. He fretted that Moffett's comments sent a larger signal of naiveté to management and would encourage them to expand postseason play without a proportional boost in pension contributions. Fed up at being ignored by the union's new leader, Miller now retaliated with an act of open insubordination, dictating a memo on the intertwined television-revenue and pension issues without the leader's clearance for distribution to the Executive Board. Moffett aide David Vaughn, spotting the attempt at an end-run, seized the document before it could be disseminated and then had the locks changed on the union's office doors to keep Miller out. When the latter stormed down to demand an explanation, a scene out of the Keystone Kops unfolded. Miller's former secretary was unable to locate him a new set of office keys, and Vaughn refused to return the draft memo and nipped at Miller's heels as the angry ex-leader stormed through the suite. Miller then redrafted the release at home and dispatched it anyway, along with a second letter blasting the new leadership for trying to censor him.[8]

Within a matter of days, veteran stars Joe Morgan and Reggie Jackson had openly rallied to Miller's side. Having vigorously stirred the pot, the outcast leader left with his wife for a vacation in Sarasota—ostensibly to escape the controversy, but with a schedule that conveniently overlapped the latter part of Moffett's and Fehr's tour of the Florida camps by a day. While the Millers were in transit from New York, Moffett summoned a subcommittee of his reps and secured a directive ordering his predecessor not to bypass the official lines of authority again but only offer his opinions when asked. Even before Miller had received the stinging rebuke, an uneasy Fehr read it to him over the phone and then met his former boss to discuss the contents. The counsel tried both to talk down Miller and at the same time defend himself, insisting that he had been in no position to stop the order—an assertion his listener summarily rejected by pointing out Fehr's initials on the document. At a conference call Fehr arranged for Miller that included reps Renko, Rogers, and Garner, the quartet tried to reproach gently their former leader for having sent the anti-Moffett memos. At this point Miller could hold his rage no longer. In a bitter tone he declared to his former subordinate, "Don, I didn't want to go off half-cocked, so I didn't say this before, when I was angry. I'll say it now that I've had a chance to think it over. I want nothing more to do with the Players Association."[9]

Miller would not be able to bring himself to keep the vow. Out of loyalty he swallowed his pride and testified for the union in a lawsuit seeking its inclusion in future broadcast negotiations. But the bitterness remained, as demonstrated in his comments to reporter Ira Berkow: "When I quit, somebody said the players would forget me in two years. Two years? It didn't take two months." But Miller's abrupt departure also started the clock ticking toward the end of Ken Moffett's tenure. As an anonymous MLBPA member described it to Jerome Holtzman, "These guys on the executive board picked Moffett and feel they have a responsibility to him. But I know this: when it comes down to the rank and file, the players will do whatever Marvin says. He's the guy who built the union. Without him, we're still peons." Moffett himself recognized that he stood no chance of surviving in his job without the blessing of the man who had preceded him, admitting afterward, "It was just a matter of time." While Miller occupied his time with tennis, the theater, and consideration of an offer to join Weirton Steel's board that he eventually rejected, the MLBPA reps' dissatisfaction with Moffett continued to mount. To their dismay, the new executive director did not appear to work very hard. His associate Nancy Broff had herself already left on paid vacation just weeks after having been brought in. Moffett and his staff consistently racked up exorbitant personal phone charges on the union's tab. Any one of these complaints might have been dismissed as merely the grumblings of dissidents looking for an excuse to jettison their leader. But even more troubling were the whispers coming from the owners and picked up by the reps that Moffett's conciliatory rhetoric was encouraging industry that it could "steamroller" the union in the next collective-bargaining showdown.[10]

The telephone call bearing the news of Ken Moffett's dismissal rang in Miller's apartment at 10 P.M. one evening just before Thanksgiving. Marvin and Terry had just returned from a month-long vacation to Greece and the south of France and his jet-lagged spouse had already retired for the night. The trip had been a welcome escape, save for the sad news from Don Fehr of Peter Seitz's death. In the arbitrator's honor, Miller had read aloud samples of their correspondence to his travel companions. On the other end of the line now, however, was the union's AL delegate Steve Renko. An inner circle of the reps had decided among themselves to fire their executive director of less than a year, and the full board was officially being polled as Renko spoke. The pitcher and several of his colleagues wanted to come over to Miller's home at once to discuss the decision. The former leader was understandably skeptical at first, given that the previous March, the board had refused to rally to his defense. Terry had no doubt what her husband's response should be, insisting, "You owe them nothing."[11]

But the Players Association was Marvin Miller's living monument—could he now abandon his men in their moment of need? After the initial pro forma response "I'm retired," he almost immediately gave in to say, "What the hell—come over." Twenty minutes later the four players had covered the short distance from the Hyatt Regency. Over the next four hours, until the wee hours of the morning, Miller methodically fielded their questions. How should they go about the formal process of firing Moffett? How should they notify him as well as staffers Broff and Vaughn? Should the dismissed be awarded severance pay? It fell upon Miller, however, to raise the obvious follow-up, "Then, what?" Who would succeed Moffett in the short run and the longer term? The former executive director noted that the union's winter meeting was due in just two weeks, and the representatives needed to have all their ducks in a row by then.

At that moment catcher Bob Boone gave voice to the question already hanging in the air—would Miller be willing to return temporarily as their leader? The veteran ballplayer cited in support of his suggestion the looming pension and Basic Agreement negotiations. To the suggestion that he return as executive director until both sets of talks had been concluded, Miller delivered an emphatic "no." Boone then asked if he would consider a more limited role chairing the union's negotiating committee. Again the answer was negative. A worried Steve Rogers pointed out that "no one else has ever led these negotiations" to insist that any other choice would still need Miller's direct guidance. Facing his supplicants' solid front, the host reluctantly agreed to help the successor within a clearly circumscribed role and if "the circumstances seem right."[12]

The key to the latter, of course, was who the players selected as an interim leader to succeed Moffett. Don Fehr had diligently patched up his relationship with Miller and was the obvious first possibility, but several players expressed concern about his relative inexperience. Would Miller be willing to serve as Fehr's right-hand man for the upcoming negotiations? After thinking ruefully about his wife's almost certain dismay at his reenlistment with the Players Association, he tentatively conceded. By the meeting's end Miller had given still more ground, agreeing to fill in as executive director until the board's winter meeting. He cautioned his listeners, though, "If you don't find anyone by then, you're on your own." The reps had one more favor to ask of him, but this time it was one Miller savored. Would he personally be willing to come down to the office and be present when Moffett and his team received their "pink slips?" As he escorted out his late-night intruders, he let out a sigh and answered, 'Why not?" When he had finally adjourned to bed and briefed Terry on all of the night's events, her reply was squarely on target—"Marvin, you've flunked retirement."[13]

As promised, Miller joined the reps to deliver notice to Ken Moffett. As he walked down the familiar route to the MLBPA headquarters, however, his purpose was nearly discovered by a young CNN reporter named Keith Olbermann, who was walking home in the opposite direction. Sensing in Miller's no-nonsense demeanor that this was not a time to interrupt even to say hello, Olbermann unwittingly missed a scoop. Miller later acknowledged thinking at the time, "It was fortunate that that damn-fool kid reporter didn't recognize me." After the firings, Miller returned as interim executive director for three weeks until his successor could be named. Against his advice, the reps agreed to accept a settlement of a breach-of-contract suit brought by Moffett, Broff, and Vaughn granting the trio combined severance of $210,000 over two years. At the union's winter meetings, Fehr was chosen as acting leader while retaining his counsel post. Recognizing the daunting challenge, he noted to reporter Joe Durso, "When Moffett left with bargaining so close, we had to move fast," and he added, "It was Superman, Marvin Miller, or me, and Superman and Marvin didn't want it [the executive directorship]." In conclusion he admitted, "I'm still a lawyer who still isn't used to being a client."[14]

Miller was prepared to assist the interim chief but was studious to limit his role to that of advisor and panelist on the bargaining team. Helping him bury the hatchet with Fehr over real or perceived slights was the industry's abrupt decision to challenge the union over the issue of baseball's recreational-drug policy. In the latter years of Miller's tenure as Players Association leader, drug controversies had occasionally surfaced, usually prompted by a management-cast suspicion of an individual player for marijuana or cocaine use. When the union had asked for hard evidence of actual violations, however, nothing had followed. But in 1982 San Diego had suspended Alan Wiggins for a month following a cocaine-possession arrest, and Cardinals outfielder Lonnie Smith had voluntarily submitted to drug treatment for his habit. The following year had seen a further surge in drug controversies, involving Dodger reliever Steve Howe and the Kansas City Royals quartet of Willie Wilson, Vida Blue, Jerry Martin, and Willie Aikens. After the season Bowie Kuhn issued one-year suspensions to all and the union challenged the sentences in grievance arbitration. Miller insisted that the unilateral penalties were "way out of line" because specific punishments for drug violations had not been mutually agreed upon in collective bargaining and the commissioner had not waited for the players' due process to play out before imposing the verdicts.[15]

By 1984, however, the number of on-field employees undergoing drug treatment or convicted in court of offenses in the last five years climbed to sixteen persons. The deposed Ken Moffett now chose to add his voice to management's attacks on the Players Association. The ex–executive director accused his predecessor personally of having orchestrated his dismissal at the hands of a "kangaroo court" of player reps, and went on to accuse those he identified as Miller's principal allies, Don Fehr and Mark Belanger, of seeking his ouster specifically because of Moffett's willingness to work with the owners on a joint drug policy including the random testing of players. According to the union's ex-leader, his union adversaries had been more concerned about the impact of a toughened drug policy on the contracts of implicated players than they had with the safety of the membership.

Although Moffett denied having supported any proposal that would have put the union in the awkward position of policing its own members, his successors doubted his disavowal. It was true that Fehr and Miller alike were determined to protect their membership's due-process and privacy rights from the threat of random testing. They insisted that any industry recreational-drug program require an unambiguous finding of just cause before any individual test, as well as a guarantee that the union could appeal any such order via the grievance-arbitration process. When Moffett claimed that four to five members per squad—more than one hundred men total—were using illegal drugs, Fehr publicly challenged his veracity, pointedly asking, "How does he know?" The former chief then fired back that according to his own sources, the FBI had conducted secret investigations and obtained photographs of players openly using cocaine in team clubhouses before and even during games.[16]

Despite the explosive nature of Moffett's charges and his aspersions against Miller, the latter refrained from public comment even to friendly ears in the sporting press. Privately he attributed his uncharacteristic silence to the predilection of the media and owners to portray him otherwise as some puppet master pulling Don Fehr's strings at a time the interim leader was seeking to establish credibility. Nonetheless, the drug controversy had put the union's officialdom—including Miller—on the defensive. In response, the Executive Board consented to negotiations for a new policy while the union pressed ahead with grievances against Kuhn's suspensions. Arbitrator Richard Bloch upheld the union's position in the Martin and Wilson cases, limiting the players' penalties to May 15 of the new season and effectively forcing the commissioner to similarly shorten Aikens's sentence. Vida Blue, however, remained under his one-year ban as a cocaine procurer, as did Howe for being a repeat drug offender. Later in the 1984 season Atlanta pitcher Pasqual Perez drew a similar one-year suspension and follow-up probation for cocaine possession. But again arbitrator Bloch overturned Kuhn's sentence on grounds that it had never been proven the pitcher had actually used the drugs in question.[17]

The end result of the first real test of the "post-Miller" Players Association was the ironically named Joint Drug Policy that applied to illegal hard drugs but not marijuana or to prescription substances such as amphetamines. Players who came forward to seek treatment drew no penalty for a first offense but were subject to escalating sanctions for additional violations. A club suspecting a player of drug abuse could confront him, and if he denied the charge or confessed but refused treatment, the dispute went to a three-person medical panel similar to a grievance-arbitration committee. Players undergoing treatment would be placed on the inactive list with full pay for up to thirty days, then receive half-pay for an additional month's care if required, and would remain entitled to the minimum salary over any regimen running beyond sixty days. The union formally recognized the commissioner's authority to suspend any industry employee who had been convicted of drug offenses, with penalties starting at a year's suspension without pay. Kuhn could similarly punish any employee caught with illegal substances on stadium grounds. The Players Association retained the right, however, to file grievances in any case involving a member if it believed the commissioner had overstepped his authority or violated the performer's due-process rights.[18]

As the drug controversy swirled in early 1984, Miller's focus instead remained upon the pending Basic Agreement talks. He missed the first formal negotiating session because of a conflict with a prescheduled visit to his ninety-four-year-old mother in Florida, but he was back for the next as part of a union bargaining team that also included Fehr and old colleague Dick Moss. Lee MacPhail now headed up the PRC team, backed by lawyers Barry Rona and Lou Hoynes. No significant progress was expected, however, until the clubs had their new commissioner in place. The owners had already settled on entrepreneur and Los Angeles Olympics organizer Peter Ueberroth as Kuhn's replacement, but his assuming charge awaited the end of the Games. Prior to the selection, one candidate—Miller years later still refused to break a confidence and say if it had been Ueberroth—had actually sought his opinion on whether to pursue the position. Now, the commissioner-in-waiting, who Miller described as a "talented rogue," launched a charm offensive directed at the former executive director. Although Miller was loath to admit it, his distaste for industry patriarchs and romantics alike was matched by a weakness for adversaries who came across as sophisticated realists, and Ueberroth skillfully projected that impression. While MacPhail offered up hardline proposals, the commissioner-elect privately disparaged his bosses to Miller and Fehr as "jerks," all the while professing a sincere desire to understand the union point of view and volunteering to lift the suspensions of legends Willie Mays and Mickey Mantle for ties to casinos.[19]

Whether unaware of or opting as the "bad cop" to ignore the new commissioner's courtship of the union, the PRC demanded major concessions both on salaries and on the share of broadcast money allocated to the pension. The Astros' John McMullen advised the rank and file to "get rid of Miller and Fehr," and Peter O'Malley tried to have drug-testing clauses inserted in individual player contracts in violation of the Joint Drug Policy. With the National Basketball Association having successfully won a player salary cap, baseball now was pressing for something similar. As in past negotiations, real bargaining only came late and was influenced by a commissioner intervention. In February 1985, Ueberroth privately relayed to the union that he was willing to consider means of payroll restraint other than a salary cap, and to underscore his belief in the industry's purported economic stress he compelled the clubs to release their financial statements. The two sides then dueled over the industry's true health, with the owners claiming to have lost $27 million the year before and MLBPA-consultant Roger Noll countering that they had made $25 million.[20]

With the talks still stalled as the regular season began, reps voted to participate in the upcoming All-Star Game but set a second-half strike date of August 6. As the deadline neared, Ueberroth launched a public-relations offensive calling upon the union to cancel the strike, endorsed a cap on salary-arbitration awards save for those in a narrow "superstars" category, and backed a $44-million yearly pension contribution that fell halfway between each side's positions. The commissioner added the threat that starting on August 10, every day the parties failed to strike a pension deal each would forfeit a million dollars, with the money going to amateur baseball. Peter O'Malley later insisted, though Miller did not believe him, that in laying down his gauntlet the commissioner was not acting at the PRC's behest but instead out of personal hubris that he could personally orchestrate a "napkin deal." The Dodgers owner quickly added, "Marvin Miller doesn't do napkin deals." Similar grandstanding by past commissioners who claimed impartiality while paid by the clubs had always gotten Miller's goat, and this was no exception. Accordingly, he slammed Ueberroth with the rhetorical question, "What fans elected him?"[21]

Ueberroth and the PRC now both suggested that Miller was the real obstacle to a settlement. It was true that he had drawn an unyielding line in the negotiations, insisting that fundamentally the union should never agree to givebacks. Some PRC officials believed that Fehr might not be as rigid and, that if they could isolate Miller from the discussions, a compromise agreeable to the clubs might be possible. Ironically, at least one legendary hard-liner secretly sided with the union's old lion. Charley Finley covertly relayed to player rep Buck Martinez, "You tell Marvin to stick to his guns. . . . You guys are doing the right thing." But with the talks at a crucial juncture, Fehr assented to a meeting with Barry Rona at Lee MacPhail's 5th Avenue apartment without Miller—a development that infuriated the latter. In fairness to Fehr, he faced the uncertainty of the membership's willingness to proceed with a strike over the size of what would regardless be a hefty pension increase, and over preserving salary arbitration for two-year men when the average player earned $370,000 and accordingly had much to lose in a work stoppage. In addition, fully half the union membership had not been around for the 1981 strike and had no memory of that prior struggle. Miller grudgingly conceded years later that by 1985 "the players had lost touch with their own history." Even current performers who had been 1981 strike supporters, such as Bob Boone, were now nearing the end of playing careers and hoping for future opportunities as coaches or managers. Painfully for Miller, Boone now threw back in his old leader's face the cautionary point the latter had emphasized in the past—"If 30% of the players don't want to strike, that's a losing proposition."[22]

As the strike deadline drew nearer, the bargainers escaped media scrutiny by alternating negotiating sessions between the Helmsley Building and Miller's apartment. Defying a Ueberroth threat to employ "best interests" powers to prevent the walkout, the union struck as scheduled. Just two days later, however, the two sides had a deal, albeit one that to Miller contained troubling givebacks. Just after the final details had been hammered out, the commissioner barged in with the disappointed demeanor of one who had arrived to save the day only to find his presence unnecessary. Ueberroth still managed to claim a share of credit for purportedly having pushed the parties into the deal. The next day, showing he had not lost his romantic touch, Ueberroth ordered flowers be delivered to Terry Miller. Her bemused husband observed, "I remember looking at the flowers and feeling sorry for whoever he ran against when he finally decided to go into politics."[23]

One positive in the 1985 Basic Agreement for the union was the dropping of big-league-player compensation to clubs that lost free agents—the very policy management had provoked a fifty-day strike to get just four years ago. The pact also included a $60,000 minimum salary and major benefit increases. On the other hand, however, the MLBPA had accepted a one-year increase in the service time required of salary-arbitration eligibility and a share of national broadcast money for the pension well below the one-third Miller had demanded in the past. Instead, the benefit plan would receive an average annual 18 percent over six years with $25 million retroactively applied to 1984, $35 million each year from 1985 through 1988, and $39 million in 1989. Even at the lower contribution level, however, the deal meant 1987 pension payouts of $91,000 per year to ten-year veterans that had reached age sixty-two, fully retroactive pension gains for big-league players of 1975 forward, and prorated earnings of 40 to 50 percent for earlier performers. As a show of good faith for having claimed economic distress to justify lower percentage pension contributions, Ueberroth and the owners had also promised to commit $20 million out of the television package to an emergency fund for small-market clubs.[24]

Miller would forever insist that the 1985 pact was a weak one in which for the first time since his arrival the Players Association had taken "backward steps." The claim was technically untrue, because in the 1981 negotiation he had personally retreated slightly on the issue of free-agent compensation. Nonetheless, he faulted Fehr for having failed to sustain adequately the membership's historical memory and the consequences of any retreat, and he feared that further erosion loomed on the horizon. Years later he continued to maintain that "the minute we relaxed, we were greasing the skids for failure." But diverting him for the moment from additional second guessing was an unusual task he had agreed to take on. The Boston Red Sox had become embroiled in a nasty partnership quarrel, with majority owners Jean Yawkey and Haywood Sullivan seeking to buy out rival stakeholders led by longtime trainer Buddy LeRoux. Before the buyout could be consummated, the opposing sides had to agree upon the club's value and with it the proper price of a buyout. Miller was approached by the LeRoux faction's lawyer—former Watergate defense-attorney James St. Clair—to be its expert on an arbitration panel charged with determining the proper figure.[25]

Although he was sixty-eight years old and again exhausted from negotiations, Miller consented. His decision partly stemmed from a sense of obligation to LeRoux for his support during son Peter's earlier leg recuperation, which had included the trainer's suggestions of therapists. At first, the Yawkey-Sullivan faction sought to block Miller's appointment, and when that failed they demanded a promise from him not to leak club financial information to outsiders—by which they meant the MLBPA or agents—or else incur a $50,000 fine. The demand, however, was thrown out by a judge. Speaking from his union vantage point, Don Fehr relished the irony that in light of the clubs' recent poverty claims, "We do think it is interesting that when an ownership group needs a fair valuation of a worth of a franchise, Marvin's judgment is trusted."[26]

Settling on an acceptable franchise value took another month, with Miller commuting between Boston and New York and smoking three packs of cigarettes a day, downing endless cups of coffee, and getting little sleep. His opposite number was former Houston general manager Tal Smith, while former baseball salary arbitrator Robert Stutz constituted the panel's deciding vote. Pushing his clients' interest in a low price, Smith advocated a number far below the $55 million current record sales figure of the Detroit Tigers. While Stutz generally favored a more generous figure than Smith, his refusal to set forth a clear rationale for any number frustrated Miller. But when he in turn informed his clients of his dissatisfaction with what they were being offered, he was stunned to hear that they were content with Stutz's figure of $50 million and ready to settle. At the panel's next session, Miller proposed to his fellow arbiters that they adopt the best-offer method of salary arbitration to set the final figure, with Stutz choosing between the other two's submissions. He insisted, however, that even if they did not adopt the "either-or" method in their next conference call, they should still agree on a final verdict at that time. When both other participants rejected Miller's "best-offer" method, he then announced acceptance of Stutz' valuation, which carried by a two-to-one vote.[27]

Miller physically was about to hit a wall, but he ignored warning signs and refused to tell his wife about them. Shortly after Labor Day, after playing tennis he still felt poorly half an hour past finishing. Sitting down heavily in a chair, he smoked a Marlboro and felt the discomfort finally ease. Several weeks later, during a chilly afternoon in early October, a more strenuous workout with a club pro triggered a terrible tightness in his chest that left his arm tingling and gave him difficulty breathing. Again seated outside when the second attack occurred, when he looked around for help he found himself alone. He managed to drag himself to the players' lounge, where other club members sat socializing unaware of his condition. After a few minutes the symptoms again waned. He went home, rationalized the renewed occurrence as simply the product of fatigue, and again kept it to himself.[28]

The "third strike" came later the same month at home while watching a playoff game after dinner. Suddenly unable to get his breath, he tried to hide his surging pain. But it shot down both arms, and his fingers lost feeling. The frightened Terry immediately called 911. Within minutes an ambulance had arrived, nitroglycerin had been placed under his tongue, and he had been wheeled on a gurney to an emergency vehicle and rushed to New York Hospital. After two negative electrocardiograms, a third then indicated, "Heart attack under way." Presented a variety of immediate options, Miller chose catheterization, and a probe was fed up to his heart from an artery near his groin. Remaining alert throughout the procedure, which began after midnight, he exchanged baseball banter with his medical team. Fortunately, the procedure revealed he had suffered no severe heart damage and bypass surgery was not necessary. After two weeks in the hospital and a battery of stress tests, his doctors placed him on beta blockers, ordered him to give up cigarettes, and released him. A chain smoker for half a century, he drew upon a strong force of will and quit cold turkey. He then resumed tennis two weeks later. Nonetheless, even he conceded that his body had emphatically told him it was time to "get out of the ballgame."[29]

Miller's brush with mortality made him all the more conscious of his legacy and sensitive to any slights from those deemed insufficiently appreciative. It now grated upon him that when Don Fehr suggested he author a personal history of the Players Association as a reminder to the membership of its heritage, the union's follow-up offer consisted of but a $1,000–2,000 per month retainer and a small, windowless office. Adding to his resentment was that Fehr, who had hinted at his own possible departure and return to a private law practice, had since gained removal of the interim tag from his title and been awarded a pay increase to $500,000. With his ego bruised, Miller declined the book offer and also resigned for good his job as a formal consultant to the union.[30]

Despite the hurt that eventually faded, Miller remained committed to protecting his monument, his union, from outside attack or internal wavering. Despite his protestations, he still craved the respect of others and needed to feel needed by those he had served. And he still believed that the union he had molded could benefit from his wisdom. He would no longer play an active leadership role in the Players Association, or serve on its bargaining teams. But his door remained open and his phone number available whenever his union brethren or the press chose to seek him out. It made him feel he was relevant—and he was determined to remain so.

Part Three

Defender of the Faith
(1986–2012)

"The big things—how we think, what we value—
those you must choose yourself. You can't let anyone—
or any society—determine those for you."

—Morrie Schwartz to Mitch Albom,
Tuesdays with Morrie

Fifteen

Living Memory

By 1986 it had been twenty years since Marvin Miller had been selected to revive the moribund Major League Baseball Players Association. For sixteen years he had led it through trials and triumphs. After stepping down as its executive director he had continued to serve it as a consultant, had retired and then unretired, and had joined the union's bargaining team for the 1985 Basic Agreement negotiations. Prompted by reminders of his mortality and what he perceived as the ingratitude of others, he had once more retreated from the arena. But to the surprise of no one who knew him, Miller's second "retirement" again soon turned active. Immediately after the conclusion of the Basic Agreement negotiations, Peter Ueberroth had steered the owners in a policy of collusion to undermine the free-agent system. Starting with the 1985–1986 offseason crop, stars suddenly found their old teams extending nonexistent or miniscule raises and other clubs refusing to bid. Recognizing the telltale signs of an illegal conspiracy, the MLBPA filed a grievance that would become known as Collusion I. Desiring to illustrate Players Association solidarity in support of its embattled free agents, Don Fehr summoned Miller from retirement to address a union mass meeting in Chicago, and the aging warhorse dutifully heeded the call.[1]

At the same October 1985 meetings at which Ueberroth had called upon the owners to curb their passion for free agents, he had also secured their support for a drive to impose mandatory random drug testing of players for illegal recreational substances. Over the spring of 1986, with the backdrop of a Pittsburgh trial of a clubhouse caterer/cocaine dealer who implicated twenty-three performers, Ueberroth unilaterally tried to impose his four-times-a-year testing regimen. The union quickly filed a grievance on the grounds any change in the existing Joint Drug Policy required negotiations with the MLBPA. When Thomas Roberts ruled against the commissioner, the PRC then attempted to fire the arbitrator. Fehr and Miller both suspected that the motive behind the sudden effort to dismiss Roberts actually had less to do with the drug issue than preventing him from hearing the union's free-agency grievance. At a similar stage of the Messersmith-McNally grievance cases a decade before, a previous commissioner had been deterred when he had advocated a similar strategy. Now it was Ueberroth who had chosen to trot out the dubious gambit and, as Miller had forecast on the prior occasion it failed, leaving Roberts to preside over the Collusion I hearings.[2]

The clubs' conspiracy to thwart free agency would continue for at least two more seasons. The union filed separate grievances for each group of eligibles, and at each set of hearings—the first before Roberts in the fall of 1986 and the latter pair before successor George Nicolau—Miller took the stand as the Players Association's lead witness. Each time he recited how at the owners' own insistence, Basic Agreements since the 1970s had prohibited either side from "acting in concert" to distort the free-agent marketplace. He also recalled that, as late as the most recent 1985 negotiations, the PRC had hinted at "concerted action" by the clubs by claiming it was somehow "not concerted action if you really had a need to do it," and he had demonstrated some "explosive reactions" to that idea.[3]

Miller did not limit his salvoes to the hearing room. Finding himself once more in the media spotlight, he castigated the owners' bad faith and disregard for the game's integrity. He characterized their collective refusal to bid on stars as a greater stain upon baseball than the 1919 Black Sox scandal, portraying it as "an agreement not to field the best teams possible . . . to fixing not just games but entire pennant races, including all post-season series." Responding to industry assertions that the existence of such a conspiracy was impossible given the need for dozens of officials to guard its secrecy, he countered by pointing to Organized Baseball's decades-long "gentlemen's agreement" that had excluded African Americans. In separate rulings on September 21, 1987, August 31, 1988, and July 8, 1990, Roberts and Nicolau would find that the clubs, the two league presidents, and Ueberroth all had violated the 1985 Basic Agreement, and an out-of-court damage settlement awarded repeat free agency for specific victims and assessed total monetary damages of $280 million.[4]

The Millers in retirement (Brad Trent/Tamiment Library, NYU)

Although Miller's official status as retired had remained during the collusion-grievance battles, he now felt vindicated by the union as its gray eminence, sounding board, and champion. He insisted he was not required to clear his pronouncements with MLBPA officialdom beforehand, but he did regularly touch base with Fehr to ensure he did not undercut official union positions. In his emeritus role he continued not only to assail collusion but also the owners' continued claims of financial hardship and occasional efforts to shrink rosters. In short, he was retired from public life—except when he chose not to be. The absence of daily official responsibilities gave him more freedom to travel, including an inaugural trip to Japan to see his new grandson. There he noted approvingly the homage shown to that society's elders, and he basked in the welcome extended by the likes of Tsuneo Watanabe, advisor to prime ministers and sponsor of postseason competitions between U.S. and Japanese major-leaguers.[5]

Despite the march of time, Miller also occasionally received new offers to consult or even head up other unions. He limited himself, however, to offering his solicitors private advice. In 1987, for example, he fielded an entreaty from the NFL Players Association, whose most recent gambit to win true free agency via a strike had failed miserably. He counseled them to pursue an alternative stratagem of filing an antitrust lawsuit against professional football given its lack of a baseball-style exemption, and then issued public statements backing the effort. He cited football's annual college draft as a restraint of trade, and he pointed to the suspicious coincidence that under the NFL's purported free-agency system only one player out of two thousand had actually changed teams voluntarily within the past ten years. Privately, he continued to despair of the football union's ever becoming a serious organization given its continued refusal to hire an experienced trade unionist as its leader rather than individuals with questionable credentials and ill-prepared ex-players. Grudgingly acknowledging that progress had been made in salaries—which had risen to a $214,000 average by 1987—he attributed the gains less to the NFLPA but to the periodic threats of rival football leagues.[6]

When not responding to the occasional entreaties from former colleagues, other unions, or reporters, he fit in twice-weekly tennis sessions and vacations with Terry. But he avidly kept up with current developments not only in baseball but within the broader labor movement through the *New York Times*. When he felt circumstances dictated, he could reliably be counted on to give full-throated endorsement of a Players Association line in the sand, criticism for any perceived backsliding, and withering blasts at commissioners or other management figures. Stung by the attacks on him in Bowie Kuhn's 1987 memoir *Hardball*, Miller relished word of the ex-commissioner's recent travails, including the bankruptcy of his law firm and his flight to Florida from creditors.[7]

The deaths of loved ones and adversaries were equal reminders of his advancing age, despite the varying feelings they stirred. In 1987, the person he had arguably held deepest in his heart and who had shaped his personality more than anyone—his mother—passed away in Florida at the impressive age of ninety-seven. He thought back upon how he had inherited her gumption and her passion for learning, and he recalled a story from one of her last trips to see him in New York. When a fellow passenger had seen Gertrude waiting patiently for her boarding call, the former had asked solicitously, "Aren't you afraid to be traveling all by yourself?" In true Wald fashion she had replied unhesitatingly, "I'm not travelling by myself. . . . I've got a whole plane full of people going with me." Two years later, his reaction was quite different at the news of the sudden passing of a man he had never stopped hating. Shortly after A. Bartlett Giamatti's election as Peter Ueberroth's successor, the new commissioner had vigorously pursued career hit-leader Pete Rose—by then the Reds' manager—on gambling charges. Miller had risen to the defense of "Charley Hustle" and accused the commissioner and his investigator John Dowd with trampling upon the player's due-process rights. When Giamatti abruptly died of a heart attack mere days after announcing Rose's banishment from the game, Miller uncharitably refused to extend any compassion toward a man he saw as a self-righteous hypocrite who had willingly done the bidding of collusion-minded owners.[8]

Despite such ill-considered incivility toward past or present antagonists, however, Miller now commanded not fear alone but hard-earned respect even from men on the other side of baseball's labor/management divide. When Giamatti was succeeded by friend and adviser Fay Vincent, the new commissioner saw the wisdom in inviting the former MLBPA chief to lunch, expressing personal humility and retaining the union-friendly former agent Steve Greenberg—son of Tigers Hall of Famer Hank Greenberg—as an aide. Despite the olive branches, however, the honeymoon was brief. For Miller it ended with the Loma Prieta earthquake of 1989 that disrupted the World Series. Thrust into the spotlight by the emergency, Vincent's calm in handling the crisis garnered laudatory press coverage but to Miller fed a fresh case of "commissioneritis." He would later write of Vincent, "I thought he had the potential to become the best commissioner since I started with the Players Association. He was more intelligent than Bowie Kuhn, more interested in the game and the problems of the industry than Peter Ueberroth—who often looked like he was counting the house when speaking at baseball functions—and far less pompous and righteous and less of a dilettante than A. Bartlett Giamatti." But the old lion insisted that from that October in Oakland, a man "with some sense of balance and humor about his situation" had morphed into someone who "actually began to take seriously the role the media assigned him."[9]

Vincent's "commissioneritis," as Miller described it, constituted a wild card for the Players Association in the next round of bargaining for a Basic Agreement. Many indicators pointed to another protracted showdown. Having traded away the salary-arbitration rights of two-year men in its last such negotiation, the union was now determined to have them restored in the aftermath of collusion. Fehr and his membership were furious at the owners' bad faith that had rewarded them in the short run with lower payrolls and larger profit margins. Fueled also by a lucrative new television contract, a three-year 16 percent attendance rise, and a 150 percent jump in club licensing money, as early as the first spring after collusion's initiation the owners had claimed that the number of organizations losing money had shrunk from twenty-one just two years earlier to only four. Instead of citing red ink, baseball officialdom now freely admitted to profits over $100 million in 1986 and double the level the next season on revenues of over $900 million. By 1988 the figure surpassed $1 billion. In contrast to the clubs' ill-gotten bonanza, for the first time since Miller's arrival on the scene more than two decades earlier, player salaries in 1986 had flatlined as a share of club revenues and had dropped 5 percent more the next year to just one-third of big-league income. Free-agents' pay had fallen 16 percent in 1987 in one year alone and the mean player salary had stood still.[10]

The ongoing arbitration rulings against three years of owner bad faith did carry the promise of penalties in the hundreds of millions of dollars. But Peter Ueberroth had also left the clubs the huge national television pact that included $1.1 billion from CBS and $400 million from ESPN for 1990–1993 and effectively doubled each club's share to $14 million. As richer organizations accordingly indulged themselves in a one-time spending spree in the winter of 1989–1990—which finally triggered a rebound in the players' share of industry revenues to 43 percent—the PRC's "small-market" chairman Bud Selig of Milwaukee pressed for the complete elimination of salary arbitration, its replacement with a "pay-for-performance" scale for younger performers, and adoption of an NBA-style salary cap set at 48 percent of club revenues. From the sidelines Miller assailed the proposal and praised his union's rediscovered militancy. "Why should labor accept," he posed, "a system that doesn't permit management to pay an individual as much as it wants?" Even with wealthy clubs' profligacy, the aggregate big-league payroll of $388 million for 1990 still paled in comparison to the majors' $1.5 billion income. Repeating his time-honored demand for a coequal union role in broadcast negotiations, Miller argued, "No legitimate union representing the interests of its members could agree to accept a fixed percentage of revenue without having a significant voice on all the decisions that affect revenue." If small-market owners could not keep up with their richer brethren because of the widening disparity in local broadcasting money, the clubs had the means to address their revenue-inequality problem by redistribution among themselves rather than demanding that any leveling come from the share paid to the players.[11]

Anticipating a showdown, the union had amassed a $70 million strike fund and had secured an additional $50 million infusion from its licensing proceeds. Miller admitted the figures gave him a "nice feeling" in allowing him to claim, "For the first time, the players are independent and will be at a point where they can weather a lockout or strike better than the owners." To further assist the MLBPA's cause, he gave public endorsement to a union trial balloon of a rival player-backed league in the upcoming season should the clubs lock out their performers. When a handful of owners signaled their individual intentions to do exactly that by inserting "lockout clauses" into player contracts, Miller again emerged from behind the curtain to label these gambits violations of Basic Agreement language that only allowed special covenants if they "actually or potentially" provided benefits to players.[12]

Nonetheless, the PRC moved ahead with a spring-training lockout. Miller then offered the "friendly" advice through a reporter that "to have a meaningless lockout to support regressive proposals is to shoot yourself in the foot." He further warned the owners of the union's approaching Executive Board meeting, telling them, "If the players come out of that meeting mad, forget it." With the confrontation threatening to spin out of control, Fay Vincent now intervened. Insisting that if he had been commissioner at the time, collusion "wouldn't have happened under my watch," Vincent called for a halt to the lockout and a union pledge not to initiate a regular-season strike. To Miller's irritation, however, Vincent also injected his own settlement proposal, which suggested abandonment of the PRC salary-cap plank but keeping the status quo on the salary-arbitration eligibility standard for another three years. Refusing to credit the commissioner with some independence for having challenged the lockout, Miller insisted upon depicting Vincent's intervention as one that served his masters' interests whether they realized it or not.[13]

By mid-March the PRC had still not given up on its lockout. At the same time, cracks were emerging in the MLBPA's solidarity, with the most noticeable examples veterans Paul Molitor and Bob Boone. The two dissidents had been covertly sounding out other players on their commitment to the union demand to restore the two-year salary-arbitration standard. To Fehr the behavior was selfish, since Molitor had just reupped for big money with Milwaukee and Boone had inked a $2 million pact with Kansas City. EPSN's Peter Gammons then reported that not only had Molitor been secretly conversing with Bud Selig but that the two men had sketched out details of a settlement that included keeping the current arbitration qualification. The executive director immediately summoned his old boss to fly down to Florida for a showdown in just two days before the union's Executive Board.[14]

In a reprise of past glory, it was Miller's turn to again deliver a forceful history lesson to the MLBPA reps at a moment of crisis. He privately felt more sympathy for Molitor than for Boone, because the former had been squeezed by his personal contract situation with Selig and his union responsibilities. Boone, however, was another matter. Ever since the catcher had given his stalwart support during the 1981 strike, he had appeared to backslide. As had been the case in 1985, the veteran catcher's freelancing was now undermining the union's cause. At a preliminary meeting of Fehr, Miller, the union's bargaining panel, and the two dissidents, Molitor denied the Gammons article and insisted that no deal had been discussed or agreed upon with Selig. He went on to maintain that in talking with his owner—a fact he did not deny—he had only sought to impress upon the PRC chair the need for more reasonable proposals, but he did confess joining with Boone to poll other players on the union's salary-arbitration proposal. Boone proved more defiant, and Miller accordingly gave him no quarter. Prefacing his verbal assault with the words, "In the 1981 strike you were magnificent," the former chief bluntly continued, "I have to conclude from your actions now that you aren't the same man I knew." Boone fired back, asserting that he was the same man but the issues were not and criticizing "going to the mat" for a two-year arbitration threshold. Miller then scolded, "I think you've forgotten how important principle is in these cases." The 1981 strike, he argued, had been about the same fundamental principle—preserving the union's gains for those who would come after. The stormy session then concluded with neither man yielding.[15]

The next morning, at the aptly named Summit Hotel before an audience of players that had swollen to twice the usual number, Miller literally rose to the occasion. Enveloped in silent attention so complete one could have heard a pin drop, he avoided the rancor of the day before and calmly called upon his listeners to remain true to the principle of solidarity. "It is not my place to tell you what to do," he started, "but it's clear to me that what's happened the past few days has hurt." He then insisted that "a settlement has already been de-layed, and the settlement you get won't be as good as it could have been. But whatever happens, you'll get a better deal staying together. I'll tell you what I've told ballplayers from the beginning. Stay solid, and you can have anything that's reasonable and fair." He reminded them that any failure to back positions that had been "democratically arrived at" would result in their reps' "permanent loss of credibility." He ended with a rallying cry: "If you waver, you can count on one thing: the owners will never again take the player representatives seriously. The issue here is no longer just salary arbitration. It's the future effectiveness of the union."[16]

After Miller left the room, a four-hour pep rally ensued. By its end the as-sembled men—including Boone and Molitor—had endorsed their negotiators' recommendation to reject the PRC offer. Fehr emerged from the session joking that the attendees had "finally received" and repudiated the "ESPN offer." Individual players then took several more hours expressing support for the union to the press. With the membership having restored its resolve, by late the next Sunday night with the help of agent Randy Hendricks, the two sides had reached a compromise on salary arbitration. The top 17 percent of performers by service time with at least two but less than a full three years' tenure would regain the right to have pay disputes heard by an arbitrator. Overall, the proposed four-year pact would also guarantee twenty-five-man active rosters, boost the minimum salary to $100,000, and raise the owners' yearly pension contribution to $58 million. Deferring action on a player salary cap, the 1990 Basic Agreement instead called a joint-study committee on the economic state of the industry with a final report due in 1991. While Miller endorsed the pact as "a good settlement," he also issued an ominous foreboding. Rejecting the poverty claims of small-market owner hawks, he insisted that the recent confrontation had contradicted the usual logic that disputes arose "when an industry is in financial difficulty." He then warned, "If you can have a dispute when profits are in the hundreds of millions of dollars and at an all-time high, you can have a dispute *anytime* . . . such as when the Basic Agreement comes up for negotiation again."[17]

The 1990 pact was a modest, yet significant, union victory. When paired with the announcement of the $280 million collusion settlement and the resumption of real free-agent bidding, the developments once more set salaries soaring. Given the union's new victory after half a decade of Ueberroth-era setbacks—a literal reversal of fortune that stung the owners—it was arguably not the time to poke a stick in management's eyes and invite a thirst for vengeance. But in his status as an outside consultant and champion of the union rather than a day-to-day participant, Miller no longer was in sufficient proximity to gauge the consequences of his seeming vindictive and arrogant. Having suffered slings and arrows from the likes of Bowie Kuhn over many years, the former executive director now chose the opportunity provided by the release of his autobiography to strike back at those who had crossed him. As he saw it, the time was overdue to "set the record straight." With the assistance of the *Village Voice's* Allen Barra, he now did so in a volume appropriately entitled *A Whole Different Ball Game*.[18]

If Miller hoped that his personal account of the baseball revolution would be welcomed as a corrective of gross distortions and would heighten respect for what he had accomplished, he was disappointed. Although the book sold reasonably well—more than 100,000 copies in initial hardback and paperback versions—it drew only mixed reviews. At his editors' insistence he omitted a serious discussion of the first half-century of his life, including the more contentious parts of his childhood, his radicalism of the 1930s and 1940s, and his struggles to advance in the labor movement. Instead the final product was more an anecdotal history of his leadership of the Players Association and a slash-and-burn attack on tormentors past and present. While reviewers generally validated his claim to a central role in transforming the national pastime, they criticized his occasional intemperateness and even cruelty. In the words of *New York Times* reviewer James Edward Miller, Miller's account too often descended to "a bitterly unrestrained attack on his opponents that frequently diminishes its author."[19]

Bowie Kuhn was an obvious target for Miller's acerbic wit, but George Steinbrenner also drew the author's scorn for the lack of courage shown in 1981 and for the more recent persecution of star Dave Winfield. At the same time, Miller dubbed Fay Vincent's disciplinary hearing against Steinbrenner a "star chamber" and attributed the subsequent suspension of "The Boss" to the spite of rival owners over the Yankees magnate's lavish player spending. In general, Vincent came in for a large helping of criticism as an overreaching moralist with a raging case of commissioneritis. But the most intemperate verbal attacks were those Miller directed at Bart Giamatti. Once more assailing the deceased commissioner for his prior role in collusion, his arbitrary use of power in the Pete Rose matter, and his firing of gay umpire Dave Pallone over a private scandal—though here too the victim was not spared the author's indictment as a former scab—Miller even implied that Giamatti's death by heart attack had been a self-inflicted consequence of guilt from his Rose vendetta. At the time of the commissioner's death, Terry Miller had privately penned a harsh postmortem in her e.e. cummings lower-case style, suggesting that the dead man had delivered on his Faustian bargain. In his book Miller chose to incorporate the composition into his anti-Giamatti indictment. Despite pleas from the deceased's loyalist Vincent, relayed to Miller by Don Fehr, to have the offending section struck, the author had adamantly refused.[20]

And yet in marked contrast to the thin skin he displayed in print toward those, living or dead, he viewed as enemies, Miller modestly kept out of public view his touching kindness toward the struggling Curt Flood. When the players' union feted Miller on the release of his memoir with a party at Mickey Mantle's New York restaurant, the retired outfielder and his wife were among the invited guests. Having hosted the Floods for breakfast that morning, the Millers placed the couple at the head table along with baseball "sabermetrician" Bill James (who had contributed a forward for the book) and old ally Dick Moss. When Flood was eventually diagnosed with the throat cancer that would take his life on Martin

Luther King Day 1997, Miller frequently called the patient to offer personal words of encouragement, with Flood's spouse relaying phone messages to her now-voiceless husband for him to compose replies for her to vocalize back.[21]

Within the ranks of baseball management, continued grudging respect merged with the suspicion that Miller still pulled the MLBPA's strings from behind the scenes. The public behavior of union officialdom toward him occasionally reinforced such thoughts. The union's general counsel, Gene Orza, on one occasion responded to a postspeech question of his opinion of the former executive director with a wordless deep bow. Don Fehr retained Miller's son Peter as a consultant to Japanese baseball executives even though his father had never requested the favor nor been told of it in advance. At the 1992 annual meeting of the National Academy of Arbitrators, Miller was invited as the convention's keynote speaker, and the list of those seated at the dais included former and current baseball adjudicators Tom Roberts, Richard Bloch, and George Nicolau as well as former Steelworker colleague and Academy president David Feller. An additional empty chair had also been placed at a position of honor at the head table—a symbol of respect to the deceased Peter Seitz.[22]

Respect and power also carried with it the loss of any image Miller or his union might have had as an underdog. Former rep turned manager Phil Garner understood the necessity of the changes but still complained about the multitude of rules that made it harder to carry out player transactions. Ted Simmons, now a general manager, found himself in the uncomfortable position of a defendant in a union grievance, charged with releasing a player for economic rather than performance reasons. To critics, the Players Association and by extension Miller now seemed not just powerful but vengeful toward those who had crossed it. Barry Rona, the PRC negotiator during collusion who had since been fired by Fay Vincent, was denied union accreditation when he sought to become a player agent. When he sought to overturn the action, Miller personally testified at length against him, but an arbitrator ruled in Rona's favor.[23]

With their huge salaries, combined with the recreational drug scandals of the 1980s, players too sometimes appeared arrogant and dismissive of fans and even their predecessors' past sacrifices. In 1976 the average major-league ballplayer had earned a salary eight times that of an ordinary American worker. By 1991 the comparison had soared to forty-seven times higher. Doug DeCinces—who had made the transition from player to union activist under Miller to heading a licensing company—explained, "The real problem comes in the young players . . . who don't know who Marvin Miller is, what the history is, where this all came from. . . . They just know if they play and do well, they'll make a lot of money.

I think the Players Association has a major task in educating them." Offering his own critical perspective of the union by the early 1990s, sportscaster Bob Costas conceded that initially "it was clear that first Miller and then Fehr-Orza were right about almost everything." Acknowledging the union's past reputation for consistent albeit blunt-spoken honesty that had contrasted sharply with management falsehoods and obfuscations, he admitted, "A whole generation of us pretty much grew up reading from the gospel according to Marvin Miller and analyzed almost everything through that prism." But by the 1990s, his underlying sympathies had changed. While he agreed that "the owners are still screwed up" and their positions often were still "dishonest or disingenuous or poorly thought out," it was also clear to him that "if the owners ever got their act together and presented a clear and reasonable vision for the reform of the game, that [the union] would still resolutely resist it."[24]

In the words of sportswriter Howard Bryant, the underdog union that Marvin Miller had once commanded now saw as its mission "not the dismantling of a historically unfair system" but "the maintaining of an empire." And as with empires generally, a mix of overconfidence and disdain for one's adversaries could become a dangerous self-delusion. In the MLBPA's past confrontations with the industry, it had not been solely the talents of Miller or Fehr alone—as skilled as they were—or even the membership's ability to enforce solidarity that had guaranteed victory, but also the disunity and ineptitude of the owners and the undercutting of management by commissioners. But now the small-market majority of baseball ownership had begun to consolidate its political power in ways that made continuation of such self-inflicted wounds less likely. In the aftermath of the 1990 lockout, nine new owners entered the big leagues from a business background more antilabor than that of the 1960s and 1970s and with track records of crushing unions. Following the industry's 1990 defeat and the erosion of support for Vincent over his fumbled handling of franchise-expansion fees and increased revenue sharing from "superstation"-owned clubs, the self-described "last commissioner" was canned in September 1992. Bud Selig, chairman of the owners' Executive Council, effectively became his replacement. No longer would a commissioner hired by the clubs but not necessarily of them meddle in labor negotiations. The PRC then hired Richard Ravitch, a man who had previously bumped heads with New York's powerful municipal unions as head of Gotham's public-transit system, as its new negotiator. Ravitch pressed for relief to the small markets through greater revenue sharing in exchange for the promise to the rich of compensatory savings in the form of a player salary cap.[25]

Reinforcing the arguments of Selig, Ravitch, and their management supporters was a sudden drop in forecasted national television revenue because of the recession of the early 1990s. For all clubs the changes in baseball economics since the 1960s had tied team spending to television money growth from local and national sources. Demonstrating just how tight the linkage had become, broadcast revenue from 1971 to 1990 had climbed by 1,742 percent as player salaries had risen a virtually identical 1,741 percent. "Small-market" organizations, increasingly defined by their more limited regional broadcast revenue, were especially dependent upon the income they received from national contracts, while wealthier teams continued to extend their edge through larger and larger local cable deals not subject to the same level of sharing. Even though overall major-league revenues had risen to $1.9 billion and the average franchise value had jumped to more than $100 million, these aggregates cloaked mounting revenue disparities between clubs while overall industry profits had shrunk by more than one-half in two years. In contrast major-league pay had risen sharply with the collapse of collusion to a level of 55 percent of industry revenue in 1992 and 58 percent in 1993. Added to this background as a likely trigger of renewed labor-management confrontation was the failure of the joint-study committee created by the 1990 Basic Agreement. After a year's delay in producing a report, the panel argued vaguely for greater revenue sharing between clubs but reached no consensus on whether doing so required payroll sacrifice. Symptomatic of the panelists' divisions and confusion, they failed to call Miller as a historical witness—an omission for which former union counsel Dick Moss, who was summoned, chided them.[26]

Baseball owners' alarm at their television-money forecasts virtually guaranteed that they would seek a hard bargain with the Players Association. That a small-market owner was now the top industry executive also effectively removed the possibility this time of salvation through a commissioner intervention. At Kohler, Wisconsin, past setting of the longest work stoppage in American history (a UAW strike of eight and a half years), in August 1993 the owners' small- and large-market factions initially failed to forge unity over revenue sharing and a salary cap. Half a year later, however, they had closed ranks behind a proposal in which the wealthiest ten organizations would pay into a revenue-sharing fund, a ten-member "middle class" would neither pay into nor receive money from the pool, and the poorest eight teams would receive payments on a sliding scale. Armed with the hard-won consensus, the clubs then pressured the union for a salary cap, and management hard-liners rammed through a requirement of a three-fourths supermajority for ratifying a new labor pact.[27]

As the industry pushed the union toward the cliff of a player strike, individual owners insisted that Marvin Miller still called the MLBPA's shots and demanded the players free themselves from him. Even George Steinbrenner joined in the accusations, insisting, "The shadow of Marvin Miller is there. I never believed Marvin Miller retired. An old warhorse like that . . . no way is he not in the picture." Other executives more indirectly blamed the former union chief by asserting that Don Fehr's refusal to accept the industry's terms stemmed from a need to free himself from Miller's shadow by proving his own bona fides. Although Miller was playing no direct role in the negotiations, it was true that he was publicly pressing his successor not to yield an inch. In *Sport* magazine that spring, he reminded readers anew of management's past bad faith in sponsoring collusion, and he chided the owners for demanding that players bear the burden of their calls for increased revenue sharing. With the union also adamantly rejecting anything resembling a salary cap, the inevitable consequence was the start of a player strike on August 12, 1994.[28]

Once the strike had begun, Miller labored to project a public air of confidence to the press. He insisted that, having stuck together in the past, the players would do so again this time. He solely blamed the owners for having forced the season's halt, and as proof he offered the clubs' decision to increase the voting majority they required for a deal, insisting that their broader aim was to "destroy the union." Attacking Selig as a figurehead and trumpeting Fehr's experience, he maintained that if the players would "simply keep their cool" and remember their essential value, they would eventually prevail. But as no quick resolution emerged and both sides' losses mounted, the rest of the regular season as well as the playoffs and World Series fell by the wayside. Reflecting fans' mounting anger, big-league licensing sales fell by 15 percent, and the clubs' financial hit from the combination of cancelled games and rescinded television money reached $364 million by year's end. The players in turn lost 4/15ths of their 1994 season pay—an average of $300,000 per man.[29]

While Fehr carried on with his union's life-and-death struggle, Miller found his negotiating talents circumscribed to staring down a car dealer in Manhattan. "This," he quipped to a reporter, "is the only bargaining I do these days." He did offer his endorsement of a familiar union gambit of threatening a rival player-sponsored circuit to pressure the owners to yield. At a celebration hosted by *Sports Illustrated* recognizing its choices as the forty most influential men in sports over the last four decades, Miller was saluted for having "most dramatically elevated and altered the games we play and watch." Admitting that he was fielding an "unbelievable" number of press inquiries about the strike, when asked why he responded bluntly if not modestly, "Well, it's easy to figure out." As the work stoppage dragged on, the owners readied a formal declaration of a bargaining impasse, which they intended to succeed with a unilateral imposition of a salary cap. With Miller's public endorsement, the union then filed NLRB failure-to-bargain charges against the clubs with the aim of securing a ruling blocking the clubs that would enable the membership to return to work and possibly also even result in a mass declaration of player free agency. After the mutual displays of hardball, both sides then agreed to mediation by former Secretary of Labor William Usery. But in a show of defiance, the clubs removed from their "final" offer earlier "carrots" of a guaranteed minimum $1 billion industry payroll, revived earlier hard-line positions of a salary cap set at 50 percent of major-league revenues and complete elimination of salary arbitration, and added a proposal of a "luxury tax" on any team payrolls exceeding $34 million. Based upon 1994 salary figures, eight clubs would owe $20 million or more to their brethren. Seven organizations—including Bud Selig's Brewers—would avoid the levy entirely.[30]

To Miller's astonishment and dismay, a desperate Players Association then agreed in principle to a system of player-payroll taxation and redistribution. The union's former leader lamented to Toronto's *Globe and Mail,* "I would never have proposed that—not in a million years. I think Don and the players will live to regret that one. It was plain appeasement." In the spring of 1995, the owners then tried to hire replacement players, only to be blocked by an NLRB injunction. On March 31, 1995, federal judge Sonia Sotomayor—who in 2009 would become the first Latina justice of the U.S. Supreme Court—enjoined the magnates from unilaterally imposing their bargaining proposal and effectively maintained the 1990 Basic Agreement indefinitely. With the owners stymied in their hopes of unilaterally imposing a new order and the union willing to return to work while bargaining continued, on April 26, 1995, the strike ended some 232 days after it had begun.[31]

Despite the Sotomayor ruling and the players' subsequent return, three months later there had still been no serious bargaining progress. In August 1995 Miller wrote Fehr on the strike's anniversary for a progress report. His protégé's clever yet pessimistic response summed up his frustration—"Re-read Cervantes. Except when you do, superimpose the notion that Don Quixote *knows* he is in a useless endeavor. So it goes. Any ideas? Don." Major-league baseball would struggle on for over a year longer, after the end of the 1996 season, before a new Basic Agreement was achieved. When a tentative pact that would have imposed so-called "luxury" taxes in 1997–1999 of 35 percent on club's salaries in excess of $51 million at first and then rising to $59 million seemed close late in the campaign, the White Sox's Jerry Reinsdorf initially joined forces with small-market colleagues to defeat it. Claiming to oppose the deal because he supported expanding the number of tax-paying clubs beyond the specified maximum of five that included his team, after leading the charge to block ratification he then turned around and signed slugger Albert Belle to a $55-million five-year deal.[32]

From the sidelines, Miller assailed Reinsdorf's blatant hypocrisy and accurately predicted that the magnate's suckered colleagues might well exact revenge by ratifying the very deal they had previously been conned into voting down. Urging them to do exactly that, the former executive director warned owners not to even consider a new spring-training lockout in 1997. "I can't believe they'd be stupid enough to try that," he offered, adding, "But think of the most stupid thing possible, and they usually do it." This time Miller was thankfully proven wrong. In a 24–4 vote the owners reversed themselves and approved the new Basic Agreement and its three years of luxury tax, no such levies in 2000 and 2001, and revenue sharing starting at $70 million from the thirteen richest clubs to the poorest thirteen.[33]

With a new Basic Agreement belatedly restoring labor peace through 2001, baseball gradually returned to a deceptive normality. Aided by new Arizona and Tampa Bay expansion teams, the industry regained the attendance it had lost. Fans now flocked to see a startling offensive explosion, highlighted by Mark McGuire's and Sammy Sosa's 1998 chase of Roger Maris's single-season home-run record. A new five-year television deal with Fox, ESPN, and NBC delivered $2.1 billion that further eased industry anxieties. As for player pay, which had stood at a prestrike average of $1.17 million only to drop to $900,000 in strike-shortened 1994, even with luxury taxes on high-salary clubs the individual mean rebounded to $1.4 million in 1998 and nearly $2 million by 2000. By that same year the majors' highest-payroll clubs were spending over $90 million each—more than double prestrike levels—and twenty-one teams claimed higher pay than that of the biggest 1993 spender. Ironically, for those clubs at the payroll bottom, the hope that increased revenue sharing by and luxury taxes on the profligate would render their own organizations more competitive did not happen. From 1995 through 1999 every World Series champion still ranked in the industry's top seven spenders.[34]

As a nation of baseball watchers reveled in the sport's exciting and lucrative new "power surge," Marvin Miller once more receded from media attention. With peace guaranteed to 2002, it seemed that save for occasional inquiries on tamer topics or other sports' labor fights, the octogenarian legend would remain out of public sight or mind. When he resurfaced, most assumed, it would be prompted by occasions that served to highlight his long career and its accomplishments. If that was his own expectation too, before long he would find himself plunging headlong once more into controversy as the public defender of unpopular accused baseball stars. As a result, to his frustration and dismay, he would find himself an increasingly solitary figure—a Don Quixote tilting at windmills—more frequently denounced for holding controversial opinions than honored for his achievements.

Sixteen

Lightning Rod

Back in 1983 an anonymous baseball official had declared, "The only way Marvin Miller will ever get into the Hall of Fame is through the public entrance." But in the years immediately following his retirement from the Players Association, such sentiments had seemingly mellowed. Even Dick Young endorsed his selection. Miller himself was less optimistic, seeing Cooperstown as a company town controlled by his adversaries in management. In the aftermath of the Pete Rose gambling scandal and banishment from Hall of Fame consideration, the retired MLBPA leader had recommended the union create its own place of honor, with the costs of such a facility paid out of player licensing revenues. Although the organization did not follow the advice, in 1997 it did inaugurate an annual honor in his name recognizing an active ballplayer for distinguished public-service work within his community.[1]

As the old millennium now yielded to the new, more tributes came his way. In 2000 he was inducted into the International Jewish Sports Hall of Fame, and on Miller's eighty-third birthday that same year, sportscaster Bob Costas extended his personal well-wishes. The announcer praised the old lion's "keen intelligence and unshakeable honesty" and described Miller as "one of the significant figures in baseball history." Costas even apologized for fans' tendency to blame Miller and the union for "every pain-in-the-ass .250 hitter making six million dollars a year," likening the criticism to "blaming Alexander Graham Bell for call waiting." The honeymoon between the two men, however, did not last past the end of the 2000 baseball season. In his book *Fair Ball,* Costas attacked the Players Association for opposing the pairing of more revenue sharing with salary restraints, leading Miller to square off politely with him on Charlie Rose's interview program. Afterward in print the gloves came off, with the MLBPA's former leader assailing the broadcaster for promoting management's line and thereby acting unprofessionally while claiming to be an impartial journalist. Costas fired back in kind, accusing Miller of being "constitutionally incapable of letting go of the wars he has already fought and won" and "seeing all baseball issues through the narrow prism of circumstances that no longer apply." He then concluded, "I guess Marvin Miller will remain in his encampment, railing at the heretics."[2]

Nor was it just Costas who seemingly had concluded that the former players' chief was a divisive—or worse, outdated—symbol of baseball's labor wars. In 1999 and 2000, columnists and former ballplayers of Miller's era promoted his inclusion in the Hall of Fame by its Veterans Committee—a fifteen-member panel dominated by industry and media traditionalists. Ira Berkow offered a litany of baseball heroes in Miller's corner, and Cooperstown inductee and former MLBPA leader Senator Jim Bunning claimed the two proudest moments of his baseball career had been his perfect game and his role in choosing Miller to lead the Players Association. Home-run king Henry Aaron insisted that "Marvin Miller is as important to the history of baseball as Jackie Robinson," and Robin Roberts—who had grown more critical of both his former leader and the union over time—still concurred. "I don't know of anyone who changed the game more than Marvin Miller," he stated. "He deserves to be in the Hall of Fame." In his 1999 induction speech in Cooperstown, pitcher Nolan Ryan went out of his way to include Miller among those he thanked for helping his career. The next year, Miller's coauthor Allen Barra became the main torchbearer of the induction campaign, supported by such seemingly unlikely champions as Costas, George Steinbrenner, and Buzzie Bavasi. But on both occasions the Veterans Committee as a whole refused to consider him, offering the weak excuse that a subgroup responsible for screening nominations had been unable to agree upon whether Miller qualified in the "executives" category.[3]

Ignoring his snubs, Miller continued to live an active retirement marked by occasional broadsides at owner greed and private work in behalf of both his old union and others. He contributed a foreword to a new edition of the 1955 novel *Men in Spikes*, written by *Eight Men Out* author Eliot Asinof. Hip-replacement surgery forced him to give up ice skating, but he still attended weekly tennis sessions. Owing to his renown as the man who had defeated baseball's perpetual reserve clause, he was approached by the Boston chapter of the American Federation of Radio and Television Artists (AFRTA) for his advice with a similar problem. In the Beantown media market, on-air personalities who quit their studio employers for greener pastures were barred from taking a similar job with a rival for a minimum of one year. Miller counseled AFRTA local leader Ashley Adams to lobby the state legislature for remedial action rather than pursue a strike. The chapter's decision to heed Miller's advice paid off with passage of a bill granting the broadcast personalities their own version of free-agent rights.[4]

While baseball's next round of labor strife still lay some years in the future, Miller found the media seeking his views on other sporting labor controversies. In early 1999 NBA players folded before an owner lockout and agreed to a cap on individual salaries, even though their old contract had three years remaining. Not surprisingly the former baseball-union chief skewered the NBAPA and basketball commissioner David Stern alike in the *New York Daily News*. While he assailed Stern's hypocrisy for having used the media to deliver an ultimatum of a player-membership vote on management's proposal while enforcing a gag order on the owners, Miller still offered no excuses for the union's lack of spine. "I'm not even tolerant when this kind of thing happens to people who make ordinary salaries," he said, and added, "When you have people making millions of dollars proving to have no guts, then that's awful." In uncharacteristically salty public language, Miller concluded with the following advice, "Once your negotiating committee has authority, you don't pay any attention to the crap coming out of Stern's mouth. You just tell him to go screw."[5]

Hitting closer to home that same year was another union defeat that reinforced his continued conviction that baseball had not reconciled itself to the reality of labor organizations in its midst—the crushing of the majors' Umpires Association. Even though a dissident faction had already surfaced within his AL ranks, Richie Phillips still chose a high-risk gambit to force serious negotiation for a new contract. Because the old pact expiring at the end of 1999 included a no-strike pledge, the MLUA chief advised his men to submit individual resignations en masse, assuming that the forced shortage of umps would force the leagues' hands. But AL and NL officials turned the tables on him by accepting the resignations and then hiring twenty-eight nonunion replacements. As the incredulous Miller pointed out to a *Rocky Mountain News* reporter, the umpires union had acted in dubious legality anyway because the existing pact had barred either side from taking "concerted" disruptive action. But worse still, the ill-considered resignation strategy had handed the leagues the very weapon with which to remove the union members it wanted gone. Proving Miller's point, the majority of the "retired" umps never regained their jobs. An angry rank and file then voted to decertify and fire Phillips. As Miller summarized the sorry state of affairs, "This is a comedy, except it's a tragedy."[6]

The war between baseball and its umpires was a portent of things to come. By 2001, the home-run heroics of Barry Bonds were offering an exciting distraction from the gathering storm. But on the morning of September 11, 2001, the attentions of all Americans—including those of Marvin and Terry Miller—were brutally wrenched from ordinary affairs when nineteen terrorists of Osama bin Laden's Al Qaeda network seized control of four airliners. Two of the planes then smashed into the World Trade Center in Lower Manhattan. The ensuing fires and collapses of the Twin Towers killed nearly three thousand people, including firefighter and former Tiger farmhand Mike Weinberg. A third plane plunged into the Pentagon, while the fourth disintegrated upon contact in a Pennsylvania farm field after its passengers heroically denied the hijackers control of the aircraft. From their Upper East Side apartment, the Millers like other New Yorkers watched, heard, and literally smelled the unfolding horror. Below and to their south, stunned soot-covered pedestrians trudged up the island or eastward across the Brooklyn Bridge. Clouds of stinking particulates permeated offices and residential buildings the length of Manhattan for months to come, including the Millers' high-rise.[7]

Along with the rest of the nation, baseball enlisted in the effort to pull Americans together. Commissioner Selig rescheduled games tabbed for 9/11— the first regular-season postponements for nonlabor reasons since the D-Day invasion—and postponed the owners' quarterly meetings. After a week's hiatus the season resumed. An exciting World Series generated a major upset as one of baseball's newest franchises, the Arizona Diamondbacks, bested the heavily favored Yankees. Once the postseason had concluded, however, labor friction reheated. Having extended an olive branch shortly after 9/11 that the clubs would not lock out the players next spring training, less than a week after the Series ended and just three days before a scheduled bargaining session, the owners declared their intent to eliminate two franchises.[8]

What lay behind management's hardball stance were the financial disparities between rich and poor clubs that the recession and 9/11's economic shocks now threatened to exacerbate. Back in the spring of 2000 a Blue Ribbon Commission consisting of twelve club executives and four outside panelists—former Senator George Mitchell, Yale president Richard Levin, conservative columnist George Will, and former Fed chairman Paul Volcker—but without any union representatives had issued findings emphasizing the industry wealth divide and forecasting long-term disaster. The report provided the owners a blueprint for a bargaining agenda by rejecting an across-the-board salary cap but calling for a new 50 percent luxury tax on club payrolls over $84 million, an annual "competitive-balance" draft permitting the eight worst teams to claim players from outside the forty-man rosters of the eight top clubs, and an amateur draft that would include foreign players and offer weak teams additional selections.[9]

Marvin Miller had singled out Bud Selig as an object of particular scorn ever since the latter had orchestrated the cabal that had ousted Fay Vincent and then forced the 1994 showdown. He now accused the commissioner of blatant conflict of interest in championing the Blue Ribbon recommendations and calling for franchise contraction. Selig's "small-market" Brewers—nominally run by his daughter Wendy—would directly benefit from the policies he was pushing for, and Minnesota—one of the teams speculated to be on the chopping block—just happened to be a franchise close to the Brewers' home market. Contraction would cost the Players Association eighty active and reserve positions, reallocate a mere $2 million more each in broadcast revenue to the surviving franchises, and burden the latter at the same time with an estimated $10 million in buyout costs. Even the buyout could be construed as Selig's repayment of a past favor by Twins owner Carl Pohlad, because Pohlad's investment company in 1995 had floated the Brewers a $3 million loan to prevent its bankruptcy at that time.[10]

Despite blistering attacks by Miller and others, the commissioner stuck to his guns. While the union pursued a restraint-of-trade grievance to block contraction, during the offseason the growth in player salaries slowed to 5 percent—less than half that of the previous year. On February 5, 2002, a day after the Minnesota Supreme Court upheld an injunction blocking removal of the Twins franchise, Selig announced the delay of contraction for at least a year. In all other respects, however, he held fast to the industry's hard-line proposals, including the hiking of clubs' shared local revenue to 50 percent and luxury taxes at the same percentage upon any team payroll exceeding $98 million. The Players Association took a month before countering with an offer that only raised teams' shared-revenue percentage to 22.5 percent from the existing 20 percent and rejected the restoration of luxury taxes. Buttressing the union's stance was Forbes' annual report on major-league finances, which found a $75 million operating profit for the industry rather than a loss and twenty organizations making money instead of Selig's claimed five.[11]

As the two sides wrangled, 2002 played out as the worst season since strike-plagued 1994, tarnished not just by contraction talk but continued terrorism fears, rumors of performance-enhancing-drug scandals, unseemly family in-fighting over deceased legend Ted Williams's remains, and a tied and suspended All-Star Game. Once more Miller as the union's living memory used his media contacts to support the MLBPA and urged it to maintain an uncompromising posture. He insisted to *USA Today*'s Ian O'Connor that the owners' demands were "all designed to do one thing: cut payroll." He went further, however, insisting that the industry's ultimate goal was nothing less than breaking the Players Association. As he saw it, the union would be cooperating in suicide if it accepted the owners' luxury-tax demands, explaining, "So if the union ratifies a deal that would guarantee a lower payroll than if you had no union at all, what person in his right mind would pay dues to that organization?" When another reporter countered that a $42,000-a-year laborer could not grasp multimillionaire players striking in such perilous times, Miller stopped him short: "But that's because the guy making $42,000 is misinformed." He then recited the longstanding talking point that the union was only directly responsible for negotiating the level of the minimum salary, while arbitration only determined the pay of ten to twelve players more each season. The vast majority of members' pay owed to their or their agents' own bargaining. In these individual negotiations no one was holding a gun to an owner's head to agree to a particular sum.[12]

With agonizing slowness, the two sides finally began to make progress. Selig agreed to rule out a spring lockout, and the union responded in kind by deferring setting a strike date and accepting the concept of a worldwide prospect draft. Shyam Das, the arbitrator hearing the MLBPA's pending grievance against the owners, in turn delayed a ruling to give the bargainers more time. On the central issues of revenue sharing and payroll taxes, the clubs were still demanding 50 percent levels but indicated a willingness to at least phase in the percentages. But the Players Association refused to accept anything that high, insisted that larger shares within a smaller overall redistribution pool go only to weak teams rather than be equally allocated among all clubs, and proposed luxury-tax thresholds that effectively exempted all but a few teams from ever paying the levies. According to the figures offered by the union, the owners' offer translated into a $300 million shift to small-market clubs while the players' proposal equaled $228 million.[13]

Once more the media sought out Miller for his perspective, and as usual he was anything but shy in obliging them. To *USA Today* he acknowledged the renewed press attention, observing, "I try not to turn anybody down because I feel the facts are not really getting out, and that is no different from the past." To him the biggest misconception was that it was the players who were seeking revolutionary changes and had precipitated the crisis, not management. He noted with skepticism that nowhere in the clubs' demands for higher payroll taxes did they require receiving teams to actually spend the dollars transferred to them. He then fired back, "This may be the first monopoly in the history of free enterprise to complain about a lack of competition. This is the equivalent of a man who murders his parents and asks for mercy because he's an orphan. . . . If you truly believe you have unbalanced competition and you want to change it, you wouldn't knock out competitors—you would add them [through franchise relocation] in the best markets. Then you would let economic competition take place."[14]

In a similar conversation with the *Kansas City Star*'s Joe Posnanski, Miller again refused to give a single inch either to the owners or to fan sensitivities. Regarding the latter, the retired executive director was undiplomatic in his critique. "Fans have absolutely no right to have any say in the terms and conditions of players," he declared, and added by way of comparison, "I don't think a car buyer has any right to have any input whatsoever on the wages and benefits of automobile employees." Insisting "fans have never related" to ballplayers, he added, "People don't know the issues. They don't understand. Even President Bush doesn't understand. He said he would be 'outraged' if there was a strike. Ask the President if he's in favor of a tax that would discourage companies from paying higher salaries. Ask him that. He's as ignorant as the rest of them." Citing the plight of cities in which "schools are crumbling and bridges need repair," he lamented, "Fans don't understand that the largest pocketbook issue that faces them is the tax money being used for essentially free stadiums for wealthy owners." Expressing contempt for even the term "luxury tax," Miller went on, "There's a very clever name. It sounds harmless. Of course, that doesn't describe what it is. It is a penalty, and a large one, which is designed to prevent clubs from hiring people and prevent them from paying people what they should get on the open market." Closing with critical comments at media coverage of the impasse, he bemoaned, "I can't tell you how many times I've heard that this or that is the end of baseball" and blasted the "plague on both your houses" editorializing as "lazy" and "intellectual dishonesty."[15]

While he delivered his calculated public outrage, privately Miller was urging Fehr to consider a different tack—turning the tables on management demands for payroll restraint by insisting in return that the industry agree to minimum club-payroll requirements. On that concept, however, Fehr was more the free-labor-market purist than his predecessor, rejecting Miller's argument that in principle, mandated minimum payrolls expressed in dollars or revenue percentages were no different than federal minimum wages. The union leadership also feared with some justification that if it advanced such a proposal, it would then give the MLBPA's adversaries greater logical ammunition to demand a hard salary cap rather than an indirect drag on payroll.[16]

By August 15, the owners were holding to a 50 percent luxury tax but had raised its starting threshold to $102 million and were amenable to a 37.5 percent first-year phase-in. The union had countered with a 15 to 30 percent sliding scale based upon contract year and the number of prior threshold violations, with levies starting at the $130 million mark in 2003 and peaking at $150 million in 2005. When the clubs rejected the offer, the union set a strike date of August 30. In hopes of splitting off big-market clubs from their poorer brethren, Fehr dispatched a letter, ostensibly to his membership but intended for leaking, asserting that under management's proposal the Yankees would lose $87 million, the Mets and Red Sox $34 million each, and the Seattle Mariners $32 million. After the antagonists agreed to defer a worldwide draft by naming a study committee, PRC negotiator Rob Manfred offered a new revenue-sharing proposal that lowered the total transferred sum to $270 million, and the union in turn gave consent to a "straight-pool" system of equal team distribution. The union's withdrawal of its prior offer of a $235 million minimum yearly redistribution in favor of phased-in amounts starting at but $172.3 million in 2003, however, infuriated the owners.[17]

With the Players Association's strike just days away, the clubs lowered to 36 the percentage of local revenue subject to distribution and raised their proposed tax thresholds to $107 million in the first three years and $111 by 2006. The payroll tax for a club's "first offense" was dropped from 50 percent to 35 percent, with 5 percent increases for each subsequent violation. Selig personally entered the thrice-daily bargaining sessions, the owners once more raised the threshold to $112 million, and the union lowered its counteroffer to $120 million. One day before the deadline, the two issues still unresolved were the payroll-tax percentage and the question of whether the levy would remain in place through the last year of the contract. The latter issue carried major import, because if the tax terms stayed to the end of the deal they would constitute the status quo even after expiration until replaced by a new Basic Agreement.[18]

In the wee hours of August 30 the two sides reached agreement. Showing greater relief than jubilation, Selig and Fehr congratulated each other on avoiding an exhibition-season or regular-season interruption. Luxury-tax thresholds would start at $117 million in 2003 and climb to $136.5 million by 2006. Club first offenses would be penalized at a 17.5 percent rate in 2003 and 22.5 percent in the years 2004–2005. "Second strikes" by clubs would cost 30 percent in 2004–2006, and a third consecutive year of violation in 2005 or 2006 would trigger a 40 percent penalty. The percentage of local revenue shared between the clubs was boosted from 20 percent to 34 percent. Instead of the owners securing an $85 million fund under the commissioner's control for emergency aid to franchises, the Basic Agreement cut out all but $10 billion and replaced most of the difference with a complicated second-stage surtax imposed on clubs that were net payers to the primary revenue-sharing pool.[19]

To an unhappy Marvin Miller, the union had again traded basic principles for temporary security, and he labeled the reinstitution of the payroll taxation system a "poison apple." Immediately after the announcement of the new deal and again in an afterword to a new edition of *A Whole Different Ball Game*, he criticized his union's collective loss of historical memory and attributed the erosion to the fact the membership no longer included men with first-hand knowledge of the bad old days. He flatly rejected the owners' proclamations of present and future financial calamity and the notion that the new pact would restore competitive balance. Drawing distinctions between spring-training and regular-season interruptions, he also challenged the idea that baseball had been crippled by labor strife since the 1960s. He argued that in his fifteen years at the MLBPA's helm, the lost time from in-season strikes had been but three-tenths of 1 percent of industry work days. Accordingly he described his period of leadership as the "most peaceful in American industry in converting from non-union to union status," and he blamed all the subsequent strife on the industry's continued refusal to accept the reality. Once more he assailed Selig personally for conflicts of interest as both a team investor and the sport's commissioner, and he accused him of having deliberately maneuvered his colleagues into backing a special-interest agenda contrary to the industry's overall best interests.[20]

On the field and at the gate, however, the big-league economy contradicted Miller's view of the 2002 pact as a bad deal. Reassuring the union's leadership, individual salaries and team payrolls both continued their upward climb despite the renewed taxation. Aggregate revenues reached $4.1 billion by 2004, and player pay still claimed more than one-half of it. Fueled by George Steinbrenner's Yankee Entertainment and Sports (YES) cable network, New York's payroll alone soared to more than $184 million—twice that of 2000—as early as 2004, and by 2006 it stood just short of $200 million. By 2005 the major-league-average salary smashed through the $2 million barrier and drove toward $3 million. Attendance, television ratings, and even on-field competitive balance improved, with eight different teams winning the World Series in the new millennium's first decade. In 2007 the two sides would again avoid a work stoppage by reaching a deal ensuring labor peace through 2011 while boosting tax thresholds and setting payroll levies at 22.5 percent for one-time overspending and 30 percent and 40 percent for each next violation.[21]

As the 2000s moved forward, however, it was not the perpetuation of salary-drag schemes and revenue-sharing formulas that placed Miller most at odds not only with his traditional adversaries but even his own union. Instead it was the issue of drugs—not recreational substances but chemical compounds lumped together under the labels "steroids" or "performance-enhancing drugs" (PEDs). Beginning in the late 1980s and then accelerating in the late 1990s in the aftermath of baseball's middecade train wreck, anecdotal evidence pointed to a dramatic surge in PED use by players hoping to juice performance and with it pay. As far back as 1990 the federal government had banned the nonmedical use of anabolic steroids, but the 1994 Dietary Supplements Health and Education Act (DSHEA) had opened a huge loophole by lifting the burden of proof of the latter products' safety and efficacy before reaching market. Although the owners had raised the matter of random testing as early as 1994, the union had never been presented a formal proposal and viewed the subject as one intended merely to put it on the defensive as management pressed for payroll restraint. In the aftermath of the 1996 settlement—which did not include a new performance-drug policy—baseball had enjoyed a suspicious but restorative power surge highlighted by Mark McGuire's seventy and Sammy Sosa's sixty round-trippers in 1998 and Barry Bonds's shattering of those same marks just three years later.[22]

Prior to 2002 baseball's drug policies had been focused exclusively on illegal recreational drugs such as cocaine and had permitted individual testing only after just-cause findings by a three-person medical panel. Having never been persuaded when he had led the players that amphetamines aided their performances—although many in the membership clearly disagreed and acted accordingly—Miller viewed the new performance-drug controversy through what was arguably an outdated prism. He blithely dismissed as rubbish the claims of steroids' central role in the dramatic offensive explosion and viewed the controversy as a modern-day media-driven witch hunt. With a perspective shaped by his own earlier experience with blacklisting and the knowledge that the national pastime's earlier recreational-drug hysteria had eventually faded after a decade of sensational headlines, the ex–executive director decried random testing as "a perfect tool for harassing an employee if you want to, somebody you don't like, somebody you may have signed to a too-good contract." The very idea of forcing compulsory urine testing on employees struck Miller as a blatant violation of a worker's privacy rights and his constitutional protections against self-incrimination. Accordingly he insisted, "You can't search a man's person, his house or garage until after you get a search warrant from a judge. I don't think you should be allowed to search his bladder or his bloodstream either."[23]

Save for such occupations as police officer, firefighter, or airline pilot involved in protecting the public, random drug testing without individual cause was debatable policy. But how far also did the union's duty to protect the health of its members extend, even if the effort infringed upon privacy rights? As Chicago White Sox player rep Kelly Wunsch—a supporter of random testing—noted, did not the use of PEDs by fellow players force those not wanting to do so to risk falling behind and losing their jobs? And what substances should be included in any proposed industry crackdown? Creatine, a supplement taken in pill or powder form, presented no apparent long-term dangers and boosted the user's level of adenosine triphosphate (ATP)—the molecule responsible for muscular quickness in transitioning from inactivity to action such as running or swinging a bat. Androstenedione, a "precursor" drug made notorious by its discovery in Mark McGuire's locker in 1998, produced testosterone like a steroid but was not technically illegal under the 1990 law. More potent substances that did fall under the statute, including Winstrol and Deca-durabolin, built muscle even more rapidly but carried greater risks of dangerous side effects.[24]

The lack of precision in the science of PEDs in the late 1990s and early 2000s spurred arguments similar to those of an earlier era about tobacco. Medical experts generally concurred that steroids boosted performance but were also genuinely dangerous. They increased the torque of a batter's swing; built bulk that could help a hitter "muscle" out home runs, strengthened a pitcher's leg, shoulder, and back muscles to add velocity to his fastball; and speeded up athletes' recovery from muscle pulls and tears. But the added mass also put potentially career-shortening stress on tendons and joints. More seriously, lab-animal studies suggested disturbing linkages between the use of the powerful drugs and heart, liver, pituitary, and kidney diseases, tumors, and genital dysfunction. The phenomenon of "'roid rage"—escalated aggression in steroid users—had also begun to enter the literature, and some doctors even suggested a link between the drugs' chemical effects on developing brains in young people and increases in depression and other psychiatric disorders. But what could not be proven conclusively, given the multitude of other variables, was steroids' direct causal role in any one individual's symptoms, especially when they did not become evident for years.[25]

While Miller grudgingly refused to rule out entirely the possibility of adverse effects from steroids and other PEDs, he was only willing to endorse the idea of a stepped-up membership-education program. Whether he agreed with the public notion of ballplayers as role models or not, however, by the early 2000s the emerging popular view of athletes using PEDs was that they were not like other workers in being justified in claiming privacy rights comparable to those in other non–public safety occupations but instead were objects of emulation with a higher obligation. Fans watched the new generation of bulked-up athletes and overlooked the laudable results of advances in athletic training and nutritional science to see them all as selfish egoists using shortcuts, cheapening records, severing the sport's statistical links to past eras, and encouraging the young to similarly take foolish risks with their bodies.[26]

The American baseball industry had initially imposed year-round random testing for illegal recreational drugs on minor leaguers in the Ueberroth era. Under Selig, organizations now expanded the minor-league program in 2001 to include steroids, with the result an alarming 11 percent positive rate. During the subsequent 2002 Basic Agreement negotiations—a coincidence that only fed union suspicions of management's motives on the issue—front-page headlines aided by industry leaks proclaimed the existence of a similar major-league problem. Just-retired slugger Jose Canseco publicly claimed that at one time the share of big-league steroid users had been an astounding 85 percent. In a *Sports Illustrated* story of June 3, 2002, former NL MVP Ken Caminiti admitted to his earlier abuse and put the current level at 50 percent. A former general manager claimed that as early as 1996 some 40 percent of big-league performers had been taking PEDs, and he blamed management and labor alike for ignoring the problem out of a shared fear than if "you start testing, the home runs will drop and so will attendance." Belated disclosure of a winter 2000 meeting of Selig with team physicians revealed doctors' estimates of likely users at that time of 10 percent to 15 percent. Pitcher Curt Schilling admitted to personally knowing teammates who had asked not to be patted on the rump upon crossing home plate because of soreness where they had self-injected. Barry Bonds also now faced a gathering cloud of suspicion that his 2001 home-run record had been the product of at least four years' chemical enhancement.[27]

The flood of disclosures fueled a growing split within the Players Association's ranks over steroids, with an increasing share of the membership willing to accept some testing to prove their innocence and guard their livelihoods from juiced competitors. A *USA Today* story released six weeks after the Caminiti disclosures revealed that according to a mid-June poll of the membership, only 17 percent of the rank and file opposed independent steroid testing while 79 percent favored it. Forty-four percent admitted to sensing pressure to use the substances to keep up with those already doing so. With little choice given the mounting pressure from Congress as well as within the union, the MLBPA leadership yielded to a new steroid-testing policy. In the spring of 2003 all major-league players would take part in "anonymous-survey" testing to establish a baseline figure of steroid use. Individual-level confidentiality was promised, with no penalties to be assessed upon anyone with a positive result. If 5 percent or more results turned up positive then or any subsequent "survey" year, mandatory random testing with individual sanctions would follow the next two seasons. If in follow-up years the positive rate fell back to 2.5 percent or lower, the mandatory testing regimen and individual punishments would cease and survey sampling would resume. Those caught by a test and subject to discipline would be required to undergo treatment for the first offense, with repeat violations drawing punishments starting at fifteen-day suspensions and $10,000 fines and peaking with one-year bans and $100,000 levies. Because of player concerns that clubs would manipulate the testing process to back out of expensive contracts, a joint owner-union committee assigned the testing and record keeping to the outside firms Comprehensive Drug Testing and Quest Diagnostics.[28]

Miller adamantly opposed the union's decision to yield to either survey testing or mandatory random tests with punishments, though the plan's penalties—based upon those of the majors' recreational-drug policy—seemed overly lenient to critics on the other side. For years, not just for Miller but the current Players Association leadership as well, the larger principle—one that had now been rejected not just by a majority of the public but also by the union's own rank and file—had been that no employee organization should ever allow itself to be bullied into the untenable position of endorsing or enforcing limitations upon the privacy rights of individual members, especially when federal law permitted such substances as androstenedione and the stimulant ephedrine to be sold to the general population. All the while, however, the continuing drip of negative headlines kept the Players Association on its heels.

With the backdrop of still-fresh collective-bargaining battles and a baseball PED image problem looming larger with each new revelation, in February 2003 the Hall of Fame Veterans Committee prepared to announce the results of its most recent round of Cooperstown balloting. Since the previous election the panel had been revamped to include all fifty-eight living Hall of Fame players, forty-one of whom had been MLBPA members during Miller's tenure, along with twenty-four broadcasters and writers. The former executive director would still have to survive a first-round cut to fifteen candidates and then be chosen as one of ten selections made by each voter on 75 percent of the ballots. Mere days before the vote, Baltimore pitcher Steve Bechler collapsed and died from a spring-training heart attack after having taken ephedra diet pills—a drug already linked by the FDA to 155 U.S. deaths. Following a similar tragedy eighteen months earlier involving offensive lineman Korey Stringer of the Minnesota Vikings, the NFL had already banned the substance. By year's end Congress would follow suit, and then do the same with androstenedione the following spring.[29]

With a pall still hanging over the balloting, the Veterans Committee results were tabulated and announced. To the shock and dismay of friends and supporters, Miller only received the support of thirty-five panelists. Hall of Famer Joe Morgan proclaimed his astonishment, and Joe Torre declared it "a shame." Particularly unforgivable were the refusals of two ex-player members, Mike Schmidt and Reggie Jackson, who had profited handsomely from Miller's successful struggles for free agency. Schmidt refused to offer any explanation for leaving his former union leader off his ballot, and Jackson expressed the selfish view that the Hall should be reserved for performers only. Putting forth a brave front, the disappointed candidate insisted he did not care. With bravado he pointed to his induction into a different place of honor, the Baseball Reliquary, whose "Shrine of the Immortals" recognized the "rebels, radicals, and reprobates" of the national pastime. "They honor anti-establishment people," Miller noted, chuckling. "That's me." Later that summer, in connection with his donation of his papers to the labor archives of alma mater New York University, Miller was featured in a special photographic exhibit on his life and career. But friend and coauthor Allen Barra cogently observed that, while "Marvin likes his outside status in baseball," it remained the case that "the fact that he didn't receive more support from the players wounded him."[30]

Miller viewed with undisguised contempt Bud Selig's newly appointed role as PED-crackdown champion, given his and other owners' previous indifference to player use of "greenies" (amphetamines). In September 2003 the aggregate results of the majors' survey testing suspiciously leaked to the media, and the percentage of positive testers—between 5 and 7 percent—triggered mandatory individual urine sampling in 2004 with penalties. Pointing to a drop in minor-league positives from 9 percent in 2001 to 4 percent by 2003, the commissioner now pressed for the year-old Basic Agreement to be reopened to make the big-leagues' infant testing regimen permanent as well as require more frequent testing and tougher sanctions. In October, FBI agents raided offices of the Bay Area Laboratory Cooperative (BALCO), a company suspected of dispensing "designer drugs" to various ballplayers including Jason Giambi and Barry Bonds. Later that winter a San Francisco federal grand jury compelled testimony under oath from forty BALCO-linked performers. With the media and public assailing the accused, President George Bush even included a reference to the steroids issue in his 2004 State of the Union address, and John McCain grilled Fehr and Selig in hearings by the Senate Commerce Committee.[31]

More and more baseball players scrambled to separate themselves from their implicated brethren. But swimming against the tide, Miller defiantly defended Barry Bonds and condemned what he labeled violations of the star's due-process rights, insisting, "This is a whole made-up furor that doesn't have a basis. The media is beginning to act like the Ayatollah in Iran, thinking they're the guardians of civic behavior." In the new edition of his autobiography, he kept up the assault, accusing Bush, McCain, and Attorney General John Ashcroft of politically motivated meddling and hypocrisy in not at the same time proposing a tobacco ban. Miller even questioned the validity of claims that performance drugs were primarily responsible for baseball's offensive explosion, arguing that the requisite physical attributes for hitting, including hand-eye coordination and quick reflexes, were not enhanced by steroids.[32]

Having once more shown a willingness to tilt at windmills in defense of principle, Miller now received greater respect from foreign dignitaries than from Americans—a fact demonstrated on a postseason trip to visit his son and attend an all-star game between U.S. and Japanese squads. Back in the States, in January 2004 he was feted by a host of labor notables at the annual Peggy Browning Fund dinner—so named after the first union official ever appointed to the NLRB, and that sponsored internships for promising law students with labor organizations. That same year, his old high school honored him by adding his name to James Madison's Wall of Distinction, where he joined such luminaries as Ruth Bader Ginsburg, Barry Commoner, Irwin Shaw, and "Judge Judy" Sheindlin, among others. Even at his old educational institution, however, the memory of his accomplishments had required jogging. When the nominating committee had notified ex-player Frank Torre—Joe's older brother—of his own selection, it had been his refusal to accept unless the panel also inducted Miller that had led to the invitation. In June, Marvin and Terry Miller traveled to Cooperstown to keynote the annual symposium "Baseball and the American Culture," but he found himself fielding awkward media questions about his Hall of Fame chances. With his typical directness he refused to rate them highly, admitting, "The votes are not there." As one scribe in attendance put it, "The two octogenarians barely caused one head to turn, looking like yet another couple taking a holiday in Cooperstown. . . . Rarely had the Baseball Hall of Fame hosted such a baseball legend with less fanfare."[33]

Unknown to Miller, his old subordinate Don Fehr had reluctantly agreed to reopen the 2002 Basic Agreement drug provisions. Although the bargaining was essentially complete by the end of the summer, news of the revision was not released until Commissioner Selig announced it in January 2005. Now there would be year-round testing and punishments for the length of the pact, including ten-day suspensions without pay for a first offense, thirty days for a second, sixty for a third, a year's suspension for a fourth, and disposition of fifth-time violators left to Selig. It was the first time in MLBPA history that it had consented to an early reopening of a contract—a fact that galled Miller almost as much as the substance of the retreat. To an old-line unionist like him, any reopening of an active pact at management's demand was an unforgivable sin; one reminiscent of Reagan-era labor humiliations when, intimidated by the administration's busting of PATCO, other federal employees had been bullied into drug testing and then private-sector workers in various industries.[34]

The same month as the rollout of baseball's revision of its performance-drug policy, supposedly confidential BALCO grand jury testimony leaked to the press, including Jason Giambi's open admission of steroid use and Barry Bonds's incredible claim of having taken PEDs without realizing so that put him at risk of perjury charges. Before the Boston chapter of the Baseball Writers' Association of America, a lonely but defiant Miller unloaded on the new drug policy. To his audience he repeated the controversial claim that regardless of what players themselves believed, steroids did not enhance performance. "If someone tells me bulking up and putting muscles on muscles helps a linebacker, I might buy it. Does bulking up help a professional wrestler? Maybe. Would it improve a nightclub bouncer? Maybe so. If you tell me it will help somebody become the governor of California, maybe. But hitting major-league pitching more often and farther is a far cry." Pausing to inject a brief caveat—"I'm not going to say I know . . . I don't"—he continued, "I'm going to say neither does anyone in this room nor anyone else now. There has never been any kind of decent testing of the same player . . . for example, with and without steroids, over a stretch of time so you can judge his performance . . . none. And until we get some evidence of a concrete nature instead of someone's opinion, that's my view." Once more he called for an end to the "witch hunt" directed at certain stars, to the continuing demand that the union enforce stiffer penalties of its own upon its members, and to the implied collective guilt of universal testing. He demanded the sport return to a process by which a suspecting club could present its evidence before an impartial medical committee, and pointed out that, in the past, organizations had refused to bring such accusations forward. "Of course clubs don't do it," he continued. "What's a club owner supposed to do, bring a player before the committee because of probable cause, and when asked what the probable cause is, say, 'He's hitting too many damn home runs?'"[35]

According to the industry's own statistics from the first year of mandatory individual testing, the positives rate had already fallen to 2 percent, and the minor-league number had plunged to barely over 1 percent. Although some of the improvement was attributable to successful masking or other evasion tactics, a strong case could be made that ballplayer fear of discovery and the growing underground concerns of PED side effects had already produced a major decline in steroid use. But fed by still more sensational disclosures, the outcry for even greater sanctions would not be contained. In March 2005, following Jose Canseco's depictions of rampant use in his autobiography *Juiced,* the self-confessed user joined reluctant witnesses Mark McGuire, Sammy Sosa, and Rafael Palmeiro and management and union officials for a public grilling before the House Government Reform Committee. The unconvincing denials and obvious evasions from all the players but Canseco led to more threats of federal legislation and a second reopening of the performance-drug policy. Testing now was expanded to cover precursor drugs and masking agents, amphetamines were added to the list of banned substances, and penalties escalated to fifty-day suspensions without pay for first infractions, one hundred days for second offenses, and lifetime bans for "third strikes." The new provisions were even carried beyond the Basic Agreement's 2006 expiration to the end of 2008. A thoroughly disgusted Miller mocked, "I expect that in the next go-round we will perhaps see that spitting on the clubhouse floor will be at least two lifetime penalties to be served consecutively." In fact, the 2007 Basic Agreement would extend the existing sanctions through 2011.[36]

For his defiant and even vituperative defense of high-profile players already convicted in the court of public opinion, Miller was increasingly finding his unorthodoxy mocked as the views of a crank. Typical was the condemnation from Bob Costas, who claimed the former executive director's views on steroids would have to "move up several notches to qualify as drivel." In truth, his stance now did seem driven as much by ideological dogma as by what he had always prided himself upon—his willingness to challenge conventional thinking and embrace new realities. It was as if with advancing age and detachment from the everyday demands of leading the Players Association, the more he had fallen back upon the reflexive convictions of his youth. He was unquestionably brave in taking his own slings and arrows by defending unpopular ex-heroes, but his defiance had taken a toll upon his living monument, the Players Association, as well as his own reputation. That price, when added to the thirst for payback by those made the subject of past bargaining-table humiliations or publicly taken to task for being part of a "kept press," meant that due recognition of Marvin Miller for his central role in reshaping baseball and professional sports generally faced an uncertain future.

Seventeen

Awaiting the Call

As his ninetieth birthday approached, Marvin Miller's intellect and tongue both remained as sharp as ever. Remarkably, he still managed a set of tennis on a weekly basis. But arthritis now limited his performances on the piano, multiple bouts of atrial fibrillation had led to being placed on a blood thinner, and his eyesight had grown dimmer. Nonetheless, outside the media spotlight, leaders of other unions still sought his counsel when they encountered fresh difficulties. In 2006, with baseball reporter Murray Chass serving as unofficial go-between, the Association of Minor League Umpires contacted him seeking tactical advice for their effort to secure pay raises, higher per diems, and improved health benefits that had not budged since the late 1990s.[1]

Later that same year, with a new Veterans Committee vote pending, Miller's supporters once more hoped that he would receive his long-overdue recognition in Cooperstown. As Joe Morgan wrote at the time, "There are 61 living Hall of Famers [the number of ex-players now on the committee] who should know how much he contributed to the improvement of the game." Even Reggie Jackson indicated that this time he would support his old leader. But yet again, Miller fell short—this time by a mere ten votes. Putting on a brave face to friends, he pointed out the consolation that in any other election a 63 percent vote constituted a landslide victory.[2]

In March, barely three months after the Veterans Committee election in which he had received fifty-one votes to Bowie Kuhn's fourteen, Miller's old adversary passed away from pneumonia at the age of eighty. In marked contrast to the harsh words the two men had exchanged over the years—and choosing to look past the former commissioner's recent support for the antievolution "intelligent-design" cause in Pennsylvania—Miller extended a posthumous olive branch upon the news of Kuhn's death. "He always meant well in terms of the way he performed," he stated for the media. "I always thought he had a marvelous sense of humor. . . . I think that helped him in a lot of ways, and in my case it eased things a bit when there was tension between us." He again reiterated his belief that what had been at the heart of their professional confrontations had not been matters of personality but his opponent's sincere if wrongheaded "misinterpretation" of his actual powers—in short, Kuhn's "commissioneritis."[3]

Prompted by stinging criticism of the most recent snub of Miller, Hall of Fame sponsor and Singer heiress Jane Forbes Clark indicated that yet more changes to the Veterans Committee would be considered, starting with the vote for the induction class of 2008. But when the institution announced its adjustments it became clear that Miller stood even less chance of selection—and Kuhn far greater. Returning to a composition closer to the one that had been jettisoned in 2001, the Veterans Committee would no longer consist of all living Hall of Fame players and media inductees present and voting, but instead a twelve-member group of baseball executives and writers meeting to cast ballots in even-numbered years. Those selected to the committee included three former players—Monte Irvin, Harmon Killebrew, and Bobby Brown—two of whose on-field careers had completely preceded Miller, and all three subsequently hired to club or league employment; one former and five current front-office executives, including John Harrington (Boston), Jerry Bell (Minnesota), Bill DeWitt (St. Louis), Bill Giles (Philadelphia), David Glass (Kansas City), and Andy MacPhail (Baltimore); and three longstanding print journalists, none of whom hailed from the more union-friendly territory of New York City—Paul Hogan (*Philadelphia Daily News*), Rick Hummel (*St. Louis Post-Dispatch*), and Hal McCoy (*Dayton Daily News*). The dozen panelists could vote for up to four names out of a list of ten finalists, with the support of three-quarters of them required for election. In the words of *CNN Money*'s Chris Isidore, the change in the electorate was tantamount to changing the location of home plate after a runner had rounded third base.[4]

To the surprise of no one, Miller was passed over in late 2007 in favor of not just one but two deceased former adversaries—the appropriately paired Bowie Kuhn and Walter O'Malley. The meager vote total of the former executive director, however—just three tallies—was a gratuitous slap. Even Bud Selig, the frequent target of Miller's barbs in recent years, nonetheless claimed to be

surprised given his antagonist's "important impact on the game." But he added
cryptically, "Maybe there are not a lot of my predecessors who could agree with
that." Selig's predecessor Fay Vincent, referring to those in management he
deemed primarily responsible for keeping Miller from his due, now lamented,
"There are old men trying to turn back time, to reverse what has happened. Theirs
is an act of ignorance and bias. I am ashamed for them. I am ashamed that they
represent our game." Reporter Murray Chass, who had covered the majors for
nearly forty years, called the verdict "a joke," and Jim Bouton questioned, "How
did these people vote, and why are their votes kept secret? And why aren't there
more players on that committee?"[5]

When asked for his own reaction, Miller offered, "I think it was rigged, but
not to keep me out. It was rigged to bring some of these in." Publicly keeping up
a mien of indifference, in the spring he dispatched a letter to the president of the
Baseball Writers' Association of America, the organization ostensibly in charge
of Hall of Fame election procedures, requesting he no longer be considered. He
wrote, "Paradoxically, I'm writing to thank you and your associated for your part
in nominating me for Hall of Fame consideration, and, at the same time, to ask
that you *not* do this again." Claiming "anti-union bias" on the part of "the powers
who control the Hall," he continued, "I find myself unwilling to contemplate one
more rigged Veterans Committee whose members are handpicked to reach a
particular outcome while offering the pretense of a democratic vote." Labeling
the process "an insult to baseball fans, historians, sportswriters, and especially
to those baseball players who sacrificed and brought the game into the 21st
century," he ended, "At the age of 91, I can do without farce."[6]

With or without Miller's blessing, it now appeared unlikely that he would ever
receive his place of honor in Cooperstown. Besides the lingering determination
of old enemies to deny him recognition while he lived, media figures linked him
as well as his union with baseball's unfolding PED scandal and judged his defense of accused users with as much scorn as the players themselves. Following
Selig's appointment of former U.S. Senator George Mitchell—a distinguished
public servant but one with a conflict of interest as a Red Sox shareholder—to
conduct an investigation and deliver a report on the history of baseball's "Steroid Era," in December 2007 the final findings were released. The result was not
only a detailed airing of the industry's previously known "dirty laundry" but
new revelations as well, most notably involving pitcher Roger Clemens. A little
over a year later at the start of 2009, Yankee star Alex Rodriguez was subjected
to the media microscope upon the leak of his 2003 survey-year test results revealing he had used performance-enhancing substances. By midseason, Boston's

David Ortiz was "outed" and his ex-teammate turned Dodger Manny Ramirez drew a fifty-game suspension for a more recent positive. Facing tough questions over why, since the start of mandatory random testing and penalties in 2004, the union had not destroyed its copy of a list of 2003 survey-year positives, Executive Director Fehr reminded reporters that a BALCO-related subpoena had been issued just eight days after the Players Association had initially received the document. Destruction of the material then or later could have exposed the union to possible federal charges, and consequently the MLBPA had both sought to quash the subpoena and maintain the records in the meantime. Despite the association's legal efforts to block them, prosecutors had obtained additional warrants and had seized the information directly from the testing companies.[7]

Miller could find no fault in Fehr's failure to protect his members' confidentiality, responding to an inquiring reporter that "under these circumstances, if you just ignore what's going on and you destroy records, you're running a terrible risk of being charged with obstruction of justice." But he was genuinely outraged at what he saw as the trampling of individuals' privacy rights and constitutional protections against self-incrimination. He was especially sympathetic to Alex Rodriguez, who he remembered fondly for having crashed a 2006 MLBPA All-Star break dinner in Pittsburgh along with his spouse to personally thank the former executive director for enabling them to afford a lavish vacation home. In separate interviews in February and March 2009 with ESPN.com and the *New York Times,* Miller reiterated his disapproval of the union's earlier decision to accept even survey testing. He recalled telling his wife at the time, "This is such an error; you're going to see players go to jail before this is over." He continued, "It was clear that the government was going to get involved, and when the government gets involved, they will pick out targets and the media just goes along with it." Dismayed that the Justice Department of a Democratic administration had now opted to appeal a court ruling blocking the prosecution from using seized evidence in Barry Bonds' perjury trial, he added, "I expect the right-wing Republicans like Bush to act in a certain way. . . . I do not expect President Obama and his appointees to do the same."[8]

When Miller was asked why it was only now, fully a half-dozen years after the initial survey testing, that Rodriguez's results had been leaked, the former player leader linked the circumstance with the Bonds case and blamed both on prosecutors' desire for "publicity and big names." He went on, "If they suspect they are not going to be able to railroad Bonds into jail, now they're looking at A-Rod. They have unlimited resources, and their determination to get somebody is more important than doing what's right." In August, an appeals court ruled that the government did not have the legal right to seize players' survey-year records save for those related to ten performers specified in the original search warrant. Although it was unlikely that the Supreme Court would reverse the lower court's opinion, David Ortiz nonetheless noted that the ruling had come too late to spare his reputation, and Atlanta's Chipper Jones concluded, "We've already got a number [of positive survey-test takers] out there. It's not going to be over until it's all out there."[9]

Not just Miller but current union officials continued to insist not only that the extent of the steroid plague had been overblown but that its on-field consequences had also been overstated. In support of their argument they noted that per-game home run rates had not diminished since the onset of PED testing. Other evidence, however, pointed to a contrary conclusion. In the history of big-league baseball prior to 1996, there had never been more than two fifty-homer sluggers in the same year, and that number only on three occasions. By contrast, during the steroid years of 1996 through 2002, only one season—ironically Bonds's record-setting campaign of 2001—had produced fewer than two men with fifty round-trippers each, and in two of the campaigns there had been as many four players attaining that mark. While acknowledging the contributory factors of smaller ballparks, a tighter baseball, improved nutrition and weight training, a narrower strike zone, and expansion-diluted pitching, a more persuasive explanation for the lagging decline of the overall home-run rate was the persistence of club efforts to seek power hitters at every position, even though now no one was likely to reach the stratospheric heights of a McGuire, Sosa, or Bonds.[10]

Miller remained utterly unpersuaded. "I have a personal belief," he asserted, "that there's no such thing as a magic pill or magic injection. I don't know that there's any scientific evidence that there's a performance-enhancing drug. Players take it because they think it does. That's a far cry from saying that it does. Where is the evidence that requires testing?" Careful to absolve his successor for his inability to stem the hysteria, Miller admitted, "Don has faced some problems that I never had to." Chief among them in his mind was the modern-day reality of a membership without memories of the preunion days and increasingly prone to take their rights and fortunes for granted. He still insisted, however, that were he in charge of the MLBPA he would "tell owners at the first opportunity we want to negotiate an end to this." Assailing the current policy as a nightmare, he posed a worst-case scenario: "You get a false positive and then people are questioned in another context—'Were you a user?' They say no. And then you get a news leak—a leak of a leak as it were—and it turns out you tested positive. If you say anything under oath, you could go to jail and still be an innocent man."[11]

In his fervent opposition to baseball's drug-testing regimen and the popular rush to condemn the accused, Miller also resorted to an old argument that those on the other side of the issue saw at best as a straw man, that tobacco—which killed 400,000 Americans a year—represented a worthier target for a prohibition campaign. Ironically, at the same time, he clung to an even weaker line of defense reminiscent of cigarette industry arguments by refusing to accept the scientific consensus that at least some forms of PEDs were dangerous. He supported his contrarian assertion by making another straw-man argument: "There's not one single documented death from the use of steroids . . . so that's a hypocritical lie." He went on to accuse experts in the field and affiliated laboratories with financial conflicts of interest because of their paid participation in expanded sports-testing programs, and insisted that while "it's a witch hunt in baseball for sure . . . it also extends to cycling and the Olympics. And the victims are the athletes. They're obviously the ones being hunted down here."[12]

Inviting still greater scorn, Miller even rejected the overwhelmingly popular notion that as societal role models to youth, athletes bore a special obligation to voluntarily accept the hard line against steroids. Blaming instead the spread of PED use among youngsters more on the media and the drug industry, he argued, "What the propagandists have done is confuse young people that they could become great stars like these and all you have to do—and it's so easy, no work involved—is just find yourself a pusher who's got some steroids and you've got it made." When pressed harder the old lion would only concede regarding the banned substances, "Maybe they do cause real harm and death, but no one has demonstrated it yet." When asked to provide a policy alternative, he suggested that the union and industry jointly retain their own scientific experts to study whether or not steroids actually boosted athletic performance or caused genuine harm. But he admitted that such an approach would take years to provide satisfactory answers, and as for more timely recommendations, for the present he could only say, "I don't know."[13]

If Miller could not offer an acceptable alternative to the existing testing regimen, he nonetheless had raised fundamental if unpopular questions. In certain eerie respects, baseball's "war on PEDs" had come to resemble the nation's war on terrorism. Both struggles had been going on for approximately a decade against an unconventional enemy. Both sets of adversaries had been cited to justify large-scale intrusions upon the privacy rights of Americans; in the terror war the wholesale "mining" of electronic communications, in professional sports the comprehensive invasion of athletes' bodies through urine and eventually blood testing. Both had produced a diminution of the enemy but could not guarantee its eradication. Given that reality, could victory ever be declared in either conflict, and with it wartime necessities wound down, or were the changes irreversible?

The year 2009 would become probably the most difficult year of Marvin Miller's long and strenuous life. Although he was inducted into the National Jewish Sports Hall of Fame early in the year, in March his beloved Terry suffered a severe stroke. Despite fighting on bravely for months, first in a hospital, then a rehabilitation facility, and finally at home under nurses' care, complications to her respiratory system and likely additional strokes led to her passing on October 27 at the age of ninety. After first obtaining permission from the grieving spouse, Joe Morgan announced the sad news on the broadcast of that post-season's first World Series contest. Following Terry's request that her death be treated with modest dignity, additional public notice was limited to a short listing in the *New York Times* of November 8 that recalled her multiple roles as "educator, psychologist, tennis player, swimmer, enthusiast of life" and "warm, considerate friend to many." In keeping with her wishes, her body was donated to Mount Sinai Hospital for medical research.[14]

Adding to the season of gloom, Cooperstown had still not called Miller's name and likely would not in his lifetime. In voting in December 2009, seven members of a twelve-man Executive/Pioneer Committee consisting of former players Robin Roberts and Tom Seaver; baseball writers Rick Hummel, Hal McCoy, and Phil Pepe; and management figures John Harrington, Jerry Bell, Bill DeWitt, Bill Giles, David Glass, Andy MacPhail, and John Schuerholtz cast ballots for him—still two tallies short of the required number. Compared with the panel that had rejected him in late 2007, the new committee actually contained one more baseball executive and one fewer ex-player, although, in the persons of Roberts and Seaver, individuals more likely to support their former executive director.[15]

Old age had been unsparing in its measure of disappointment and sorrow. But despite the respective hurts from continued snubs and profound personal loss, Miller still drew solace from the acknowledgements, whether positive or negative, of his impact upon the national pastime and the wider world of professional sports. As Allen Barra had noted back in 2003, the legendary broadcaster Red Barber had listed him along with Babe Ruth and Jackie Robinson as one of the three most important men in baseball history. The late Arthur Ashe had similarly saluted him for having done more with less fanfare for the welfare of the black athlete than any man in modern sport. Even his critic Bob Costas ranked him with Branch Rickey as the two unmatched giants of the national pastime. His enduring impact could be seen in the remarkable growth of the baseball economy over four decades and in the enduring power of the union he had rescued from obscurity and impotence. In 1967 the average player salary had stood at $19,000 and the baseball industry's revenues at $50 million. By 2011 major-league revenue exceeded $7 billion, the average player drew pay in excess of $3 million, and current performers and retirees alike enjoyed the most comprehensive health and pension benefits of any unionized workforce on the planet. To take but one individual example, ex-pitcher turned U.S. Senator Jim Bunning earned a $175,000 annual pension from baseball that was larger than his federal governmental salary.[16]

Would the union Miller had led to such dizzying heights uphold his legacy? Longtime observers such as Murray Chass privately doubted it, questioning if the current generation of players could be roused to act when necessary. Miller himself lamented the continued erosion of memory and solidarity and what he saw as the union's modern tendency to embrace deal making for its own sake. He did not blame the union's leadership personally for what he saw as the MLBPA's faded militancy, but he worried what additional erosion might occur in a post-Fehr era. In the absence of new leadership that had been nurtured in the broader trade-union movement with its class-conscious traditions, would the Players Association become just another meek spokesman for professional athletes, or even worse a company union again? While his former colleague Dick Moss insisted both as praise and cautionary, "Marvin will never die," would his combative spirit live on after him? When Fehr had announced in mid-2009 his intention to retire the next year and introduced his successor, Michael Weiner—who had been with the MLBPA since the late 1980s and its general counsel since 2004—at a staff gathering Miller was invited to attended, the latter admitted that he had met the new executive director-in-waiting "a number of times" but did not "know him well at all." Extending Weiner the benefit of any doubts, Miller added, "I think that he's a bright guy. . . . He's certainly not lacking in experience. He's got the background for it."[17]

Miller held greater worries for the broader American labor movement. Despite U.S. unions' steadily diminishing membership and political clout, he took some encouragement from the emergence of leaders such as the AFL-CIO's Richard Trumka. He remained convinced, however, that essential to a real revival of organized labor in the absence of an economic collapse bigger than the current Great Recession was the rediscovery of an uncompromising political activism. It was up to labor itself, he believed, to force a transformation in electoral reality that would make workers once again feared and followed. As he had proclaimed before his Peggy Browning Fund audience back in 2005, America's labor movement had allowed itself to become the least overtly political of any in the Western world. Hearkening back to his youth, he called for the creation of a European-style Labor Party in America, rooted in working-class voters and willing to "reward our friends and punish our enemies" rather than embracing centrism. Citing the adverse trends of recent times as proof, he insisted, "A lessening political influence and role gets followed by reduced union membership, which in turn leads to and is followed by a similar reduction in political influence, and on and on like that." Halting labor's political death spiral was essential to achieving such national goals as adequate wages for all, universal health care, the end of upper-class control of taxation, and the protection of American consumers and workers alike.[18]

But was a revival of the old notion of a radicalized labor movement realistic for the present? Was it a formula for success or Naderite political suicide? Was the retired Miller in this and other ways unwittingly giving credence to the crude caricature of him that the late Bowie Kuhn and others had drawn—a man with "a deep hatred and suspicion of the American right and of American capitalism . . . an old-fashioned, nineteenth-century trade unionist who hated management generally and the management of baseball specifically"? Would labor in sports or elsewhere advance in the twenty-first century through an overt embrace of the ideological zeal of the Popular Front years? Or was what was needed now not the youthful Marvin Miller but instead an updated version of the Miller of the 1960s and 1970s, a man who had merged principle with hard-headed pragmatism? At the Steelworkers, that approach had brought its membership greater security in spite of the gradual contraction of America's share of the steel industry and the effects of modernization on its employment. In baseball he had similarly won the players greater profit sharing with the owners while at the same time enhancing their workplace due-process rights. In pressing for higher minimum pay, generous pensions, independent grievance and salary arbitration, and free agency for veteran players while modifying but not eliminating the reserve clause, he had ushered in a revolution of prosperity and security with remarkably modest disruption and without bankrupting the industry.[19]

Fighting similar good fights in the future, however, was now the task of younger men. After his wife's death, Miller now retreated further from public view, partly to avoid undermining the MLBPA's new leadership. When Mark Mc-Guire as part of an orchestrated 2010 reentry into baseball as a hitting instructor issued a carefully calibrated confession in which he admitted having used not only androstenedione but also steroids and HGH, the former executive director declined comment. When management's Rob Manfred announced that HGH blood testing would begin in the minors in midseason—an obvious precursor to a push for similar policies at the big-league level—Miller again held his tongue. When unrelated events focused popular attention on former MLBPA leaders-turned-critics Jim Bunning and Robin Roberts, their former chief displayed a softer tone in the brief phone interviews he granted. In Bunning's case the senator had become a center of controversy for his quixotic Senate filibuster of an unemployment-benefits extension at a time when the national jobless rate hovered at 10 percent. Miller scolded the ex-pitcher's seeming heartlessness on the subject, but he then tempered the criticism by reminding the interviewer of Bunning's past role in ending the union's color barrier by backing Pittsburgh's Roberto Clemente as a rep, as well as the ex-pitcher's expression of sympathy at Terry's death the year before. When Roberts passed away in May 2010 at the age of eighty-three, Miller similarly put aside their prior sniping and released a statement through the union paying tribute to the hurler's contributions in reviving the MLBPA and facilitating Miller's initial election as executive director.[20]

In mid-July that same year, Miller's old antagonist and occasional ally George Steinbrenner also died from a heart attack. The passing of "the Boss" prompted calls for the immediate induction of both Miller and the Yankee magnate into the Hall of Fame. To *Bloomberg News,* Miller stated of Steinbrenner, "I'm going to miss him. . . . I don't mean he was pro-union in any sense of the word, but he was clearly not of the school of the hard line owners that felt that unions were treasonous." When Allen Barra similarly asked for his reaction for an upcoming column in the *Wall Street Journal,* he replied, "Baseball owners pay lip service to competition and free enterprise, then shudder when they set it in action. Not George. He embraced the idea of competition and made baseball a better game." He added whimsically, "Baseball executives quickly found out they didn't have as much time for golf. They got to their offices a little earlier."[21]

With his own mortality brought into focus by the passing of Roberts and Steinbrenner, Miller's thoughts understandably returned to the matter of his legacy. How would he be remembered by friends and foes alike? One reassuring indication was a special Web site that had been created by former player Bob Locker called ThanksMarvin.com. Timed to coincide with Miller's ninety-third birthday, the online site included moving testimonials from eighty-five of his former players, Allen Barra, off-Broadway playwright Mike Folie—who had interviewed him for his play *American Pastime* about the Curt Flood saga—and even management opponent Fay Vincent. Most surprising were the contributions of Bud Selig and especially Ray Grebey, who not only offered a brief salute but links to letters he had written in 2009 and 2010 to the Hall of Fame demanding Miller's induction to Cooperstown. When asked by Murray Chass about such campaigning, however, the subject of their pleas neither endorsed nor repudiated them but offered the cautionary opinion, "In my view the time has passed."[22]

Hopes of Miller's supporters were temporarily raised when the Hall of Fame in July 2010 announced more changes to its Veterans Committee election processes. Instead of appointing separate panels to vote on candidates in different occupational categories, the Hall now formed distinct committees based upon eras labeled "Pre-integration" (1871–1946), "Golden" (1947–1972), and "Expansion" (1973 on). For the latter category—the one to which Miller's case was assigned—a sixteen-member panel was appointed consisting of seven current Hall of Fame players (Johnny Bench, Eddie Murray, Jim Palmer, Tony Perez, Frank Robinson, Ryne Sandberg, and Ozzie Smith), one former manager (Whitey Herzog), four media representatives (sportswriters Bob Elliott, Tim Kurkjian, Tom Verducci, and Ross Newhan), and four executives (Jerry Reinsdorf, Andy MacPhail, Bill Giles, and David Glass). Seventy-five percent support—twelve votes—would be required for election. When the committee met in early December, however, Miller fell short by a single tally. With the panel not scheduled to vote again until late 2013, it was now likely that induction to Cooperstown would never happen during his lifetime.[23]

Accordingly, Don Fehr called the result "a sad day for anyone who is or had been a major-league player," and added the opinion that the vote "says more about them [the committee] than it does about Marvin." Current Executive Director Michael Weiner remarked that his feelings were those of "frustration, disappointment, and sadness," and he reasserted that the Hall of Fame had "squandered a chance to better itself as an institution." For his part, an angry Miller released a statement through the Players Association claiming, "Many years ago those who control the Hall decided to rewrite history instead of recording it. . . . The aim was to eradicate the history of the tremendous impact of the players union on the progress and development of the game as a competitive sport, as entertainment, and as an industry." To reporters he added with biting sarcasm, "A long time ago, it became apparent that the Hall sought to bury me long before my time. . . . It is an amusing anomaly that the Hall of Fame has made me famous by keeping me out."[24]

Battling a raspy voice and dealing with restricted mobility from a stroke that now necessitated the use of a cane, half a year later Miller could still not completely cloak the sting of his latest rejection despite a brave front. When asked by a *Sporting News* reporter whether he intended to watch the July 24 induction ceremonies on television, he responded, "Maybe I'll watch it . . . depends on if I get a better offer." Fondly remembering his departed wife's talent for injecting humor into his arguments and for spurring him on into combat, he now confessed he no longer had the desire to debate the "Hall of Fame foolishness" any longer. Asserting that "considering who runs the place, not being part of it gives me credibility as a union leader," he added, "That's how I hope it stays long after I'm gone." He concluded by insisting, perhaps too strongly, "I still say I don't want to belong to any club that would have me. . . . Even when I'm dead."[25]

To the leaders of other sports unions, who found their organizations under siege to slash pay in the recession-mired America, Miller still carried great credibility for what he had accomplished. Having sought out the former executive director's advice two years earlier before taking a comparable position with the NFLPA, DeMaurice Smith faced a football industry eager to reinstitute a salary cap at a much lower level after not having had one in 2010. Describing Smith's predecessor Gene Upshaw as a "friend of mine" but "no labor leader and he wasn't going to be one if he lived to be 3,000," Miller called the football owners' lockout threat "stupid," praised Smith's instincts, and insisted that "no legitimate union could ever agree to a salary cap." When NFL management did order the lockout, Smith's union decertified itself, players filed an antitrust suit, a federal court issued an injunction halting the lockout, the NFLPA reconstituted, and the two sides reached a deal in August 2011. Despite Miller's earlier advice to hang tough, the NFLPA's new pact sharply cut its share of industry revenue for salaries to 47 percent and limited rookie pay, though it did set aside $50 million for medical research and $1 billion for retiree pensions.[26]

The NFLPA was not alone among sports unions in accepting forced givebacks in the era of austerity. Later that same year a comparable scenario played out between the NBA and its players that resulted in a similar reduction of performers' pay percentage and higher luxury taxes. In November 2011 the Major League Baseball Players Association itself avoided a work stoppage by accepting a new five-year pact that extended luxury taxes on payrolls, added a new cap on the amounts organizations spent on amateur signees, took tentative steps toward similar restraints on signings of international prospects, added an additional round to the postseason, and initiated HGH blood testing and fifty-game suspensions for first offenses beginning February 2012. In return Miller's old union managed one notable advance—reducing the percentage of free agents whose signings mandated the highest level of draft-pick compensation from their new clubs. Following Don Fehr's unusually brief retirement from the labor battlefield and return as head of the NHLPA, an 113-day owner-initiated lockout in fall 2012 produced a ten-year contract limiting the length of individual hockey players' deals and cut each team's payroll cap from more than $70 million in 2012–2013 to $64.3 million the following year.[27]

If sports unions were in retreat, ironically some of baseball's former stars who had found themselves at the center of legal storms over accused PED use scored unexpected court victories. After years of delay, in December 2011 Barry Bonds received just thirty days' house arrest and two years' probation for a conviction on a single obstruction-of-justice count for misleading testimony before the BALCO grand jury. Roger Clemens, implicated in steroid use by personal trainer Brian McNamee as well as the Mitchell Report and subsequently indicted in August 2010 on six counts of perjury, making false statements, and obstructing a congressional inquiry, stunningly was acquitted of all charges in June 2012.[28]

Whatever the verdicts of juries, the court of public opinion was not likely ever to deliver similar exonerations to Bonds, Clemens, and the others like them who had been the diamond heroes of the period now disparaged as the "Steroid Era." Marvin Miller, however, despite faltering health could still be relied upon to come to the defense of his men—past and present—and to skewer those he still viewed as the enemies of workers, whether in sports or in the larger society. In April 2012, barely more than a week after his ninety-fifth birthday, he was invited to the NYU Law School for a symposium on the 1972 baseball strike—the first in the history of American sport. As he rode to the occasion with his son, he tellingly observed that this would be his "last hurrah." At the event, George Mason University School of Law professor Ross Davies unveiled a portrait of the former executive director, the first of its kind other than a jurist or lawyer to be hung in the halls of the United States Supreme Court. Introduced by his old colleague Dick Moss, Miller began by remarking that while it was improper to celebrate a strike, it was acceptable to recognize the results of one. He then delivered a history lesson of more than an hour on the history of players' rights and the meaning of the 1972 labor action, including his description of baseball's first commissioner, Kenesaw Mountain Landis, as a Klansman; his condemnation of the industry's past policies of racial exclusion; and his characterization of the owners' collusion against free agents in the 1980s as worse than the 1919 Black Sox scandal.[29]

Miller moved on to deliver a similar attack on America's current business titans. "Let's take chief executive officers of important corporations, or the stock

Miller with successor executive directors Michael Weiner
and Donald Fehr (Peter Miller)

exchange or Wall Street firms," he began. "The typical way that compensation is set is for the board of directors, most of whom have been appointed directly by the CEO, decide what the CEO's salary should be, or they have a committee, a compensation committee composed of board members." He then pointed to the conflict of interest inherent in other companies' executives sitting on corporate boards and using their positions to create a context for their own demands for higher pay, as well as the lack of accountability exerted by shareholders who footed the bills. With Weiner and Moss at his side and Fehr in the audience, Miller then made the contrast with modern-day ballplayers such as Alex Rodriguez whose salaries were both more justifiable and more accountable. "There always has been and is a rule that no contract of a player is valid unless it is signed by the franchise owner or somebody designated by the franchise owner in his place," he observed. "In other words, no salary is put on paper and becomes valid until the man who is going to pay for it, the owner of the franchise, has signed the contract. A better check and balance you can't find anywhere."[30]

It was his last public appearance. Growing noticeably weaker, he underwent tests in August that revealed incurable liver cancer. The remainder of his life would be measured in weeks, or at most months. If the truest measure of a man lay in how he dealt with his own mortality, Miller was determined not to be found wanting. With courage, dignity, and even humor he went about the business of notifying old friends, colleagues, and adversaries. Ringing Fay Vincent, he told his now good friend not to view the news as tragic. "He was 95," the former commissioner would recall his opposite number saying, "and the last two years had been difficult. The call was as remarkable as Marvin was." In mid-November Keith Olbermann stopped by to see him and swap stories, but he found that Miller wanted to talk less about himself than about his fears of the loss of individual freedom in the society he would soon depart. Among the last besides family to see him was coauthor and stalwart defender Allen Barra, and Miller had two things in particular to relate. First off, Sandy Koufax had called to thank his old leader for what he had done for baseball, and all the former executive director had been able to think of at the time was how much money the left-hander could have made if his career had occurred later. "Sandy's always been a class act," Miller stated, "but can you imagine Sandy Koufax as a free agent?" He then related a second story for his guest's consumption—his account of Alex Rodriguez's similar expression of gratitude at the 2006 All-Star festivities.[31]

Miller then had one final word for Barra. Referring to the Hall of Fame, he pointedly requested, "If they vote me in after I'm gone, please let everyone know it is against my wishes and tell them if I was alive I would turn it down." Later, in his own tribute to his friend, the writer would later add the postscript—"OK, MLB, you've been warned." But was it what Miller truly wanted? His reputation for blunt honesty argued so. But was it pride talking instead of rational consideration? Or was he—even now—truly his father' son, the *hondler*, who knew his intended targets so well that by saying he did not want the honor, it would actually lead his adversaries to do something he secretly desired—if only out of spite.[32]

The end came in the early hours of November 27, 2012. In accordance with his wishes, there was to be no elaborate funeral or public displays of emotion. Like that of his wife, his body would be donated to Mount Sinai Hospital for the aid of others. From his former colleagues and those who had covered him, the tributes now came flooding in. Michael Weiner—fighting his own brave battle against inoperable brain cancer—issued a statement in which he declared, "It is with profound sorrow that we announce the passing of Marvin Miller. . . . All players—past, present, and future—owe a debt of gratitude to Marvin, and his influence transcends baseball. Marvin, without question, is largely responsible for ushering in the modern era of sports, which has resulted in tremendous benefits to players, owners, and fans of all sports." Don Fehr added his words of tribute, "Marvin possessed a combination of integrity, intelligence, eloquence, courage and grace that is simply unmatched in my experience. . . . All of us who knew him will miss him enormously." Fehr's brother Steve, an MLBPA consultant, remembered the departed above all as a teacher: "He was just so eloquent. He could always calmly articulate the situation, whatever it was, and he could talk on the players' level." DeMaurice Smith described Miller as "a mentor to me," and added, "Marvin exemplified guts, tenacity, and an undying love for the players he represented." But perhaps the baseball columnist Joe Posnanski captured the essential spirit of his subject best. Recalling his own sometimes-combative encounters with Miller and gently taking issue with those who had maintained that the old lion should have tempered his views and yielded some of his ideological ground, Posnanski summed up the departed as "a true believer to the last. And it's the true believers who change the world."[33]

Baseball industry officialdom of past and present also weighed in with its own tributes with varying levels of enthusiasm. Unquestionably sincere in his words was Joe Torre, the former player and rep turned manager and eventually MLB's executive vice president of baseball operations, who stated, "I was proud to be one of the players that sat alongside him." Genuine too was Fay Vincent, who described his friend of recent years as "the most important baseball figure of the last fifty years." In a combination of moving tribute and call to arms published in the *New York Times,* the "last Commissioner" said of Miller, "His death should give rise to some serious feelings of regret by those who failed to elect this good man . . . to membership in the Baseball Hall of Fame. More than anyone else, he transformed baseball." Vincent concluded, "The shame of his rejection should greatly embarrass those who voted to exclude him." Peter Ueberroth, for his part, concurred "without question," saying simply, "He changed the game of baseball." He added the personal note, "He was very tough, but he was very fair in the end." More muted were the comments of Bud Selig, who managed, "Marvin Miller was a highly accomplished executive and a very influential figure in baseball history. . . . He made a distinct impact on this sport."[34]

The most comprehensive and heartfelt send-off, however, appropriately came from Miller's daughter Susan. On the *Thanks Marvin* Web site she composed a eulogy with a style that her literary-minded mother no doubt would have approved:

A sweet and gentle man, polite, old-school, dapper, distinguished, egalitarian, good sense of humor, easygoing (sometimes), erudite, logical and meticulous problem solver—small-town Brooklyn boy, son of a . . . schoolteacher and a garment district salesman . . . did good! But he was also a fierce competitor whom you did not wish to cross—or be across from, whether at the bargaining table or on the tennis court or in the middle of an argument. "Eyes on the prize" and "playing the point" (i.e., not getting ahead of oneself) were always top of mind with him. It is in Loving Remembrance that his Family and extended family of fans, sportswriters, labor union members, baseball players, steelworkers, etc. feel deeply the impact of his loss.

Another bright light from a bygone era has been extinguished. Hopefully the afterglow will still be far-reaching when people stand up for what's right, just, equal . . . and in some cases long overdue.[35]

Even in death, however, fresh controversies threatened to overshadow Miller's life and legacy. One day after his death, the Hall of Fame released its player ballot for 2013, and for the first time among the candidates for induction were the poster children of the "Steroid Era"—Barry Bonds, Sammy Sosa, and Mark McGuire. On January 9 the results were released, and no one reached the necessary vote threshold. Two days later, major-league baseball announced in conjunction with the Players Association that HGH blood testing would now take place in the upcoming regular season, and the World Anti-Doping Agency would maintain records of each player's baseline ratio of testosterone to epitestosterone for comparison with later samples. On the twenty-third, wire-service stories reported that in the past year, labor-union membership in the United States had reached its smallest percentage since the 1930s and private-sector unionization its lowest in ninety-seven years. A week after that, press reports again linked Alex Rodriguez to PEDs, citing records from a Miami antiaging clinic operated by Anthony Bosch listing such various banned substances as HGH, testosterone cream, IGF-1 (an insulin-production stimulant), and GHRP (a trigger of growth hormones) next to the slugger's name. Over the coming days more than twenty major-leaguers would similarly be implicated, including 2011 NL MVP Ryan Braun.[36]

In the midst of the turmoil, on the evening of January 21, 2013—later in the same day as Barack Obama had been publicly sworn in to another term as president—450 people packed into NYU's Tishman Auditorium to say their final goodbyes to Marvin Miller. Hosting the tribute was Weiner, and it featured speakers included the MLBPA's director of player relations Tony Clark, Don Fehr, Jim Bouton, Murray Chass, Phil Garner, sports historian Charles Korr, Buck Martinez, Joe Morgan, Dick Moss, Steve Renko, Steve Rogers, and Rusty

Staub. Among those in the audience were industry representatives Rob Manfred, Katy Feeney, and Phyllis Merhige; Federal Mediation and Conciliation Service director George Cohen; Japanese Players Association executive-director Toru Matsubara; Miller's children Peter and Susan; and former players Dave Winfield, Reggie Jackson, Keith Hernandez, Steve Garvey, Ted Sizemore, and David Cone, among others.[37]

As Weiner stated in his opening remarks, "We're here to honor . . . a giant of American labor." In a fashion no doubt Miller would have personally approved, it was an occasion for swapping stories, for looking back and renewing memories— and for rallying the troops behind a noble cause. After listening to clips from interviews the old lion had given—whose voice cast an unmistakable aura of his presence among them—the tales began. Especially for those who had been union members or reps during Miller's tenure, it was an opportunity to demonstrate their love for their departed leader through championing his long-overdue recognition in Cooperstown. To heartfelt laughter, Jim Bouton decried Bowie Kuhn's inclusion so long as Miller remained outside, insisting, "that's like putting Wile E. Coyote in the Hall of Fame instead of the Road Runner" and adding that Kuhn had been "0 for 67" in his battles with their leader. To Don Fehr, the union itself was his mentor's legacy: a "symbol of what a union could be if it was run right." Moss reiterated the familiar theme, "He was a great teacher." A fiery Rusty Staub demanded, "Every time somebody signs one of these wonderful contracts . . . I think before they get the first check they should have to write an essay on Marvin Miller." Buck Martinez similarly called his former chief's absence from the Hall of Fame "a travesty," but Murray Chass, drawing both laughter and applause, predicted—incorrectly, as it turned out—the legend's vindication at the next induction election later in 2013, and added, "The owners are now safe. Now they won't have to fear what Marvin will say in Cooperstown."[38]

A decade earlier, at a time when his Hall of Fame prospects had seemed more certain, Miller had been asked what words he thought his plaque should contain. After pausing momentarily to collect his thoughts, he had responded as follows:

> He was the leader of the first true union in the history of the game, and work- ing closely with the players he helped form the structure of what had been termed one of the strongest and best unions in the country. And contrary to certain beliefs, the arrival of the players union coincided with, and was instru- mental in, the greatest prosperity and expansion the game has ever seen.[39]

Despite the national pastime's continuing problems, Miller's description of the game and of the role he had played in making it so remained fundamentally true. Long gone was the era of romantic ballyhoo that had cloaked miserly paternalism. In its place—owing to him more than any other man—had risen an industry, one that for both better and worse was recognized as such by all. Modern fans were realistic to the point of cynicism about their diamond heroes, but they still could and did cheer them for their capacity to inspire through their feats of on-field brilliance. The main difference now was that those athletes were being rewarded commensurate with their centrality in their sport. They had always really been the heart of the game, but now they were compensated accordingly. That reality, above all else, offered living testament to the legacy forged by the scrawny boy from Brooklyn with the bum right arm.

Notes

Chapter 1. A Brooklyn Boyhood

1. Marvin Miller, *A Whole Different Ball Game: The Inside Story of the Baseball Revolution*, 2nd ed. (Chicago: Ivan R. Dee, 2004), x; Marvin Miller interview with the author, November 15, 2005.

2. Malvin Wald interview with the author, May 28, 2006; Miller interview with the author, June 27, 2006; *The WPA Guide to New York City* (New York: The New Press, 1939), 514–15.

3. *WPA Guide,* 109; Miller interview with the author, November 15, 2005, June 13, 2006; Peter Miller to the author, August 16, 2007; "Marvin Miller Oral History Interview: American Jewish Committee Project," Marvin and Theresa Miller Papers, WAG.165 (henceforth Miller Papers), Box 5, Folder 11, Tamiment Library/Robert F. Wagner Labor Archives, Eleanor Holmes Bobst Library, New York University Libraries.

4. *WPA Guide,* 109; "Oral History Interview," Miller Papers, Box 5, Folder 11.

5. *WPA Guide,* 110–12; Miller interview with the author, January 24, 2006; Wald interview with the author, May 28, 2006.

6. Miller interviews with the author, November 29, 2005, May 30, 2006, June 27, 2006; Wald interview with the author, June 17, 2006; *WPA Guide,* 116; "Oral History Interview," Miller Papers, Box 5, Folder 11.

7. Miller interviews with the author, May 30, 2006, June 13, 2006; Thelma Miller Berenson interview with the author, June 21, 2006.

8. Miller interviews with the author, January 24, 2006, June 13, 2006; Wald interview with the author, May 28, 2006; "Oral History Interview," Miller Papers, Box 5, Folder 11.

9. Miller, *Whole Different Ball Game,* 15; *WPA Guide,* 243, 249; Wald interview with the author, May 28, 2006.

10. Miller, *Whole Different Ball Game,* 12, 15; Wald interview with the author, May 23, 2006; Miller interview with the author, May 30, 2006; "Oral History Interview," Miller Papers, Box 5, Folder 11.

11. Miller interview with the author, November 29, 2005; "Oral History Interview," Miller Papers, Box 5, Folder 11.

12. Miller interview with the author, May 30, 2006.

13. Miller, *Whole Different Ball Game,* 14; Miller interview with the author, November 29, 2005; "Oral History Interview," Miller Papers, Box 5, Folder 11.

14. Miller, *Whole Different Ball Game,* 14; Miller interview with the author, November 15, 2005; Berenson interview with the author, June 21, 2006; "Oral History Interview," Miller Papers, Box 5, Folder 11.

15. Miller, *Whole Different Ball Game,* 12; Miller interviews with the author, November 15, 2005, November 29, 2005, May 30, 2006; Wald interview with the author, May 28, 2006.

16. *WPA Guide,* 431–39, 471–75, 480–93; Miller interview with the author, May 30, 2006.

17. Miller interview with the author, May 30, 2006; Wald interview with the author, May 28, 2006; "Oral History Interview," Miller Papers, Box 5, Folder 11.

18. Miller, *Whole Different Ball Game,* 16; Wald interviews with the author, May 23, 2006, May 28, 2006; Miller interviews with the author, November 15, 2005, May 30, 2006; "Oral History Interview," Miller Papers, Box 5, Folder 11.

19. Wald interview with the author, May 28, 2006; *WPA Guide,* 478.

20. Miller, *Whole Different Ball Game,* 12; "Oral History Interview," Miller Papers, Box 5, Folder 11.

21. Miller, *Whole Different Ball Game,* 12; Miller interview with the author, May 30, 2006; "Marvin Miller: A Baseball Giant who never played the game . . .," *Sports Collector's Digest,* June 23, 1995, in Marvin Miller Subject File, National Baseball Library, Cooperstown, N.Y.

22. Miller interview with the author, May 30, 2006; "Oral History Interview," Miller Papers, Box 5, Folder 11.

23. Berenson interview with the author, June 21, 2006; "Oral History Interview," Miller Papers, Box 5, Folder 11.

24. Miller, *Whole Different Ball Game,* 16; Miller interviews with the author, November 15, 2005, November 29, 2005; "Oral History Interview," Miller Papers, Box 5, Folder 11.

25. Miller interviews with the author, November 29, 2005, May 30, 2006; Wald interview with the author, May 28, 2006; "Oral History Interview," Miller Papers, Box 5, Folder 11.

26. Miller, *Whole Different Ball Game,* 15; Miller interviews with the author, November 29, 2005, May 30, 2006, June 13, 2006; Wald interview with the author, May 28, 2006.

27. Miller, *Whole Different Ball Game,* 13; Miller interviews with the author, November 29, 2005, December 13, 2005, May 30, 2006; Wald interview with the author, May 28, 2006.

28. *WPA Guide,* xxxi, 104–7, 116–20; Miller interview with the author, May 30, 2006.

29. Miller, *Whole Different Ball Game,* 12–13; Miller interview with the author, May 30, 2006; "Oral History Interview," Miller Papers, Box 5, Folder 11.

30. Miller, *Whole Different Ball Game,* 13; "Oral History Interview," Miller Papers, Box 5, Folder 11.

31. Miller interviews with the author, November 15, 2005, November 29, 2005, December 13, 2005, June 27, 2006.

32. Miller, *Whole Different Ball Game,* 14.

33. Miller, *Whole Different Ball Game,* 15; Miller interviews with the author, November 15, 2005, November 29, 2005, June 13, 2006.

34. Miller, *Whole Different Ball Game,* 13–14; Miller interview with the author, June 13, 2006; *WPA Guide,* 109–10.

35. Miller, *Whole Different Ball Game,* 14; Miller interviews with the author, November 29, 2005, June 13, 2006; "Oral History Interview," Miller Papers, Box 5, Folder 11.

36. Miller, *Whole Different Ball Game,* 12, 16; Miller interviews with the author, November 29, 2005, May 30, 2006, June 13, 2006; "Oral History Interview," Miller Papers, Box 5, Folder 11.

37. Miller interviews with the author, November 15, 2005, November 29, 2005, June 13, 2006; Berenson interview with the author, June 21, 2006.

38. Miller, *Whole Different Ball Game,* 15; Miller interviews with the author, November 15, 2005, November 29, 2005, May 30, 2006.

Chapter 2. Hard Times

1. Wald interview with the author, May 28, 2006; Miller interview with the author, May 30, 2006; "Oral History Interview," Miller Papers, Box 5, Folder 11; Miller, *Whole Different Ball Game,* 15–16.

2. Miller interviews with the author, November 15, 2005, June 13, 2006; "Oral History Interview," Miller Papers, Box 5, Folder 11; Miller, *Whole Different Ball Game,* 14; David M. Kennedy, *Freedom From Fear: The American People in Depression and War, 1929–1945* (New York: Oxford University Press, 1999), 88.

3. Miller interview with the author, June 27, 2006; *WPA Guide,* 579.

4. Miller to the author, October 25, 2005; "Oral History Interview," Miller Papers, Box 5, Folder 11.

5. Miller interviews with the author, November 15, 2005, November 29, 2005.

6. "Oral History Interview," Miller Papers, Box 5, Folder 11; "Marvin Miller Interview for Fay Vincent," Miller Papers, Box 10; Miller interview with the author, November 15, 2005.

7. Miller interviews with the author, November 29, 2005, December 13, 2005; "Oral History Interview," Miller Papers, Box 5, Folder 11.

8. Miller interview with the author, November 15, 2005; Marvin Miller Interview for Fay Vincent," Miller Papers, Box 10.

9. Miller interviews with the author, November 15, 2005, November 29, 2005; "Oral History Interview," Miller Papers, Box 5, Folder 11.

10. Miller interviews with the author, November 15, 2005, November 29, 2005, December 13, 2005.

11. Miller interviews with the author, November 15, 2005, June 27, 2005; "Oral History Interview," Miller Papers, Box 5, Folder 11.

12. Miller, *Whole Different Ball Game,* 16.

13. Miller interview with the author, November 15, 2005.

14. Miller interviews with the author, November 15, 2005; "Oral History Interview," Miller Papers, Box 5, Folder 11.

15. Miller interviews with the author, November 15, 2005, June 13, 2006, June 27, 2006.

16. Miller interview with the author, November 29, 2005; Miller, *Whole Different Ball Game,* 16; "Oral History Interview," Miller Papers, Box 5, Folder 11.

17. Miller interviews with the author, November 15, 2005, November 29, 2005, June

13, 2006, June 27, 2006; Miller, *Whole Different Ball Game,* 16; *Miami Student* (campus newspaper), January 21, 1936, February 14, 1936, January 8, 1937, January 12, 1937, January 15, 1937.

18. "Oral History Interview," Miller Papers, Box 5, Folder 11.

19. Ann Cox to the author, December 4, 2005; Miami of Ohio varsity football team photo, *Recensio—1936* (Miami of Ohio school yearbook); Miller interview with the author, December 13, 2005.

20. Miller interviews with the author, November 15, 2005, November 29, 2005.

21. Miller interviews with the author, November 15, 2005, May 30, 2006, June 13, 2006, June 27, 2006, "Oral History Interview," Miller Papers, Box 5, Folder 11.

22. Miller interviews with the author, November 15, 2005, November 29, 2005, June 13, 2006, June 27, 2006.

23. Miller interview with the author, November 15, 2005.

24. Miller interviews with the author, November 15, 2005, December 13, 2005, June 27, 2006.

Chapter 3. Avenues of Discovery

1. Marvin Miller interviews with the author, November 29, 2005, December 13, 2005, August 1, 2006; Kennedy, *Freedom From Fear,* 298–319; *WPA Guide,* 112, 500; Robert H. Zieger, *The CIO, 1935–1955* (Chapel Hill: University of North Carolina Press, 1995), 22–65, 81, 179–80.

2. Miller interview with the author, June 27, 2006; *WPA Guide,* 133–34.

3. Miller interviews with the author, December 13, 2005, June 27, 2006; *WPA Guide,* 494.

4. Miller interviews with the author, June 27, 2006, August 1, 2006; Terry Miller to the author, June 20, 2006.

5. Miller interviews with the author, November 29, 2005, December 13, 2005; "Oral History Interview," Miller Papers, Box 5, Folder 11.

6. Miller interview with the author, November 29, 2005; "Oral History Interview," Miller Papers, Box 5, Folder 11; Kennedy, *Freedom From Fear,* 350–61.

7. Miller interview with the author, November 29, 2005; "Oral History Interview," Miller Papers, Box 5, Folder 11

8. Miller interviews with the author, November 29, 2005, December 13, 2005, June 27, 2006.

9. Miller interviews with the author, November 29, 2005, June 27, 2006; *WPA Guide,* 69, 72, 86; Peter Miller to the author, June 18, 2006.

10. Miller interview with the author, June 27, 2006; Terry Miller to the author, June 20, 2006, August 8, 2006; *WPA Guide,* 627–48.

11. Miller interviews with the author, November 29, 2005, December 13, 2005.

12. Miller interviews with the author, November 29, 2005, December 13, 2005, June 27, 2006.

13. Miller interviews with the author, June 27, 2006, September 5, 2006; Kennedy, *Freedom From Fear,* 400–440.

14. Miller interviews with the author, November 29, 2005, December 13, 2005.

15. Miller interviews with the author, November 29, 2005, December 13, 2005, June 27, 2006; Miller, *Whole Different Ball Game,* 20, 22–23; Terry Miller essay, *Passager: A Journal*

of Remembrance and Discovery, Winter 1993, in "footprints . . . fingerprints . . . reprints . . . the book of Terry/Theresa," Miller Papers, Box 11.

16. Miller interview with the author, November 29, 2005.

17. Miller interviews with the author, November 29, 2005, June 27, 2006; "Marvin Miller Interview for Fay Vincent," Miller Papers, Box 10.

18. Miller interviews with the author, November 29, 2005, June 27, 2006.

19. Miller interviews with the author, November 29, 2005, June 27, 2006.

20. Miller interviews with the author, November 29, 2005, December 13, 2005; "Finding Aid for the Frieda Wunderlich Papers, 1920–1941: Biographical Sketch," University Libraries, University at Albany, State University of New York.

21. Terry Miller to the author, August 5, 2006; Miller interview with the author, August 1, 2006.

22. Miller interview with the author, August 1, 2006; Robert Briffault, *Reasons for Anger* (New York: Robert Hall, 1937).

23. Robert H. Zieger and Gilbert H. Gall, *American Workers, American Unions: The Twentieth Century*, 3rd ed. (Baltimore: Johns Hopkins University Press, 2002), 104–17; Kennedy, *Freedom From Fear*, 482–83.

Chapter 4. Working for Victory

1. Kennedy, *Freedom From Fear*, 616–18; John Morton Blum, *V Was For Victory: Politics and American Culture During World War II* (New York: Harcourt Brace, 1976), 117–23.

2. Marvin Miller interviews with the author, November 29, 2005, December 13, 2005.

3. Blum, *V Was For Victory*, 122, 227–28; Kennedy, *Freedom From Fear*, 619–20, 640; Terry Miller to the author, June 20, 2006; James B. Atleson, *Labor and the Wartime State: Labor Relations and Law During World War II* (Urbana: University of Illinois Press, 1998), 44–45; Zieger and Gall, *American Workers, American Unions*, 117–18, 132–33.

4. Miller interview with the author, November 29, 2005; Blum, *V Was For Victory*, 94; Kennedy, *Freedom From Fear*, 621, 626, 645.

5. Miller interview with the author, November 29, 2005; Blum, *V Was For Victory*, 222; Kennedy, *Freedom From Fear*, 626–28; Terry Miller interview with the author, May 2, 2006.

6. Miller interview with the author, November 29, 2005.

7. Miller interview with the author, November 29, 2005.

8. Miller interviews with the author, November 29, 2005, December 13, 2005; Zieger and Gall, *American Workers, American Unions*, 131; Atleson, *Labor and the Wartime State*, 46.

9. Miller, *Whole Different Ball Game*, 19–20; Miller interview with the author, November 29, 2005; Blum, *V Was For Victory*, 140; Zieger and Gall, *American Workers, American Unions*, 127–28, 136–37; Atleson, *Labor and the Wartime State*, 103–22.

10. Miller interview with the author, November 29, 2005; Kennedy, *Freedom From Fear*, 640–43; Zieger and Gall, *American Workers, American Unions*, 129–30, 132, 134, 138–39; Atleson, *Labor and the Wartime State*, 130–50.

11. Miller, *Whole Different Ball Game*, 19–20; Miller interviews with the author, November 29, 2005, December 13, 2005.

12. Miller interview with the author, December 13, 2005; Atleson, *Labor and the Wartime State*, 55–77.

13. Examples of Miller's cases at the War Labor Board include "Allegheny County Milk

Exchange and Milk and Ice Cream Salesmen, Drivers, and Dairy Employees, AFL," Case 111–11501-HO (December 11, 1944); "Erie Resistor Corporation and United Electrical, Radio, and Machine Workers of America, Local 631, CIO," Case 111-11589-HO (December 28, 1944); "Baldwin Locomotive Works and United Steelworkers of America, Local 1940, CIO," Case 111-14196-D (April 25, 1945); and "Christian and Company and Milk and Ice Cream Salesmen, Drivers, and Dairy Employees, Local 205 of the IBTCWHA, AFL," Case 111-14525-HO (May 14, 1945), Miller Papers, Box 1, Folder 14.

14. "Continental Diamond Fibre Company and United Mine Workers of America, District 50, Local 12952, Independent," Case 111-16325-D (September 1, 1945), Miller Papers, Box 1, Folder 14.

15. "Labor Standards Association of Pittsburgh and Hotel and Restaurant Employees International Alliance and Bartenders International League of America, Local 237, AFL," Case 111-14063-HO (July 20, 1945), Miller Papers, Box 1, Folder 14.

16. Blum, *V Was For Victory*, 95, 135, 138; Terry Miller to the author, May 28, 2006; Terry Miller interview with the author, May 2, 2006; Seymour S. Cohen to the author, May 24, 2006.

17. Terry Miller to the author, May 28, 2006; Terry Miller interview with the author, May 2, 2006.

18. Terry Miller to the author, May 28, 2006; Terry Miller interview with the author, May 2, 2006.

19. Terry Miller to the author, May 28, 2006; Terry Miller interview with the author, May 2, 2006; Miller interview with the author, November 29, 2005; Miller, *Whole Different Ball Game*, 20–21; Kennedy, *Freedom from Fear*, 808, 849–52.

Chapter 5. Issues of Loyalty

1. Miller, *Whole Different Ball Game*, 21; Nelson Lichtenstein, *State of the Union: A Century of American Labor* (Princeton, N.J.: Princeton University Press, 2002), 100–101; Zieger and Gall, *American Workers, American Unions*, 145–51.

2. M. J. Miller to Joseph N. Smith, Director, Wage Stabilization Division, "Confidential: National Wage Stabilization Board, Third Region, Memorandum to the Board," Case 3-1-1030, Campbell Soup Company, Camden, N.J., Food, Agricultural, Tobacco, and Allied Workers, Local 80, CIO, Miller Papers, Box 1, Folder 5.

3. Zieger and Gall, *American Workers, American Unions*, 153–54; Terry Miller interview with the author, May 2, 2006; Terry Miller to the author, May 8, 2006; Terry Miller, "Election Day—What's On Our Minds As We Go To The Polls," *Union Reporter*, November 1946, 2–3, in "footprints . . . fingerprints . . . reprints . . .," Miller Papers, Box 11.

4. Marvin Miller interview with the author, November 29, 2005, December 13, 2005; Miller, *Whole Different Ball Game*, 21.

5. Miller interview with the author, November 29, 2005; Lichtenstein, *State of the Union*, 114.

6. Lichtenstein, *State of the Union*, 103–4, 111–13, 118–22; Zieger and Gall, *American Workers, American Unions*, 155–56.

7. Miller interviews with the author, November 29, 2005, December 13, 2005; Terry Miller interview with the author, May 2, 2006; Miller, *Whole Different Ball Game*, 21; Terry Miller

articles, "Is Einstein A Good Jew?" *American Jewish Outlook,* April 1947, 8–9, "American Booby Traps," *American Jewish Outlook,* July 1947, 7, 15, "A Tale of Arabian Knights," *Southern Jewish Outlook,* September 1947, 5, 18, October 1947, 7, 10, "The Day We Sabotaged UN," *Southern Jewish Outlook,* April 1948, 7, 28–29, "What About Menachem Begin?," *Southern Jewish Outlook,* February 1949, 5, 11–12, in "footprints . . . fingerprints . . . reprints . . .," Miller Papers, Box 11.

8. Zieger and Gall, *American Workers, American Unions,* 159–62; Blum, *V Was For Victory,* 252–54.

9. Zieger and Gall, *American Workers, American Unions,* 162–63.

10. Zieger and Gall, *American Workers, American Unions,* 173–75; Blum, *V Was For Victory,* 279–300; Lawrence Lader, "The Wallace Campaign of 1948," *American Heritage Magazine* 28, no. 1 (December 1976), American Heritage.com.

11. Miller interviews with the author, November 29, 2005, December 13, 2005.

12. Zieger and Gall, *American Workers, American Unions,* 176; Lader, "The Wallace Campaign of 1948."

13. Miller interview with the author, November 29, 2005.

14. Lader, "The Wallace Campaign of 1948."

15. Miller interview with the author, November 29, 2005; "American Labor Party: 1948 Fall Primary Petitions," in "footprints . . . fingerprints . . . reprints," Miller Papers, Box 11.

16. Miller interview with the author, December 13, 2005; *New York Times,* November 4, 1948; Lader, "The Wallace Campaign of 1948."

17. Miller interview with the author, November 29, 2005; Zieger and Gall, *American Workers, American Unions,* 144; Lichtenstein, *State of the Union,* 122–23; Gary Gerstle, "The Crucial Decade: The 1940s and Beyond," *Journal of American History* 92, no. 4 (March 2006): 1298.

18. Miller interviews with the author, November 29, 2005, December 13, 2005; Miller, *Whole Different Ball Game,* 21.

19. Zieger and Gall, *American Workers, American Unions,* 177–78; Miller interview with the author, January 24, 2006.

20. Miller interviews with the author, November 29, 2005, December 13, 2005.

21. Miller interviews with the author, November 29, 2005, December 13, 2005; Terry Miller interview with the author, May 2, 2006.

22. Miller, *Whole Different Ball Game,* 21.

23. Kennedy, *Freedom From Fear,* 305–6; Miller, *Whole Different Ball Game,* 22.

24. Miller interviews with the author, November 29, 2005, December 13, 2005.

25. Miller interview with the author, December 13, 2005.

26. Miller, *Whole Different Ball Game,* 22.

Chapter 6. Technician

1. Marvin Miller interviews with the author, January 24, 2006, February 7, 2006, February 21, 2006; "Man of Steel," *Time,* July 9, 1956; John Helyar, *The Lords of the Realm: The Real History of Baseball* (New York: Ballantine Books, 1994), 18.

2. Miller interviews with the author, January 24, 2006, February 7, 2006; Zieger and Gall, *American Workers, American Unions,* 196.

3. Peter Miller to the author, June 1, 2006; Jim Thomas interview with the author, June 14, 2006; "Oral History Transcripts: Marvin J. Miller" (H. Golatz interview), Pt. 1, Labor Oral History Collection, United Steelworkers of America Archives (henceforth USWA Archives), Historical Collections and Labor Archives, Pennsylvania State University Libraries.

4. Miller interview with the author, January 24, 2006; "Oral History Transcripts: Marvin J. Miller" (Golatz interview), Pt. 1, USWA Archives; "Marvin Miller Interview for Fay Vincent," Miller Papers, Box 10.

5. Ben Fischer interview with the author, June 27, 2006; Ben Fischer obituary, *Pittsburgh Post-Gazette,* November 15, 2006; Peter Miller to the author, June 27, 2006; "Marvin Miller Interview for Fay Vincent," Miller Papers, Box 10.

6. "Oral History Transcripts: Marvin J. Miller" (Golatz interview), Pt. 1, USWA Archives; "Marvin Miller Interview for Fay Vincent," Miller Papers, Box 10; Miller, *Whole Different Ball Game,* 187–88; Helyar, *Lords of the Realm,* 18.

7. Ben Fischer interview with the author, June 27, 2006; Miller interviews with the author, January 24, 2006, February 7, 2006.

8. Miller interviews with the author, January 24, 2006, February 7, 2006; "Man of Steel," *Time,* July 9, 1956; Miller, *Whole Different Ball Game,* 23.

9. Miller interviews with the author, January 24, 2006, February 7, 2006; Marvin Miller to James G. Thimmes, "Foundries," January 11, 1951, Philip Murray Papers, Catholic University of America; "Oral History Transcripts: Marvin J. Miller," Pt. 1, Otis Brubaker and Marvin Miller to I.W. Abel, September 10, 1954, USWA Research Department: Marvin J. Miller, 1948–1972," Box 1, Folder 1, USWA Archives.

10. Miller interview with the author, January 24, 2006.

11. Peter Miller to the author, June 1, 2006, June 7, 2006; Miller interviews with the author, January 24, 2006, May 30, 2006; Terry Miller to the author, May 8, 2006; Stefan Lorant, *Pittsburgh: The Story of an American City* (Pittsburgh: Esselmont Books, 1999), 373–447.

12. Peter Miller to the author, June 1, 2006; Terry Miller, "Correspondence," *New Republic,* May 5, 1952; "Around the USA," *The Nation,* April 4, 1953, "Letter to the Editor," *Pittsburgh Post-Gazette,* March 30, 1955, in "footprints . . . fingerprints . . . reprints," Miller Papers, Box 11.

13. Miller interviews with the author, December 13, 2005, February 7, 2006; "Oral History Transcripts: Marvin Miller" (Golatz interview), Pt. 1, USWA Archives; "Marvin Miller Interview for Fay Vincent," Miller Papers, Box 10.

14. Ben Fischer interview with the author, June 27, 2006; Miller interviews with the author, January 24, 2006, February 7, 2006; "Marvin Miller Interview for Fay Vincent," Miller Papers, Box 10; 'Steelworkers' Brain Trust," *Wall Street Journal,* February 8, 1965.

15. Miller interview with the author, February 7, 2006; Peter Miller to the author, August 16, 2007.

16. Miller interview with the author, February 7, 2006.

17. Peter Miller to the author, June 1, 2006; Terry Miller to the author, May 2, 2006; Terry Miller, "Ladies Day Out," *The Blue Print,* February 1952, *Brookline Journal,* June 9, 1955, June 28, 1955, in "footprints . . . fingerprints . . . reprints," Miller Papers, Box 11.

18. Peter Miller to the author, June 1, 2006, June 7, 2006, August 16, 2007.

19. Peter Miller to the author, June 7, 2006, August 16, 2007; "Oral History Interview," Miller Papers, Box 5, Folder 11.

20. Miller interview with the author, June 27, 2006; "Guide to the Camp Tamiment Photographs: Historical/Biographical Note," Tamiment Library/Robert F. Wagner Labor Archives, NYU Libraries.

21. Terry Miller to the author, August 10, 2006; Miller interview with the author, May 30, 2006; Peter Miller to the author, June 7, 2006.

22. Peter Miller to the author, June 1, 2006, June 7, 2006; Miller interviews with the author, January 24, 2006, February 7, 2006.

23. Miller interview with the author, January 24, 2006; "Oral History Transcripts: Marvin J. Miller" (Golatz interview), Pt. 1; Otis Brubaker, "Guaranteed Annual Wage," *Labor Law Journal,* June 1953, reprint in USWA Research Department: Marvin J. Miller, 1948–1972, Box 2, Folder 16, USWA Archives.

24. Miller interview with the author, January 24, 2006; Otis Brubaker, "Long-Term Employment Trends in the Basic Steel Industry," March 3, 1961, in USWA Research Department: Marvin J. Miller, 1948–1972, Box 2, Folder 5, USWA Archives.

25. Miller interview with the author, January 24, 2006; "Certain 1955 Wage and Employment Distribution Statistics for the Major Basic Steel Companies," Research Department to David McDonald, January 2, 1957, USWA Research Department: Marvin J. Miller, 1948–1972, Box 5, Folder 14, USWA Archives; "Steelworkers' Brain Trust," *Wall Street Journal,* February 8, 1965.

26. Miller interviews with the author, January 24, 2006, February 7, 2006, February 21, 2006; Research Department, "Long-Term Trends in the Basic Steel Industry," March 1959, USWA Research Department: Marvin J. Miller, 1948–1972, Box 7, Folder 1, USWA Archives.

27. Miller interviews with the author, January 24, 2006, February 7, 2006; "Oral History Transcripts: Marvin J. Miller" (Golatz interview), Pt. 1, USWA Archives.

28. Miller interview with the author, February 7, 2006; "Oral History Transcripts: Marvin J. Miller" (Golatz interview), Pt. 1, Pt. 3, USWA Archives.

29. Ben Fischer interview with the author, June 27, 2006.

30. Miller interview with the author, February 7, 2006; "Oral History Transcripts: Marvin J. Miller" (Golatz interview), Pt. 1, USWA Archives.

31. David McDonald to Ben Fischer, April 15, 1960, in USWA Research Department: Marvin J. Miller, 1948–1972, Box 4, Folder 13, USWA Archives.

Chapter 7. A House Divided

1. "Steelworkers' Brain Trust," *Wall Street Journal,* February 8, 1965; Helyar, *Lords of the Realm,* 19; "Oral History Interview," Miller Papers, Box 5, Folder 11.

2. Miller interview with the author, February 21, 2006; "Oral History Transcripts: Marvin J. Miller" (Golatz interview), Pt. 1, USWA Archives; *Steel Labor,* June 1960, 7.

3. Helyar, *Lords of the Realm,* 19; "Oral History Transcripts: Marvin J. Miller" (Golatz interview), pt. 1, USWA Archives; Jim Thomas interview with the author, June 14, 2006; "Steelworkers' Brain Trust," *Wall Street Journal,* February 8, 1965; Ben Fischer interview

with the author, June 27, 2006; "U.S. Steel Agreement," January 4, 1960, Miller Papers, Box 1, Folder 6; "Has Steel Industry Bargaining Really Started?" *Steel,* January 21, 1963.

4. "News Flash—USWA," March 5, 1962, "Human Relations Committee—Collective Bargaining Provisions in the Steel Industry Showing the Chronological Development of the Human Relations Committee, 1960–1963," Miller Papers, Box 1, Folder 6.

5. "Oral History Transcripts: Marvin J. Miller" (Golatz interview), Pt. 1, Pt. 3, USWA Archives; Miller, *Whole Different Ball Game,* 188; Helyar, *Lords of the Realm,* 19.

6. "Oral History Transcripts: Marvin J. Miller" (Golatz interview), Pt. 3, USWA Archives.

7. Miller interview with the author, February 7, 2006, February 21, 2006; "Steelworkers' Brain Trust," *Wall Street Journal,* February 8, 1965.

8. Edgar F. Kaiser to Marvin J. Miller, March 28, 1962, Marvin J. Miller to the Editor, *New York Times Magazine,* November 19, 1963, Miller Papers, Box 1, Folder 11; "Oral History Transcripts: Marvin J. Miller" (Golatz interview), Pt. 3, USWA Archives.

9. *New York Times,* April 1, 1962, April 2, 1962; "Has Steel Industry Bargaining Really Started?" *Steel,* January 21, 1963; *Steel Labor,* July 1963.

10. "Oral History Transcripts: Marvin J. Miller" (Golatz interview), Pt. 3, USWA Archives; Hugh Francis Moore to Marvin Miller, January 19, 1963, Box 1, Folder 8, "Transcripts of Speeches before Mass Membership of Fontana Workers," December 17, 1992, Miller Papers, Box 1, Folder 9; *The Ingot,* January 21, 1963.

11. *Detroit Free Press,* April 26, 1963; Miller interview with the author, May 30, 2006; "The Kaiser-Steel Union Sharing Plan," Studies in Personnel Policy, No. 187: A Research Report from the Conference Board (1963), Miller Papers, Box 1, Folder 9; "Labor Force Employment and Earnings," U.S. Department of Commerce, Bureau of the Census, 86th ed. (1965), 238–40.

12. "Oral History Transcripts: Marvin J. Miller" (Golatz interview), Pt. 3, USWA Archives; Miller interview with the author, February 7, 2006; "Steelworkers' Brain Trust," *Wall Street Journal,* February 8, 1965.

13. Miller, *Whole Different Ball Game,* 28; *New York Times,* May 26, 1963.

14. Miller, *Whole Different Ball Game,* 28; "Steelworkers' Brain Trust, *Wall Street Journal,* February 8, 1965.

15. Miller interview with the author, May 16, 2006.

16. Terry Miller interview with the author, May 2, 2006; Peter Miller to the author, June 7, 2006, August 16, 2007.

17. Jim and Cookie Thomas interviews with the author, June 14, 2006.

18. "Oral History Transcripts: Marvin J. Miller" (Golatz interview), Pt. 3, USWA Archives; "Alan Wood Steel Company—Labor Agreement of July 1, 1965 with USWA," Miller Papers, Box 1, Folder 2.

19. "Oral History Transcripts: Marvin J, Miller," (Golatz interview), Pt. 3, Archives; "Alan Wood Steel Company—Labor Agreement . . ." Miller Papers, Box 1, Folder 2.

20. "Oral History Transcripts: Marvin J. Miller" (Golatz interview), Pt. 2, USWA Archives; Miller, *Whole Different Ball Game,* 23; Helyar, *Lords of the Realm,* 18; Miller interview with the author, February 7, 2006; " Man of Steel," *Time,* July 9, 1956.

21. "Oral History Transcripts: Marvin J. Miller" (Golatz interview), Pt. 1 and 2, USWA Archives; "Oral History Interview," Miller Papers, Box 5, Folder 11.

22. Helyar, *Lords of the Realm*, 20; Miller interview with the author, February 7, 2006.

23. Miller, *Whole Different Ball Game*, 31–32; Miller interview with the author, February 7, 2006.

24. Jim Thomas interview with the author, June 14, 2006; Ben Fischer interview with the author, June 27, 2006; Miller, *Whole Different Ball Game*, 23–24.

25. "Oral History Transcripts: Marvin J. Miller" (Golatz interview), Pt. 2, USWA Archives; Miller, *Whole Different Ball Game*, 24.

26. "The Man Steel is Watching," *Business Week*, March 27, 1965; "Oral History Transcripts: Marvin J. Miller" (Golatz interview), Pt. 1, USWA Archives; Ben Fischer interview with the author, June 27, 2006; Miller, *Whole Different Ball Game*, 24, 32; Miller interview with the author, February 21, 2006.

27. Miller, *Whole Different Ball Game*, 25.

28. Miller, *Whole Different Ball Game*, 5, 26–28.

29. Richard Moss interview with the author, July 3, 2006; "Former Players Honor Marvin Miller," Associated Press, January 22, 2013; Miller, *Whole Different Ball Game*, 30.

30. Jim Thomas interview with the author, June 14, 2006; Helyar, *Lords of the Realm*, 20; Miller interview with the author, February 21, 2006; Marvin Miller notes (ca. December 1965), Box 1, Folder 1, Marvin Miller to Joseph P. Molony, April 21, 1966, Miller Papers, Box 1, Folder 4.

31. Miller, *Whole Different Ball Game*, 4, 30–31.

32. Miller, *Whole Different Ball Game*, 4–5.

33. Miller interview with the author, December 13, 2005.

Chapter 8. A Fresh Start

1. Marvin Miller interview with the author, May 6, 2006; Miller, *Whole Different Ball Game*, 3–6; John Helyar, *Lords of the Realm*, 21; Robert F. Burk, *Much More Than a Game: Players, Owners and American Baseball Since 1921* (Chapel Hill: University of North Carolina Press, 2001), 148.

2. Miller interview with the author, May 16, 2006; Miller, *Whole Different Ball Game*, 6–7; Helyar, *Lords of the Realm*, 15–17; Charles P. Korr, *End of Baseball As We Knew It: The Players Union, 1960–81* (Urbana: University of Illinois Press, 2002), 31, 46; "Relentless, Resolute—That's Miller," *Sporting News*, February 15, 1969.

3. Miller, *Whole Different Ball Game*, 8; "Miller-Led Players Show Huge Economic Gains," *Sporting News*, March 23, 1974.

4. "Marvin Miller Interview For Fay Vincent," Miller Papers, Box 10; Miller, *Whole Different Ball Game*, 40; *Jewish Daily Forward*, September 13, 2004.

5. Korr, *End of Baseball*, 28.

6. Miller, *Whole Different Ball Game*, 8–9.

7. Marvin Miller interview with the author, February 21, 2006; Miller, *Whole Different Ball Game*, 3, 9–10; Korr, *End of Baseball*, 35; Peter Miller to the author, August 16, 2007; "Miller-Led Players . . .," *Sporting News*, March 23, 1974.

8. Robin Roberts with C. Paul Rogers III, *My Life in Baseball* (Chicago: Triumph Books, 2003), 219–20; Marvin Miller to Robin Roberts, December 30, 1965, Miller Papers, Box 3, Folder 52.

9. Miller interview with the author, November 29, 2005, February 21, 2006; Miller, *Whole Different Ball Game,* 33–34; Korr, *End of Baseball,* 31–33.

10. Miller, *Whole Different Ball Game,* 34; Helyar, *Lords of the Realm,* 21–23; Korr, *End of Baseball,* 35–36.

11. Miller, *Whole Different Ball Game,* 35, 40–41; Korr, *End of Baseball,* 39; "In Praise of Those Who Got Others a Share," *New York Times,* July 2, 1991.

12. Miller, *Whole Different Ball Game,* 36–37.

13. Miller interview with the author, February 21, 2006.

14. Miller, *Whole Different Ball Game,* 38–39, 41–43; "Miller Confident Despite Players' Rising Opposition," *Sporting News,* March 26, 1966.

15. Miller interview with the author, February 21, 2006; Miller, *Whole Different Ball Game,* 43–46.

16. Miller, *Whole Different Ball Game,* 47–48.

17. Miller interview with the author, February 21, 2006; Miller, *Whole Different Ball Game,* 49–53; "Relentless, Resolute . . .," *Sporting News,* February 15, 1969; "Oral History Transcript," Miller Papers, Box 5, Folder 11.

18. Miller interview, February 21, 2006; Miller, *Whole Different Ball Game,* 54–55.

19. Miller, *Whole Different Ball Game,* 55–56; "In Praise of Those . . .," *New York Times,* July 2, 1991.

20. Miller interview, February 21, 2006; Miller, *Whole Different Ball Game,* 57–60.

21. "Major League Baseball Players Association Press Release," April 15, 1966, Miller Papers, Box 3, Folder 52; Miller, *Whole Different Ball Game,* 60–62.

22. Miller interview, May 30, 2006; Miller, *Whole Different Ball Game,* 63–64.

23. Miller, *Whole Different Ball Game,* 65–66.

24. "Major League Baseball Players Association Press Release," May 4, 1966, in United Steelworkers of America, Research Department: Marvin J. Miller, Box 8, Folder 1, USWA Archives; Miller, *Whole Different Ball Game,* 66–68; Korr, *End of Baseball,* 46–47.

25. Miller, *Whole Different Ball Game,* 68–69.

26. Marvin Miller to All Club Player Representatives, May 10, 1966, USWA Research Department: Marvin J. Miller, Box 8, Folder 1, USWA Archives; Miller, *Whole Different Ball Game,* 69.

27. Miller, *Whole Different Ball Game,* 70–71.

28. Miller, *Whole Different Ball Game,* 72–73; Helyar, *Lords of the Realm,* 26–27; Korr, *End of Baseball,* 49–50.

29. Miller interview, February 21, 2006; Miller, *Whole Different Ball Game,* 74–75.

30. Miller, *Whole Different Ball Game,* 76; Korr, *End of Baseball,* 47–48.

31. Miller, *Whole Different Ball Game,* 77; Burk, *Much More Than a Game,* 153.

32. Miller, *Whole Different Ball Game,* 78; Terry Miller interview with the author, May 2, 2006.

33. Miller, *Whole Different Ball Game,* 79–82; Miller interview with the author, February 21, 2006.

34. "Story Inaccurate, Miller Asserts," *Sporting News,* August 6, 1966.

35. Richard Moss interview with the author, July 3, 2006; Korr, *End of Baseball,* 50–51.

36. Miller, *Whole Different Ball Game,* 83–4.

37. Miller, *Whole Different Ball Game,* 142–47.

38. Miller interview with the author, February 21, 2006; Korr, *End of Baseball,* 54.

39. Miller, *Whole Different Ball Game,* 86–92.

40. Miller interview with the author, February 21, 2006.

Chapter 9. Securing the Basics

1. Marvin Miller interview with the author, February 21, 2006; Richard Moss interview with the author, July 3, 2006; Miller, *Whole Different Ball Game,* 154–55; "Relentless, Resolute—That's Miller," *Sporting News,* February 15, 1969; George Frazier IV, "That Guy in New York Trying to Destroy the Reserve Clause," *Jock,* April 1970.

2. Korr, *End of Baseball,* 57–58; Miller interview with the author, February 21, 2006; Peter Miller to the author, August 14, 2008.

3. "The Birds Would Warble—For a Fee," *Sporting News,* March 25, 1967; Helyar, *Lords of the Realm,* 27; Korr, *End of Baseball,* 58–59.

4. Miller, *Whole Different Ball Game,* 95, 153; Miller interview with the author, February 21, 2006; *New York Times,* February 12, 1967; Helyar, *Lords of the Realm,* 29–30, 32–33, 35–36.

5. Miller, *Whole Different Ball Game,* 156; *Sporting News,* April 8, 1967; Burk, *Much More Than a Game,* 155–56; Korr, *End of Baseball,* 70–71.

6. Major League Baseball Players Association, "Average Salaries in Major League Baseball, 1867–1982," Miller Papers, Box 5, Folder 29.

7. Miller, *Whole Different Ball Game,* 96–97; Michael Burke, *Outrageous Good Fortune: A Memoir* (Boston: Little, Brown, 1984), 276–78; Korr, *End of Baseball,* 60.

8. Miller, *Whole Different Ball Game,* 159–60; Miller interview with the author, May 2, 2006.

9. Miller, "Goals," July 28, 1967, Statement of Policy," Miller Papers, Box 4, Folder 19.

10. Miller interview with the author, December 13, 2005; Peter Miller to the author, June 15, 2006; "Marvin Miller," *Sports Collector's Digest,* June 23, 1995; "Marvin Miller Interview For Fay Vincent," Miller Papers, Box 10; Helyar, *Lords of the Realm,* 84–85.

11. Major League Baseball Players Association, *Newsletter,* June, September 1967, Miller Papers, Box 3, Folder 47; Korr, *End of Baseball,* 65–66; "Marvin Miller," *Sports Collector's Digest,* June 23, 1995.

12. Marvin Miller interview with the author, December 13, 2005; Richard Moss, "Miller Proved Almost Ideal as Baseball's Union Chief," *New York Times,* January 2, 1983; "Marvin Miller Interview for Fay Vincent," Miller Papers, Box 10.

13. Peter Miller to the author, June 15, 2006; Helyar, *Lords of the Realm,* 85–87; *Washington Post,* February 11, 1990.

14. Miller interview with the author, February 21, 2006; Korr, *End of Baseball,* 56.

15. Peter Miller to the author, June 15, 2006; Helyar, *Lords of the Realm,* 33–34.

16. Miller, *Whole Different Ball Game,* 95–96, 161; Miller interview with the author, February 21, 2006; Buzzie Bavasi, *Sports Illustrated,* May 22, 1967.

17. Miller, *Whole Different Ball Game,* 162; Burk, *Much More Than a Game,* 157.

18. Helyar, *Lords of the Realm,* 36–37.

19. *Sporting News,* September 2, 1967, September 9, 1967.

20. *Sporting News,* September 23, 1967.

21. Helyar, *Lords of the Realm*, 88.

22. Miller, *Whole Different Ball Game,* 163; Miller interview with the author, May 15, 2006; *New York Times,* November 30, 1967; *Sporting News,* December 16, 1967; Korr, *End of Baseball,* 69.

23. *Sporting News,* December 16, 1967; Korr, *End of Baseball,* 70; Helyar, *Lords of the Realm,* 36.

24. Miller interview with the author, February 21, 2006.

25. *St. Louis Post-Dispatch,* January 2, 1968; *Boston Record-American,* January 26, 1968; *Sporting News,* December 30, 1967, February 3, 1968.

26. Miller interview with the author, February 21, 2006; Miller, *Whole Different Ball Game,* 97–98,163: Korr, *End of Baseball,* 71–73.

27. Miller, *Whole Different Ball Game,* 145–48; Korr, *End of Baseball,* 74; Helyar, *Lords of the Realm,* 90.

28. Miller, *Whole Different Ball Game,* 148–50; Weston Merchandising Corporation and MLBPA, "Licensing Agreement," September 9, 1967, Miller Papers, Box 3, Folder 35.

29. Miller, *Whole Different Ball Game,* 92–94, 150.

30. *Sporting News,* March 30, 1968.

31. Miller, *Whole Different Ball Game,* 164; *Sporting News,* September 28, 1968.

32. *Sporting News,* June 15, 1968, September 28, 1968.

33. Terry Miller interview, May 2, 2006; Terry Miller to the author, May 28, 2006; *West Side News,* May 30, 1968, in "footprints . . . fingerprints . . . reprints," Miller Papers, Box 11.

34. Miller, *Whole Different Ball Game,* 149–50.

35. Helyar, *Lords of the Realm*, 81–82.

Chapter 10. Taking On the Plantation

1. Burk, *Much More Than a Game,* 158, 160; Helyar, *Lords of the Realm,* 88–92.

2. Miller, *Whole Different Ball Game,* 240; *Sporting News,* August 17, 1968, September 21, 1968, January 31, {correct year—1969?}; *Chicago American,* September 19, 1968; Korr, *End of Baseball,* 74–75.

3. Miller, *Whole Different Ball Game,* 98–99; *Sporting News,* November 30, 1968, December 28, 1968.

4. Miller, *Whole Different Ball Game,* 100.

5. Major League Baseball Players Association, "Press Release," January 17, 1969, January 22, 1969, Miller Papers, Box 2, Folder 9; *Sporting News,* January 18, 1969, January 25, 1969, February 1, 1969, February 8, 1969; *Utica Observer,* February 9, 1969; Miller, *Whole Different Ball Game,* 101–3; Bowie Kuhn, *Hardball: The Education of a Baseball Commissioner* (New York: Times Books, 1987), 35; Helyar, *Lords of the Realm,* 95–98.

6. Miller, *Whole Different Ball Game,* 103–4, 166, 284; *Sporting News,* February 15, 1969, February 22, 1969; *New York Times,* February 19, 1969, February 21, 1969.

7. Miller, *Whole Different Ball Game,* 167; Kuhn, *Hardball,* 40.

8. Miller, *Whole Different Ball Game,* 105; *Boston Herald-Traveler,* February 26, 1969, *Sporting News,* April 12, 1969.

9. Peter Miller to the author, August 24, 2010.

10. *Sporting News,* May 3, 1969; Helyar, *Lords of the Realm,* 101–2.

11. *Sporting News,* May 10, 1969, May 24, 1969.

12. Miller interview with the author, March 14, 2006; Miller, *Whole Different Ball Game,* 98, 167, 240; *Cincinnati Enquirer,* May 24, 1969; *Sporting News,* June 7, 1969; Korr, *End of Baseball,* 76–82; Helyar, *Lords of the Realm,* 130.

13. Miller, *Whole Different Ball Game,* 98, 168–69.

14. MLBPA memo, "Joint Study of the Reserve Clause (1970)," Miller Papers, Box 3, Folder 10; Korr, *End of Baseball,* 82–83.

15. Miller interview with the author, March 14, 2006; Brad Snyder, *A Well-Paid Slave: Curt Flood's Fight for Free Agency in Professional Sports* (New York: Viking Press, 2006), 16–19; Lee Lowenfish, *The Imperfect Diamond: A History of Baseball's Labor Wars,* rev. ed. (New York: Da Capo Press, 1991), 106–7; Helyar, *Lords of the Realm,* 105–8.

16. Miller interview with the author, March 14, 2006; Snyder, *Well-Paid Slave,* 19–27; *Sporting News,* January 24, 1967.

17. Miller interview with the author, March 14, 2006; Snyder, *Well-Paid Slave,* 27–30.

18. Marvin Miller to Bowie Kuhn, August 1, 1969, Kuhn to Miller, August 22, 1969, Box 3, Folder 31, Miller to Kuhn, September 3, 1969, Box 2, Folder 27, Miller Papers; Miller, *Whole Different Ball Game,* 105, 294; Kuhn, *Hardball,* 80–81.

19. Miller, *Whole Different Ball Game,* 185–87; Snyder, *Well-Paid Slave,* 69–81; Korr, *End of Baseball,* 86–89, 94–95.

20. Miller interview with the author, March 14, 2006; Peter Miller to the author, August 16, 2007; Snyder, *Well-Paid Slave,* 83–91.

21. Snyder, *Well-Paid Slave,* 95.

22. Korr, *End of Baseball,* 84.

23. Miller, *Whole Different Ball Game,* 191–92; Snyder, *Well-Paid Slave,* 94–106; Kuhn, *Hardball,* 83–85; Korr, *End of Baseball,* 89.

24. Snyder, *Well-Paid Slave,* 107–9; Korr, *End of Baseball,* 97.

25. Miller interview with the author, March 14, 2006; Korr, *End of Baseball,* 92–92, 96–99; Kuhn, *Hardball,* 80, 296; Carl Yastrzemski to Marvin Miller, January 15, 1970, Miller to Yastrzemski, January 22, 1970, Miller Papers, Box 8, Folder 20.

26. Miller interview with the author, March 14, 2006; Snyder, *Well-Paid Slave,* 122–24, 135; Jay H. Topkis, "Monopoly in Professional Sports," *Yale Law Journal* 58 (1949): 691.

27. Miller interview with the author, March 14, 2006; *Sporting News,* November 29, 1969, December 27, 1969.

28. Helyar, *Lords of the Realm,* 109–10.

29. Miller interview with the author, March 14, 2006; Burk, *Much More Than a Game,* 164.

30. *Sporting News,* April 4, 1970; Helyar, *Lords of the Realm,* 113–14.

31. Miller, *Whole Different Ball Game,* 239–40; *New York Daily News,* May 25, 1970, May 26, 1970; *Sporting News,* June 13, 1970, June 20, 1970.

32. Miller interview with the author, March 14, 2006; Miller, *Whole Different Ball Game,* 198, 276–77; Snyder, *Well-Paid Slave,* 145–54, 179, 182, 188.

33. Miller, *Whole Different Ball Game,* 366–67; Snyder, *Well-Paid Slave,* 157–68, 184.

34. Miller, *Whole Different Ball Game,* 197; Snyder, *Well-Paid Slave,* 192–93.

35. Miller, *Whole Different Ball Game,* 200; Snyder, *Well-Paid Slave,* 198–201.

36. Dick Young, *New York Daily News,* May 23, 1970.

37. Marvin Miller, "Salary, 1970–72," Miller Papers, Box 5, Folder 30; Kuhn, *Hardball,* 73.

38. Burk, *Much More Than a Game,* 166, 169–71.

39. Helyar, *Lords of the Realm,* 115.

40. Miller, *Whole Different Ball Game,* 194; Kuhn, *Hardball,* 87; Marvin Miller to Justice Arthur J. Goldberg, June 3, 1970, September 21, 1971, Goldberg to Miller, October 12, 1971, Arthur J. Goldberg Papers, Box I:94, Library of Congress, Washington, D.C.; Snyder, *Well-Paid Slave,* 236, 254–55, 266; *Sporting News,* November 13, 1971.

41. Korr, *End of Baseball,* 91–92.

42. Miller, *Whole Different Ball Game,* 108, 131–41.

43. *Sporting News,* April 17, 1971, May 22, 1971, November 20, 1971; Korr, *End of Baseball,* 99–100.

44. Peter Miller to the author, June 21, 2006, August 16, 2008, August 17, 2008; "Oral History Interview," Miller Papers, Box 5, Folder 11; *Sporting News,* November 20, 1971.

Chapter 11. Earning Respect

1. Marvin Miller interview with the author, March 14, 2006; Miller, *Whole Different Ball Game,* 203–4; Marvin Miller to All Players, Managers, Coaches, and Trainers, August 11, 1971, September 4, 1971, Miller Papers, Box 2, Folder 3; Burk, *Much More Than a Game,* 172–74; Korr, *End of Baseball,* 103–5.

2. Miller interview with the author, March 14, 2006; *Sporting News,* January 8, 1972; Helyar, *Lords of the Realm,* 116.

3. Miller interview with the author, March 14, 2006; *Sporting News,* April 8, 1972.

4. Miller, *Whole Different Ball Game,* 205–7; *New York Daily News,* March 23, 1972, April 2, 1972.

5. Miller interview with the author, March 14, 2006; Miller, *Whole Different Ball Game,* 208; *Sporting News,* April 1, 1972.

6. Miller, *Whole Different Ball Game,* 208–9.

7. Miller, *Whole Different Ball Game,* 109, 205; Kuhn, *Hardball,* 106.

8. Miller interview with the author, March 14, 2006; Miller, *Whole Different Ball Game,* 210–11; Korr, *End of Baseball,* 106–8.

9. Miller interview with the author, March 14, 2006; *Sporting News,* April 15, 1972; Helyar, *Lords of the Realm,* 120–23; Korr, *End of Baseball,* 109–10.

10. Miller, *Whole Different Ball Game,* 212–15.

11. Miller, *Whole Different Ball Game,* 217–19; *New York Times,* April 15, 1972; *Sporting News,* April 15, 1972.

12. Helyar, *Lords of the Realm,* 125; *Binghamton Press,* April 6, 1972; "Cincinnati Reds News Release," April 6, 1972, Marvin Miller Subject File, National Baseball Library, Cooperstown, N.Y.

13. Miller, *Whole Different Ball Game,* 220–21; Helyar, *Lords of the Realm,* 129.

14. *Sporting News,* April 22, 1972; Burk, *Much More Than a Game,* 176–77.

15. Miller, *Whole Different Ball Game,* 222–23; Korr, *End of Baseball,* 102; Kuhn, *Hardball,* 107.

16. *Sporting News,* April 29, 1972.

17. Marvin Miller to Buzzie Bavasi, June 22, 1972, Miller to Thomas A. Yawkey, June

23, 1972, Miller to Francis Dale, May 5, 1972, Miller Papers, Box 2, Folder 28; Korr, *End of Baseball*, 115–16.

18. Marvin Miller to Wes Parker, April 24, 1972, Miller Papers, Box 2, Folder 28; Korr, *End of Baseball*, 116–18; Miller, *Whole Different Ball Game*, 206; *Sporting News*, April 22, 1972; *New York Times*, May 21, 1972; *New York Daily News*, May 20, 1972.

19. *Sporting News*, June 3, 1972, June 10, 1972, June 24, 1972.

20. Miller, *Whole Different Ball Game*, 194–200; Snyder, *Well-Paid Slave*, 267–74; Korr, *End of Baseball*, 121–22.

21. Snyder, *Well-Paid Slave*, 308, 313–14; *Sporting News*, July 8, 1972; Helyar, *Lords of the Realm*, 134–35.

22. Miller interview with the author, March 14, 2006; Helyar, *Lords of the Realm*, 130–33; Korr, *End of Baseball*, 133–36.

23. Miller, *Whole Different Ball Game*, 240; Korr, *End of Baseball*, 137.

24. Miller, *Whole Different Ball Game*, 110–11; Korr, *End of Baseball*, 123.

25. Miller interview with the author, March 14, 2006; *Sporting News*, December 16, 1972, December 23, 1972; *San Francisco Chronicle*, December 8, 1972; *New York Times*, December 8, 1972; "Notes," Bargaining Session of October 30, 1972, Miller Papers, Box 4, Folder 23.

26. Miller interview with the author, March 14, 2006.

27. Korr, *End of Baseball*, 122, 128.

28. Miller interview with the author, March 14, 2006.

29. Snyder, *Well-Paid Slave*, 314; *New York Times*, February 14, 1973; *Sporting News*, March 3, 1973; Korr, *End of Baseball*, 130.

30. Helyar, *Lords of the Realm*, 160–61.

31. Burk, *Much More Than a Game*, 186–87.

32. *New York Daily News*, March 5, 1973; *Boston Herald-American*, March 14, 1973; *Sporting News*, February 8, 1973, March 10, 1973, March 31, 1973, April 14, 1973; *New York Times*, March 13, 1973, March 17, 1973; Marvin Miller to Reuben Askenase, April 17, 1973, Buzzie Bavasi to Miller, November 7, 1973, Miller to Bavasi, November 12, 1973, Miller Papers, Box 2, Folder 30; Korr, *End of Baseball*, 140–41.

33. "Oral History Interview," Miller Papers, Box 5, Folder 11, Miller to N. E. Beyer, April 26, 1973, Box 2, Folder 30; *Sporting News*, May 26, 1973, August 11, 1973.

34. Miller interview with the author, March 14, 2006; Miller to Johnny Bench, May 14, 1974, Miller Papers, Box 2, Folder 31; Korr, *End of Baseball*, 137–40.

35. *Boston Herald*, October 18, 1973; *New York Times*, December 12, 1973.

36. Miller, *Whole Different Ball Game*, 371–74; *Sporting News*, October 6, 1973, December 15, 1973, February 16, 1974.

37. Miller, *Whole Different Ball Game*, 375–76; *Sporting News*, May 16, 1974.

38. Peter Miller to the author, August 17, 2008; *New York Times*, March 23, 1974.

39. "Oral History Interview," Miller Papers, Box 5, Folder 11; *Sporting News*, April 27, 1974; Miller interview with the author, March 14, 2006; Miller, *Whole Different Ball Game*, 240–41; Snyder, *Well-Paid Slave*, 318.

40. *Sporting News*, October 12, 1974; Miller interviews with the author, March 14, 2006, April 18, 2006; Miller, *Whole Different Ball Game*, 111–13, 228–29; Helyar, *Lords of the Realm*, 141–48.

41. Miller interview with the author, March 14, 2006; Korr, *End of Baseball*, 142–44.

42. Miller, *Whole Different Ball Game,* 231–33; Kuhn, *Hardball,* 139; J. Carlton Cherry to Jerry Kapstein, December 17, 1974, Miller Papers, Box 1, Folder 15.

43. Miller, *Whole Different Ball Game,* 234–35; Kuhn, *Hardball,* 140.

44. Kuhn, *Hardball,* 142.

45. Miller interview with the author, March 14, 2006; Kuhn, *Hardball,* 143; Helyar, *Lords of the Realm,* 150–59.

Chapter 12. Emancipation

1. Kuhn, *Hardball,* 154; Miller, *Whole Different Ball Game,* 243; Helyar, *Lords of the Realm,* 164; Korr, *End of Baseball,* 132; Snyder, *Well-Paid Slave,* 318–19.

2. Miller interview with the author, May 16, 2006; *Chicago Tribune,* May 16, 1975; *Sporting News,* August 23, 1975.

3. *Sporting News,* May 10, 1975; Korr, *End of Baseball,* 171–72.

4. Miller interview with the author, March 14, 2006; Korr, *End of Baseball,* 147–48, 150; Burk, *Much More Than a Game,* 193–95.

5. Miller interview with the author, March 14, 2006.

6. Helyar, *Lords of the Realm,* 166–67.

7. Miller interview with the author, March 14, 2006; Helyar, *Lords of the Realm,* 168–69; Korr, *End of Baseball,* 152–53.

8. Burk, *Much More Than a Game,* 197.

9. Miller interview with the author, March 14, 2006; Miller, *Whole Different Ball Game,* 116, 245–46.

10. Kuhn, *Hardball,* 155–58.

11. Korr, *End of Baseball,* 154–56.

12. Jim Bouton, *Ball Four Plus Ball Five: An Update, 1970–1980* (New York: Stein and Day, 1981), xii; Helyar, *Lords of the Realm,* 170–79.

13. Korr, *End of Baseball,* 157–58; Kuhn, *Hardball,* 160.

14. Miller interview with the author, March 14, 2006; Miller, *Whole Different Ball Game,* 251–52; Kuhn, *Hardball,* 155, 160; *Sporting News,* January 10, 1976; *Kansas City Royals Baseball Corp. v. Major League Baseball Players Association and Golden West Baseball Company, et al.,* United States District Court for the Western District of Missouri Western Division, no. 75-CV-712-W-1, January 26–28, 1976; Korr, *End of Baseball,* 159–67.

15. Miller interview with the author, March 14, 2006; Korr, *End of Baseball,* 168–69; *Sporting News,* August 2, 1975, October 18, 1975, October 25, 1975; November 8, 1975.

16. Miller interview with the author, March 14, 2006; Korr, *End of Baseball,* 175–76, 177–79.

17. Miller interview with the author, March 14, 2006; Helyar, *Lords of the Realm,* 181–82; Korr, *End of Baseball,* 182–83.

18. Burk, *Much More Than a Game,* 201.

19. Miller interview with the author, March 14, 2006; Miller, *Whole Different Ball Game,* 255–59; Kuhn, *Hardball,* 161–62; *Sporting News,* February 7, 1976; *Chicago Sun-Times,* February 15, 1976.

20. Miller, *Whole Different Ball Game,* 260–62, 269; *Sporting News,* February 21, 1976; Helyar, *Lords of the Realm,* 183–85.

21. *Sporting News,* March 13, 1976; Decision of the United States Court of Appeals, Eighth Circuit, in *Kansas City Royals v. MLBPA,* No. 76-1115, March 9, 1976.

22. Miller, *Whole Different Ball Game,* 262–63; *Sporting News,* March 6, 1976.

23. *New York Daily News,* March 17, 1976; *Sporting News,* March 20, 1976; Korr, *End of Baseball,* 180–81.

24. Miller, *Whole Different Ball Game,* 271.

25. Miller, *Whole Different Ball Game,* 264; Kuhn, *Hardball,* 163–64.

26. "Basic Agreement—Players Association Proposal," April 19, 1976, Miller Papers, Box 4, Folder 26; Miller, *Whole Different Ball Game,* 252–53; Kuhn, *Hardball,* 165.

27. Miller team meeting notes, "24 Meetings—May 13–June 21, 1976," Miller Papers, Box 4, Folder 26.

28. Miller, *Whole Different Ball Game,* 377–79; Kuhn, *Hardball,* 177.

29. Kuhn, *Hardball,* 181; *Chicago Sun-Times,* June 19, 1976; *Sporting News,* July 3, 1976; Helyar, *Lords of the Realm,* 201–3.

30. Miller, *Whole Different Ball Game,* 266–68; Helyar, *Lords of the Realm,* 208.

31. Burk, *Much More Than a Game,* 205.

32. Kuhn, *Hardball,* 167.

33. Kuhn, *Hardball,* 168; Helyar, *Lords of the Realm,* 181.

34. "Statement of Marvin Miller to House Select Committee on Professional Sports," August 2, 1976, Miller testimony notes, House Select Committee, October 1976, Miller Papers, Box 3, Folder 16, "Clubs First Draft—September 23, 1976," Box 4, Folder 26; *Sporting News,* October 8, 1976.

35. *Sporting News,* November 5, 1976; Burk, *Much More Than a Game,* 206–7.

36. Korr, *End of Baseball,* 188–89.

37. Burk, *Much More Than a Game,* 208.

38. Miller, *Whole Different Ball Game,* 151.

39. Burk, *Much More Than a Game,* 209–12.

40. Miller interview with the author, March 14, 2006.

Chapter 13. Holding the Line

1. *Sporting News,* March 18, 1978, April 1, 1978; Miller, *Whole Different Ball Game,* 280.

2. Miller, *Whole Different Ball Game,* 272–75; Miller to Jerry Kapstein, November 16, 1976, Box 1, Folder 15, Miller to Rick Burleson, Carlton Fisk, and Fred Lynn, January 14, 1977, Miller Papers, Box 2, Folder 33; Jerry Crasnick, *License to Deal: A Season on the Run with a Maverick Baseball Agent* (New York: Rodale, 2005), 135–36; *New York Daily News,* January 27, 1977, January 28, 1977; *Sporting News,* February 12, 1977; *New York Times,* January 29, 1977.

3. Miller, *Whole Different Ball Game,* 277–79; Miller interview with the author, April 4, 2006; Crasnick, *License to Deal,* 139; *Sporting News,* March 19, 1977, December 24, 1977, June 10, 1978; *New York Times,* February 27, 1977.

4. Miller interview with the author, April 4, 2006.

5. Miller interview with the author, April 4, 2006; Burk, *Much More Than a Game,* 212–13.

6. Miller interview with the author, April 4, 2006; Kuhn, *Hardball,* 304.

7. Marvin Miller to Coaches and Trainers, August 21, 1978, Miller Papers, Box 2, Folder 19; *New York Daily News,* June 11, 1979; Burk, *Much More Than a Game,* 218–19.

8. Miller to George Cantor, April 27, 1979, Miller Papers, Box 2, Folder 35.

9. Miller, *Whole Different Ball Game,* 280; Miller interview with the author, April 4, 2006; Howard Bryant, *Juicing the Game: Drugs, Power, and the Fight for the Soul of Major League Baseball* (New York: Viking Press, 2005), 43.

10. Miller, *Whole Different Ball Game,* 275–76; Miller to John J. Gaherin, February 18, 1983, Miller Papers, Box 2, Folder 39; *Sporting News,* August 13, 1977; Helyar, *Lords of the Realm,* 230–31.

11. Miller interview with the author, April 4, 2006; Kuhn, *Hardball,* 333; Lowenfish, *Imperfect Diamond,* 227–28.

12. Miller interview with the author, April 4, 2006; Kenneth Jennings, *Balls and Strikes: The Money Game in Professional Baseball* (New York: Praeger, 1990), 41–42.

13. *New York Daily News,* February 25, 1979, February 27, 1979; Miller, *Whole Different Ball Game,* 281, 285; Helyar, *Lords of the Realm,* 232–34; Burk, *Much More Than a Game,* 214–18.

14. Marvin Miller to Charles D. Feeney, April 26, 1979, Miller Papers, Box 2, Folder 35; Helyar, *Lords of the Realm,* 238; Bryant, *Juicing the Game,* 37.

15. Miller, *Whole Different Ball Game,* 281, 295; Miller notes, "1979," Miller Papers, Box 4, Folder 28.

16. Miller, *Whole Different Ball Game,* 116–18, 285; Miller interview with the author, April 4, 2006; Kuhn, *Hardball,* 335; Helyar, *Lords of the Realm,* 231, 235–37.

17. Miller, *Whole Different Ball Game,* 298.

18. Jennings, *Balls and Strikes,* 43–44; Lowenfish, *Imperfect Diamond,* 228.

19. Miller interview with the author, April 4, 2006; Burk, *Much More Than a Game,* 223–24; Korr, *End of Baseball,* 191–94.

20. Miller, *Whole Different Ball Game,* 290, 296–97; Miller interview, April 4, 2006; Miller to MLBPA Executive Board, March 24, 1980, Miller Papers, Box 5, Folder 1; Jennings, *Balls and Strikes,* 45–46; Ray Grebey, *Sporting News,* May 17, 1980.

21. Miller interview with the author, April 4, 2006.

22. Helyar, *Lords of the Realm,* 239–40.

23. Miller, *Whole Different Ball Game,* 300; Korr, *End of Baseball,* 200–201.

24. Marvin Miller to All Members of the MLBPA, "Tentative Agreements," May 29, 1980, Miller Papers, Box 5, Folder 2; Miller interview with the author, April 4, 2006; Miller, *Whole Different Ball Game,* 120, 291; Jennings, *Balls and Strikes,* 48–49.

25. Miller, *Whole Different Ball Game,* 119; Helyar, *Lords of the Realm,* 243; Don Baylor with Claire Smith, *Don Baylor* (New York: St. Martin's Press, 1989), 167–69.

26. Miller, *Whole Different Ball Game,* 127–28; Kuhn, *Hardball,* 304–6; *Sporting News,* August 23, 1980.

27. Miller, *Whole Different Ball Game,* 291–92, 297–98; Miller notes of Joint Study Committee, December 16, 1980, Miller Papers, Box 5, Folder 1; Korr, *End of Baseball,* 205–9.

28. C. Raymond Grebey to Marvin Miller, February 19, 1981, Miller Papers, Box 5, Folder 1; Helyar, *Lords of the Realm,* 274–75.

29. Miller, *Whole Different Ball Game,* 287–88, 297–98; Miller interview with the author, April 4, 2006; Donald Fehr to C. Raymond Grebey, February 27, 1981, Miller Papers, Box 5, Folder 1.

30. Miller, *Whole Different Ball Game,* 120–23, 125, 289, 291–92; Helyar, *Lords of the Realm,* 277–79; Jennings, *Balls and Strikes,* 52–59.

31. Miller, *Whole Different Ball Game,* 125, 381–82; Kuhn, *Hardball,* 355.

32. Miller, *Whole Different Ball Game,* 299, 382; Miller interview with the author, April 4, 2006; Kuhn, *Hardball,* 347–49; Murray Chass interview with the author, September 4, 2008; Donald Peterson to Marvin Miller, June 17, 1981, Miller Papers, Box 6, Folder 17.

33. *New York Times,* July 2, 1981; Korr, *End of Baseball,* 214–15, 217, 224–26; A. Bartlett Giamatti, *New York Times,* June 16, 1981; Giamatti to Miller, February 22, 1982, Miller Papers, Box 2, Folder 38.

34. *New York Times,* July 9, 1981; Helyar, *Lords of the Realm,* 289–90; Baylor, *Don Baylor,* 169.

35. Miller interview with the author, April 18, 2006; Miller, *Whole Different Ball Game,* 309–10.

36. Miller, *Whole Different Ball Game,* 311–14; Miller interview with the author, April 4, 2006; Kuhn, *Hardball,* 354–57; Helyar, *Lords of the Realm,* 293–99; Baylor, *Don Baylor,* 170–71; Korr, *End of Baseball,* 217–20.

37. Chass interview with the author, September 4, 2008; Miller interview with the author, April 4, 2006; Korr, *End of Baseball,* 221; Helyar, *Lords of the Realm,* 300–302; Lowenfish, *Imperfect Diamond,* 245–46.

38. Miller, *Whole Different Ball Game,* 120, 124, 286, 314–17; Kuhn, *Hardball,* 355, 358–59; *Sporting News,* September 12, 1981; Helyar, *Lords of the Realm,* 303–4.

39. *Sporting News,* August 15, 1981; Andrew Zimbalist, *Baseball and Billions: A Probing Look Inside the Business of Our National Pastime* (New York: Basic Books, 1994), 22.

40. "August J. Busch," August 6, 1981, Miller Papers, Box 2, Folder 16; Helyar, *Lords of the Realm,* 305–6.

41. Miller, *Whole Different Ball Game,* 120–22, 302; Miller, "The Union's Strength Is Established," *New York Times,* August 16, 1981; Korr, *End of Baseball,* 222, 230.

42. Miller, *Whole Different Ball Game,* 125, 323; Miller interview with the author, April 4, 2006, May 16, 2006; Peter Miller to the author, June 21, 2006.

43. Miller interview with the author, April 4, 2006; Joe Durso WQXR broadcast, August 7, 1982, Miller Papers, Box 2, Folder 38.

Chapter 14. Flunking Retirement

1. Gerald W. Scully, *The Business of Major League Baseball* (Chicago: University of Chicago Press, 1989), 39, 153; Reggie Jackson with Mike Lupica, *Reggie: The Autobiography* (New York: Villard Books, 1984), 292; *New York Times,* January 22, 1982, January 24, 1982; Helyar, *Lords of the Realm,* 583; Kuhn, *Hardball,* 381; "Before the Subcommittee on Monopolies and Commerce and Law of the Committee on the Judiciary, U.S. House of Representatives: Prepared Statement of Marvin Miller," February 24, 1982, Miller Papers, Box 8, Folder 7.

2. *Sporting News,* February 13, 1982, February 27, 1982; Malvin Wald interview with the author, June 10, 2006; Jane Leavy to Marvin Miller, 7/2/81, Miller Papers, Box 3, Folder 32.

3. Miller, *Whole Different Ball Game,* 328.

4. Miller interview with the author, April 4, 2006.

5. Miller, *Whole Different Ball Game,* 323; Kenneth Moffett to Marvin Miller, June 23, 1982, Miller Papers, Box 4, Folder 1; Lowenfish, *Imperfect Diamond,* 250.

6. Miller, *Whole Different Ball Game,* 324, 329–30; Miller interview with the author, April 4, 2006; Jack Sands and Peter Gammons, *Coming Apart At the Seams: How Baseball Owners,*

Players & Television Executives Have Led the National Pastime to the Brink of Disaster (New York: Macmillan, 1993), 48–50; Jennings, *Balls and Strikes*, 60.

7. Miller interview with the author, April 4, 2006; Ben Fischer interview with the author, June 27, 2006; Burk, *Much More Than a Game*, 236.

8. Miller, *Whole Different Ball Game*, 325–26; Miller to MLBPA Executive Board, "Interim Service," March 3, 1983, "The Players' Right to Know," March 7, 1983, Miller Papers, Box 4, Folder 1; Lowenfish, *Imperfect Diamond*, 249, 251–52.

9. Miller interview with the author, April 4, 2006.

10. *New York Post*, November 5, 1983; David L. Robertson to Marvin Miller, August 25, 1983, Miller Papers, Box 2, Folder 39, MLBPA Executive Board to Kenneth Moffett, November 22, 1983, Box 4, Folder 1, Miller notes, February 20, 1984, Box 4, Folder 2.

11. Miller interview with the author, April 4, 2006.

12. Miller, *Whole Different Ball Game*, 322–23.

13. Miller interview with the author, April 4, 2006.

14. Keith Olbermann, "Marvin Miller, the Man Who Reinvented Baseball," *Baseball Nerd* (keitholbermann.mlblogs.com); *Wall Street Journal*, November 2, 1984; Miller, *Whole Different Ball Game*, 334–35; "Minutes of MLBPA Executive Board," December 6–8, 1983, Miller Papers, Box 1, Folder 15, Miller notes, "Moffett," February 22, 1984, Box 4, Folder 1; Kuhn, *Hardball*, 311–12; Burk, *Much More Than a Game*, 236–38.

15. Miller interview with the author, April 4, 2006; Kuhn, *Hardball*, 307–8.

16. *Washington Post*, February 22, 1984; *Newsday*, February 23, 1984; Sands and Gammons, *Coming Apart*, 51.

17. Donald Fehr, "Memorandum to All Player Representatives," August 7, 1984, Miller Papers, Box 3, Folder 1.

18. "Memorandum of Agreement (Joint Drug Policy)," 1984, Miller Papers, Box 1, Folder 8.

19. Miller, *Whole Different Ball Game*, 385–86; *New York Times*, November 18, 1984; Helyar, *Lords of the Realm*, 345, 583–84.

20. Sands and Gammons, *Coming Apart*, 61–62.

21. Lowenfish, *Imperfect Diamond*, 257–58; Burk, *Much More Than a Game*, 247–48.

22. Miller, *Whole Different Ball Game*, 335–38; "Former Players Honor Marvin Miller," Associated Press, January 22, 2013.

23. Miller interview with the author, April 4, 2006.

24. Miller, *Whole Different Ball Game*, 339–40.

25. Miller interview with the author, April 4, 2006; *Detroit Free Press*, September 6, 1987; Sands and Gammons, *Coming Apart*, 112.

26. Miller, *Whole Different Ball Game*, 341–42; Donald Fehr to MLBPA Player Representatives, August 14, 1985, Miller Papers, Box 2, Folder 12.

27. Miller interview with the author, April 4, 2006; Bryant, *Juicing the Game*, 289.

28. Miller, *Whole Different Ball Game*, 343–44.

29. Miller, *Whole Different Ball Game*, 345–46.

30. Sands and Gammons, *Coming Apart*, 10.

Chapter 15. Living Memory

1. Helyar, *Lords of the Realm*, 351–59; Bryant, *Juicing the Game*, 292.

2. Burk, *Much More Than a Game*, 251–52.

3. Miller, *Whole Different Ball Game,* 346, 391–92; Miller interview with the author, April 18, 2006; "Arbitration Decisions, 1984–86," "In the Matter of the Arbitration Between MLBPA and the Twenty-Six Major League Baseball Clubs," Grievance No. 86-2, June 26, 1986, 166, Miller Papers, Box 1, Folder 25, "Arbitration Decisions, 1987–1988," Box 1, Folder 26.

4. Miller, *Whole Different Ball Game,* 351; Sands and Gammons, *Coming Apart,* 80; Bryant, *Juicing the Game,* 12–13.

5. Peter Miller to the author, June 21, 2006; December 21, 1986.

6. *Sporting News,* February 24, 1986; *Boston Globe, Kansas City Star,* October 23, 1987; Bryant, *Juicing the Game,* 74.

7. Miller, *Whole Different Ball Game,* 129.

8. Thelma Miller Berenson interview with the author, June 21, 2006; "Oral History Interview," Miller Papers, Box 5, Folder 11; Miller, *Whole Different Ball Game,* 393–94, 396–99; *New York Times,* February 13, 1990; Burk, *Much More Than a Game,* 263–66.

9. Miller, *Whole Different Ball Game,* 403–4; Bryant, *Juicing the Game,* 17.

10. Burk, *Much More Than a Game,* 254, 256, 259; Zimbalist, *Baseball and Billions,* 170.

11. Burk, *Much More Than a Game,* 260, 267; Helyar, *Lords of the Realm,* 441–43.

12. Jennings, *Balls and Strikes,* 67–68; *Kansas City Star,* February 13, 1990.

13. Miller, *Whole Different Ball Game,* 355; *New York Times,* February 25, 1990.

14. Miller, *Whole Different Ball Game,* 357; Randal A. Hendricks, *Inside the Strike Zone* (Austin, Tex.: Eakin Press, 1994), 28; Helyar, *Lords of the Realm,* 448–9.

15. Miller, *Whole Different Ball Game,* 356–59; Miller interview with the author, April 4, 2006, May 2, 2006; Hendricks, *Inside the Strike Zone,* 29.

16. Miller, *Whole Different Ball Game,* 360–61; Miller interview with the author, May 2, 2006; Korr, *End of Baseball,* 259; Helyar, *Lords of the Realm,* 450.

17. Burk, *Much More Than a Game,* 273; Miller, *Whole Different Ball Game,* 362.

18. Allen Barra to the author, April 7, 2009, April 16, 2009; Lee Lowenfish to Donald Fehr, August 31, 1995, Miller Papers, Box 3, Folder 38.

19. Miller, *Whole Different Ball Game,* 85, 393–94; *New York Daily News,* July 20, 1991; *Sporting News,* July 15, 1991; Allen Barra to the author, April 7, 2009, April 16, 2009; James Edward Miller, "Labor's Last Heavy Hitter," *New York Times Book Review,* July 14, 1991.

20. Miller, *Whole Different Ball Game,* 293–94, 382–85, 394–98.

21. Snyder, *Well-Paid Slave,* 343–36.

22. Peter Miller to the author, June 22, 2006; Helyar, *Lords of the Realm,* 442, 584.

23. Helyar, *Lords of the Realm,* 584–85.

24. Bryant, *Juicing the Game,* 383–84.

25. Burk, *Much More Than a Game,* 274–81; Hendricks, *Inside the Strike Zone,* 137; Bryant, *Juicing the Game,* 46; Helyar, *Lords of the Realm,* 588–93.

26. Burk, *Much More Than a Game,* 274.

27. Burk, *Much More Than a Game,* 284–86.

28. *New York Daily News,* January 7, 1992; Bryant, *Juicing the Game,* 42; Roger G. Noll, "Baseball Economics in the 1990s," August 1994, Miller Papers, Box 5, Folder 10; Marvin Miller, "Baseball Revenue-Sharing: Brother, Can You Spare a Dime?" *Sport,* May 1994.

29. *Boston Globe,* February 17, 1995, April 12, 1995; Burk, *Much More Than a Game,* 287–89.

30. *New York Daily News,* December 23, 1994; *Upper East Side Resident,* October 26–November 1, 1994, Miller Papers, Box 10, Folder 14.

31. *Inside Sports,* August 1996; Burk, *Much More Than a Game,* 292–93.

32. Donald Fehr to Marvin Miller, August 8, 1995, Miller Papers, Box 2, Folder 45; *New York Daily News,* December 23, 1994; *Chicago Sun-Times,* December 24, 1996.

33. *Chicago Sun-Times,* December 24, 1996; *USA Today,* November 22, 1996.

34. Bryant, *Juicing the Game,* 154–55.

Chapter 16. Lightning Rod

1. ESPN.com, June 26, 2003; *Boston Globe,* August 9, 1991; *New York Times,* November 28, 2012.

2 Allen Sharman to Marvin Miller, September 20, 2000, Bob Costas to Miller, April 17, 2000, Miller Papers, Box 2, Folder 46; *Street and Smith's Sports Business Journal,* July 16–22, 2001.

3. Ira Berkow, "Marvin Miller, Hall of Famer," *New York Times,* February 15, 1999; Bryant, *Juicing the Game,* 383–85; *Ft. Worth Star-Telegram,* August 15, 1999; Allen Barra, Marvin Miller's Fame is Subject to Interpretation," *New York Times,* January 20, 2000.

4. Marvin Miller interviews with the author, May 16, 2006, May 30, 2006; Eliot Asinof, *Man on Spikes* (Carbondale: Southern Illinois University Press, 1998).

5. *New York Daily News,* January 10, 1999.

6. *Rocky Mountain News,* August 4, 1999; *Toronto Globe and Mail,* July 29, 1999; Bryant, *Juicing the Game,* 223–24.

7. Marvin Miller interview with the author, May 2, 2006.

8. *Sporting News,* September 24, 2001, October 19, 2001; *USA Today Baseball Weekly,* September 1926, 2001.

9. *Sporting News,* November 5, 2001, November 19, 2001; *USA Today Baseball Weekly,* January 26–February 1, 2000, September 19–26, 2001; *Baseball America,* August 7, 2000.

10. *Minneapolis Star-Tribune,* November 14, 2001; *Dallas Morning News,* November 4, 2001; *Sporting News,* November 19, 2001; *USA Today,* January 9, 2002; *Baseball America,* February 4–17, 2002.

11. Associated Press, November 7, 2001, November 10, 2001, November 16, 2001, November 27, 2001, February 4, 2002, February 5, 2002, February 14, 2002, March 13, 2002, March 26, 2002, April 2, 2002, April 3, 2002; *USA Today,* November 27, 2001, December 14, 2001, January 11, 2002, February 5, 2002, April 4, 2002, April 17, 2002; *USA Today Baseball Weekly,* December 19–25, 2001, December 26, 2001–January 1, 2002, May 22–28, 2002, July 17–23, 2002; *Baseball America,* January 7–20, 202, February 4–17, 2002, March 4–17, 2002; *Sporting News,* February 4, 2002, August 26, 2002; Reuters, March 28, 2002; *Sports Illustrated,* April 8, 2002.

12. *USA Today,* July 10, 2002.

13. Associated Press, July 9, 2002, July 10, 2002, July 12, 2002, July 20, 2002, July 24, 2002; *Baseball America,* July 8–21, 2002, July 22–August 4, 2002; *USA Today,* July 23, 2002; *USA Today Baseball Weekly,* July 10–16, 2002.

14. *USA Today,* August 16, 2002; *Philadelphia Daily News,* May 21, 2002; Marvin Miller interview with the author, April 18, 2006.

15. Joe Posnanski, "True Believer," *Sports on Earth* (mlb.com), November 27, 2012.

16. Marvin Miller interview with the author, April 18, 2006.

17. *USA Today Baseball Weekly,* August 9, 2002; Associated Press, August 16, 2002, August 17, 2002, August 20, 2002, August 21, 2002, August 23, 2002, August 24, 2002, August 25, 2002; *USA Today,* August 14, 2002, August 15, 2002, August 16, 2002, August 21, 2002, August 22, 2002, August 23, 2002.

18. Associated Press, August 26, 2002, August 28, 2002, August 29, 2002; *USA Today,* August 29, 2002.

19. *USA Today,* August 29, 2002, August 30, 2002.

20. USA Today, August 30, 2002; Miller, *Whole Different Ball Game,* 416–20, 423–24.

21. "USA Today Salaries Databases: 2000, 2004, 2006," USAToday.com; *Sports Illustrated,* July 5, 2004; *Baseball America,* August 2–15, 2004; *USA Today Sports Weekly,* August 11–17, 2004; *USA Today,* September 4, 2009.

22. Christopher Hayes, *Twilight of the Elites: America After Meritocracy* (New York: Crown Publishers, 2012), 77–85.

23. *USA Today,* July 10, 2002, August 16, 2002; Posnanski, "True Believer," *Sports on Earth* (MLB.com), November 27, 2012.

24. Hayes, *Twilight of the Elites,* 85–86.

25. For discussion of various performance drugs and their benefits and risks, see Bryant, *Juicing the Game,* 181–87.

26. Marvin Miller interview with the author, May 2, 2006; *USA Today,* August 16, 2002.

27. *Sports Illustrated,* June 3, 2002; *Sporting News,* June 10, 2002; *USA Today,* June 14, 2002, July 8, 2002; Associated Press, June 18, 2002; *USA Today Baseball Weekly,* June 5–11, 2002.

28. Bryant, *Juicing the Game,* 256–73; Associated Press, August 30, 2002.

29. Allen Barra, "Is It Miller Time At Baseball Hall of Fame?" *Wall Street Journal,* February 25, 2003, *Sporting News,* September 9, 2002; Associated Press, February 21, 2003, February 27, 2003; *Sports Illustrated,* March 3, 2003.

30. ESPN.com, February 26, 2003; *Jewish Daily Forward,* July 11, 2003.

31. *Tampa Tribune,* March 17, 2004; Bryant, *Juicing the Game,* 331; Miller, *Whole Different Ball Game,* 421–22.

32. Miller interview with the author, May 2, 2006; Bryant, *Juicing the Game,* 332–36.

33. "Noted Alumni of James Madison High School," nycenet. April 1, 2006; Miller interview with the author, May 16, 2006; *Albany Times-Union,* June 3, 2004; *Utica Observer-Dispatch,* June 3, 2004.

34. Bryant, *Juicing the Game,* 335–38.

35. *Boston Globe,* January 14, 2005; Bryant, *Juicing the Game,* 384–85.

36. *Tampa Tribune,* March 17, 2004; *USA Today,* May 2, 2005; Bryant, *Juicing the Game,* 385.

Chapter 17. Awaiting the Call

1. Marvin Miller interview with the author, May 2, 2006.

2. *New York Times,* December 2, 2006; Joe Morgan to the author, November 8, 2006.

3. Miller interview with the author, November 15, 2005; *USA Today,* March 16, 2007.

4. *USA Today,* February 27, 2007; *New York Times,* February 28, 2007; Chris Isidore, "Miller's Time? Don't Count on it Yet," CNN.com, November 30, 2007; *USA Today,* November 30, 2007.

5. Allen Barra, "Runnin' Scared, Once Again, One of Baseball's Greatest Is Kept from Cooperstown," *Village Voice,* November 27, 2007; Associated Press, December 3, 2007; *New York Times,* December 4, 2007, December 8, 2007.

6. *USA Today Sports Weekly,* December 9–15, 2009; Allen Barra, "R.I.P., Marvin Miller: Baseball's FDR," Salon.com, November 28, 2012.

7. Associated Press, December 13, 2007, August 27, 2009; ESPN.com, February 10, 2009.

8. Miller interview with the author, May 2, 2006; ESPN.com, February 10, 2009; *New York Times,* March 1, 2009.

9. *New York Times,* March 1, 2009; Associated Press, August 27, 2009.

10. "Home Runs: Single Season," Baseball-Reference.com, August 19, 2014.

11. ESPN.com, February 10, 2009; *New York Times,* March 1, 2009.

12. ESPN.com, February 10, 2009; *New York Times,* March 1, 2009.

13. Bryant, *Juicing the Game,* 383–85; SI.com, June 23, 2009.

14. Peter Miller to the author, November 5, 2009; "Theresa Miller," Death Notices, *New York Times,* November 8, 2009.

15. John Pessah, "Baseball Screws Marvin Miller Again," *Fair Play* (trueslant.com), December 7, 2009; *Chicago Tribune,* December 8, 2009.

16. Marvin Miller interview with the author, February 21, 2006, May 16, 2006; Allen Barra, "Is It Miller Time At Baseball's Hall of Fame?" *Wall Street Journal,* February 25, 2003; Peter Miller, "The Paradoxical Marvin Miller," *New York University Journal of Legislation and Public Policy* 16, no. 2 (Spring 2013): 350.

17. Marvin Miller interview with the author, April 18, 2006, May 2, 2006; Murray Chass interview with the author, November 4, 2008; SI.com, June 23, 2009; Associated Press, June 23, 2009.

18. Marvin Miller interview with the author, May 2, 2006; Remarks by Marvin Miller, "The Peggy Browning Fund Honors Marvin Miller," peggybrowningfund.org, January 28, 2004.

19. Kuhn, *Hardball,* 77.

20. *USA Today Sports Weekly,* January 13–19, 2010; Associated Press, July 22, 2010; *Sports Illustrated,* March 15, 2010; *The Biz of Baseball,* May 6, 2010.

21. David Lariviere, "Miller and Steinbrenner Should Go Into Hall of Fame Together," Forbes.com, July 14, 2010; Allen Barra, "The Yankee Capitalist," *Wall Street Journal,* July 14, 2010; Bloomberg.com, July 13, 2010.

22. Murray Chass, "Miller Not in Hall But in Vincent Book," *Murray Chass . . . On Baseball* (murraychass.com), March 3, 2010; Ray Grebey to the Board of Directors, Baseball Hall of Fame, December 8, 2009, Grebey to Ms. Jane Forbes Clark, February 22, 2010, *Thanks, Marvin* (thanksmarvin.com).

23. Associated Press, December 6, 2010.

24. Associated Press, December 6, 2010.

25. Lisa Olson, "Petty malice keeps Marvin Miller out of baseball's Hall of Fame," Sporting News.com, July 14, 2011.

26. Terrence Moore, "Take It From Marvin Miller: NFL Owners, Players in Trouble," aolnews.com, February 16, 2011; Michael David Smith, "Marvin Miller rips NFL union for ever agreeing to a salary cap," nbcsports.com, April 12, 2011; Associated Press, June 30, 2011.

27. Ronald Blum, "AP Source: MLB players, owners reach verbal deal," Associated Press, November 19, 2011.

28. Reuters, December 16, 2011; Associated Press, August 19, 2010; Kevin Kaduk, "Roger Clemens verdict: Not guilty on all six counts," *Yahoo! Sports* (sports.yahoo.com), June 18, 2012.

29. Larry Ruttman, *American Jews and America's Game: Voices of a Growing Legacy in Baseball* (Lincoln: University of Nebraska Press), 210; "NYU Law Honors Marvin Miller on 40th Anniversary of the First Strike in Sports History," *NYU School of Law News*, April 26, 2012; Peter Miller, "The Paradoxical Marvin Miller," 351; Marvin Miller, "Remarks: Reflections on Baseball and the MLBPA," *New York University Journal of Legislation and Public Policy* 16, no. 2 (Spring 2013): 352–66.

30. "Marvin Miller blasts corporate pay," Associated Press, April 25, 2012.

31. Fay Vincent, "Miller Earned Respect as He Stood for Players' Rights," *New York Times*, November 27, 2012; Keith Olbermann, "Marvin Miller: The Man Who Reinvented Baseball," *Baseball Nerd* (keitholbermann.mlblogs.com); Allen Barra, "R.I.P, Marvin Miller, Baseball's FDR," Salon.com, November 28, 2012.

32. Barra, "R.I.P., Marvin Miller," November 28, 2012.

33. "Michael Weiner: The Good Fight," ESPN.com, November 21, 2012; *New York Daily News*, November 27, 2012; *Yahoo! Sports* (sports.yahoo.com), November 27, 2012; Joe Posnanski, "True Believer," *Sports on Earth* (mlb.com), November 27, 2012.

34. *Thanks, Marvin* (thanksmarvin.com); Associated Press, November 27, 2012; *New York Times*, November 28, 2012.

35. *Thanks, Marvin* (thanksmarvin.com).

36. Associated Press, January 9, 2013, January 11, 2013, January 23, 2013, January 30, 2013.

37. *Philadelphia Sports Examiner*, January 15, 2013.

38. Associated Press, January 22, 2013; *New York Times*, January 22, 2013; *New York Daily News*, January 22, 2013; *Hardball Talk* (nbcsports.com), January 22, 2013.

39. ESPN.com, February 26, 2003.

Selected Bibliography

Manuscript Collections

Arthur J. Goldberg Papers, Manuscript Division, Library of Congress, Washington, D.C.

Marvin and Theresa (Terry) Miller Papers (WAG.165), Tamiment Library/Robert F. Wagner Labor Archives, Elmer Holmes Bobst Library, New York University Libraries, New York, NY

Marvin Miller Subject File, National Baseball Hall of Fame and Library, Cooperstown, N.Y.

Philip Murray Papers, Catholic University of America, Washington, D.C.

Peter Seitz Arbitration Files, 1954–1983, Kheel Center for Labor-Management Documentation and Archives, M. P. Catherwood Library, Cornell University, Ithaca, N.Y.

United Steelworkers of America Papers, Historical Collections and Labor Archives, Special Collections Library, Pennsylvania State University, University Park, Pa.

University Archives, Miami University of Ohio, Oxford, Ohio.

Interviews with the Author

Thelma Miller Berenson, June 21, 2006

Murray Chass, September 4, 2008

Ben Fischer, June 27, 2006

Marvin Miller, November 15, 2005, November 29, 2005, December 13, 2005, January 24, 2006, February 7, 2006, February 21, 2006, March 14, 2006, April 4, 2006, April 18, 2006, May 5, 2006, May 16, 2006, May 30, 2006, June 13, 2006, June 27, 2006, August 1, 2006, September 5, 2006

Terry Miller, May 2, 2006

Richard Moss, July 3, 2006

Jim Thomas, June 14, 2006

Cookie Thomas, June 14, 2006

Malvin Wald, May 23, 2006, May 28, 2006

Correspondence with the Author

Allen Barra

Seymour Cohen

Donald Fehr

Alice Levy

Marvin Miller

Peter Miller

Terry Miller

Joe Morgan

Richard Moss

Collective Bargaining Agreements and Legal Documents

Arbitration between American and National Leagues of Professional Baseball Clubs (Oakland Athletics, Div. of Charles O. Finley & Co., Inc.) and Major League Baseball Players Association (James A. "Catfish Hunter), Decision No. 23 (December 13, 1974)

Arbitration between the Twelve Clubs Comprising the National League of Professional Baseball Clubs and the Twelve Clubs Comprising the American League of Professional Baseball Clubs (Los Angeles Club and Montreal Club) and Major League Baseball Players Association (John A. Messersmith and David A. McNally), Decision No. 29, Grievance Nos. 75-27, 75-28, 66 LA 114 C (Seitz, 1975).

Basic Agreement between the American League of Professional Baseball Clubs and the National League of Professional Baseball clubs and the Major League Baseball Players Association (1968, 1970, 1973, 1976, 1981).

Constitution and By-Laws of the Major League Baseball Players Association (July 21, 1967).

Curtis C. Flood, Petitioner, v. Bowie K. Kuhn, et al., Respondents, No. 71-32, *U.S. Supreme Court Reporter,* 407 U.S. 258 (1972).

Curtis C. Flood, Plaintiff, v. Bowie K. Kuhn, et al., Defendants, U.S. District Court, Southern District of New York, 70 Civ. 202 (1970).

Kansas City Royals Baseball Corporation, Plaintiff, v. Major League Baseball Players Association, Defendant, and Golden West Baseball Company, et al., Plaintiff- Intervenors, No. 75CV-712-W-1, 409 F. Supp. 233, U.S. District Court, Western District of Missouri (1975).

Kansas City Royals Baseball Corporation, Plaintiff-Appellant, et al. v. Major League Baseball Players Association, Defendant, Counter-Claim Plaintiff-Respondent, No. 76-1115, 532 F.2d 615, U.S. Court of Appeals, Eighth Circuit (1976).

Newspapers, Magazines, and Web Sites

Albany Times-Union

aolnews.com

Associated Press

Atlanta Journal-Constitution

Baseball America

Baseball Nerd (keitholbermann.mlblogs.com)
Baseball-Reference.com
Binghamton Press
The Biz of Baseball
Bloomberg.com
Boston Globe
Boston Herald
Boston Herald-American
Boston Herald-Traveler
Boston Record-American
Business Week
Chicago American
Chicago Sun-Times
Chicago Tribune
Cincinnati Enquirer
CNN.com
CNNSI.com
Deadspin.com
Detroit Free Press
ESPN.com
Fair Play (trueslant.com)
Forbes.com
Ft. Worth Star-Telegram
Hardball Talk (nbcsports.com)
The Ingot
Inside Sports
Jamesmadisonalumni.org
Jewish Daily Forward
Jock
Kansas City Star
Labor Law Journal
Los Angeles Times
Minneapolis Star-Tribune
Murray Chass . . . On Baseball (murraychass.com)
nbcsports.com
New York Daily News
New York Post
New York School of Law News
New York Times
The New Yorker
Newsday
nyce.net
peggybrowningfund.org
Philadelphia Daily News

Philadelphia Sports Examiner
Rocky Mountain News
Reuters
St. Louis Post-Dispatch
Salon.com
San Francisco Chronicle
Sport
Sporting News (sportingnews.com)
Sports Collector's Digest
Sports Illustrated (SI.com)
Sports on Earth (MLB.com)
Steel
Steel Labor
Street and Smith's Sports Business Journal
Thanks, Marvin (thanksmarvin.com)
Time
Toronto Globe and Mail
USA Today (USAToday.com)
USA Today Baseball Weekly
USA Today Sports Weekly
Upper East Side Resident
Utica Observer-Dispatch
Village Voice
Washington Post
Wall Street Journal
Yahoo! Sports (sports.yahoo.com)

Books, Journals, and Articles

Albom, Mitch. *Tuesdays With Morrie: An Old Man, A Young Man, and Life's Greatest Lesson* (New York: Broadway Books, 1997).

Asinof, Eliot. *Man on Spikes* (Carbondale: Southern Illinois University Press, 1998).

Atleson, James B. *Labor and the Wartime State: Labor Relations and Law During World War II* (Urbana: University of Illinois Press, 1998).

Bavasi, Buzzie, with John Strege. *Off the Record* (Chicago: Contemporary Books, 1987).

Baylor, Don, with Claire Smith. *Don Baylor* (New York: St. Martin's Press, 1989).

Blum, John Morton. *V Was for Victory: Politics and American Culture During World War II* (New York: Harcourt, Brace, 1976).

Bouton, Jim. *Ball Four Plus Ball Five: An Update, 1970–1980* (New York: Stein and Day, 1981).

Briffault, Robert. *Reasons for Anger* (New York: Robert Hall, 1937).

Bryant, Howard. *Juicing the Game: Drugs, Power, and the Fight for the Soul of Major League Baseball* (New York: Viking Press, 2005).

Burk, Robert F. *Much More Than a Game: Players, Owners and American Baseball Since 1921* (Chapel Hill: University of North Carolina Press, 2001).

Burke, Michael. *Outrageous Good Fortune* (Boston: Little, Brown, 1984).

"A Celebration of Baseball Unionism," *New York University Journal of Legislation and Public Policy* 16, no. 2 (Spring 2013): 317–82.

Costas, Bob. *Fair Ball: A Fan's Case for Baseball* (New York: Thorndyke Press, 2000).

Crasnick, Jerry. *License to Deal: A Season on the Run with a Maverick Baseball Agent* (New York: Rodale, 2005).

Dolson, Frank. *Jim Bunning: Baseball and Beyond* (Philadelphia: Temple University Press, 1998).

Durocher, Leo, with Ed Linn. *Nice Guys Finish Last* (New York: Simon and Schuster, 1975).

Flood, Curt, with Richard Carter. *The Way It Is* (New York: Trident Press, 1971).

Gerstle, Gary. "The Crucial Decade: The 1940s and Beyond," *Journal of American History* 92, no. 4 (March 2006).

Hayes, Christopher. *Twilight of the Elites: America After Meritocracy* (New York: Crown Publishers, 2012).

Helyar, John. *The Lords of the Realm: The Real History of Baseball* (New York: Ballantine Books, 1994).

Hendricks, Randal A. *Inside the Strike Zone* (Austin, Tex.: Eakin Press, 1994).

Jackson, Reggie, with Mike Lupica. *Reggie: The Autobiography* (New York: Villard Books, 1984).

Jennings, Kenneth. *Balls and Strikes: The Money Game in Professional Baseball* (New York: Praeger, 1990).

Kaat, Jim. *Still Pitching* (Chicago: Triumph Books, 2003).

Kennedy, David M. *Freedom From Fear: The American People in Depression and War, 1929–45* (New York: Oxford University Press, 1999).

Korr, Charles P. *The End of Baseball As We Knew It: The Players Union, 1960–81* (Urbana: University of Illinois Press, 2002).

Kuhn, Bowie. *Hardball: The Education of a Baseball Commissioner* (New York: Times Books, 1987).

Lader, Lawrence. "The Wallace Campaign of 1948," *American Heritage* 28, no. 1 (December 1976).

Leavy, Jane. *Sandy Koufax: A Lefty's Legacy* (New York: HarperCollins, 2002).

Lichtenstein, Nelson. *State of the Union: A Century of American Labor* (Princeton, N.J.: Princeton University Press, 2002).

Lorant, Stefan. *Pittsburgh: The Story of an American City* (Pittsburgh: Esselmont Books, 1999).

Lowenfish, Lee. *The Imperfect Diamond: A History of Baseball's Labor Wars*, rev. ed. (New York: Da Capo Press, 1991).

MacPhail, Lee. *My Nine Innings: An Autobiography of Fifty Years in Baseball* (Westport, Conn.: Meckler, 1989).

Malraux, Andre. *Man's Fate (La Condition Humaine)* (New York: Random House, 1961).

Miller, Marvin. *A Whole Different Ball Game: The Inside Story of the Baseball Revolution*, 2nd ed. (Chicago: Ivan R. Dee, 2004).

Ruttman, Larry. *American Jews and America's Game: Voices of a Growing Legacy in Baseball* (Lincoln: University of Nebraska Press, 2013).

319

Snyder, Brad. *A Well-Paid Slave: Curt Flood's Fight for Free Agency in Professional Sports* (New York: Viking Press, 2006).

Topkis, Jay H. "Monopoly in Professional Sports," *Yale Law Journal* 58 (1949): 691–712.

Ueberroth, Peter. *Made in America* (New York: William Morrow, 1985).

Vincent, Fay. *It's What's Inside the Lines That Counts: Baseball Stars of the 1970s and 1980s Talk About the Game They Loved* (New York: Baseball Oral History Project, Simon and Schuster, 2010).

———.*The Last Commissioner: A Baseball Valentine* (New York: Simon and Schuster, 2002).

Winfield, Dave, with Tom Parker. *Winfield: A Player's Life* (New York: W.W. Norton, 1988).

The WPA Guide to New York City (New York: New Press, 1939).

Zieger, Robert H. *The CIO, 1935–1955* (Chapel Hill: University of North Carolina Press, 1995).

Zieger, Robert H., and Gilbert H. Gall. *American Workers, American Unions: The Twentieth Century*, 3rd ed. (Baltimore: Johns Hopkins University Press, 2002).

Zimbalist, Andrew. *Baseball and Billions: A Probing Look Inside the Business of Our National Pastime* (New York: Basic Books, 1994).

———. *In the Best Interests of Baseball?: The Revolutionary Reign of Bud Selig* (New York: Wiley, 2006).

Index

Marvin Miller, 30–32, 37–38, 174; death of, 274, 276–77; political views of, 31, 34, 38–40, 54, 57, 60–63, 76, 131–32; role as mother, 54–55, 65, 75–77, 154; wartime employment of, 45, 47–48, 52–54
Milwaukee Braves, 101
Milwaukee Brewers, 165, 208–9, 238, 247, 254
minimum salary, of major-league players, 99, 119–21, 125–26, 128, 147, 166, 168, 182, 190–91, 204, 206, 227, 241, 255
Minnesota Twins, 103, 107, 156, 159, 181, 187, 191, 201, 205, 254
Mitchell, George, 253, 270
Mitchell, James, 80
Mitchell Report, 270, 280
Moffett, Kenneth, 205–7, 210–11, 217–24
Molitor, Paul, 239–40
Molony, Joseph, 94
Montreal Expos, 152, 163, 179–80
Morgan, Joe, 219, 263, 268, 274, 284
Moss, Richard, 117, 122, 126, 139, 151,197, 225, 245, 275, 280–81, 284; agent practice of, 199, 217; Basic Agreement negotiations (1968), 119–21, 128; Basic Agreement negotiations (1970), 148; Basic Agreement negotiations (1976), 188, 191; Flood litigation and, 142, 144, 149–50, 152, 242; hiring by Players Association, 114–15; Hunter arbitration case and, 173; Messersmith-McNally arbitration case and, 179–82; pension talks (1972), 157–58; work at Steelworkers union, 93–94, 108
Murray, Eddie, 278
Murray, Phillip, vii, 33, 64–70, 74–75, 91
Murrow, Edward R., 75
Musmanno, Michael, 74
"Murphy money," 125, 168

National Academy of Arbitrators, 102, 243
National Basketball Association (NBA), 121, 181, 225, 238, 252, 279
National Basketball Association Players Association (NBAPA), 121, 252, 279
National Broadcasting Company (NBC), 137, 153, 216, 219, 248
National Football League (NFL), 121, 176, 200, 263, 279
National Football League Players Association (NFLPA), 177, 236, 279

National Hockey League Players Association, 121, 280
National Jewish Sports Hall of Fame, 274
National Labor Relations Board, 120–21, 126–27, 153, 171, 182, 191, 205, 208–9, 213, 216, 247, 264
National League of Professional Baseball Clubs (NL), 105, 111, 113, 119–20, 122, 131, 134, 145, 151, 178, 180, 187, 201, 213, 252, 261, 284
National War Labor Board, 46, 48–52, 55–57, 65–66, 124–25
Nazi-Soviet Pact, 38
Newcombe, Don, 198
New Deal, 27, 60, 63
Newhan, Ross, 278
New School for Social Research (NYU), 42
New York City Welfare Department, 39–42
New York Giants (baseball), 11–12
New York Mets, 120, 131, 136, 138, 176, 196, 257
New York Rangers, 12
New York Times, 19, 97, 104, 144–45, 162, 218, 236, 242, 271, 283
New York University, 31, 33–34, 42, 65, 263, 280, 284
New York World Fair of 1939, 37
New York Yankees, 11–12, 107, 118, 120, 128, 139, 172, 174–75, 187–88, 191, 205–7, 216, 242, 253, 257–58, 270
Nicolau, George, 234, 243
Niekro, Joe, 211
Niekro, Phil, 211
Nixon, Richard M., 80, 101–2, 114, 156, 158, 163–64, 217
Nixon, Russ, 126
no-strike pledge, in World War II, 46, 48, 56
Noll, Roger, 235
Norris, Frank, 34
North American Aviation, 43

Oakland Athletics, 139, 159–60, 170–71, 173–74, 187–88, 191, 201
O'Connor, Ian, 255
Obama, Barack, 271, 284
Odets, Clifford, 33, 159
O'Donnell, John, 213
Office of Civilian Supply, 47

Robert F. Burk is an emeritus professor of history at Muskingum University and the author of *Never Just a Game: Players, Owners, and American Baseball to 1920* and *Much More than a Game: Players, Owners, and American Baseball since 1921.*

Sport and Society

The University of Illinois Press
is a founding member of the
Association of American University Presses.

Composed in 10.5/14 Chaparral Pro
with Archer display
by Jim Proefrock
at the University of Illinois Press
Manufactured by Cushing-Malloy, Inc.

University of Illinois Press
1325 South Oak Street
Champaign, IL 61820-6903
www.press.uillinois.edu